THE HOUSE OF THE CYLINDER JARS

The House of the Cylinder Jars

Room 28 in Pueblo Bonito, Chaco Canyon

EDITED BY PATRICIA L. CROWN

University of New Mexico Press   Albuquerque

© 2020 by the University of New Mexico Press
All rights reserved. Published 2020
Printed in the United States of America

ISBN 978-0-8263-6177-6 (cloth)
ISBN 978-0-8263-6178-3 (electronic)

Library of Congress Control Number: 2020941429

COVER ILLUSTRATION Bird's-eye view of Room 28 in August
1896. Photograph by Richard Wetherill. HEE 105, Image
#411881, American Museum of Natural History Library

DESIGNED BY Mindy Basinger Hill

COMPOSED IN 12.25 / 14 pt Chapparral Pro

To all who made Chaco their home

To Chip, my partner in life

And to Dabney Ford, for making this research possible

Contents

Illustrations

ILLUSTRATIONS

Tables

Acknowledgments

This volume details the results of the reexcavation of Room 28 in Pueblo Bonito, Chaco Canyon. Financial support for the project was provided by the National Endowment for the Humanities (RZ-51417-13), the National Geographic Society (9276-13), the University of New Mexico (UNM), and the Friends of Chaco. My thanks to NEH program officer Lydia Medici and NatGeo program officers Christopher Thornton and Matthew Piscitelli. The field portion of the research was conducted in the Chaco Culture National Historical Park. We could not have completed the fieldwork without the help of the park staff, particularly archaeologist Dabney Ford and chief ranger Don Whyte. Dabney and Don provided support and advice throughout the project, and we were very fortunate that they were part of the staff that summer. CCNHP staff members Roger Moore, Rechanda Lee, and G. B. Cornucopia also provided help and advice (and sometimes pizza). Under Garry Joe's skilled supervision, the Chaco stabilization crew (Robinson Lewis, Willard Martinez, Wilmer Martinez, Harold Suina, James Yazzie) installed safety scaffolding, built a portable garage over the room, created "sheep pens" for our backdirt, set up a bucket-o-matic to lift dirt out of the deep room, hauled away tons of rock, and backfilled the room after we left. Harold Suina used his expert masonry skills to rebuild a filled door that had collapsed. Chip Wills and I oversaw an intrepid crew of UNM graduate students (Leigh Cominiello, James Davenport, Scott Gunn, Jacque Kocer, Jennie Sturm) and one undergraduate, Yvonne Green. Their patience and good humor made the hot enterprise fun. Brenda Shears volunteered her time and enthusiasm. UNM faculty member Emily Lena Jones joined us in the field and then returned to conduct the inventory of human remains. UNM safety engineer Robert Dunnington visited twice and provided solutions that made it possible for us to continue to work under difficult conditions. Back in Albuquerque, the UNM Department of Anthropology staff, particularly JoNella Vasquez and Jennifer George, handled the finances for the project.

After the fieldwork was completed, analysis of the materials collected in 2013 and the materials collected in 1896 began. Research assistant Jacque Kocer conducted the analysis of the 2013 chipped stone, ground stone (with help from undergraduate Curtis Randolph), gullet stones, and ornaments, and she ran the flotation samples in preparation for the analysis. Katherine Brewer analyzed the historical artifacts. Research assistants Stephanie E. Franklin and Caitlin S. Ainsworth analyzed the faunal material under the supervision of Emily Lena Jones. Dr. Jones and Caitlin S. Ainsworth also completed the inventory of the human remains. Cyler Conrad conducted analysis of the eggshells. Cyler Conrad and Marian Hamilton prepared some bird and rabbit bones for stable isotope analysis, which was conducted at UNM in the laboratory of Seth Newsome. Research assistant Jill Jordan conducted the scanning electron microscope analysis of some ceramics and plaster samples from Room 28, a project that continues with Katharine Williams, both in the laboratory of Michael Spilde. Specialists Karen Adams (macrobotanical materials) and Susie Smith (pollen) completed their analyses with funding from the NEH. The NEH grant provided funding for trips to the American Museum of Natural History in 2014 and the National Museum of the American Indian in 2016 to analyze the 1896 Room 28 collections. Hannah Mattson accompanied me on the trip to AMNH, and her previous dissertation analysis of the ornaments from Room 28 was incorporated into our research outlined here. At AMNH, David Hurst Thomas gave us access to the Room 28 collections, and Anibal Rodriguez supervised our work. We could not have completed this portion of the study without the excellent staff at AMNH, particularly Barry Landua (systems manager and manager of digital imaging) and Kendra Meyer (digital lab manager, Department of Library Services). At NMAI, I worked with Lisa Anderson and Veronica Quiguango, both of whom made my research time a pleasure. Nathan Sowry (reference archivist, NMAI) was wonderfully responsive to my request for permission to use digital images. Diane Tyink, archivist for the Maxwell Museum of Anthropology, provided access to the George Pepper photographs in its collection. At Harvard's Peabody Museum of Archaeology and Ethnology, Cynthia Mackey of the Office of Rights and Reproductions provided help with an image request. At the Robert S. Peabody Institute of Archaeology, Marla Taylor provided help with my image request.

I had previously analyzed all of the cylinder jars from Room 28 on research visits to AMNH in 2003 and 2007, a research visit to NMAI in 2007, and a research visit to the Peabody Museum at Harvard in 2009. These visits were facilitated by David Hurst Thomas, Lori Pendleton, and Anibal Rodriguez (AMNH), Patricia Nietfield (NMAI), and Steven LeBlanc (Peabody). The material from Rooms 53 and 56 discussed in this volume was analyzed during research trips in 2008, 2017, and 2018. I am indebted to Bonnie Sousa and Marla Taylor of the Peabody Institute of Archaeology for their help with the Moorehead collections and to David Hurst Thomas and Anibal Rodriguez for their help with the AMNH collections.

NEH and UNM funding also supported cataloging of the materials in the National Park Service system for curation at the Chaco Collections at the University of New Mexico. Under the expert and patient supervision of Wendy Bustard, graduate students Jacque Kocer, Jill Jordan, and Katherine Brewer cataloged the artifacts collected in 2013 so that future researchers can access them.

Compiling this volume has involved the hard work of the contributors over the last several years. I am grateful to all of them for their efforts and patience. At the University of New Mexico Press, Clark Whitehorn, James Ayers, and Sonia Dickey helped shepherd the volume to print. Steve Lekson and Barbara J. Mills provided helpful comments on an earlier draft of the volume. Merryl A. Sloane provided exceptional copyediting.

Finally, I could not have completed this volume without the support of my family, particularly my partner in research, Chip Wills, who was there throughout the process, providing good counsel and his vast understanding of Chaco. My wonderful children, Carson Alice Wills and Andrew Keith Wills, suffered through years of listening to me natter about Room 28 and cylinder jars; hopefully, they now will see where studying one question in depth can lead.

THE HOUSE OF THE CYLINDER JARS

PATRICIA L. CROWN

CHAPTER ONE

Room 28 in Pueblo Bonito
Background, Research Questions, and Methods

In 1896, William McKinley beat William Jennings Bryan in the US presidential election, Guglielmo Marconi applied for a patent for the radio, Wilhelm Roentgen identified X-rays, miners discovered gold in the Klondike, Giacomo Puccini's *La Bohème* premiered in Turin, John Philip Sousa penned "The Stars and Stripes Forever," Greece hosted the first modern Olympics, and Queen Victoria continued her reign in England. And in June in a sandstone canyon located in the northwestern part of the Territory of New Mexico, the Hyde Exploring Expedition (HEE) began excavating Pueblo Bonito. Led by George Pepper, a 23-year-old archaeologist from New York, and Richard Wetherill, a rancher from Colorado, the HEE crew consisted primarily of Navajo men hired in Chaco, and the work was financed by Talbot and Fred Hyde, brothers whose fortune came from soap.

Around August 10, George Pepper and Richard Wetherill commenced excavations in Room 28 of Pueblo Bonito. They numbered rooms as they worked, and Room 28 was the 28th opened during that season. This room is located on the northern side of Pueblo Bonito, sandwiched between the West Court and what is called the northern burial cluster (figure 1.1). Initially, the Navajo workers found only burned roofing and walls in the two-story room, and they encouraged Pepper to move elsewhere (Pepper 1920). But on August 20, 1896, a worker identified only as Juan uncovered the first known Chacoan cylinder jar in Room 28. The Chacoan cylinder jar is a distinctive form that is approximately 2.5 times as tall as it is wide (Crown 2018; figure 1.2). Over the following nine days, they discovered another 111 cylinder jars along with numerous bowls and pitchers in a large pile on the western end of the room and in smaller groups in other parts of the room, eventually totaling 174 whole vessels. The room had burned and collapsed, burying the vessels with debris. On August 29,

they finished excavating Room 28 and removed stone masonry from a sealed doorway in the north wall of the room. George Pepper entered the adjacent room (Room 32) through the doorway and from there moved through another doorway into Room 33, the room with the two richest burials in Pueblo Bonito. This ended the 1896 excavation of Room 28, but for the next several weeks, it served as a staging area for the excavations in the adjacent Rooms 32 and 33. Fill from those rooms was thrown into Room 28, where it was searched for artifacts. Pepper was not thorough about recording where backdirt from any rooms ended up, but it appears that the fill from Rooms 32 and 33 was eventually tossed out of Room 28 in order to keep the room clear and to make it easier to search for small artifacts by placing the fill outside Richard Wetherill's tent.

In 2009, nutritional chemist Jeff Hurst and I discovered residues of cacao (chocolate) drinks absorbed into the fabric of Chaco cylinder vessels from Pueblo Bonito (Crown and Hurst 2009). This discovery was the first evidence of cacao north of the Mexico border, but it raised a number of additional questions, including how and why Chaco residents obtained cacao from more than 2,000 km away. Cacao grows in the tropics and could not grow in Chaco Canyon, so it had to be acquired at the source, brought by traders, or exchanged hand to hand across the distance between Chaco and the nearest *Theobroma cacao* trees.

Another important question concerned how Pueblo Bonito residents consumed cacao. I believed that a way to answer this lay in further study of the cylinder jars and the contexts in which they have been found. There are only around 200 known Chacoan cylinder jars, and 112 of those were found in Room 28, a room consumed by fire sometime in the AD 1100s. I believed that reopening Room 28 might answer some basic questions about the

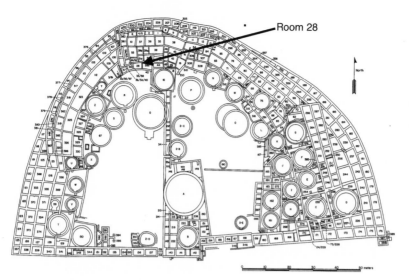

FIGURE 1.1. Map of Pueblo Bonito with location of Room 28. Base map courtesy of Thomas C. Windes. Image created by Drew Wills.

FIGURE 1.2. Chacoan cylinder jar (AMNH H/3414). Courtesy of the Division of Anthropology, American Museum of Natural History. Photograph by Patricia Crown.

room, particularly when and why it burned and why so many jars were placed there. Discussions with staff at the Chaco Culture National Historical Park (CCNHP) about reopening the room began in 2009; I then submitted a draft proposal in May 2010 and a second proposal in March 2011 that responded to comments from park personnel. The revised proposal was sent to the Tribal Consultation Committee, which has 22 member tribes, for comments and to three senior southwestern archaeologists for peer review. I received comments from representatives from Acoma Pueblo, the Hopi Tribe, Ysleta del Sur Pueblo, and the Pueblo of Zuni. I also received comments from archaeologists Eric Blinman, Barbara Mills, and Steve Plog. I again revised the proposal based on these comments and resubmitted it to the CCNHP and the New Mexico State Historic Preservation Office. The work was approved in October 2011 by the CCNHP and the New Mexico SHPO. I then sought and received funding from the National Endowment for the Humanities (RZ-51417-13) and the National Geographic Society (9276-13). Our Archaeological Resources Protection Act permit (13-CHCU-01) was signed on April 15, 2013.

Excavations began on June 4, 2013, and continued until July 13. Chip Wills and I supervised a crew of five UNM graduate students (Leigh Cominiello, James Davenport, Scott Gunn, Jacque Kocer, and Jennie Sturm) and one undergraduate (Yvonne Green from Amherst College). While our permit was issued for a thirty-day field season, excavations were halted and a consultation was held in the middle of the season due to the inadvertent discovery of isolated human remains, which had been tossed into Room 28 with backfill from another room. Pepper and Wetherill had not found any human remains in Room 28 in 1896, so finding them in 2013 was a surprise. The human remains included several toe bones found in a tin can, so they were clearly thrown into Room 28 in the late 1800s. The consultation determined that we could resume work, but a reburial of the human remains was scheduled for immediately before the project ended. The need for consultation reduced the number of project days to 23. In addition, the CCNHP wanted all human remains inventoried prior to reburial (but not documented in any other way, including photography), so Emily Lena Jones of the University of New Mexico was hired to complete the inventory while we were working in the field.

The funded research included reopening Room 28 to the level where the HEE excavators stopped work and also some new excavation beneath the floor to document any earlier surfaces. It also included analysis of all material recovered from the room during our excavations as well as material from the 1896 excavations. The latter analysis required research visits to the American Museum of Natural History in New York City and the storage facility for the National Museum of the American Indian in Suitland, Maryland. Analysis of all of the artifacts excavated from Room 28 in the 1890s was deemed necessary to enlarge our understanding of the suite of material used in cacao drink preparation and consumption.

The basic research questions included how, why, and when the room was abandoned, with the goal of situating the ritual drinking of cacao and the abandonment of the cylinder jars in the broader life history of Pueblo Bonito. The research was expected to improve our appreciation for the social and cultural conditions surrounding the acquisition of cacao from cultures in Mesoamerica and was part of an NEH initiative to enlarge Americans' understanding of other times, cultures, and beliefs within current US borders, focusing in this case particularly on rituals that demonstrate the great historical depth of the exchange of goods and ideas with Mesoamerican peoples. The project was also expected to have a significant impact on the public interpretation of Pueblo Bonito, the most visited site in Chaco Canyon.

In the remainder of this chapter, I present the original research design that guided the reopening of Room 28 and the methods used in the excavations. Specific methods used in the analysis of the artifacts and ecofacts from Room 28 are presented in the individual chapters that report the results of those analyses.

RESEARCH DESIGN AND QUESTIONS

The focus of the Room 28 reexcavation was how Ancestral Puebloan populations in Chaco Canyon in what is now New Mexico performed two specific rituals that engaged long-distance exchange for chocolate, special equipment and knowledge, and, based on the number of cylinder jars, perhaps scores of participants. The first ritual involved consumption of cacao drinks in cylinder jars. The second included the caching and burning of most of the known cylinder jars in Room 28. Both rituals were believed to date sometime between AD 1000 and 1140.

Ritual is a universal human behavior involving a set of fixed actions conducted in a prescribed order according to customs; rituals are often used in religious practice, such as sacred ceremonies, but also in secular practice. Rituals characterize the lives of people throughout the past and present. Gaining a fuller understanding of ritual activity in Chaco is particularly important because current interpretations of the archaeology of the canyon emphasize the primacy of ritual activity in explaining the cultural florescence there. Many Chacoan scholars consider the canyon to have been a major religious center

(Fritz 1978; Judge 1989; Lekson 2006; Sofaer 1997; Stein and Lekson 1992; Toll 1991), designating it a "rituality" (Yoffee 2001) with a "sacred economy" and evidence of "high devotional expression" (Renfrew 2001). The National Park Service promotes this vision in its visitor brochure: "From AD 850 to 1250, Chaco was a hub of ceremony, trade, and administration for the prehistoric Four Corners area—unlike anything before or since." Despite an almost universal acceptance of this view of Chaco, little scholarship has delineated the nature of the beliefs, ceremonies, and rituals associated with any religion there. In other words, scholars recognize the importance of sites such as Pueblo Bonito in the ritual life of the Ancestral Puebloans who inhabited Chaco Canyon, but they have rarely identified the nature of any specific rituals that occurred there.

Recent advances in methods and theory provide frameworks for evaluating ritual activities in the past. In particular, careful analyses of stratigraphic sequences and deposits often reveal processes such as dedication and termination rituals (Freidel and Schele 1989; Harrison-Buck et al. 2007; McAnany and Hodder 2009; Mills 2008; Mock, ed. 1998; Pagliaro et al. 2003; Stanton et al. 2008; Walker 2002; Walker et al. 2000). Advances in dating methods offer the opportunity to evaluate the timing of novel ritual behavior. Residue analysis demonstrates the presence of specific substances consumed in ritual activity. Combining multiple lines of evidence permits us to determine when and how two types of ritual activity occurred in Chaco: the consumption of cacao drinks in cylindrical jars and the termination ceremonies associated with the last use of most of these vessels.

To examine ritual in Chacoan society, the plan of work was to (1) reexcavate Room 28 (originally excavated in 1896), where more than 60% of all known cylinder jars were cached; (2) examine the remaining stratigraphy on the west end of the room that overlaid the cylinder jar cache to determine the sequence of events surrounding the burning and collapse of the room; (3) extract datable material from the room; (4) extract pollen and macrobotanical samples to search for ritual use of plants; (5) determine if the original excavators found the floor of the room and excavate to that floor if they did not; (6) analyze all artifacts extracted from the 1896 and new excavations; (7) analyze organic residues from a sample of artifacts found in the room; and (8) interpret the nature of the ritualized deposits associated with Room 28 at Pueblo Bonito.

The Bonito phase (ca. 850–1140) in Chaco Canyon is one of the most prominent and debated examples of rapid social transformation in the archaeology of North America (Altschul 1978; Bernardini 1999; Bustard 1996, 2003; Crown and Judge 1990; Kohler 1998; Lekson 1999, 2006; Mills 2002; Neitzel 1999, 2003a; Vivian 1990; Wills 2001). Within a short period of time, perhaps only one to two generations, a regional population of dispersed farming households gave rise to aggregated settlements socially anchored by a dense cluster of large stone buildings in Chaco Canyon called "great houses." Labor estimates for the construction of individual great houses exceed several hundred person-hours (Lekson 1984) and bear testimony to the unprecedented amount of energy and organization that marks a shift from small undifferentiated social networks to large segmentary corporate groups (Kantner 1996; Saitta 1997; Sebastian 1992). Archaeologists have studied this striking change for more than 100 years and since the 1940s have known with considerable confidence the span in calendar years during which great houses appeared, were occupied, and were abandoned. Researchers have devoted much effort to understanding the role or function of great houses in their final or completed form (e.g., Cameron and Toll 2001; Heitman and Plog 2005; Plog and Heitman 2010; Renfrew 2001), but they have been hampered by a limited number of excavations at great houses, which were primarily conducted before current standards of fieldwork were established, and sometimes by the inadequate publication of results.

Archaeologists consider Pueblo Bonito to be the center of the Chaco world (Neitzel, ed. 2003). The largest and most completely excavated of the great houses in Chaco Canyon also produced the largest assemblage of whole artifacts. Two major expeditions excavated most of the site in the 1890s and 1920s, providing extensive collections housed at the Smithsonian Institution and the American Museum of Natural History. These excavations revealed a concentration of objects that has not been duplicated in excavations of other great houses (Heitman and Plog 2005:90). These collections form the basis of much of what is known about the Chacoan material world. Pueblo Bonito is thus not only the center of the Chaco world, but also the center of Chaco archaeologists' world. Discussions of subjects such as a possible Mesoamerican connection and ritual activity rely on this material because the preponderance of clearly Meso-american objects and identifiable ritual objects in the Chaco world come from Pueblo Bonito.

Pueblo Bonito was excavated by two major expeditions. For the Hyde expedition in the late 1890s, Richard Wetherill worked with George Pepper to excavate approximately half of the rooms in Pueblo Bonito (Pepper 1905, 1909, 1920). They packed and shipped the artifacts from their work to eastern museums, and most are curated at the American Museum of Natural History in New York City, with a smaller collection at the National Museum of the American Indian in Washington, DC. A second expedition funded by the National Geographic Society in the 1920s excavated most of the remaining rooms in the site under the supervision of Neil Judd (1954, 1964). Those artifacts are curated at the National Museum of Natural History in Washington, DC. Smaller projects have included opening two rooms by the Phillips Academy in Andover, Massachusetts, in 1897 (Moorehead 1906), stabilization and tree-ring sampling by the National Park Service (Windes and Ford 1992), and the reopening of trenches placed through the trash mounds south of Pueblo Bonito by the University of New Mexico in 2004–2008 (Crown, ed. 2016; Wills et al. 2016).

As already mentioned, reopening Room 28 offered an exceptional opportunity to examine two distinct and identifiable rituals: the drinking ritual associated with the cylinder jars and the termination ritual. Room 28 is known primarily for the recovery of more than half of all known Chacoan cylinder jars (Crown 2018; Toll 1990; see also Washburn 1980). Cylinder jars are now known to have been used in consuming drinks made from cacao brought more than 2,000 km from the tropics of Mesoamerica (Crown and Hurst 2009; Crown et al. 2015; Washburn et al. 2011) or from holly brought from the Gulf coast or Mexico (Crown et al. 2015). Room 28 contained 112 cylinder vessels together with pitchers and bowls, which were found in discrete and apparently orderly groupings. Other artifacts in the room in 1896 included grinding stones, sandstone jar lids, a variety of other objects (chipped stone knives, bone awls, bone "implements," a wooden stick, yucca cord, and a wooden "piece"), and non-utilitarian pigments and ornaments (shell beads, shell bracelets, a crystal, mica, iron ore, turquoise, copper ore, and a copper object) (Pepper 1920:112–28). Further analysis of these objects offers the opportunity to examine the nature of the drinking ritual involving the cylinder jars.

Cacao would have been brought from Mesoamerica as beans or semi-processed tablets of chocolate, and additional processing of either form would be required to make chocolate drinks. Processing would include grinding the nibs or tablets to make a paste, then stirring water and other additives into the paste to make a drink, which was followed by some means of creating a froth on the drink (probably by pouring from jar to jar). Alternatively, historical records indicate that holly drinks were created by toasting the leaves and twigs, then brewing a tea by heating the toasted plants in water (Merrill 1979). The elixir was then frothed, much like cacao drinks. Because they were found together with the cylinder jars in Room 28, the ground stone and wooden implements found in Room 28 may have been used in preparing drinks or in the drinking ritual. Examination of these implements for evidence of use in preparing elixirs would help to determine the range of objects associated with drink preparation in Chaco Canyon. While the use of the cylinder jars found in Room 28 is roughly dated to around AD 1000–1140 based on the range of ceramic designs on the pots, refining the dating of the placement of the cache of cylinder jars would provide a stronger date for cacao and holly use and exchange. The broader question in this case is what the material associated with this largest collection of cylinder jars tells us about ritual drinking.

The second ritual of interest here involved the caching of the cylinder jars and other vessels in the room followed by burning of the room. Prior to the reexcavation, a possible explanation was that the vessels represented items stored in a room that accidentally burned (Crown and Wills 2003; Toll 1990; although see Akins 2001). However, Barbara Mills (2008) suggested that the large group of vessels was the remains of a termination ritual. Common in Mesoamerica (Mock, ed. 1998) but recognized also in the US Southwest (Adams 2016; Mills 2008; Walker 1995, 2002), termination rituals brought permanent closure to rituals, objects, constructions, or features. Many cultures believe that some objects or buildings must be given life—animated or ensouled—to empower them; termination rituals reverse the processes that originally animated or brought to life those objects, rooms, and sites through destruction and "decharging" (Stanton et al. 2008). Such rituals might involve the retirement of objects considered too powerful to be discarded in the manner of normal ob-

jects (Mills 2004, 2008) and/or deconsecration of ritual spaces (Creel and Anyon 2003; Mills 2008; Walker et al. 2000). Termination rituals occur in ethnographic contexts under several different circumstances: when the last practitioner capable of performing a ritual died; when a village or town was abandoned; in association with cyclical ritual destruction of objects or structures (as when a ritual cycle was complete) prior to rebuilding; or when enemies occupied or sacked a site and wished to cleanse it. In all cases, the goal was to remove sacred power from objects and structures. The special nature of many of the objects found in Room 28 in 1896 indicates shared features with termination rituals elsewhere, but we only know about the material part. The nonmaterial parts of the ritual, including placement of the objects, burning the structure, and depositing additional material above them, can only be determined through careful analysis of the surrounding stratigraphy. Through such careful analysis, a project research goal was to determine whether this was indeed a termination ritual, the type of termination ritual it was, and when it occurred.

To answer these questions, it was necessary to reopen Room 28. The field notes, photographs, journals, and publications created by Richard Wetherill and George Pepper based on the 1896 excavations provided all of the information we had in 2013 about this important room beyond the artifacts and a single tree-ring date. Unfortunately, these left many issues unanswered. Photographs of the room combined with Pepper's (1920) published description of his excavations indicated a complex series of formation processes. We knew the following events occurred but did not know the order: the room was constructed and used, the room was partitioned, artifacts were placed in the room, the door to the adjoining burial room was closed, the room burned, the room flooded, the room filled with trash, and the upper partition wall was built.

According to Pepper (1920), the Room 28 fill was unremarkable. The fill included fallen walls and "accumulated debris." Pepper described evidence of the room having burned: blackened walls, reddened plaster/adobe, red vitrified sand, and posts turned to charcoal. He noted that the western portion of the room had filled with sand that had both blown in and washed in before the ceiling fell, helping to preserve the ceramics in the room. He also thought that the cylinder jars had been forced from their "well-laid pile" and sometimes crushed "by the weight of the debris that the burning of the ceiling beams precipitated upon them" (Pepper 1920:117).

There were several reasons to question this interpretation of the events. First, the HEE photographs reveal a highly uneven surface with vessels sitting at various depths on the undulating surface. Second, careful reading of the expedition artifact catalog at the American Museum of Natural History reveals that Pepper found masses of broken cylinder jars both 3 feet (91 cm) above the "floor" and "a few feet below the surface." Because the "floor" on which the cache was found was only 1.22 m below the surface, the actual mass of pottery apparently extended from about 30 cm below the 1896 surface to 1.22 m below the surface; in other words, the cache may have been part of a much larger pile of pottery, the upper levels of which were crushed and sandwiched in a 1 m layer. Third, the photographs reveal burned wooden beams in, around, and *under* the vessels in the cache. Fourth, my examination of the cylinder jars in the cache showed that most were exposed to fire, but the fire damage was often on the *underside* of the pots rather than on the surface facing up (it is possible to determine which surface faced up both from the photographs and from silt lines still visible on the unwashed pots themselves). Where charred wood is visible in the photographs, the pots in physical contact with the wood are burned on the vessel walls that contacted the wood. All of this patterning suggests that the pots were originally resting on a wooden structure that burned while the pots were in contact with it. But what was the wooden structure—a bin, shelving, or the upper-story floor? In other words, were the pots actually placed in the lower story of Room 28 or on the floor of the upper story (Room 28b)? The answer to this question is critical for understanding the cultural and natural processes that created the cache and associated stratigraphy.

Prior to the reexcavation, the only additional information we had came from the photographs and from the descriptions of the adjoining Rooms 55 on the west and 28a on the east. Beginning with Room 55, the cache of cylinder jars partly underlaid a mass of material that formed the foundation for a later masonry wall that partitioned an upper story of Room 28 into Room 28b to the east and Room 55 to the west. Pepper had to partially undercut this mass of material to retrieve some of the cylinder jars. Thus, Pepper's notes suggest that lower Room 28 and lower Room 55 were once a single large room, making Pepper's description of what he

found in lower Room 55 relevant here. In lower Room 55, Pepper (1920:215–16) noted that the western wall was debris, but the remains of a floor were found 4 feet (1.2 m) below the western (upper cross) wall; this was not an intact lower-room floor, but an upper-story floor that had collapsed into the room. Pepper described east-west beams, cedar bark covering, and pieces of adobe that represented this fallen upper floor. Only sterile sand to a depth of 4 feet (1.2 m) lay below these floor beams. The presence of this floor was of interest because its depth seemed to fit well with the level at which the cache of vessels was found in Room 28, again suggesting the possibility that the cylinder jars were originally resting on an upper-story floor that collapsed during the fire.

Pepper found that Room 28a to the east of Room 28 was separated from Room 28 by a masonry partition wall that was 1.22 m high on the Room 28 side, but 2.59 m high on the Room 28a side. In describing Room 28a, Pepper (1920:126) stated that this dividing wall "extended to the ceiling of the lower room which was 8½ feet [2.59 m] from the floor at this end. The base on which the wall rested was composed of large stones. The room was floored at this depth (8½ feet) and had been filled in, and another floor put down at the bottom of the dividing wall or at a depth of 6 feet [1.83 m] from the ceiling." If there were floors in Room 28a at 1.83 m and 2.59 m below the former ceiling, it is possible that Pepper never reached the actual floors in Room 28 on the other side of the partition wall, instead stopping at 1.22 m. His published description of Room 28 and his diary entries in the Chaco Research Archive indicate that on August 28, 1896, Pepper and Wetherill completed removing the cache of pottery from Room 28; on August 29, they packed up the pottery for shipment, measured the floor, and broke through a sealed door to adjacent Room 32. They then used Room 28 only as a location to temporarily throw backdirt while excavating Rooms 32 and 33. There is no indication that they ever excavated below the level of the cache in Room 28. Since the cache was only 1.22 m below the ceiling, I believed there was a strong possibility that additional floors were still present in Room 28 at .61–1.37 m below the level at which Pepper stopped working in this room.

From Pepper's description, it was clear that although the room burned and many perishable objects may have been lost, preservation was fairly good, with charred posts standing almost a meter high and wooden objects buried in sand left uncharred. Pepper did not state whether he removed the charred posts, leaving open the possibility that they remained in the room and could be dated by tree-ring dating.

The later excavator of other portions of Pueblo Bonito, Neil Judd (1954:22–28), raised questions about Pepper's interpretation of Room 28 and provided a thorough re-interpretation of the series of events that led to the archaeological strata found by Pepper. My own inter-pretation of the notes, photographs, and artifacts is quite different from both Pepper's and Judd's. All three interpretations are outlined in table 1.1.

In the research design, I argued that determining the actual dating and sequence of events was critical because the large cache of cylinder vessels found in Room 28 was associated with the importation and consumption of cacao from Mesoamerica. Dating the room and exam-ining the other artifacts in the room provided the best opportunity for enlarging our understanding of drinking rituals in Chaco Canyon. The charred material in con-tact with the jars offered the possibility of obtaining information on room construction prior to the fire and a terminus post quem (date after which the cache must have been placed); radiocarbon dating of any charcoal in

TABLE 1.1. **Three interpretations of events in Room 28 of Pueblo Bonito from construction to abandonment**

	PEPPER 1920	JUDD 1954	CROWN 2011
EVENT 1	Room 28 constructed late 800s to early 900s	Room 28 constructed late 800s to early 900s	Room 28 constructed late 800s to early 900s
EVENT 2	Room 28 remodeled	Room 28 remodeled and construction debris pushed into room	Room 28 remodeled
EVENT 3	partition wall built between Rooms 28 and 28a	clean sand placed over debris and new floor laid at doorsill level	partition wall built between Rooms 28 and 28a
EVENT 4	clean sand fills western half	partition wall built between Rooms 28 and 28a	drifting sand blows into lower-story room
EVENT 5	cylinder jars and other objects placed in room	cylinder jars and other objects placed in lower Room 28, AD 1025–1050	doorway to adjacent Room 32 sealed
EVENT 6	door to Room 32 sealed	sand blows into room, covering artifacts	cylinder jars and other objects placed in upper-story room and room burned as termination ritual
EVENT 7	room burned	room burns	room open to elements (evidence of wet silt deposited on vessels)
EVENT 8	room flooded	door to Room 32 sealed	additional debris dumped into room and upper story built, creating Rooms 28b and 55, around AD 1083
EVENT 9	room filled with trash	upper story burned, walls and roofing dumped into lower room through an opening	
EVENT 10	upper partition wall built between Rooms 28 and 55	upper-story walls rebuilt on south	
EVENT 11		upper partition wall built between Rooms 28 and 55, AD 1071–1083	
EVENT 12		corridor left in debris in lower Room 28 to access adjacent Room 51a to the north	

TABLE 1.2. **Expectations of the Pepper, Judd, and Crown models for the caching and burning events in Room 28**

	PEPPER	JUDD	CROWN
EXPECTATIONS FOR FLOOR BENEATH CYLINDER JARS	clearly defined floor at level of cylinder jars	a clearly plastered floor at level of doorsills	no evidence for a floor at level of cylinder jars
EXPECTATIONS FOR STRATIGRAPHY	clearly defined floor in the stratigraphy of the dirt between Rooms 28 and 55 at level of cylinder jars	a layer of blown sand below level of cylinder jars	evidence that debris from the falling burned roofs was below level of cylinder jars as well as above
EXPECTATIONS FOR POSTS	no charring of posts below level of cylinder jars	burned material above level of cylinder jars, but not at or below that level	burned material mixed in with layers at which Pepper found cache; charring of posts below level of cache
EXPECTATIONS FOR LOWER FLOOR	no evidence for a lower floor up to 1.5 m below final excavation level	lower floors likely exist	evidence for lower floors at 0.3 and 1.3 m below final excavation level

the room constructed over the burned room and overlying the main cache of jars might provide a terminus ante quem (date before which the cache must have been placed). Having both sets of dates should bracket the cache. Finally, bracketing the placement of the cache also would provide a date for the likely termination ritual involving the placement of the cache and burning of the room. Scholar Barbara Mills (2008) has argued that a termination of the Room 28 cache occurred at the end of the Pueblo Bonito occupation in the late 1100s. Without absolute dates to indicate when the room burned, we could not determine whether this dating is correct or not. Only through additional excavation, careful examination of stratigraphy, and obtaining dates could we hope to resolve this ongoing debate concerning the dating of the room and cache. Teasing apart the actual sequence required examining the stratigraphy and presence of features, such as floors, in addition to obtaining datable material. Expectations for the three models are presented in table 1.2.

In addition to determining the sequence of events that created the stratigraphy and artifact placement in Room 28, our research sought to determine the nature of the probable ritual activity associated with these events, including whether these were use-and-abandonment processes or part of a termination ritual. It is possible that the vessels were simply stored in Room 28 between uses. The room might have burned with the vessels left inside, or the room might have been abandoned before it burned. In either event, the association of the cache,

burning, and abandonment might be coincidental rather than purposeful. As mentioned, some researchers have suggested that the cache and burning represent a termination ritual (Mills 2008:108). They might represent a desecratory termination ritual enacted when victors of a conflict or later occupants of Pueblo Bonito wanted to remove sacred power from the objects or site by piling the vessels up and setting the room ablaze. Alternatively, existing occupants of Pueblo Bonito might have held a reverential termination ritual if the last practitioner capable of performing the ritual associated with the cylinder jars died, perhaps as the population of Pueblo Bonito dwindled (Mills 2008:105), if abandonment of the site was planned, or in association with the cyclical ritual destruction of objects or structures prior to rebuilding. Determining which of these three scenarios is correct required careful examination of stratigraphy, dating, residues on vessels, defacement of vessels, and marks on room walls. Table 1.3 presents the specific expectations for each scenario, based in part on models derived from reverential and desecretory termination ritual activity in Mesoamerica.

EXCAVATION METHODS

A year prior to our beginning the excavation, graduate student Jennie Sturm conducted tests with ground-penetrating radar in the room. Using this technique, we hoped to determine the depth to the floor and whether there was intact wood in the room. The results indicated what we thought were intact charred posts (Sturm and Crown 2015), which later turned out to be cobble-lined postholes.

With the research design as a guide, the plan had been to excavate the room to the level at which the HEE stopped working, record that surface, and then excavate beneath it to sterile soil. Unfortunately, several factors constrained the 2013 excavations in Room 28, requiring us to alter our plans. As mentioned above, our permit allowed 30 days of excavation, but the need for a consultation in the middle of the field session reduced the actual excavation to 23 days. In addition, the room required considerable stabilization as we worked. Scaffolding and screw jacks had to be placed to hold back the unstable upper-story west wall, which rested entirely on debris, and the upper-story north wall, which leaned precariously into the room. The HEE had found the north wall unstable in 1896 as well, noting that it slanted to the south over Room 28 (Pepper 1920:209). Robert Dunnington, a safety engineer from the University of New Mexico, served as our advisor as we followed OSHA regulations during the excavations. By the time the project was over, we had five screw jacks and ten scaffolds holding back various parts of the walls, which made entering and exiting the room a challenge: we ducked under some metal poles and climbed over

others. In addition, we had to leave one quadrant of the room only partially excavated because the walls were too unstable to support a ladder; our only egress was steps cut into the deposits in the northeastern quadrant of the room. For safety, over the final ten days, only two individuals worked in the room simultaneously, with one crew member stationed at the surface as a spotter monitoring the walls for signs of imminent collapse. The door in the south wall to the West Court had been filled with rubble, which collapsed while we were working in the room. The park stabilization crew filled it with masonry and mortar, but this prevented our completely excavating the step leading to the doorway. The north doorways also remained blocked because they were too unstable to clear. The door into Room 32 was particularly unstable, so we left an area around the door unexcavated to keep it from collapsing. We wore hard hats and safety vests, and I conducted an inspection daily to monitor wall cracks with calipers before anyone entered the room. A Quonset hut–shaped garage was erected over the excavations for security and safety. It kept tourists from entering the excavations and inadvertently falling into the room. We hired a guard who kept people out when we were not present during weekends and in the evenings until the park closed.

Room 28 is 8.89 m^2 in size, and the depth to the floor

TABLE 1.3. **Interpretive framework, including expectations for evidence of abandonment, desecratory termination, and reverential termination ritual**

	ABANDONMENT OR ACCIDENTAL FIRE	DESECRATORY TERMINATION RITUAL	REVERENTIAL TERMINATION RITUAL
TIMING OF BURNING	later than placement of cylinder jars	contemporary with placement of cylinder jars	contemporary with placement of cylinder jars
EVIDENCE OF OTHER RITUAL OBJECTS	lack of other ritual offerings	lack of clear scattering of ritual offerings (shell, turquoise) amid cache	scattered offerings (shell, turquoise) amid cache
OBJECTS IN CACHE	collection of objects go together and are normal for the room context	objects in unusual context and do not necessarily belong together as a coherent assemblage	most objects belong together as an assemblage used in a single ritual
TREATMENT OF OBJECTS	objects complete when left	objects broken, scattered, defaced	objects complete prior to deposition or broken in place, not defaced
SURFACES AND WALLS	untouched	scarred, cut open, defaced	untouched
ARTIFACT ORIGINS	normal range of items, mostly local	high percentage of exotic items	high percentage of exotic items
DEPOSITION OF CLEAN MATERIAL	no sterile sand or wood ash deposited prior to burning	sterile sand or wood ash deposited prior to burning	sterile sand or wood ash deposited prior to burning

was about 2.6 m below the present ground surface. The room was filled with a matrix that included chunks of masonry and backdirt; we excavated the fill in arbitrary 20 cm levels. For the upper levels, we screened 90% of the fill using quarter-inch mesh and 10% using eighth-inch mesh. When we reached Level 8, the quantity of tiny ornaments increased, and it became necessary to alternate eighth-inch mesh with window screen–size mesh. Historical photographs of the room in 1896 were used to help determine when we were approaching the original depth of the cylinder jar cache. We collected all artifacts and bagged them in the field by artifact type.

The backfill was a mix of two different deposits: one was heavily reddened from burning and with abundant charred wood and burned adobe; the other showed no burning but had preserved wood and many chunks of sandstone masonry. Initially, we combined these distinct matrices in our levels, but by Level 8, we excavated them separately: the designation "Level 8" referred to the burned matrix, and "Level 8a" referred to the unburned matrix. The burned fill required more careful excavation because of the abundant charred chunks of wood, which we took for tree-ring samples. Removing these carefully also slowed us down; we removed 1,969 pieces of charred and unburned wood from the fill. The burned fill gradually disappeared, so from Level 11 (2.2 m below the surface) to the floor, each level was given a single number designation. The remaining unburned fill extended from the surface to the floor. It had large chunks of masonry, and one layer (located at the top of Level 10/10a, 1.8 m below the present ground surface) had dozens of flat-lying building stones; a whole metate was found directly above this level.

These backfill layers showed considerable evidence of disturbance after they had been tossed into Room 28. In particular, we found large numbers of articulated rodent and rabbit skeletons and one complete rodent nest in the backdirt. These were not bagged as separate skeletons due to a lack of time, but they were notably common in some levels. Because they were burrowing animals, these skeletons provide evidence of the mixing of deposits after the backdirt was thrown into Room 28 in 1897. The condition of the artifacts provides further evidence of disturbance. Burned artifacts were recovered from the unburned backfill and unburned artifacts from the burned backfill, so clearly there was some movement of artifacts between the two deposits after they were placed in Room 28. Because of this, the burned matrix is not

always discussed separately from the unburned matrix in the chapters of this volume because it was not always clear where the items we recovered originated. When it was clear, that separation is made in the chapters; otherwise, we simply discuss the assemblage as a whole.

The Room 28 floor was easy to distinguish on the western end of the room because it had been exposed to a fire, and the floor was glassy and reddened. Elsewhere, the floor was apparent only as a slightly harder surface with flecks of gypsum in it. When the floor was reached, that surface and associated features were documented in detail, including mapping and photographs. Floor features were mapped and bisected for stratigraphy.

We divided the room into quadrants for the subfloor excavation. As discussed above, although we had intended to subfloor the entire room, time constraints and safety concerns made that impossible. We subfloored the southeast quadrant because it was adjacent to the eastern wall, which was the wall that Pepper indicated was deeper on the Room 28a side than on the Room 28 side, and I wanted to verify whether that was true or not. The subfloor excavation followed the natural stratigraphy when possible. However, much of the subfloor consisted of minute layers that were visible in stratigraphic profile but virtually impossible to follow with a trowel. When we found a clearly defined surface, we excavated it separately. Otherwise, we used 20 cm arbitrary levels. When we reached the base of Level 15 (at 3 m below the present ground surface) in the southeast quadrant, it became apparent that we did not have time to excavate the entire quadrant, so a 50 × 50 cm unit was excavated in the northeast corner, and the deposits proved to be sterile. To ensure that there were no deeper cultural deposits, we excavated another 1.1 m and then augered another 90 cm. No artifacts or charcoal were found in either the small unit or the auger.

Once the entire room was cleared, a very high resolution terrestrial laser scanner (lidar) was used to document all walls and features. Jed Frechette from the Albuquerque company Lidar Guys conducted this scanning. Wetherbee Dorshow of Earth Analytic, a company based in Santa Fe, used a gigapan to photograph the entire room to create a three-dimensional model. This was done for complete documentation of the room at the request of the National Park Service for conservation purposes. Chaco Culture National Historical Park archaeologists have stated that Room 28 will never be opened again, so this complete documentation will

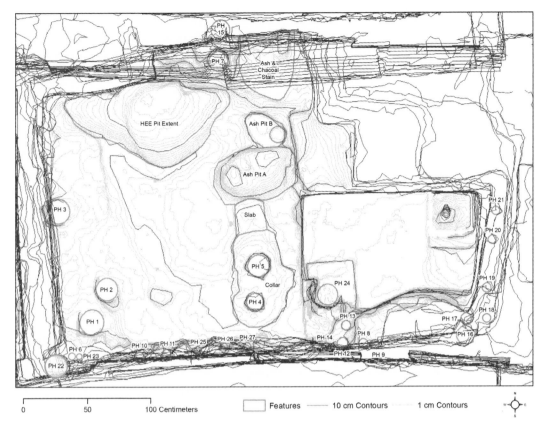

FIGURE 1.3. Map based on lidar scanning of Room 28 showing the deep test unit in the southeast corner and the features. Image by Jed Frechette and Drew Wills, Lidar Guys.

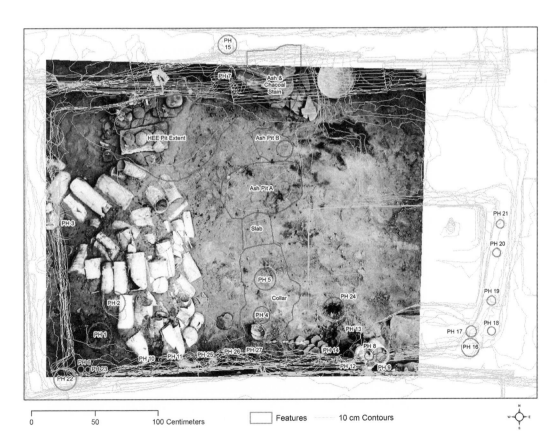

FIGURE 1.4. Lidar-scanning map draped over a historic bird's-eye photograph of Room 28 by Richard Wetherill. Catalog no. 88.42.14. Courtesy of the Maxwell Museum of Anthropology, University of New Mexico. Image by Jed Frechette and Drew Wills, Lidar Guys.

permit future generations to view the room walls and surfaces using the lidar images. Figure 1.3 is a map of the excavated room based on the lidar and showing all features, and figure 1.4 shows the same map draped over one of the historic photographs of the room.

Datable material was taken from all remaining posts. Where possible, this included both tree-ring samples, which were sent to the Laboratory of Tree-Ring Research, and charcoal samples, which were sent to the AMS (accelerator mass spectrometry) dating facility, both at the University of Arizona. Rex Adams and Karen Adams identified wood species for any posts that were not dated. Archaeobotanical samples, including both isolated finds and larger samples, were collected in the field. All of the contents of thermal features were bagged for flotation analysis. Pollen samples were taken only from the floor level down to sterile soil, because the fill was likely contaminated from the 1890s excavations. Pollen samples were taken from under any flat-lying rocks, from two columns in the subfloor unit, and from a 50 cm grid over a surface found in the subfloor unit. Some ceramics were removed with latex gloves and immediately placed in aluminum foil for residue analysis.

OUTREACH

Room 28 is located on the main path taken by visitors through Pueblo Bonito, so it was critical that we plan some kind of ongoing outreach to park visitors during the excavations. The park roped off the area of the excavations and backdirt piles, and staff members placed an exhibit we designed in front of the ropes to explain what we were doing. Visitors tended to come in waves, so one crew member was assigned to explain the project to the public throughout each day. Ranger-led tours of Pueblo Bonito were scheduled at 10 a.m. and 2 p.m., and we typically met those tours as they came through the area and talked to them about what we were doing. The walls were too precarious to allow all visitors to view the excavations, so most visitors were given a talk and shown photographs of the excavation area.

I had planned to use a GoPro camera system to show visitors the excavations in real time. Coupled with an iPad with Bluetooth wireless technology, the plan was to attach the camera to one of the excavators and then have the iPad available for visitors to watch the excavations as they occurred. This plan did not work because the ma-

sonry walls of Room 28 blocked the Bluetooth signal and because the bright sun made images on the iPad screen impossible to see. Even with an umbrella shading it or a darkened box with the iPad inside, it was not possible to view the iPad images on a sunny day in Chaco. So, this plan failed. We estimated that around 2,000 visitors, including groups from France, England, Germany, and Slovenia, stopped by the excavations during our work.

ANALYSIS

The excavation crew sorted and counted artifacts in the evening. All artifacts were taken to the University of New Mexico for processing, analysis, cataloging, and curation. Analyses followed standard procedures and are described in the chapters that follow. Cataloging was completed after the artifacts were analyzed, and we followed the NPS procedures established for Chaco collections. All of the artifacts and samples removed from Room 28 in 2013 are now curated at the Hibben Center on the UNM campus by CCNHP. Samples were sent to specialists for analysis, including pollen and archaeobotanical analysis.

During the summer of 2014, Hannah Mattson and I traveled to the American Museum of Natural History to analyze the materials excavated from Room 28 in 1896. In February 2016, I traveled to the National Museum of the American Indian to analyze the materials they curate from Room 28. I had previously analyzed the cylinder jars from the room, and Mattson (2015) had analyzed the ornaments as part of her dissertation research, so our analyses focused on the remaining materials. They took three weeks to complete.

As a project permitted by the National Park Service, copies of all electronic files, including photographs, and data generated by this project were turned over to the CCNHP. Electronic databases are available to the public and interested scholars through the NPS. All artifacts and samples are available for study by qualified scholars and to view by appointment by the public.

SUMMARY

This volume provides information about Room 28's architecture (chapter 2), ceramics (chapter 3), chipped and ground stone (chapter 4), ornaments (chapter 5), textiles (chapter 6), fauna (chapter 7), eggshells and gastroliths (chapter 8), archaeobotanical remains (chapter 9), pollen (chapter 10), and historical artifacts (chapter 11). We provide significant amounts of detail in each chapter, so the casual reader may wish to skip to chapter 12, which summarizes the results and provides interpretations. Appendixes provide additional results and data, including photographs of all vessels and lists of macrobotanical remains and human remains. The excavations answered all of our questions about Room 28 and showed how its use shifted from a domestic space to a storage room for ritual objects. But in addition, the backfill thrown into Room 28 from multiple nearby rooms reveals much about the use of those rooms.

In addition to this volume, publications arising from the 2013 Room 28 excavations include studies of polydactyly at Pueblo Bonito (e.g., a six-toed-foot impression in the plaster of Room 28) (Crown et al. 2016); the ritual use of birds (Ainsworth et al. 2018); stable isotope analysis of rabbit bones (Hamilton et al. 2018); the use of cylinder jars in drinking rituals in Chaco (Crown 2018); and the complex architectural sequence of Pueblo Bonito (Crown and Wills 2018).

Current interpretations of Chaco Canyon place ritual activity at the center of explanations for the cultural florescence in the eleventh century, yet little has been known of the specifics of such ritual activity. This study enlarges our understanding of past rituals and beliefs in Chaco Canyon. The drinking ritual associated with the cylinder jars suggests historical depth in the exchange of goods and ideas with Mesoamerican peoples. It provides strong confirmation that luxury foods, including cacao, were an important part of the economic fabric of cultures within what are now the US borders long before Europeans set foot on American soil.

Understanding the termination of the cylinder jars and Room 28 at Pueblo Bonito adds important insight into the social history of the great houses in Chaco. On the one hand, termination signals the end of the use of cylinder jars as drinking vessels; given the likely status signaling that accompanied the drinking of cacao, this cessation must have been a charged event, perhaps an actual crisis for the community. On the other hand, accurately dating the termination ritual and closure of the room makes it possible to situate the event in Pueblo Bonito's life history, allowing a more comprehensive perspective that connects the termination to episodes of construction and destruction, possible cycles of ritual renewal, subsistence change, and even periods of abandonment.

PATRICIA L. CROWN

CHAPTER TWO

The Architecture and Sequence of Use of Room 28

Dynamic. That word best describes the space occupied by Room 28 and the environment surrounding it. People living at Pueblo Bonito responded to their own changing needs as well as to the changing environment by modifying and using that space in different ways over time, forming a complex use and construction history. Evidence for my reconstruction of this history comes from stratigraphy, thermal features, postholes, walls, doorways, artifacts, and dates. In this chapter, I review the long history of use of the space that Pepper (1920) and Wetherill designated Room 28. I begin with the material that underlies the room, followed by the construction and use of the room, and finally the strata that indicate construction over Room 28.

The number designations of Room 28 are confusing. From the surface, the Hyde Exploring Expedition (HEE) designated Room 28 as a long, narrow room stretching westward from the apex of Pueblo Bonito. However, not far below the surface, they encountered a wall that separated that room into two. The room to the east became Room 28a and the room to the west became Room 28. And once Room 28 was excavated, Pepper (1920) believed that it stretched to the west below three numbered rooms: upper Room 28b, Room 55, and Room 57. Our reexcavation efforts focused only on the part originally described as lower Room 28. We did not touch deposits in Rooms 28a, 55, or 57, so in this chapter I describe only the portion of Room 28 that occupies the western end of Room 28b and the eastern end of what Pepper believed was a long room that included Rooms 55 and 57. Figure 2.1 shows the early and late versions of the room space as described by Pepper.

PRE-ROOM COURTYARD

As mentioned in chapter 1, in his description of the adjacent Room 28a, Pepper (1920:126–27) noted the presence of two floors: one located at the bottom of the partition wall that separated Room 28 from Room 28a at 1.83 m and another floor at 2.59 m. At the lower depth, he described the partition wall as resting on a base of large stones. Based on this description of the room just east of Room 28 and the wall partitioning the two rooms, I assumed that Room 28 would also have multiple floors and that the shared partition wall would have an identical base of large stones on the Room 28 side. We excavated deeply in the southeast quadrant to confirm this situation by digging alongside the partition wall and were surprised to find neither multiple floors nor a base of large stones beneath the partition wall. Instead, the pre–Room 28 side of the partition wall was apparently a courtyard or plaza area immediately west of the deeper floor found in Room 28a.

Our excavations then located sterile soil to determine the level at which the space was originally used for cultural activities. Sterile soil was reached at a depth of 96.6 m (using the arbitrary datum established on the Pueblo Bonito West Mound and set at 100 m). We augered down from 96 m to 94.98 m just to confirm the lack of any cultural materials. A control pollen sample taken at 95.75 m confirmed the lack of economic plants at this depth (see Smith, this volume). At this depth, the deposits consist of gray clay mixed with yellow sand. At 95.95 m, the deposits change slightly to yellow sand but remain sterile, with no charcoal or artifacts. We can compare this depth to sterile with other parts of Pueblo Bonito. Our excavations in and between the two mounds south of Pueblo Bonito reached depths below 93 m before reaching sterile deposits. Neil Judd (1964:figure 14;

Pithouse 2) found a slab-lined pit structure at 94.74 m in depth about 80 m south of Room 28 on his B–B' north-south trench through Pueblo Bonito. This was one of two pit structures Judd located in the north-south trench through the West Court of Pueblo Bonito, indicating occupation of the site in Basketmaker III. However, although these habitation structures indicate occupation during Basketmaker III, there is no evidence of features or structures in the area upon which Room 28 was built during this early time period. The ground surface under Room 28 was about 2 m higher than the pit structures, creating a slope of around 2.5%.

At least one and probably two structures were built closer to Room 28 later in time (Crown and Wills 2018). As noted above, George Pepper (1920:126–28) described a floor in the adjacent Room 28a located 0.76 m (2.5 feet) lower than the floor found at the bottom of the partition wall that separates Room 28 from Room 28a. He found that this lower floor was associated with earlier walls on the west and south sides of Room 28a. Assuming that the floors associated with the partition wall were roughly equivalent in depth (which was 97.06 m on the Room 28 side), the earliest floor in Room 28a would have a depth of around 96.3 m. There is no cultural deposit found at 96.3 m under Room 28; it seems most likely that the construction of this lower-room floor in Room 28a is contemporaneous with a level found at 96.6 m in Room 28, with the Room 28a floor excavated 30 cm into sterile sand. This almost certainly represents an architectural

form called a "tub room," which may be restricted to the San Juan Basin (Windes 1993). Tub rooms had square to rounded masonry walls with floors that included a central, bathtub-shaped depression 20–40 cm deep surrounded by shelves 15–25 cm wide (Windes 1993). A photograph of the room (Crown and Wills 2018:figure 6) shows shelf projections around the worker standing on the lower floor, supporting the idea that this was a tub room. Immediately to the south of this room and at approximately the same elevation, Judd (1964:76–77) found the possible remains of a second tub room.

The earliest cultural deposits, which begin at around 96.6 m under Room 28, constitute an occupation surface about 5 cm thick, designated Level 16. This is not a prepared floor, but an uneven, dark-stained surface with charcoal and artifacts in association. As I describe in chapter 3, ceramics from this level include Wide Neck-banded Chuska Gray Ware and Plain Cibola Gray Ware. Wide Neckbanded Gray generally dates to late Pueblo I (ca. AD 850–925; Toll and McKenna 1997:230), suggesting that this initial surface was used later than the Basketmaker pit structures. However, there are earlier ceramics found in the southeast quadrant, including sherds of La Plata/White Mound Black-on-white and Lino Gray, all dating to around AD 550–700 and found at a depth of 97.19–96.87 m. Pollen of economic taxa found on this surface at a depth of 96.65 m included maize, squash, cholla, prickly pear, and beeweed (Smith, this volume). Fauna found at this level included small mammals and

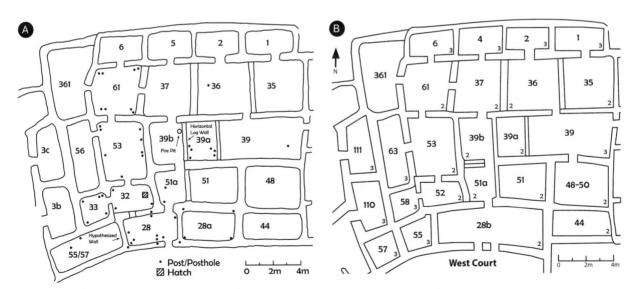

FIGURE 2.1A AND B. Maps showing the changing configuration of Room 28: (a) likely configuration of ground-floor rooms in the northern portion of Pueblo Bonito around AD 1050; (b) configuration of upper-story rooms in the same portion of Pueblo Bonito around AD 1100. Drawing by Drew Wills.

FIGURE 2.2. Level 15 in the southeast quadrant of Room 28 showing horizontal surfaces alternating with laminated sand. At this level, the area was an outdoor surface used for food processing and trash disposal. Photograph by W. H. Wills.

mice (Ainsworth et al., this volume). The fact that the ceramics are out of stratigraphic order suggests some mixing of deposits or that earlier sherds were moved to this level. The strata do not show any break suggestive of rodent, root, or human disturbance, so it is probably a situation of earlier sherds being discarded at a later time period, or possibly the ceramic dates are not accurate. Above the lowest cultural level, a 15 cm stratum of yellow sand and light charcoal sits between 96.65 and 96.8 m. Fifty-five sherds were found in this stratum, designated Level 15 (96.87–96.63 m), including Kiatuthlanna Black-on-white, Red Mesa Black-on-white, Sanostee Orange, and Abajo Red-on-orange. Together, these ceramics suggest dates between AD 700 and 1025. A flotation sample taken from an ash stain located at 96.7 m contained charred saltbush, rabbitbrush, juniper, cottonwood/willow, greasewood, corncobs, and unidentified nutshell fragments (FS 332 in Adams, this volume). Economic pollen recovered in this series of levels at 96.8 m included maize, cholla, prickly pear, beeweed, and an unidentified large grass (little barley, panic grass, or Indian ricegrass) (Smith, this volume). As described in chapter 7, large numbers of cottontails, jackrabbits, a prairie dog, small mammals, and small rodents came from this stratum, along with four bird bones. This stratum lacked any clear surfaces, but may represent trash deposited from occupation elsewhere, perhaps from the occupants of the adjacent Room 28a, together with wind- and water-deposited sand (figure 2.2).

Above this lay a series of at least eleven horizontal surfaces separated by laminated sand, at depths between 96.87 and 97.09 m. These represent use surfaces that predate Room 28. Each appears as an organic-rich brown stain with some gypsum mixed throughout. The surfaces in this area are unbroken, with no evidence of rodent disturbance or mixing. The 68 ceramic sherds found in these strata include a variety of Cibola White Ware decorated types ranging from La Plata Black-on-white to Red Mesa Black-on-white. A pollen sample taken at 96.9 m had cholla, squash, and beeweed among its economic taxa (Smith, this volume). A flotation sample taken from this level produced charred wood, including serviceberry, saltbush, mountain mahogany, juniper, and greasewood; 31 fragments of charred corncobs, cupules, and a kernel; and uncharred seeds of hedgehog cactus, prickly pear, tomatillo, butternut squash, and pinyon (Adams, this volume). Fauna from this level and the flotation sample include cottontails, jackrabbits, prairie dogs, a medium artiodactyl, small mammals, and a bird (Ainsworth et al., this volume). The rich variety of taxa at this level support the use of these horizontal surfaces for trash disposal and probably food processing. Recovery of both squash seeds and squash pollen in this series of levels is notable because evidence of squash is fairly rare in archaeological contexts.

At 96.89 m, seven sherds lay flat on one of the surfaces, including a Wide Neckbanded sherd of Chuska Gray Ware, five sherds of Red Mesa Black-on-white, and one sherd of Newcomb Black-on-white (Crown, chapter 3, this volume). This surface was soft, loamy sand mottled yellow, red, and brown, with pockets of ash and charcoal. It had abundant uncarbonized splinters of wood, indicating that modification of either roof beams or posts had occurred at this level. However, this surface does not clearly correspond with the construction of any posts or walls in Room 28, so it is possible this was a work surface associated with construction of nearby rooms.

At 97.03 m, another surface was used that had wood chips on it. This yellow clayey surface produced extraordinary amounts of cattail pollen in the four samples taken in different quadrants of the excavation. Along with the cattail, economic pollen included squash, cholla, prickly pear, beeweed, and large grass (Smith, this volume). Another pollen sample taken underneath a large flat-lying stone adjacent to two postholes in Room 28 at an elevation of 97 m produced maize, squash, cholla, beeweed, and large grass (Smith, this volume); fauna from under this stone included cottontails, jackrabbits, a small mammal, and two snake bones (Ainsworth et al., this volume). The position of the stone indicates that this material dates immediately prior to the construction of Room 28. A flotation sample (FS 511) taken at what is likely the same surface in what was later the center of Room 28 at 97.01 m produced charred fragments of serviceberry, sagebrush, saltbush, New Mexico privet, ash, juniper, and cottonwood/willow; charred corncobs and cupules; and uncharred prickly pear and cheno-am seeds (Adams, this volume). A charred corncob from this level was submitted for AMS (accelerator mass spectrometry) dating and produced a calibrated date of cal AD 776–968 (AA108161; see table 2.1 for details). More than 200 faunal elements were recovered from this flotation sample, but only a few were identifiable, and these were all cottontail rabbits or mice. Other fauna recovered immediately below the floor in the southwestern quadrant included cottontails, jackrabbits, a woodrat, small mammals, and a medium artiodactyl (Ainsworth et al., this volume). This surface likely was associated with the construction of Room 28; it is possible that the cattail was used in construction because cattail fluff or fibers from cattail leaves are mixed with clay in wattlework construction elsewhere in the world (Georgiev et al. 2013; Racusin and McArleton 2012:49). Alternatively, the cattail might have been placed as an offering just prior to laying the floor of the room. The floor of Room

28 was not perfectly flat; it was measured at 97.06 m along the eastern wall, 97.09 m in the center of the room, 97.14 m in the southwestern corner, and 97.19 m along the northern wall.

ROOM 28

Construction of Room 28 began with preparation of a surface, construction of walls, laying of posts, and construction of a ceiling/roof. Initially, Room 28 was a single story, or at least there is no evidence for multiple stories in the initial room. Here I provide descriptions of the construction of each wall, the postholes, the roof, and the floor. Plan views of the room are in figures 1.3 and 1.4. Descriptions of the floor features follow.

East Wall

The eastern wall of Room 28 was adjacent to the deep southeast quadrant excavation, so we had strong evidence for the wall construction methods. The wall consisted of what Judd (1964:60) called post-and-mud construction, "posts with mud and rocks packed between." In the case of the east wall of Room 28, the wall builders began by digging a foundation trench slightly wider than the wall down to 96.77 m. They then built a wall one course wide; this type of wall construction fits with what Lekson (1984:17) called a "simple" wall. Judd (1964:57) described such walls as "wall-wide sandstone slabs spalled around the edge with hammerstones and laid one upon another in generous quantities of mud." In the Room 28 east wall, the courses of stone were so widely separated and engulfed in mortar that it was not possible to record the actual distance between courses. The bottom courses were still covered with daub and not visible. I estimate that the wall included six to seven courses of stone, each separated by about 10 cm of mud.

In front of this masonry and mud wall, posts 6–8 cm in diameter were placed at intervals of 25–30 cm. Two were recovered in place; one was juniper and the other ponderosa. Each post or stake was placed by first using a sharpened stick, perhaps a digging stick or the post itself, to create a hole about 14 cm in width and with a conical base into the sterile sand below the surfaces described above. The hole was about 45–50 cm below floor level and extended 18 cm below the foundation trench. The lowest 12 cm of the hole was filled with gray sand and charcoal mixed together. Above this, gray clay balls filled the hole another 5 cm. Pebble-size pieces of lignite were

TABLE 2.1. **AMS dates for Room 28 samples calculated with the IntCal13 calibration curve (Reimer et al. 2013) and the computer program OxCal4.2 (Bronk Ramsey 2009)**

SAMPLE ID	CONTEXT	UNCALIBRATED RADIOCARBON AGE	+/-	D¹³C VALUE (%)	CALIBRATED AD RANGE (96%)		HIGHEST PROBABILITY (95.4%)	PROBABILITY (%)
					From	*To*		
AA108152	Posthole 24, wood, floor post	1123	23	-23.7	880	987	880–987	95.4
AA108153	Posthole 2, wood, floor post	1192	24	-24.5	769	893	769–893	95.4
AA108154	Posthole 10, wood, south wall	1184	28	-20.6	730	945	769–898	90.5
AA108155	Posthole 11, wood, south wall	1137	24	-20.6	777	982	862–982	87.3
AA108156	Posthole 15, wood, north wall	1118	26	-22.8	783	992	877–992	95.1
AA108157	Posthole 6, wood, south wall	1207	41	-24.9	687	944	687–898	92.6
AA108158	Posthole 8, wood, south wall	1170	24	-20.9	772	950	772–900	85.6
AA108159	Posthole 12, wood, south wall	1610	24	-19.9	395	536	395–476	53.3
AA108160	Posthole 14, wood, south wall	1630	24	-21.5	348	535	379–435	67.3
AA108161	corncob below floor	1153	21	-10.3	776	968	800–906	52.5

then poured into the hole, filling approximately 8 cm. The wooden post or stake was then pushed into the lignite, with lignite filling some of the space between the post and the edge of the hole (figure 2.3a and b). A thin gray lining found in the postholes suggests that a clay slurry was poured into the holes to help hold the posts in place and avoid wall cracking.

Impressions in the mud show that horizontal crosspieces of wood were attached to the posts. The crosspieces did not preserve, but the impressions of the wood look like strips of juniper. A similar wattlework wall apparently was built on the eastern, or Room 28a, side of this wall separating Room 28 from Room 28a

(Pepper 1920:126). The entire wattlework was then covered with a 10–15 cm layer of plaster that sloped at floor level. The plaster was patted into place with bare hands; handprints are particularly evident at the corners of the room, as seen in our excavations of the southeast corner (figure 2.4) and HEE photos of the northeast corner (for instance, Pepper 1920:figure 44). The builders applied the initial coats of plaster with a very wet consistency, which is apparent in the clear wattlework impressions. The final coat, or perhaps refurbishing, was less moist, as is clear from the handprints.

The wall stands 1.68 m above the floor level on the Room 28 side. There is no evidence of beam sockets in

FIGURE 2.3A AND B. East wall of Room 28:
(*a*) post-and-mud construction; (*b*) detail
of post with lignite and clay at base of posthole.
Photograph by W. H. Wills.

the wall, so the roofing material (most likely second-aries in the east-west direction that would sit on this wall) must have been placed on the open wall (Lekson 1984:30). Any trace of masonry built up between beams no longer exists. There are no openings in the wall.

South Wall

Room 28's southern wall was bonded to the eastern partition wall described in the previous section; more accurately, the top stones of the two walls interdigitate, indicating bonding of the uppermost masonry. Most of the corner is not visible behind the posts and plaster found in the corner, so we could not confirm if the entire wall was bonded.

Like the eastern wall, the southern wall is post-and-mud construction. There are many differences between the two walls, however, suggesting that they were not built simultaneously or by the same builders. The south-ern wall masonry was largely covered over with mud, much of it fired and oxidized, so that it was impossible to count courses or see the stones. Furthermore, the Pepper-Wetherill excavations appear to have damaged sections of this wall, so that it is not possible to view

FIGURE 2.4. Southeast corner of Room 28
with handprints in the plaster at the corner.
Photograph by Patricia Crown.

the entire wall in pristine condition. However, there were at least three pieces of broken ground stone used as masonry in the wall, including a broken basin metate fragment placed upside down in the wall.

The builders of the south wall then placed mud/plaster over at least some of the masonry. Finishing techniques varied over different sections of the wall. Beginning in the southeast corner, a large post (in Post-hole 16) sits just west of the corner where the east and south walls meet and just interior to the masonry (figure 2.5). It is completely embedded in plaster. This post was ponderosa and 15.5 cm in diameter at the top of the

FIGURE 2.5. Southeast corner of Room 28. *From left*, Postholes 16 and 17; rounded entry; Postholes 9, 8, 12, 14, and 13; bisected Posthole 24, and Postholes 4 and 5 surrounded by double adobe collar. The large stone in the entryway can be seen in the Hyde Exploring Expedition photographs of this location. Photograph by Patricia Crown.

FIGURE 2.6. Hyde Exploring Expedition photograph of vessels sitting on plaster adjacent to southeast doorway of Room 28. The trowel marks visible beneath the pots show the HEE's excavation of the hard plaster that surrounded the doorway feature. HEE 111, Image #411887, American Museum of Natural History Library.

posthole. A sample was taken for tree-ring dating, but it was too short to date. A second post (in Posthole 17) was just north of this and also embedded in plaster/mud (figure 2.5). This post was Douglas fir and only 8 cm in diameter. These posts abutted the south doorway into Room 28 and an elaborate, rounded masonry step, which led from the door to the floor. Posts surrounded the door and step on both the east and west sides of the feature.

On the west side of the door, five closely spaced posts were embedded in dense plaster. Fragments of wooden posts were recovered from these, and wood identification showed that four were pinyon and one juniper. A photograph from the HEE shows the posts in place and charred (figure 2.6, *left*). Interestingly, the photograph shows a cylinder jar and pitcher sitting above the floor (where the sandstone disks are resting in the center of the photograph). By comparing figures 2.5 and 2.6, it is possible to see that the cylinder jar and pitcher are sitting on the raised slab/ledge adjacent to the step into the room. The stratum surrounding these five posts, both on this small ledge and below it, is dense and hard, a combination of sand and mortar/plaster/clay that is extremely difficult to trowel. Figure 2.6 shows that Pepper and Wetherill had shaved this hard stratum with a shovel; this is unfortunate because it appears that it was part of an elaborate doorway feature that included masonry and shaped/sculpted plaster. The posts formed a T shape, and plaster surrounded them. It is not clear whether this feature and plaster continued to the ceil-

ing level or not. AMS testing of three of the posts produced varied dates, two in the interval from cal AD 379 to 476 and one at cal AD 772–900 (AA108159, AA108160, AA108158; details in table 2.1).

At the roofline above the level of the postholes sits a section of masonry built of flat blocks of sandstone with considerably less mortar between them; this section is at the roofline but only covers about 50 cm of the roofline. Adjacent to this is a section that fits Judd's (1964:57) description of many early exterior walls at Pueblo Bonito, with small stone chips pressed into the mud. Interestingly, one of Judd's (1964:57, plate 17, *lower*) examples of this type of treatment comes from the exterior of the south wall of Room 28. But the south wall of Room 28 exposed in our 2013 excavations is obviously not an exterior wall, so this method of embedding small chips of sandstone in the mud of a post-and-mud wall appears to have been used sometimes on interior walls as well. This unusual area of the wall may be a patch used to repair the wall during the long history of room use.

To the west of this set of posts is a 55 cm gap in the posts. It is unclear if Pepper and Wetherill destroyed all vestiges of the posts or not, but there are no postholes at floor level nor any post impressions in the wall. Figure 2.6 shows this gap where the sandstone jar lids are resting. There is the usual sparse masonry and thick mud wall in this area, but no wattlework apparent in front of it.

West of this gap, a series of five postholes are 15–20 cm apart (figure 2.7). Each is set in thick mud at floor

FIGURE 2.7. South wall of Room 28, showing post-and-mud construction. Three of the posts left impressions in the burned plaster to the top of the wall, and there is also a large heavily burned plaster patch to the right (west) of these impressions. Photograph by Patricia Crown.

FIGURE 2.8. Close-up of plaster patch in figure 2.7 (*top right*), showing polydactylous footprint to the left of the circular beam socket impression and modeled plaster at the top of the patch. Photograph by Patricia Crown.

level, but when constructed, the posts were apparently visible because the upper wall shows fired depressions for these posts with no outer covering of mud or plaster. In this upper area, the posts separate areas of masonry that stick out farther. This creates a pattern of post-masonry-post-masonry that fits the description by Judd (1964:60) of typical post-and-mud construction: "posts with mud and rocks packed between." It may at one time have resembled the wall of nearby Room 53 illustrated in Judd (1964:plate 20). The five posts of this part of the wall were between 7 cm and 8 cm in diameter and all pinyon. Two provided AMS dates (table 2.1) of cal AD 769–898 (AA108154) and cal AD 862–982 (AA108155). Horizontal crosspieces were apparent at 6 cm and 124 cm above the floor.

Farther to the west there is another gap (55 cm) in

the vertical posts. Toward the floor there is only unfired mud, but from the ceiling to about 50 cm above the floor there is a large square area of thick plaster, which was fired when the room burned (figure 2.8). This plastered area includes a beam socket (discussed below under "Shelving") surrounded by footprints (including a polydactylous left footprint to the left of the beam socket), a shaped design in the plaster at the top, and a number of tabular pieces of sandstone pressed into the plaster. The 23 cm long polydactylous footprint (roughly a US men's size 6 shoe) has been interpreted elsewhere (Crown et al. 2016), but the height of the beam above the floor and the positioning of this footprint directly adjacent to the beam socket suggest that the print was stamped into the fresh wall plaster by a person hanging onto the beam and swinging the foot up. The upper part of the wall plaster was damaged by the HEE excavations, but it is clear that the thick plaster was molded into a pattern here and that the pattern may have continued to the east. Burning helped preserve the plaster.

Two small vertical posts were situated to the west of the gap in Postholes 6 and 23. Post 23 was only 4 cm in diameter and juniper. Post 6 was an unknown species, but provided an AMS date of cal AD 687–898 (AA108157, details in table 2.1). It was 6.5 cm in diameter.

Finally, excavation of the south wall ended at a large post (Posthole 22). This 18 cm in diameter juniper post appeared to be in excellent shape, although charred, but apparently only heartwood remained. It provided a tree-ring date of AD 862 ++vv (explanation of the symbols for tree-ring dates is in Robinson et al. 1975:6). This post was incorporated into the south masonry wall. The posthole had a sandstone slab at the base and lignite on the slab. Three turquoise beads constituted an offering at the base of the post. I believe that this post was located at the corner of a western wall with the south wall or partition for lower Room 28. The only other large posts in this southern wall are incorporated into corners, so it seems likely that this large juniper post was part of a cross-wall that constituted a western wall for lower Room 28. Some partitions in this part of Pueblo Bonito are fairly flimsy; for instance, the partition "wall" between Rooms 39a and 39b consisted of two horizontal poles with some matting or cloth draped from ceiling to floor (Pepper 1920:198). While the HEE excavations did not locate a partition wall in this location between lower Room 28 and Room 55, the wall might either have burned/melted in the fire or been entirely engulfed in the debris that constituted the limits of the HEE excavations in this location to keep the upper-room partition wall from collapsing into lower Room 28. Unfortunately, there will probably never be a way to confirm this because the upper cross-wall makes it impossible to excavate at floor level in the area where I suggest a partition wall once stood.

North Wall

The north wall of Room 28 is Type II masonry (figure 2.9). In his interpretation of the construction sequence of Room 28, Neil Judd (1954:22–28) argued that this north wall "is a Late Bonitian veneer of second-type masonry and is abutted by the partition between 28 and 28a" (Judd 1964:66). Judd did not reexcavate Room 28 and never saw it open, so he based his interpretation on the HEE photographs, believing that the north wall of Room 28 had a veneer of Type II masonry placed in front of an earlier wall or was entirely a straight Type II replacement wall for an earlier, concave north wall to the room. Unfortunately, just about every bit of interpretation for Room 28 offered by Judd is incorrect. The eastern partition wall was unquestionably earlier than the north wall of Room 28, and all four walls of the adjacent Room 28a were Type I masonry. Therefore, the later north wall must abut the partition wall rather than vice versa. There also is no evidence of an earlier Type I wall that was replaced by the north wall. Pepper (1920) did not mention finding evidence of an earlier concave wall in the room to the north (Room 32), and the north wall visible in his photographs of the doorways from Room

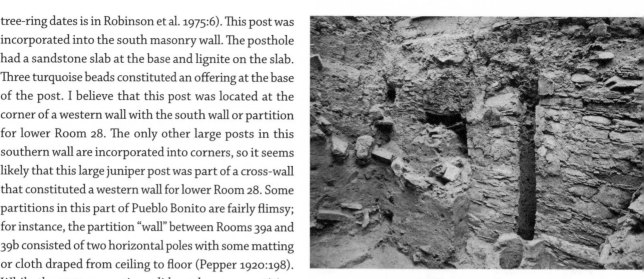

FIGURE 2.9. North wall of Room 28 showing Posthole 15 embedded in masonry, Posthole 7 connected to it with plaster, and a beam socket to the west of the unexcavated door to Room 32. Note the burned plaster over the doorway. Photograph by Patricia Crown.

28 into Room 32 and Room 51a (Pepper 1920:figure 44) shows that the north wall was a double simple wall with masonry courses lined up symmetrically. This means that the north wall of Room 28 and the south walls of Rooms 32 and 51a were all Type II masonry. There was no veneer of Type II masonry over an earlier wall and no evidence of an earlier concave wall straightened by the new north wall. Unfortunately, because the upper-room wall was leaning dangerously into Room 28, we could not uncover either doorway safely, so we were not able to examine the wall construction in either of the two doorways except by the photographs. However, we did uncover the section of the north wall between the two doorways.

The north wall consisted of 16 rows of masonry with large friable sandstone blocks separated by thin layers of chinking stones. The entire north wall had been plastered, but plaster remained only where it had hardened due to the fire. The foundation rested on dense gray clay in a shallow footing trench, with chips of sandstone from the construction process left in the clay. The entire wall from the lowest row of sandstone blocks to the roofline is only 147 cm, putting the roofline on the north side of the room at 98.66 m. The lowest blocks rest on the Room 28 floor. This means that the wall was certainly constructed after the rest of Room 28 had been in use for some time, because the foundation is not below floor level.

Both doorsills are identical in height and depth and are located three courses above the floor. The HEE removed the doorsill to Room 32 to make it easier to remove the objects from Rooms 32 and 33, making it appear that the doorsill was closer to the floor than it actually was. Halfway between the two doorways, a post was incorporated into the wall so that slightly more than half of the circumference was enclosed in the masonry and the other portion was largely covered in plaster. This post (Posthole 15) was 16 cm in diameter, ponderosa pine, and produced both a tree-ring date (AD 803–933 +vv) and an AMS date (cal AD 877–992) (AA108156; table 2.1, figure 2.9). No offerings were found in the posthole. The base of the post rested at 97.22 m on a sandstone slab a bit higher than the adjacent floor at 97.19 m. At the top of the post was a horizontal beam socket with a base at 98.37 m. Unfortunately, the north wall was pulling apart on either side of this post opening, and so it was not possible to measure the diameter of the vertical beam socket accurately. Just to the south of the post in Posthole 15 was another post in Posthole 7. The two were entirely encased and joined in plaster, at least at the base, suggesting that the posts were not visible when the room was occupied. Photographs show the post in Posthole 7 was preserved and standing about a meter above the floor when the HEE opened the room, but it had been removed by 2013.

Another horizontal beam socket hole sits to the west of the door to Room 32 (visible in figure 2.9 to the left of the doorway). Pepper (1920:129) discussed this hole in his description of the opening of Room 32. The socket shows burning, indicating that the beam was present when Room 28 burned and was not part of the unburned Room 32 roof. The base of the socket is at 98.25 m, roughly the same level as the socket on the other side of the door to Room 32.

To summarize, the north wall of Room 28 was constructed after Room 28 had been in use for some time. The entire wall was Type II masonry, rather than having a veneer of this masonry. This wall provided sockets for the room shelving described below and must have been constructed when the shelving was built to provide support for the room-wide shelving beams. It almost certainly replaced an earlier wall in basically the same location, although we did not find any earlier foundation or foundation trench. The doors to Rooms 32 and 51a may have been present prior to the construction of this wall or were added when the wall was built. Without reopening Room 32 to examine the floor for evidence of an earlier wall, we will probably never know exactly why

the north wall of Room 28 was replaced or where exactly it was originally located.

Postholes

In addition to the postholes that were embedded in walls, our excavations uncovered seven floor postholes, and an eighth post is visible in a photograph of the door to Room 51a (Pepper 1920:figure 44, *right*). Details regarding all of the postholes are found in table 2.2. Postholes were constructed in two ways. One method involved excavating a hole larger than the intended post and placing a shaped sandstone slab at the base. Offerings of beads (turquoise, bone, and/or shell) and raw turquoise were sometimes placed above the sandstone slab, and a bed of lignite was placed over the sandstone slab. The post was then placed in the hole. Cobble-size pieces of sandstone were placed in the hole encircling the post in courses, with pea-size pieces of lignite placed between the courses and between the courses and the post, to the floor surface. In many cases, an adobe collar was then packed around the post, covering the floor in a circumference of about 20 cm beyond the post. When posts had adobe collars, the collars typically surrounded two posts, creating a figure 8–shaped adobe collar that recalls the figure 8–shaped shell beads found elsewhere in Chaco. All but one of the posts constructed using this method had adobe collars; the exception was Posthole 3, which was directly under the western profile of the room. This area of the room had been heavily burned, and it is possible that a collar was present around this posthole at one time.

Figures 2.5 and 2.10 both show Posthole 24, which was bisected as part of the excavation of the southeast quadrant. The sandstone slab at the base of the posthole is visible in figure 2.10; cobble-size pieces of sandstone were placed around the post and surrounded by lignite. The lignite at the base of the post was removed before this photograph was taken.

The other method for constructing posts involved excavating a hole larger than the post, placing a sandstone slab at the base, placing the post atop the slab, and then filling the hole with dirt. This method was associated only with the large posts incorporated into walls (in Postholes 15 and 22) and the post in Posthole 7, which was completely surrounded by plaster and attached to Posthole 15 with plaster. So, it appears that posts that were incorporated into walls or surrounded entirely with plaster did not have cobble/lignite lining. Of the three

TABLE 2.2. **Room 28 posthole attributes and dates**

POSTHOLE	LINING	SPECIES	DIAMETER (CM)	TREE-RING DATE	C-14 (95.4% PROBABILITY)	BASAL SLAB	OFFERING IN POSTHOLE	ADOBE COLLAR	LIGNITE	DEPTH TO BASE	LOCATION
1	sandstone and lignite	no wood	19			sandstone	turquoise beads	collar attached to PH 22 and 2	around sandstone in lining	96.51 m	floor
2	sandstone and lignite	PP	17		769–893	sandstone	turquoise, bone, shell ornaments	collar attached to PH 1	around sandstone in lining	96.2 m	floor
3	sandstone and lignite	unknown	18			sandstone	none	none	around sandstone in lining	96.58 m	floor
4	sandstone and lignite	PNN	13			sandstone	none	collar attached to PH 5	around sandstone in lining	96.88 m	floor
5	sandstone and lignite	DF	17			sandstone	none	collar attached to PH 4	around sandstone in lining	96.42 m	floor
6	unlined	unknown	6.5		687–898	none	unknown	none	unknown	—	south wall
7	unlined	unknown	17			sandstone	beads, raw turquoise and shell	on wall side attached to PH 15	none	96.65 m	floor
8	unlined	PNN	8		772–900	on doorstep	unknown	none	unknown	96.81 m	doorway/wall
9	unlined	PNN	5			on doorstep	unknown	none	unknown	—	doorway/wall
10	unlined	PNN	7.5		769–898	sandstone	unknown	none	unknown	96.73 m	south wall
11	unlined	PNN	7.5		862–982	sandstone	unknown	none	unknown	96.73 m	south wall
12	unlined	JUN	11		395–476	none	unknown	none	unknown	96.99 m	south wall
13	unlined	PNN	8			sandstone	unknown	none	unknown	—	doorway/wall
14	unlined	PNN	7		379–435	sandstone	unknown	none	unknown	96.9 m	south wall
15	in north wall	PP	16	809–933 +vv	877–992	sandstone	none	none	none	97.22 m	north wall
16	at least partly lined	PP	15.5			unknown, post in plaster and left in corner	unknown	none	unknown	—	southeast corner, embedded in wall
17	unlined	DF	8			unknown	unknown	none	unknown	96.7 m	doorway/wall
18	unknown	PP	7			unknown, post in plaster and left	unknown	none	unknown	—	east wall
19	unlined	no wood	8			none	unknown	none	unknown	96.4 m	east wall
20	unlined	unknown	8			none	none	none	at base	96.43 m	east wall
21	unlined	JUN	6			none	none	none	at base	96.5 m	east wall

POSTHOLE	LINING	SPECIES	DIAMETER (CM)	TREE-RING DATE	C-14 (95.4% PROBABILITY)	BASAL SLAB	OFFERING IN POSTHOLE	ADOBE COLLAR	LIGNITE	DEPTH TO BASE	LOCATION
22	unlined	JUN	18	625–862 ++vv		sandstone	turquoise beads	collar attached to PH 1	at base	96.84 m	south wall
23	unlined	JUN	4			none	unknown	none	unknown	—	south wall
24	sandstone and lignite	PP	18	847–895 +vv	880–987	sandstone	none	collar	around sandstone in lining	96.3 m	floor
25	unlined	PNN	7			none	unknown	none	unknown	96.8 m	south wall
26	unlined	PNN	7			none	unknown	none	unknown	96.77 m	south wall
27	unlined	PNN	8			none	unknown	none	unknown	96.76 m	south wall

Tree-ring date symbols from Robinson et al. 1975:6.

For more information on AMS dates, see table 2.1. | DF = Douglas fir; JUN = juniper; PNN = pinyon; PP = ponderosa pine.

posts in Room 28 erected using this method, only the post in Posthole 22 had lignite, in this case placed at the bottom of the posthole. The posts in Postholes 7 and 22 had offerings, while that in Posthole 15 did not. As noted, a final post can be seen in photographs of the northeast corner of the room (Pepper 1920:figure 44, just visible on the right and more visible in later photographs of this corner of the room). That post does not have an adobe collar, although there seem to be sandstone slabs adja-

FIGURE 2.10. Bisected Posthole 24 with basal sandstone slab. Note the cobble-size pieces of sandstone that were placed around the post with lignite in between. Photograph by Patricia Crown.

cent to it to the south. We were unable to expose this portion of the room due to safety concerns.

The species of tree used for floor (as opposed to wall) posts in Room 28 included ponderosa, pinyon, and Douglas fir. Posts were visible in Postholes 1, 3, and 7 in the 1896 photographs but were not found in our excavations, so someone pulled the posts from these postholes prior to backfilling the room in 1897. Ponderosa pine from Posthole 24 provided a tree-ring date of AD 895 +vv and an AMS date of cal AD 880–987 (AA108152; table 2.1). The post in Posthole 2 provided an AMS date of cal AD 769–893 (AA108153; table 2.1).

The methods used to erect posts in Room 28 are documented elsewhere in Pueblo Bonito. Judd (1964:325) described similar methods for the posts in early Bonito Rooms 323, 325, and 326, including the presence of what he called "cones of adobe" where the posts intersect the floors. As with Room 28, there were many posts in these three rooms: eight in Room 323, seven in Room 325, and six in Room 326. The posts were all on the eastern side of these three rooms, which is the West Court side. In Room 28, the collared posts are all on the southern side of the room, which is also the West Court side. This pattern, along with the overabundance of posts in these rooms, suggests the possibility that these rooms were originally ramadas fronting rooms on the plaza or court area of early Pueblo Bonito, which were later walled in to create rooms. The adobe cones may have helped keep moisture out of the posts before the ramadas were transformed into rooms. Unfortunately, this is an interpretation that may be difficult to verify.

The use of lignite in the posts (Judd called it "shale chips") is a well-documented practice in Chaco Canyon (Heitman 2015:tables 5 and 6). As Heitman (2015:230–31) notes, packing lignite around posts may have had both functional and cosmological significance.

Doors

There are three doors in the lower portion of Room 28 and no other known openings. Two of the doors are known only through photographs because the condition of the upper-story north wall made it unsafe to expose these openings. The two doors located in the north wall are identical in construction and symmetrically placed around the exposed post in the north wall. The photographs indicate sills about 15 cm above the floor. Pepper (1920:163) described the door into Room 32 (the doorway on the west looking toward the north wall of Room 28) as 56 cm wide and 86 cm high. It had lintels of wooden strips with bark still attached. The lintels over the eastern door are not visible in the photographs, but Pepper's (1897a:Room 51a) field diagrams show that the doorway between Room 28 and Room 51a was 61 cm wide and 71 cm high.

The southern door originally fronted the West Court of Pueblo Bonito. It sits directly beneath a T-shaped doorway in the upper room (one of two doorways in the south wall; the other sits directly above the partition wall). Unfortunately, collapse of the rubble filling the lower doorway made it necessary to seal it up with new masonry, so we were unable to excavate it properly. Pepper did not provide measurements for this doorway, and the poor condition of the doorway made it impossible to get accurate measurements; it was approximately 50 cm wide. Inside Room 28, a circular step constructed of masonry and mud mortar aided movement from the floor to the door. The top of the step was a large, irregular stone, which is visible in Pepper's bird's-eye photographs of the room. Pepper's excavations in the adjacent Room 40 (a room that Judd [1954:27] stated is "nonexistent") revealed a feature probably associated with this doorway, consisting of three walls jutting out from the north wall of Room 40 in line with the door to Room 28. Pepper (1920:200) thought it might have been a small room used as a workshop because of the quantity of shell and turquoise beads found in it. In contrast, Judd (1954:27) argued that the space held stairs: "By

a flight of stone steps this south door [from Room 28] gave access to the terrace overlooking Kivas Q and R." Visible in photographs taken in 1897 (figure 2.11), this workshop or stairway space was constructed of masonry and mud to the roofline of Room 40 just south of Room 28; the outline of this feature is visible today on the surface adjacent to Room 28 and beneath the upper-story T-shaped doorway. In this case, I believe Judd is correct: it was an enclosed masonry stairway from Room 28 to the West Court or the roof of Room 40. The staircase was a small space, probably around 1.5 m east-west and 1.3 m north-south. Pepper (1920:200) mentioned that a stone slab was found in the room, and this slab is visible in the photographs. I believe the slab was a sandstone door cover for the southern doorway into Room 28.

Maps of Pueblo Bonito show similar small "bins" adjacent to early Bonito rooms, including Rooms 83, 309, and possibly 315, that front courtyards. A strong possibility is that over time deposits filled the courtyards and buried the early ground-floor room entries; stairways then were built to enclose entries to the height of the new ground level, permitting continued use of the lower-story rooms. Rising ground level is known to have been a problem at Pueblo Bonito. Tree-ring dates indicate a probable hiatus in construction at Pueblo Bonito between about AD 975 and 1040 (Windes and Ford 1996:301). When construction resumed in the 1000s, the surface of the West Court had risen so much that it was approximately level with the roofs of the first-story rooms (Crown and Wills 2018). Judd (1964:60) suggested that wind-blown sand contributed to this. Sand also piled up against the rear rooms, and new rooms were built on the accumulated sand (Lekson 1984:133). While Judd saw these deposits as natural accumulation, Stein and colleagues (2003:50) argue that occupants of Pueblo Bonito raised the surface level artificially. The deposits may represent both natural and cultural accumulation, particularly as excavation for adjacent kivas may have raised the surrounding surface level.

Floor and Floor Features

Along the western edge of the excavation, the floor of Room 28 was so burned that parts had vitrified to glass, just as Pepper (1920) stated. In areas around the postholes, the adobe collars were easy to follow. But otherwise, the floor was simply compacted sand with some gypsum, and it was not always easy to follow. As noted above, there was a surface just below the floor

FIGURE 2.11. Hyde Exploring Expedition photograph of the north wall of Room 40 (the outside of the south wall of Room 28) with blocked twin T-shaped doorways in the upper-story wall, the jutting roofline for lower Room 40, and "bin" walls surrounding a likely stairway down to the lower Room 28. Note the large sandstone slab inside the "bin" walls that may have been a door slab for the south door of Room 28. HEE 194, Image #411957, American Museum of Natural History Library.

that had many impressions of wood shavings, probably from constructing the room and shaping the posts. The gypsum at and just below floor level may have derived from mixing wall plaster or it might have been part of the floor preparation.

We located a number of features at or just below the floor, including three thermal features that had ash, charcoal, and reddened areas. These may have been used as informal hearths, but they are not lined and are amorphous in shape. They are located along the central north-south axis of the room.

The first, Ashpit A, is 25 × 20 cm in size and 21 cm deep, with slightly rounded sides, and is located roughly in the center of the excavated area. A burned cobble-size piece of sandstone was found at the northern side of the feature, and the bowl-shaped pit had ashy fill, in-

dicating use as a thermal feature. A flotation sample contained varieties of wood, two tomatillo seeds, maize fragments, and a fragment of twine (FS 362; see Adams, this volume). The only identifiable bone was a lagomorph vertebra (Ainsworth et al., this volume). Ceramics from this feature include Escavada Black-on-white, Narrow Neckbanded Gray Ware, and a Cibola White Ware with purple paint outlined in a glaze paint (Crown, chapter 3, this volume). Together, these ceramics suggest that the feature might have been used in the late 1000s or early 1100s.

Adjacent to this was a second pit (Ashpit B) filled with ash and charcoal. A circular indentation was found at the northeastern edge of this depression. The entire feature was 15 × 25 cm in size and 20 cm deep. The flotation sample from this feature produced varieties of wood, cheno-am seeds, mustard seeds, tomatillo seeds, charred maize fragments, an unknown charred fruit fragment, and many uncharred pinyon nut fragments (FS 363; see Adams, this volume). Three identifiable bones were from rabbits (two) and a small mammal (one) (Ainsworth et al., this volume). No ceramics were found in this feature.

Yet another ashy thermal feature was located adjacent to the north wall and above the foundation clay of that wall. It was shallow in depth (less than 10 cm) but covered an area 40 cm east-west by 50 cm north-south. A flotation sample taken from this feature produced varieties of wood, an *Echinocereus* cactus seed, more than 50 charred stickleaf seeds, and charred maize fragments (FS 299; see Adams, this volume). Fauna found in the feature included rabbits and a small rodent (Ainsworth et al., this volume). Only Plain Gray and unidentifiable ceramics were recovered from this feature (Crown, chapter 3, this volume).

A final floor feature may predate the floor of Room 28 because it is located at 97.02 m, lower than the average floor level of 97.09 m. However, given its location, I believe it might be associated with the room floor despite its depth. This feature is a circular depression, 8 cm in diameter at the surface and 4 cm deep and filled with red ocher. At the surface, a rounded worked sherd crafted from a Red Mesa Black-on-white bowl was pressed into

the ocher in the center of the feature. The feature is located 70 cm south of and directly centered on the doorway to Room 32. I am not aware of other features like this at Pueblo Bonito, but it clearly had some ritual significance. It resembles an eye, with the worked sherd as the pupil and the red ocher as the iris.

In addition to samples from the floor features, a flotation sample was taken from the floor adjacent to the large post pulled from Posthole 22 in the southwest corner of the room. This sample (FS 510) came from burned material found in this corner. As described in chapter 9, the sample included uncharred and charred seeds, particularly maize and tomatillo, along with many kinds of wood; fauna from this sample included cottontail rabbit, mice, other small rodents, and other rabbits (perhaps jackrabbits) (Ainsworth et al., this volume).

Roofing

The primary roof beams of lower Room 28 were placed atop the room walls, which was apparently the most common method for constructing roofs in Chaco (Lekson 1984:30). Lekson (1984:30) stated that masonry was then placed around the beams, but there is no evidence of such masonry in Room 28 and no way to know if it was originally present or not. The primaries ran north-south, across the narrowest axis of the room. At the top

FIGURE 2.12. Hyde Exploring Expedition photograph of Room 28 with cylinder jar cache. Note the roofline for the lower room (*left*) and the gap in the north wall where the roof beams once sat. HEE 104, Image #411880, American Museum of Natural History Library.

of the south wall, the roofline lay at 98.67 m (figure 2.12, *left*). At the top of the north wall, a large gap between the lower-room wall and the upper-story wall sits where the roof would have been; the bottom of this gap lay at 98.66 m. This gap is visible particularly in the HEE photographs over the door to Room 51a in the lower right-hand corner (figure 2.12). Some of the rocks visible in that gap may have served as masonry between primary beams, but there was no evidence of mortar between them. As discussed above, the north wall of Room 28 was added some time after the room was originally built, and so roof beams already spanned this area when the short north wall was built underneath it. With an average floor level of 97.09 m, the ceiling would have been 1.58 m (5' 2") above the floor.

Pepper (1920:117) described how the 1896 excavation encountered burned beams and calcined flooring. In the adjacent Room 55, Pepper (1920:216) described finding "the remains of a cedarbark floor covering and pieces of adobe floor," although it is somewhat unclear if he was talking about the ceiling/floor of the lowest room or the second story. Because this is presumably the same roof that would have covered Room 28, it is possible that Room 28 also had cedar bark covering the roofing beams, followed by adobe flooring. Unfortunately, while we encountered thousands of pieces of burned daub with roofing impressions in the backfill of Room 28 in the 2013 excavations, these probably came from the adjoining Room 28a rather than Room 28. This burned material had impressions of sticks and beams, and some of the pieces had turquoise beads and sherds embedded in the adobe. One of the sherds was identifiable as Lino Gray. The sections of roof/floor found in the room were 10–12 cm thick. A sample of 75 reed impressions found in the burned daub averaged 0.96 cm in diameter. We also recovered burned sticks in the backfill and measured a sample of them. The average diameter of 496 of these sticks was 0.77 cm. So, many of the sticks were probably roofing material, perhaps parts of rush mats, which were used as roofing material in other rooms (Judd 1964:26; Lekson 1984:31). Karen Adams analyzed a sample of the sticks and found that they included charred twigs of juniper, mountain mahogany, *Populus/Salix*, pine, saltbush, and *Chrysothamnus*. The variety of wood contrasts with the relatively narrow range of stick diameters, suggesting that builders used whatever plants offered appropriately sized sticks. The use of matting or carefully selected sticks for roofing is apparently a later building

technique at Pueblo Bonito, whereas earlier roofs had cedar bark, brush, or cornstalk closing material (Judd 1954:26). For this reason, I believe that the material we found probably belongs to the upper story (probably Room 28b), which was constructed later than Room 28, but it does shed light on roofing patterns at Pueblo Bonito. Taking all of the evidence into account, I suggest that lower Room 28 had cedar bark covering the roof beams, and the upper-story Room 28b had reed mats or sticks covering the roof beams.

Shelving

There is evidence for a shelf or room-wide platform (Judd 1954:45, 1964:29; Lekson 1984:38, 2007:15) in Room 28. Several types of evidence suggest the presence of this shelving, including beam sockets, the positions of vessels on the floor, and burned wood visible in photographs. As noted above, the primary roof beams of lower Room 28 were clearly positioned on top of the north and south walls of the room. Evidence for a shelf is found in beam sockets located below the roofline. There are two beam sockets located on either side of the door to Room 32 on the north wall and one clear beam socket located on the south wall. The area where a second beam socket should have been located on the south wall is now covered with melted daub, but it was probably present. The western pair of beam sockets sits at 98.25–98.28 m, and the bottom level of the sockets is thus around 40 cm below the roofline, which sat at 98.67 m. The socket is 16 cm in diameter, leaving about 24 cm between the top of the beam and the ceiling.

The crosspieces for the shelving may have been wooden planks. A single burned plank crafted of Douglas fir (*Pseudotsuga menziesii*, identified by Karen R. Adams and Rex K. Adams, July 22, 2019) was recovered from Posthole 1 into which it had fallen; this posthole would have been directly beneath the shelving. And an HEE photograph (figure 2.13) of the room shows what appear to be planks near that posthole, along with what may be pairs of small charred wooden beams lying under and around the cylinder jars, which may also have been crosspieces for shelving (see Lekson 1984:46). These charred beams cannot be from the ceiling because there is no daub or floor plaster associated with them.

The positioning of the cylinder jars also supports the argument that they once sat on shelving. The first layer of jars encountered by George Pepper lay in a patterned configuration, suggesting that they had been placed in

FIGURE 2.13. Hyde Exploring Expedition photograph of the fifth layer of cylinder jars excavated in 1896. There is a possible plank (*bottom left*) next to a posthole. The pairs of charred cross-pieces around the pots are interpreted in this volume as shelving. HEE 109C, Image #411897, American Museum of Natural History Library.

FIGURE 2.14. West profile of Room 28, showing late masonry wall (*beneath scaffolding*) and backfill stratigraphy beneath the wall. At the bottom in the center is Posthole 3 with a heavily reddened area just above and around it. Photograph by Patricia Crown.

an orderly manner either on the floor or on something above it that collapsed (figure 2.12). The fact that the pairs of small wooden beams were found toward the bottom of the pile of vessels strongly indicates that a wooden structure of some kind held the vessels. The charring of those wooden pieces indicates that they were exposed to air on some side (otherwise, they might smolder but not burn), and I propose that it was the underside. Furthermore, many of the vessels show blackened areas from burning that are not fireclouds from their original firing. As noted in chapter 1, because the vessels have never been washed, it is possible to use the photographs to orient the original position of each vessel as it was found, and the blackened areas are all underneath the vessels rather than on top, as we would expect if the charred pieces fell from above.

The reddened and vitrified areas of flooring indicate that the fire was started around the post in Posthole 3 (figure 2.14), directly under the shelving that held the vessels. A fire laid there would climb up the post to the shelving above, causing it to burn and collapse, depositing the pottery that was sitting on the shelving onto the floor.

Upper Story

Because the reexcavation of Room 28 was focused on the lower, early room, relatively little attention was paid to the upper story, which is still visible at the site today. Indeed, the shoring system we put in place covered most

of those upper walls. However, I can provide some information on the upper story that is relevant for the earlier room. The upper story was built using the lower-story walls in part. The upper-story Room 28b covered both Room 28a and the portion of Room 28 that we excavated. Judd (1964:23–26) stated that the north wall of the upper Room 28b was Type II masonry, while the south wall was Type IV masonry. He also stated that the west wall of the upper room, the wall that sits on debris from the burned lower room, is also Type II masonry, but it is not. Instead, that wall is a late partition that abuts both the north and south walls of the room. The floor plaster still evident along the base of this wall (figures 2.12 and 2.14) is higher than the base of the north and south walls, indicating it was added after those walls had been in use for some time. We attempted to locate the debris underlying this wall that is apparent in the photographs, but we could not. The HEE had apparently undercut it so much, first in 1896 from the Room 28 side and then in 1897 from the Room 55 side, that we could not locate any of those original layers. We cut a "window" into the stratigraphy on our last day in the field to try to find where the original debris strata were, but despite cutting in 60 cm, we only encountered backfill. It was too dangerous to undercut the wall further.

The wall construction sequence suggests that the north wall of upper Room 28b was probably constructed when the north wall of lower Room 28 was rebuilt, probably in the mid-1000s. But the south wall was constructed later. As Type IV masonry, it was probably constructed in the late 1000s. This timing suggests that the north wall of the upper story was constructed to put an upper story over Room 52 to the north, while Room 28 remained a single-story room until a few decades later. The builders placed this north wall directly over the lower story's wall/ceiling.

In contrast, the upper-story south wall was placed adjacent to rather than over the lower-story south wall. Placing a new wall adjacent to the south wall required digging out the accumulated deposits in the West Court to the south of the lower south wall of Rooms 28 and 28a and then building a new wall parallel to the old wall and rising another story above it. Evidence from the excavations in the adjoining Room 40 to the south (Pepper 1920:199) and by Judd (1964:57) in the West Court shows that both the lower- and upper-story walls are continuous and Type IV masonry when viewed from the south. While this wall sits partially atop and directly adjacent to the south wall in part of Room 28 (see figure 2.12), it is a curved wall, deviating at the eastern end of Room 28 because it curves to the south, while the walls of Rooms 28 and 28a are fairly straight east-west. The single photograph of lower Room 28a shows this deviation quite well (reproduced in Crown and Wills 2018:figure 6). Thus, when the upper-story Room 28b was constructed, a wall was built adjacent to the lower-story south wall of Room 28 that spanned two stories, creating both the south wall of Room 28b, which was the upper story of Rooms 28 and 28a, and the north wall of Room 40. Room 28b

sits largely outside the south wall of Room 28, so that there is a ledge about 30 cm wide at the roofline today. The upper story is thus slightly larger than the lower story and has a curved south wall. On the south side of this south wall, photographs (e.g., figure 2.11) show a roofline roughly at the current ground level, presumably for Room 40. The upper-story wall is 47–53 cm wide, so the double south wall of lower Room 28 must have been close to a meter wide when the second wall was added to support the upper story.

For upper Room 28b, two T-shaped doorways were built into the south wall, opening onto either the West Court or the rooftop of Room 40 (figure 2.11). One sits directly above the lower-story partition between the two rooms; the other sits directly above the door into lower Room 28. A T-shaped doorway in the north wall of Room 28b also sits atop the partition wall; because T-shaped doorways generally open onto plaza/courtyard areas (Lekson 1984:28), this northern T-shaped doorway was probably originally a door to the outside, exiting from the upper-story Room 51a across the rooftop of Room 28, prior to the construction of Room 28b. The level of the west courtyard had risen so much by the time that the upper-story Room 51a was constructed that lower Room 28 was underground and thus its roof was at the courtyard level. The south wall was then constructed later and a roof put over the room.

Both the north and south walls show evidence of fire, so they were unquestionably present when the lower room burned. The west wall lacks evidence of burning and was constructed on top of the debris of the lower room, which has a floor that was placed over that leveled debris. Whether this later room was roofed is not clear. Pepper (1920) did not describe excavating through an upper-story roof in either Room 28 or 28a. It is possible that this area remained unroofed after the fire, with the T-shaped doorways closed with masonry, the partition wall constructed, and the area used for activities such as penning turkeys (see Conrad, this volume). Alternatively, the room might have been reroofed and used, with the roof either not preserved or robbed for later use and thus not present when the HEE excavated there.

DATING ROOM 28

A primary goal in reexcavating Room 28 was understanding the sequence of construction, use, and termination. Dating the construction of the room focused on tree-ring and radiocarbon dates. Dating of the use of the room focused on evidence of remodeling and on ceramics found beneath the floor and by the Pepper excavations. Dating of the termination relied on ceramics and absolute dates to provide a terminus post quem.

Photographs taken in 1896 indicate the presence of charred posts, and the ground-penetrating radar tests conducted before the reexcavations confirmed the likely presence of at least some of these posts (Sturm and Crown 2015). As noted in chapter 1, we removed more than 1,900 samples of charred wood from Room 28, but most of this wood was from backfill and thus not from Room 28. Therefore, we concentrated our dating efforts on the posts found in the room walls and in floor postholes. The National Park Service curates all of the unanalyzed samples and hopefully funding will be found to analyze those someday. They would be helpful in dating the adjacent Room 28a.

Thirty samples were sent to the Laboratory of Tree-Ring Research at the University of Arizona. This discussion is based on the report written by Ronald H. Towner (2014). The samples included 19 ponderosa, 4 *Populus* species, 2 Douglas fir, 1 pinyon, and 2 juniper. Two samples were too rotted for species identification. Only five samples produced dates. The post from Posthole 24 (a floor posthole) dated to AD 895 +vv (meaning there is no way of knowing how far the last ring is from the true outside ring). This tree was at least 50 years old, and the posthole was 18 cm wide. The large juniper post from

Posthole 22 (a south wall post) had a date of AD 862 ++vv. In this case, the tree was found to have only heartwood and no sapwood. Unfortunately, there is no formula for determining the amount of sapwood (or missing rings) based on the heartwood in a juniper. This tree had an inner ring date of AD 625, so it was a very old juniper and fit in a posthole 18 cm in diameter. The post in Posthole 15 (in the north wall of Room 28) produced a date of AD 933 +vv. Finally, two dates came from wood recovered in the gap over the north wall that represents the roofline. At the time these were excavated, I believed they might be latillas (crossbeams) above the door to Room 51a, but after viewing more of the HEE photographs, I realized that there was no wood found in that roofline gap in 1896. Therefore, this wood, like the other wood in the backfill, probably came from the adjacent Room 28a. The two dates from this wood are AD 932 ++vv and AD 1069 +L (the L means that "a characteristic surface patination and smoothness, which develops on beams stripped of bark, is present") (for an explanation of the Laboratory of Tree-Ring Research symbols, see Robinson et al. 1975:6). While the L usually refers to a cutting date, the + means that one or more rings might be missing. So, this would be considered a near cutting date. Both of these beams are ponderosa.

Once I found out that we would acquire few dates from the tree-ring samples, I sent ten samples for AMS dating to the University of Arizona (table 2.1). This discussion is based on a report from Richard Cruz and Greg

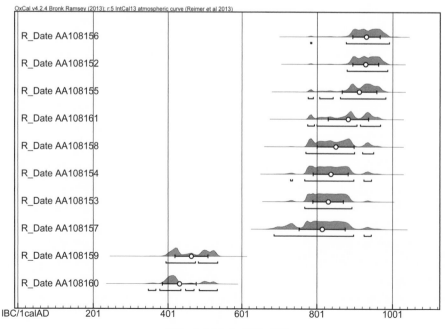

FIGURE 2.15. Calibrated posterior probability distributions for the radiocarbon dates from Room 28 posts and a corncob beneath the floor. The brackets beneath the distributions show the 1-σ and 2-σ confidence intervals. Calibrated with OxCal4.2.4/IntCal13 (Bronk Ramsey 2009; Reimer et al. 2013).

Hodgins (2016). With the exception of the corncob, all samples were collected in the field without handling and wrapped in aluminum foil. I selected the actual samples sent to the lab by cutting off the outermost rings from the posts using a new sterile razor blade for each sample.

Figure 2.15 shows the dates in chronological order from earliest to latest. A single date comes from a corncob recovered under the floor of Room 28 and should provide a date that precedes the construction of the room. Unfortunately, with a 96% probability spread from cal AD 776 to 968, the date does not provide much precision. The highest probability spread is cal AD 800–906, and this seems reasonable. Six dates come from the south wall of Room 28, which was built in a single event and does not show any signs of remodeling. These dates show a wide spread. Two dates fall in the cal AD 348–536 range, which is obviously much too early. The builders might have used old wood. These two posts were adjacent to one another in the room. The other four dates from the south wall seem more reasonable, falling between cal AD 730 and 982. Most of these cluster together in figure 2.15, with overlap particularly between AD 880 and 900. Two floor/ceiling posts come from Postholes 2 and 24; we would anticipate that these posts holding up the roof would have been placed contemporaneously. Posthole 2 dates to AD 769–893, but Posthole 24 dates to AD 880–987. Again, there is overlap in the dates between AD 880 and 893. The post from Posthole 24 also had a tree-ring date of AD 895 +vv, falling in the AMS 96% range but indicating that the actual date has to be later than AD 895. Finally, a single date came from the north wall post found in Posthole 15. Based on masonry style and bonding and abutting relationships, we would predict that this wall was built later than the rest of the room. Type II masonry is placed by Lekson (1984:19) at AD 1020–1060. The post in this wall has an AMS date of AD 783–992, the latest date in the room, and a tree-ring date of AD 933 +vv, indicating that it had to have died later than AD 933. It is, of course, possible that this post was reused from the earlier north wall, which was replaced with Type II masonry.

I interpret these dates, taken together, to indicate that the south and east walls of Room 28 were constructed sometime between AD 880 and 910, and the north wall was constructed sometime after AD 950. Lekson (1984:19) dated Type II masonry as AD 1020–1060, so it is likely that the north wall of Room 28 was constructed during that interval. As indicated in chapter 3, the ceramics found under the floor of the room include early

ceramics up to Red Mesa Black-on-white, suggesting that the room was constructed while Red Mesa Black-on-white was the dominant ceramic type (AD 875–1040; Toll and McKenna 1997:286). Unfortunately, this does not help narrow down the actual dates much, except that it's likely the north wall was added around AD 1020–1060, rather than later.

Lekson (2007:16) states that room-wide platforms appear in Chaco sites about AD 1040. Since the room-wide platform/shelving discussed above was constructed as part of the addition of the north wall, a date of around AD 1040–1060 for this addition seems reasonable.

The upper story of Room 28, designated Room 28b, was likely built at the same time as the upper stories of the adjacent Rooms 28a, 55, and 57 because these share north and south walls. There are tree-ring dates from the second stories of Rooms 55 and 57, as well as two dates from the large upper-story room (Room 28b) that spans Rooms 28 and 28a (Laboratory of Tree-Ring Research 2015). Wood from beam sockets in Room 28b dates to AD 1071 L and AD 1116 vv. The earlier date came from the west end of Room 28b and the later date from the east end of Room 28b. A Room 55 second-story west wall intramural beam dates to AD 969 vv. Two primary beams from the Room 57 second-story roof date to AD 1047 r and AD 1071 v. These dates, combined with the new tree-ring date from the fill of Room 28 of AD 1069 +L, suggest construction of the upper-story Room 28b in or close to AD 1071 (which fits with the Type IV masonry style of the south wall; Lekson 1984:19), with some remodeling after 1116.

If Room 28b was built around AD 1071, then the fire that destroyed the lower room must have occurred after this date. The whole vessels found in the room by the HEE are primarily Gallup Black-on-white, indicating they were deposited in the late AD 1000s. Pepper (1920) recovered sherds in the room in 1896 that run the gamut from Narrow Neckbanded Gray Ware and Red Mesa Black-on-white to Chaco-McElmo Black-on-white and St Johns Polychrome, but most of them came from "a few feet below surface," and the floor assemblage represents a narrower range, including Red Mesa Black-on-white and Gallup Black-on-white. The 174 whole and partial vessels found in the room include vessels from Red Mesa Black-on-white to Chaco Black-on-white. Chaco Black-on-white dates to AD 1075–1150 (Toll and McKenna 1997:334). It thus seems likely that the room burned around AD 1100, although the fire could have occurred in the first decades of the 1100s.

HISTORICAL MODIFICATIONS
TO ROOM 28

As discussed in chapter 1, Pepper and Wetherill had workers begin the excavation of Room 28 in August 1896, found the first cylinder jar on August 20, and by August 29 completed the excavations, measured the room, and removed the masonry that blocked the northwest door into Room 32. They did not subfloor the room. In his sketch of Room 28, Pepper unfortunately reversed the east and west walls and only showed one door, perhaps indicating his rush to complete the task.

So, the 1896 excavation of Room 28 took at least ten days. Of relevance to our 2013 excavations were the twin questions of where they put the backdirt from Room 28 in 1896 and where the backfill we excavated from Room 28 came from. We also discovered that during their excavations, the HEE modified Room 28, and I discuss those modifications briefly here.

As noted above, the excavation of Room 28 terminated with the opening of the closed door to the adjacent Room 32, which in turn led to Room 33. Both Rooms 32 and 33 had intact ceilings, but they were filled with deposits, and those deposits had to be removed through Room 28. Moving the fill of two rooms, particularly two rooms so packed with artifacts and burials, unquestionably had an impact on Room 28. We noted this impact in two ways. First, the doorsill of the doorway was missing and was almost certainly removed to enlarge that door and make it easier to pass through. This is apparent in the photograph of the doorway taken looking north from Room 28, which shows vessels in Room 32 (HEE 120, AMNH digital catalog 411898). Second, we found a large, shallow depression or pit adjacent to that doorway that almost certainly was caused by the Hyde group moving in and out of the room. Shovel marks outline its edges, and it measures 80 cm to the south of the doorway and 1 m along the north wall of Room 28.

In his diary for September 16, 1896, Pepper specifically stated that in working in Room 33, "Richard went inside and pitched out the dirt to Hasalufa who in turn threw it out into Room #28 where I kept it clear for him." Similarly, on September 17, 1896, Pepper wrote, "Richard went into room #33 and threw out the dirt to Hasalufa who in turn shoveled it out into #28. I kept the entrance clean and piled the dirt against the West wall—when this task was finished Richard came out and went to work clearing the balance of the dirt away from

the Eastern end of Room #32—I commenced to look over the dirt that had been thrown out and took the measurements of and numbered the articles that Richard found as he progressed with his work." At least some of the backfill was moved "near Richard's bed," but much of it was apparently "searched" in Room 28. The techniques included visual searching, but Pepper also made a screen of cheesecloth and "some old sticks" to help search for beads (Pepper 1896:entry for September 15, 1896). The diary entry for September 22 indicated that some of the crew had carried piles of sand out of Room 28. From the descriptions that followed, the piles of fill were carried to near the kitchen behind Pueblo Bonito, where the group could work together to locate beads. The season ended and the entire crew left the camp on September 23; there is no mention of backfilling Rooms 32 or 33, and they were measured on September 23 before everyone departed the camp. The records indicate then that the fill of these two important rooms was thrown into Room 28, but then at least some of it was removed to behind Pueblo Bonito. It is thus quite possible that some of the fill that we found in Room 28 was from Rooms 32 and 33, although we did not find any sherds that fit vessels from these rooms or other indications that the backdirt came from these rooms. It is also true that the backdirt from Rooms 32 and 33 would more than fill Room 28, and any backdirt piled in Room 28 had to leave open the small doorway that led to Room 32. So most of the backfill from these rooms had to be removed from Room 28. There is also no evidence that the backfill from Room 28 was returned to Room 28, so the room may have been open over the winter of 1896–1897.

Records for the following year provide additional information on how Room 28 was filled. When Pepper and Wetherill returned to Pueblo Bonito in May 1897, they discovered that Warren K. Moorehead and a group of men had hastily excavated some rooms to the north of Rooms 32 and 33 and of Rooms 53 and 56. On the first page of his field notes, Pepper stated that workers began clearing away the "piles of debris that the Moorehead expedition had left between the Northern series of rooms and the sealed suite" and that he set three Navajos to work just south of Room 28, "as there was a great amount of earth to be cleared away at this point," which they threw into nearby Kiva 16 (Pepper 1897b). The "great amount of earth" almost certainly included backfill from Room 28, which is visible along the margins of the room in the photographs of Room

28 taken in 1896. So, this backfill may have been used to fill Kiva 16.

Later in the 1897 season, the room directly east of Room 28 (Room 28a) was excavated. The only photograph of Room 28a, taken from the northeast looking southwest, shows a huge pile of dirt sloping from Room 28 toward Room 28a (Crown and Wills 2018:figure 6). Based on this photograph and the fact that Room 28a also burned, I believe that the burned fill that we found in Room 28 in 2013 came from Room 28a.

The artifacts recovered from Room 28 offer additional clues to the source of the fill found in 2013. As discussed in chapter 3, we recovered several fragments of cylinder jars in 2013 that fit jars removed from Rooms 53 and 56. Additional work comparing sherds recovered from Room 28 with ceramics recovered in Rooms 53 and 56 confirms that sherds from many vessels originally found in Rooms 53 and 56 were in the fill of Room 28 in 2013. Human remains recovered in the room indicate that backfill was thrown there from rooms that had human remains; the nearby rooms with human remains include Rooms 32, 33, 53, and 56. Pepper indicated that Moorehead threw fill from the rooms he dug over a wide area, and Kerriann Marden's 2011 dissertation documenting her reassociation of the burials from these rooms indicates that skeletal remains found over a wide number of rooms were portions of those from Rooms 53 and 56. Due to the need to rebury the human remains we recovered, we were unable to show them to Marden, but she examined the inventory list and confirmed that they could have come from the burials in Rooms 53 and 56 (Kerriann Marden, personal communication, September 3, 2015).

The recovery of portions of vessels from Rooms 53 and 56 in Room 28 proves that at least some of the backdirt from these rooms was put into Room 28, which is just two rooms south. As previously discussed, the fill in Room 28 includes portions that are heavily burned and portions that are completely unburned. As shown in figure 2.14, the burned fill overlies the unburned. The unburned portion slopes down from south to north, as if thrown from the north toward the south wall. This is the fill that likely came primarily from Rooms 53 and 56 to the north. The burned portion almost certainly came from Room 28a to the east, which burned as heavily as Room 28 (the floor was also vitrified). While the adjacent Room 55 (to the west) also burned, it was not excavated until later in the 1897 season after photographs show that Room 28 was already filled.

As documented in chapter 11, the few historic artifacts found in Room 28 are not temporally sensitive enough to distinguish whether they were thrown into the room in 1896 or 1897.

SUMMARY

Room 28 sits at the northern apex of the Pueblo Bonito arc within a series of rooms that appear more haphazardly built than much of the pueblo. This location underwent change and remodeling over the course of three centuries of use. While one of the best-documented rooms excavated by the HEE, Room 28 remains difficult to interpret because of the paucity of field records, the sloppiness of some of them (e.g., the room plan with east and west reversed), and the undocumented origin for the backfill. I have provided as much information as possible on what we found in Room 28, but the sequence of use and architecture remains speculative because we could not excavate some portions of the room and because the work of the HEE had disturbed or removed so much valuable evidence. With those caveats, I interpret the room construction in the following sequence.

Initially, the space occupied by Room 28 was an outdoor area used for various activities, including food preparation and trash disposal. Room 28a was constructed to the east before Room 28, probably in the 800s. It is possible that Room 28 began as a portal or ramada extending into the West Court from rooms to the north. Evidence for this possibility comes from the clustering of postholes, particularly with adobe collars, on the southern side of the room, which was the courtyard or plaza side. Similar clusters of collared postholes in the contemporaneous rooms fronting the court/plaza on the western side of Pueblo Bonito (Rooms 323, 325, and 326), which are also located on the court sides of those rooms, may suggest that many rooms fronting the court/plaza began as ramadas. The presence of adobe collars on these posts in these rooms indicates a specific practice for constructing posts at that time and in those positions, perhaps particularly associated with ramadas. However, the dating of the walls in Room 28 may counter this interpretation. Dates from posts in the south wall appear to be contemporaneous with the floor posts that would constitute the hypothetical ramada. So, if a ramada stood there, it did not stand in this location for long before the east and south walls were constructed.

Room 28 became a walled room sometime between

about AD 880 and 910. The room either originally encompassed Room 32 to the north or had a north wall that was later torn down. Use of the room likely included normal domestic activities as suggested by the thermal features and edible plant and animal remains (Ainsworth et al. and Adams, both this volume). Occupation may have been continuous or there may have been a hiatus in occupation (Lekson 1984:66). I believe, but cannot prove, that there was a west wall between Rooms 28 and 55, making Room 28 roughly the size and configuration of Room 28a to the east. This would make the combined room formed by lower Rooms 55 and 57 roughly the same size as well. Each of these rooms would have been roughly 8.5–9.5 m². Evidence of the presence of a western wall to lower Room 28 includes (1) Post 22 is embedded in the south wall of Room 28 on the western end of the room (wall posts in this room are generally at the corners, not in the middle of a wall); (2) the melted daub around Post 22 appears to have an orientation that would suggest a wall running north-south; (3) room-wide platforms are generally placed against walls rather than in the middle of rooms, so the shelving in Room 28 would make the most sense if it was placed against a western wall rather than in the middle of a much larger room; and (4) the fact that all of the cylinder jars fell into Room 28 rather than into Room 55 suggests there was a barrier that prevented them from rolling to the west. Having a series of four rooms (Room 44, Room 28a, Room 28, and the combined lower Rooms 55 and 57), each roughly the same size and configuration and each with straight rather than curved walls, also fits with the other rooms in this portion of Pueblo Bonito. The combined lower room beneath Rooms 55 and 57 was apparently tilted southward off of the angle of the other three rooms, which formed a straight line.

The north wall and shelf were added to Room 28 around AD 1050, with the latest tree-ring date and Type II masonry supporting this later construction event. As noted, whether the north wall replaced a wall in the same place or constituted a new configuration for the room is unknown. A second story was built over the room to the north (Room 32) with a T-shaped doorway opening onto the roof of Room 28.

Around AD 1070, a new wall was built adjacent to the south wall (on the south side facing the plaza). It created a curved wall contiguous to the straight east-west wall of Room 28. A room was constructed above Room 28

at this time. By then, deposits in the West Court had placed Room 28 underground, so the construction of this wall placed a new room at ground level. This room had twin T-shaped doorways opening to the south. The new, curved south wall had a roofline just above the level of the old doorway into lower Room 28, suggesting that a new room (Pepper's Room 40) was constructed to the south of Room 28 at this time. While Judd (1964) discounted the existence of this room, there is no reason to think that Pepper (1920) was unable to recognize a room when he encountered one. This new room included a stairway entry from the roof/ceiling down to Room 28, permitting access into the room, but with a door or hatch cover to seal it off when access was not needed. Room 28 was transformed into a dark and cool storage room.

Then, about AD 1100, the doors were sealed and the room was purposely set on fire. At some point after this, debris from the room was leveled to roughly match the former upper-story room's floor. A new west wall was set between the north and south walls of the upper room, and a plastered surface was put down. It's unclear if this space was roofed or not. Evidence of turkeys (eggs and gullet stones) suggests that the space was used as a turkey pen at some point (Conrad, this volume). Pepper did not mention finding artifacts or features on this upper-story surface.

The complex sequence of construction and use in this location illustrates how difficult it will always be to untangle the dynamic history of Pueblo Bonito. The space occupied by Room 28 was in use for as many as three centuries, used variously for trash disposal, food preparation, outdoor activities, construction, domestic activities, storage, ritual termination, and turkey penning, and many centuries later was used as a staging area for the excavation and screening of adjacent room material. There are no current reconstructions of Pueblo Bonito that accurately outline or map the use of this space (Lekson 1984; Stein et al. 2003; Wilshusen and Van Dyke 2006:241; Windes 2003; Windes and Ford 1992). How could we accomplish this when even the excavators seemed confused by the complexity of the place? Truly untangling this part of the site would require removing the upper-story walls to make it safe to remove the columns of dirt that hold them up in the lower stories. Because this will never happen, we should be cautious about interpreting the earliest uses of Pueblo Bonito. Much of the early construction remains buried.

PATRICIA L. CROWN

CHAPTER THREE

Ceramics from Room 28

In August 1896, while excavating in Room 28, George Pepper and a Navajo worker identified only as Juan uncovered the first known Chacoan cylinder jar. Excavations over the next ten days or so revealed 174 whole ceramic vessels in the room, the most of any single room in the US Southwest/Mexican Northwest: 112 cylinder jars, 24 pitchers, a corrugated jar, two effigy vessels, and 35 bowls. Room 28 gained fame particularly for the large pile of ceramics found in the southwestern corner of the room, which was excavated in five levels and contained most of the known Chacoan cylinder jars. But Pepper and Juan found more than whole vessels among the ceramics in Room 28. They also excavated and saved sherds. And our 2013 excavations recovered more than 1,000 sherds from both the backfill thrown into the room in 1897 and the subfloor excavations we completed.

I report here a complex mix of ceramics: sherds and vessels recovered in Room 28 in 1896; sherds found in Room 28 in 2013 that came from adjacent rooms; and sherds found beneath the floor in Room 28. I present these groups of materials separately and in chronological order: first, the subfloor sherds, which represent the earliest materials excavated; second, the sherds from floor features excavated in 2013; third, the sherds recovered in 1896; fourth, the whole vessels found in Room 28 in 1896, which were placed there around AD 1100; and finally, the backfill material recovered in 2013, which had been thrown in the room while adjacent rooms were being excavated. Both the room use and room excavation have complicated histories that I attempt to clarify in this chapter.

METHODS

I classified all ceramics recovered in the 2013 excavations using the same typologies used in prior University of New Mexico excavations of the trash mounds at Pueblo Bonito (Arazi-Coambs 2016; Crown 2016b; Mattson 2016a). These typologies were based primarily on the work of Goetze and Mills (1993) and Hays-Gilpin and van Hartesveldt (1998). Because these publications are widely available and comprehensive, I do not repeat the type descriptions here. The interested reader should consult the volumes cited.

I typed all sherds and created an Excel file that included information on provenience, ware type, paint type, form, vessel portion (rim or body), diameter of rims, portion of total rim circumference, weight in grams, interior and exterior use wear, whether the sherd was worked or not, and presence of residues. I also conducted analyses of all whole vessels from Room 28 housed at the American Museum of Natural History (AMNH) in 2003, 2007, and 2014; at the National Museum of the American Indian (NMAI) in 2007 and 2016; and at the Peabody Museum at Harvard University in 2009. I used the original Hyde Exploring Expedition (HEE) catalog (called the H catalog) to compile the list of all ceramics recovered from Room 28 in 1896. I recorded a variety of attributes for the whole vessels, including design style, type and ware when possible, paint type, dimensions, use wear, and residues. I was not always able to type the whole vessels because it was not possible in all cases to see the aplastic inclusions used to distinguish one ware from another. The vessels from AMNH and the Peabody Museum at Harvard still had their original field and catalog numbers, so it was easy to determine that they were found in Room 28 at Pueblo Bonito. The vessels at NMAI had been cleaned and the field numbers

TABLE 3.1. **Counts of types and forms recovered from the subfloor in Room 28 in 2013**

WARE	TYPE	BOWL	JAR	UNKNOWN FORM	TOTAL (% of grand total)	
Cibola GW	Lino Fugitive Red	—	1	—	1	(.6)
	Lino Gray	—	1	—	1	(.6)
	Plain Gray	—	49	—	49	(30.6)
	Narrow Neckbanded	—	7	—	7	(4.4)
	Wide Neckbanded	—	2	—	2	(1.2)
Cibola GW Total		—	60	—	60	(37.5)
Chuska GW	Plain Gray	—	13	—	13	(8.1)
	Narrow Neckbanded	—	2	—	2	(1.2)
	Wide Neckbanded	—	2	—	2	(1.2)
	undifferentiated clapboard corrugated narrow	—	1	—	1	(.6)
	Indented Corrugated	—	2	—	2	(1.2)
Chuska GW Total		—	20	—	20	(12.5)
Cibola WW	La Plata/ White Mound B/W	—	—	2	2	(1.2)
	White Mound B/W	—	2	—	2	(1.2)
	White Mound/Kiatuthlanna B/W	1	1	—	2	(1.2)
	Kiatuthlanna B/W	4	2	—	6	(3.8)
	Kiatuthlanna/ Red Mesa B/W	1	1	—	2	(1.2)
	Red Mesa B/W	9	13	—	22	(13.8)
	glazed	—	3	—	3	(1.9)
	unidentified	5	4	3	12	(7.5)
	white ware	6	3	3	12	(7.5)
Cibola WW Total		26	29	8	63	(39.4)
Chuska WW	Peña B/W	1	—	—	1	(.6)
	Newcomb B/W	1	—	—	1	(.6)
	unidentified	—	3	1	4	(2.5)
	white ware	—	4	—	4	(2.5)
Chuska WW Total		2	7	1	10	(6.3)
Brown ware	Woodruff Brown–Sand	—	2	—	2	(1.2)
Puerco Valley/Mogollon Brown Ware Total		—	2	—	2	(1.2)
Chuska RW	Sanostee Orange Plain	1	—	—	1	(.6)
Chuska RW Total		1	—	—	1	(.6)
San Juan Red Ware	Abajo Red-on-orange	1	—	—	1	(.6)
	Deadmans B/R	2	—	—	2	(1.2)
	unidentified	1	—	—	1	(.6)
San Juan Red Ware Total		4	—	—	4	(2.5)
GRAND TOTAL (%)		33 (20.5)	118 (73.8)	9 (5.6)	160 (100)	

B/R = Black-on-red; B/W = Black-on-white; GW = gray ware; RW = red ware; WW = white ware.

removed. In some cases, it was possible to see enough of the number to verify that a vessel was from Room 28. But in other cases, I had to rely on checking the H catalog listing of all vessels found in 1896 against those in other museum collections to decide whether an NMAI vessel was from Room 28 or not. These determinations were also checked against the original photographs of the vessels as found in situ in 1896. With one exception (discussed below), I am fairly confident that all of the vessels described here actually came from Room 28.

A note on the 1896 photographs is useful. Most of the photographs represent the undisturbed vessels as found during excavation. But Pepper seems to have reconstructed some of the vessels immediately after finding them and then returned them to their original locations for photographing. So, one must not assume that the photographs are faithful documents of the vessels as originally excavated. The HEE excavation catalog at AMNH is also flawed: the provenience listed for some vessels is inaccurate. Again, care must be taken to check exactly where vessels came from.

SUBFLOOR SHERDS RECOVERED IN 2013

We recovered 160 sherds in subfloor contexts in Room 28 during the 2013 excavations. Table 3.1 lists all of the sherds by ware, type, and form. As shown, half of the sherds were gray ware jars and the other half were mostly white ware, with some intrusive brown ware and red ware. Cibola White Ware dominated the white ware assemblage (77%), with a variety of types ranging from La Plata/White Mound Black-on-white (anywhere between AD 650 and 850) to Red Mesa Black-on-white (AD 875–1040) (Goetze and Mills 1993; Toll and McKenna 1997:286). Red Mesa is the most abundant decorated type, suggesting that Room 28 and its floor were constructed sometime during this interval (see chapter 2 for more discussion of dating). The absence of later types suggests a lack of bioturbation or intrusion from later deposits, confirming what we observed during the excavations. Although many rodent bones were recovered in Room 28, there were no burrows visible in the subfloor southeast quadrant (SEQ) excavations.

In chapter 2, I interpreted the material found in the subfloor excavations of the SEQ of Room 28 as primarily trash broadcast from earlier occupations at the site. The range of material confirms this; only a few sherds in these levels refit with one another. The variety of vessel forms is fairly narrow (bowls and jars), but apart from the absence of scoops is typical for this time period. There are no cylinder jar fragments in the subfloor contexts. Overall, the assemblage is just what we would expect from domestic trash associated with late Basketmaker III/early Pueblo I occupations in Chaco Canyon.

There is no evidence for the production of ceramics in this locale, so it is not possible to know with certainty whether the Cibola White Ware recovered here was produced in Chaco or not. There is strong evidence of ceramic production elsewhere in Chaco and Pueblo Bonito, so at least some ceramics were produced locally (Crown 2016a:214; Toll and McKenna 1997:154).

The rest of the material, representing 23% of the overall assemblage, was produced elsewhere and brought to Chaco. Of the intrusive ceramics, most (31 of 37 sherds) have a trachyte temper indicative of production in the Chuska area. Skunk Springs has been identified as a primary producer of Chuskan ceramics imported into Chaco (King 2003). The percentages of the gray ware and white ware relative to the entire assemblage (12.5% and 6.3%, respectively) are actually low compared to other Chaco sites dated before AD 920 (Toll and McKenna 1997:148), but the red and brown wares (4% combined) are relatively high compared to other sites. However, the assemblage is small and probably represents a century or more of deposition in this location, making it unlikely to be representative of any single period of time. Apart from the Chuska area, the other source areas for ceramics— Puerco Valley of the West (Fowler 1991; Hays-Gilpin and van Hartesveldt 1998) or Mogollon (Crown 2016b) and San Juan areas—are typical for Chaco in this time period.

Consumption patterns are evident in a few ways. The gray ware and brown ware sherds are all jars, and 74% of these (60 of 81) have soot residue, indicating use for cooking or other activities requiring contact with fire. None of the white ware or red ware sherds show soot, and we would not expect such decorated ceramics to have been used over a fire. Only two vessels had sufficient rim area to allow measurement of the rim diameter. These were both Red Mesa Black-on-white bowl sherds, with diameters of 15 cm and 17 cm.

Residents of early habitation structures at Pueblo Bonito discarded ceramics and other artifacts in the area where Room 28 was later built. As noted, few of the ceramics refit others found in the area; they are also small in size, with an average weight of 3.32 grams. The low density of sherds indicates that this was not a dedicated trash disposal area like the Pueblo Bonito trash mounds, but rather an area where broken ceramics were occasionally discarded or lost. None of it suggests special discard pathways for this material.

The only unusual aspect of the subfloor assemblage was the recovery of three sherds with overall clear glaze on them. While glaze paint is well known from southwestern ceramics assemblages, overall glazes have not been described previously for the prehispanic US Southwest.

To summarize, the small sherds recovered beneath the floor of Room 28 confirm construction for the room after AD 850. Prior to that time, the area was used for outdoor activities, and small ceramics were left in place rather than moved to trash piles elsewhere. The unusual recovery of glazed sherds in this context reveals new insight into ceramic technological advances by the Ancestral Puebloans.

SHERDS FROM FLOOR FEATURES EXCAVATED IN 2013

The 2013 excavation of Room 28 revealed four floor features, three interpreted as thermal features and one as a ritual feature. Although the thermal features were rich in burned organic material and bone, they held relatively few sherds (table 3.2). The nine sherds were recovered from all four locales: five sherds from Ashpit A, one sherd from Ashpit B, and one sherd from the third thermal feature. The fourth feature was a hemispherical depression in the floor filled with red ocher and with a worked sherd of Red Mesa Black-on-white pressed into the top of the ocher. This sherd was situated in the center of the feature and lying flat. As noted in chapter 2, the feature resembled an eye, with the sherd as the pupil and the ocher as the iris.

All of the sherds from the floor features were jar sherds. Four of the nine sherds were gray ware, and five were white ware. Seven were Cibola Gray or White Ware and so probably local, while two were Chuska Gray or White Ware and thus imported. The temporal range suggests about AD 900–1125. The only unusual sherd is a small pitcher sherd with a design that incorporates both specular purple hematite and a black glaze paint. Analysis with a scanning electron microscope performed by Michael Spilde and me at the Institute of Meteoritics in the Department of Earth and Planetary Sciences at the University of New Mexico shows that this sherd had a slip of combined illite and kaolinite clays. The purple

paint is specular hematite, while the black glaze paint is iron-based and bound with an illite clay to the sherd. Unfortunately, there is nothing in this analysis to indicate whether this vessel was locally made, but it could have been. This type is unusual in Chaco but present in other assemblages (Peter McKenna and Thomas Windes, personal communication, December 2015).

SHERDS FROM THE 1896 EXCAVATION

The Hyde Exploring Expedition collected some sherds from Room 28 in addition to 174 whole vessels. Some of the whole vessels were smashed when found, and George Pepper's field notes make it clear that he spent time in the field attempting to reconstruct the vessels. In some instances, accumulations of sherds were sent back to the American Museum of Natural History, where they were eventually reconstructed (or at least partially). There are drawers at the AMNH with bases of cylinder jars that fit onto partially reconstructed jar bodies found in other drawers. Here, I am not discussing such instances of sherds separated from whole vessels. Instead, in this section I focus on the sherds collected by the HEE that did not belong to any of the reconstructed vessels.

TABLE 3.2. **Ceramic sherds recovered from floor features in Room 28 in 2013**

WARE	TYPE	JAR
Cibola GW	Plain Gray	2
	Narrow Neckbanded	1
Cibola Gray Ware Total		3
Chuska GW	undifferentiated clapboard corrugated	1
Chuska Gray Ware Total		1
Cibola WW	Red Mesa B/W	1
	Escavada B/W	1
	glaze and purple polychrome	1
	unidentified	1
Cibola White Ware Total		4
Chuska WW	white ware	1
Chuska White Ware Total		1
GRAND TOTAL		9

GW = gray ware; WW = white ware.

CROWN

The sherds come from two different H catalog numbers: H/4078 and H/4147. The H catalog indicates that the sherds in H/4078 were "found a few feet below surface." Pepper (1920:117) also stated that about three feet below the surface "in the western end of the room, there appeared a stratum of broken pottery; the pieces were collected and marked, and the work proceeded." This is almost certainly the material curated as H/4078. Later, in the museum, six vessels were reconstructed from that mass of pottery (described below). The remaining material collected under this catalog number includes the sherds described here.

After the reconstruction of the whole vessels, H/4078 comprises only 24 sherds (table 3.3). Twenty of these are bowl sherds, with the remainder consisting of one cylinder jar sherd, two jar sherds, and one mug sherd. The Cibola White Ware types range from Red Mesa Black-on-white to Chaco-McElmo Black-on-white, suggesting a chronological range from possibly the late AD 800s to the early 1100s (figure 3.1). In addition to the white ware, H/4078 included one sherd each of Chuska Gray Ware, Woodruff Smudged Brown Ware, and St Johns Black-on-red. Six partial and complete vessels were reconstructed from the mass of sherds and are discussed below. None of the sherds remaining under the H/4078 catalog number fit the reconstructed vessels, although several of the reconstructed vessels are missing pieces.

Two Red Mesa Black-on-white sherds fit together and were part of a small bowl, less than 10 cm in diameter, that had a mixture of mud and feathers adhering to the exterior. We were able to confirm the presence of the feathers using a high-powered microscope at AMNH. I have not encountered this type of treatment previously, but I suspect it was an altar bowl at one time (Parsons 1939:376–77). In figure 3.1, these two sherds are visible just above and to the left of the scale.

Pepper collected an additional 15 sherds from the Room 28 floor level, which were cataloged as H/4147. They include 10 Cibola White Ware sherds: 7 bowls, a jar, and 2 scoop sherds. Cibola Gray Ware and Chuska Gray Ware jar sherds complete the assemblage.

The fact that 27 of the 39 sherds in these two lots are rim sherds (3 are handles and 9 are body sherds) suggests that the excavators selectively pulled interesting sherds to send back to AMNH, or perhaps some sherds were discarded after they reached New York. Many of the materials originally sent by the Hyde Exploring Expedition to the AMNH were later discarded, including some

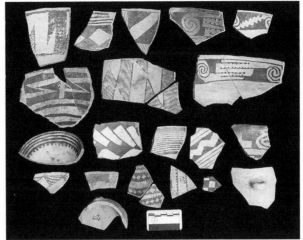

FIGURE 3.1. Sherds recovered in 1896 in the Room 28 fill. Sherds with mud and feathers on the exterior are just above and to the left of the scale. Photograph by Patricia Crown.

artifacts collected in Room 28. At any rate, the sherds in these two catalog numbers are unlikely to be representative of all of the sherds in the fill of Room 28 in 1896.

WHOLE VESSELS EXCAVATED IN 1896

Excavations in August 1896 recovered at least 174 whole or reconstructible vessels (tables 3.4 and 3.5). I was able to locate 171 and analyze 169 of these at the American Museum of Natural History, the National Museum of the American Indian, and the Peabody Museum of Archaeology and Ethnology at Harvard University. The total count may never be known for several reasons, most relating to discrepancies between the field records, the museum records, and the existing vessels in museum collections. As noted above, some vessels were reconstructed from masses of sherds found during the excavations, so they show up as one catalog number but are actually multiple vessels. Most vessels were found on or near the floor of the room (figure 3.2), and Pepper (1920) took great care in excavating and recording these as he encountered them. Vessels were cleared of matrix, photographed once without numbers, and photographed a second time with small cards with numbers set up next to them. Then, that same number was written in either graphite or red pencil on each vessel as it was removed.

The HEE found vessels in five areas of the room: one group in the fill 1 m below the surface, another group 1 m above the floor, a third group by the northeast door (figure 3.3), a fourth group by the south wall and southeast door, and the largest group in a mass of vessels

TABLE 3.3. **Sherds excavated by the Hyde Exploring Expedition in Room 28 in 1896**

LEVEL	WARE	TYPE	FORM					
			Bowl	Cylinder jar	Jar	Mug	Scoop	Grand total
Few feet below surface	Chuska Gray Ware	Patterned Indented Corrugated	—	—	1	—	—	1
	Chuska Gray Ware Total		—	—	1	—	—	1
	Cibola White Ware	Red Mesa B/W	7	—	1	—	—	8
		Puerco B/W	1	—	—	—	—	1
		Puerco-Escavada B/W	1	—	—	1	—	2
		Puerco-Puerco B/W	2	—	—	—	—	2
		Chaco B/W	1	—	—	—	—	1
		Chaco-McElmo B/W	3	—	—	—	—	3
		Reserve B/W	1	—	—	—	—	1
		unidentifiable corrugated exterior	1	—	—	—	—	1
		white ware	—	1	—	—	—	1
	Cibola White Ware Total		17	1	1	1	—	20
	Chuska White Ware	unidentified B/W	1	—	—	—	—	1
	Chuska White Ware Total		1	—	—	—	—	1
	Brown ware	Woodruff Smudged	1	—	—	—	—	1
	Puerco Valley/Mogollon Brown Ware Total		1	—	—	—	—	1
	White Mountain Red Ware	St Johns B/R	1	—	—	—	—	1
	White Mountain Red Ware Total		1	—	—	—	—	1
Few Feet below Surface Total			**20**	**1**	**2**	**1**	**—**	**24**
Floor level	Cibola Gray Ware	Narrow Neckbanded	—	—	1	—	—	1
		Corrugated	—	—	1	—	—	1
		Incised Corrugated	—	—	1	—	—	1
		Indented Corrugated	—	—	1	—	—	1
	Cibola Gray Ware Total		—	—	4	—	—	4
	Chuska Gray Ware	Patterned Indented Corrugated	—	—	1	—	—	1
	Chuska Gray Ware Total		—	—	1	—	—	1
	Cibola White Ware	Red Mesa B/W	4	—	—	—	2	6
		Red Mesa/Puerco B/W	—	—	1	—	—	1
		Puerco-Escavada B/W	2	—	—	—	—	2
		Gallup B/W	1	—	—	—	—	1
	Cibola White Ware Total		7	—	1	—	2	10
Floor Level Total			**7**	**—**	**6**	**—**	**2**	**15**
GRAND TOTAL			**27**	**1**	**8**	**1**	**2**	**39**

Sherds are in the collection of the American Museum of Natural History, H/4078 and H/4147.

B/R = Black-on-red; B/W = Black-on-white.

FIGURE 3.2. Bird's-eye view of Room 28 in August 1896. Photograph by Richard Wetherill. HEE 105, Image #411881, American Museum of Natural History Library.

FIGURE 3.3. Photograph taken in 1896 of vessels in Layer 1 by the northeast door connecting Room 28 to Room 51a. Note the burned post to the right of the pottery and handprints in the plaster on the walls. HEE 108, Image #411883, American Museum of Natural History Library.

along the southwestern portion of the room. The latter group was excavated in five layers, each numbered and photographed separately. In some cases, individual broken vessels that extended from one layer into another were (accidentally) given two separate field numbers. While reconstruction of the vessels resolved most such situations, there are more field numbers than actual vessels. In other cases, sequential numbers were skipped (for instance, numbers 148 and 162), so there never were actual vessels associated with these numbers. Three of the vessels given catalog numbers at the American Museum of Natural History are no longer present at the museum, and there is no record of where they went; I discuss these missing vessels below, but I have not analyzed them. I provide some interpretation based on the photographs of most of them taken in the field. Finally, the H catalog is sometimes incorrect. For instance, a vessel listed in the H catalog as coming from Room 32 is shown in a photograph as vessel 167 in Room 28. Because Room 28 was completely excavated before Room 32 was even opened, the vessel must have come from Room 28, making the H catalog incorrect.

Perhaps the most frustrating situation involves the vessels transferred to the Heye Foundation on January 1, 1916. These pots were subsequently transferred to the Smithsonian Institution's National Museum of the American Indian in 1989 and moved in 1999 to the Cultural Resources Center in Suitland, Maryland, where they remain today. As noted above, at some point during the last century, the vessels were thoroughly cleaned and both the field numbers and H catalog numbers removed. In addition, the provenience information for many of the HEE collections was altered; instead of indicating that the vessels came from Room 28, the NMAI catalog sometimes indicates they came from Room 33, one of the primary burial rooms in Pueblo Bonito, even though photographs confirm that they came from Room 28. Finally, three cylinder jars and two pitchers from Room 28 are in the collections of the Peabody Museum at Harvard. I found out about the two pitchers too late to analyze and include them in this volume, but there are photographs of them in the Peabody's online catalog.

Although there are some field numbers for which I have no vessels and some vessels known to have come from Room 28 for which I have no field numbers, the discussion of the assemblage here is as complete and accurate as possible.

TABLE 3.4. **All field numbers and vessels from Room 28**

FN	CATALOG NUMBER	MUSEUM	LEVEL/LOCATION	TYPE	FORM
	H/4090	AMNH	1 m below surface	Naschitti B/W	cylinder jar
	H/4091	AMNH	1 m below surface	Chaco B/W	cylinder jar
	H/4092/52110	NMAI	1 m below surface	white ware	cylinder jar
	H/4093	AMNH	1 m below surface	other B/W	partial bowl
	H/4094	AMNH	1 m below surface	white ware	cylinder jar
	H/4095*	not found	1 m below surface	unidentified	partial pitcher
	H/3428	AMNH	1 m above floor	Puerco B/W	cylinder jar
	H/3429	AMNH	1 m above floor	white ware	cylinder jar
	H/3430	AMNH	1 m above floor	white ware	cylinder jar
	H/3431	AMNH	1 m above floor	white ware	partial cylinder jar
	H/3432	AMNH	1 m above floor	white ware	cylinder jar
	H/3433	AMNH	1 m above floor	white ware	partial cylinder jar
	H/3434	AMNH	1 m above floor	Red Mesa B/W	partial gourd effigy
1	H/3212	AMNH	NE corner by door to 51a	Gallup B/W	bowl
2	H/3394	AMNH	NE corner by door to 51a	white ware	cylinder jar
3	H/3204	AMNH	NE corner by door to 51a	Gallup B/W	bowl
4	H/3223	AMNH	NE corner by door to 51a	Escavada B/W	bowl
5	H/3206	AMNH	NE corner by door to 51a	Red Mesa B/W	bowl
6	H/3203/53052	NMAI	NE corner by door to 51a	Chaco B/W	bowl
7	H/3211	AMNH	NE corner by door to 51a	Gallup B/W	bowl
8, 9	H/3425,H/3426	AMNH	NE corner by door to 51a	Gallup B/W	bowl
10	H/3207	AMNH	NE corner by door to 51a	Red Mesa B/W	bowl
11	H/3201	AMNH	NE corner by door to 51a	Red Mesa B/W	bowl
12	H/3205	AMNH	NE corner by door to 51a	Kiatuthlanna B/W	bowl
13	H/3208	AMNH	NE corner by door to 51a	Red Mesa B/W	bowl
14	H/3195	AMNH	NE corner by door to 51a	Red Mesa B/W	bowl
15	H/3199	AMNH	NE corner by door to 51a	Chaco B/W	bowl
16	H/3238	AMNH	NE corner by door to 51a	white ware	cylinder jar
17	H/3196	AMNH	NE corner by door to 51a	Red Mesa B/W	bowl
18	H/3220/52642	NMAI	NE corner by door to 51a	Kiatuthlanna B/W	bowl
19	H/3200	AMNH	NE corner by door to 51a	Red Mesa B/W	bowl
20	H/3197	AMNH	NE corner by door to 51a	Red Mesa B/W	bowl
21	H/3219/52645	NMAI	NE corner by door to 51a	Red Mesa B/W	bowl
22	H/3270	AMNH	NE corner by door to 51a	Chaco-McElmo B/W	pitcher
23	H/3214	AMNH	NE corner by door to 51a	Chaco-McElmo B/W	bowl
24	H/3202*	not found	NE corner by door to 51a	unidentified	bowl
25	H/3262	AMNH	Level 1 SW corner	Gallup B/W	cylinder jar
26	H/3260	AMNH	Level 1 SW corner	Toadlena B/W	cylinder jar
27	H/3264	AMNH	Level 1 SW corner	Gallup B/W	cylinder jar
28	H/3261	AMNH	Level 1 SW corner	white ware	cylinder jar
29	H/3419	AMNH	Level 1 SW corner	Gallup B/W	cylinder jar
30	H/3388	AMNH		sherd only	
31	H/3263	AMNH	Level 1 SW corner	Chaco B/W	cylinder jar
32	H/3252	AMNH	Level 1 SW corner	Chaco B/W	cylinder jar
33			same vessel as 36: H/3393		
34	H/3259/ PM 30-18-10/ A6919	Peabody	Level 1 SW corner	Nava B/W	cylinder jar
35	H/3417	AMNH	Level 1 SW corner	white ware	cylinder jar, base only
36	H/3393	AMNH	Level 1 SW corner	Escavada B/W	cylinder jar
37	H/3408	AMNH	Level 1 SW corner	white ware	cylinder jar
38	H/3399	AMNH	Level 1 SW corner	white ware	cylinder jar
39	H/3420	AMNH	Level 1 SW corner	white ware	cylinder jar
40	H/3416	AMNH	Level 1 SW corner	white ware	cylinder jar
41	H/3411/52108	NMAI	Level 1 SW corner	white ware	cylinder jar
42	H/3382	AMNH	Level 1 SW corner	white ware	cylinder jar
43	H/3386/52103	NMAI	Level 1 SW corner	white ware	cylinder jar
44	H/3390	AMNH	Level 1 SW corner	Gallup B/W	cylinder jar
45	H/3276	AMNH	Level 1 SW corner	Gallup B/W	pitcher
46	H/3274*	not found	Level 1 SW corner	Gallup B/W	pitcher
47	H/3282	AMNH	Level 1 SW corner	Gallup B/W	pitcher
48	H/3254/ PM 30-18-10/ A6918	Peabody	Level 1 SW corner	Brimhall B/W	cylinder jar
49	H/3421	AMNH	Level 1 SW corner	white ware	cylinder jar
50	H/3253	AMNH	Level 1 SW corner	Gallup B/W	cylinder jar

FN	CATALOG NUMBER	MUSEUM	LEVEL/LOCATION	TYPE	FORM
51	H/3413	AMNH	Level 1 SW corner	Chaco B/W	cylinder jar
52	H/3400	AMNH	Level 1 SW corner	Puerco B/W	cylinder jar
53	H/4148	AMNH	Level 1 SW corner	white ware	partial cylinder jar
54	H/3418	AMNH	Level 1 SW corner	Gallup B/W	cylinder jar
55	H/3387	AMNH	Level 1 SW corner	unidentified organic B/W	cylinder jar
56			same vessel as 85: H/3372		
57	H/3266	AMNH	Level 1 SW corner	white ware	cylinder jar
58	H/3379	AMNH	Level 1 SW corner	white ware	cylinder jar
59	H/3265	AMNH	Level 1 SW corner	white ware	cylinder jar
60	H/3385	AMNH	Level 1 SW corner	white ware	cylinder jar
61	H/3380	AMNH	Level 1 SW corner	Chaco-McElmo B/W	cylinder jar
62	H/3401	AMNH	Level 1 SW corner	white ware	cylinder jar
63	H/3277	AMNH	Level 1 SW corner	Chaco B/W	pitcher
64	H/3414	AMNH	Level 1 SW corner	Chaco B/W	cylinder jar
65	H/3410	AMNH	Level 1 SW corner	white ware	cylinder jar
66	H/3228/52055	NMAI	Level 1 SW corner	Gallup B/W	cylinder jar
67	H/3404	AMNH	Level 1 SW corner	white ware	cylinder jar
68	H/3405	AMNH	Level 1 SW corner	white ware	cylinder jar
69	H/3278	AMNH	Level 1 SW corner	Chaco-McElmo B/W	pitcher
70	H/3283/52863	NMAI	Level 1 SW corner	Gallup B/W	pitcher
71	H/3271	AMNH	Level 2 SW corner	Chaco-McElmo B/W	pitcher
72	H/3231	AMNH	Level 2 SW corner	Puerco B/W	cylinder jar
73	H/3225	AMNH	Level 2 SW corner	Gallup B/W	cylinder jar
74	H/3268	AMNH	Level 2 SW corner	Gallup B/W	pitcher
75	H/3407	AMNH	Level 2 SW corner	white ware	cylinder jar
76	H/3229	AMNH	Level 2 SW corner	Chaco B/W	cylinder jar
77	H/3406	AMNH	Level 2 SW corner	Chaco B/W	cylinder jar
78	H/3230/ PM 30-18-10/ A6921	Peabody	Level 2 SW corner	Chaco B/W	cylinder jar
79	H/3227	AMNH	Level 2 SW corner	Gallup B/W	cylinder jar
80	H/3396	AMNH	Level 2 SW corner	Gallup B/W	cylinder jar
81	H/3221	AMNH	Level 2 SW corner	Chaco B/W	bowl
82	H/3222	AMNH	Level 2 SW corner	Chaco B/W	bowl
83	H/3392	AMNH	Level 2 SW corner	Gallup B/W	cylinder jar
84	H/3232/52051	NMAI	Level 2 SW corner	Puerco B/W	cylinder jar
85	H/3372	AMNH	Level 2 SW corner	white ware	cylinder jar
86	H/3415	AMNH	Level 2 SW corner	Gallup B/W	cylinder jar
87	H/3403/52106	NMAI	Level 2 SW corner	white ware	cylinder jar
88	H/3371	AMNH	Level 2 SW corner	Gallup B/W	cylinder jar
89	H/3398/52109	NMAI	Level 2 SW corner	Gallup B/W	cylinder jar
90	H/3241	AMNH	Level 2 SW corner	Gallup B/W	cylinder jar
91	H/3402	AMNH	Level 2 SW corner	Chaco B/W	pitcher
92	H/3395	AMNH	Level 2 SW corner	white ware	cylinder jar
93	H/3389	AMNH	Level 2 SW corner	Escavada B/W	cylinder jar
94	H/3226	AMNH	Level 2 SW corner	Chaco B/W	cylinder jar
95	H/3374	AMNH	Level 2 SW corner	Gallup B/W	cylinder jar
96	H/3240	AMNH	Level 2 SW corner	Gallup B/W	cylinder jar
97	H/3289	AMNH	Level 2 SW corner	Chaco B/W	cylinder jar
98	H/3397	AMNH	Level 2 SW corner	white ware	cylinder jar
99	H/3269	AMNH	Level 2 SW corner	Chaco B/W	pitcher
100	H/3256	AMNH	Level 2 SW corner	white ware	cylinder jar
101	H/3373	AMNH	Level 2 SW corner	white ware	cylinder jar
102	H/3291	AMNH	Level 3 SW corner	white ware	cylinder jar
103			same vessel as 66: H/3228		
104	H/3383	AMNH	Level 3 SW corner	white ware	cylinder jar
105	H/3409/52105	NMAI	Level 3 SW corner	white ware	cylinder jar
106	H/3239	AMNH	Level 3 SW corner	Gallup B/W	cylinder jar
107	H/3242	AMNH	Level 3 SW corner	Chaco B/W	cylinder jar
108	H/3284	AMNH	Level 3 SW corner	Gallup B/W	pitcher
109	H/3233	AMNH	Level 3 SW corner	white ware	cylinder jar
110	H/3235/52104	NMAI	Level 3 SW corner	Chaco B/W	cylinder jar
111	H/3234	AMNH	Level 3 SW corner	white ware	cylinder jar
112	H/3251	AMNH	Level 3 SW corner	Gallup B/W	cylinder jar
113	H/3281	AMNH	Level 3 SW corner	Gallup B/W	pitcher
114	H/3243	AMNH	Level 3 SW corner	Chaco B/W	cylinder jar

TABLE 3.4. *Continued*

FN	CATALOG NUMBER	MUSEUM	LEVEL/LOCATION	TYPE	FORM
115	H/3236	AMNH	Level 3 SW corner	Chaco B/W	cylinder jar
116	H/3391	AMNH	Level 3 SW corner	Gallup B/W	cylinder jar
117	H/3209	AMNH	Level 3 SW corner	Gallup B/W	bowl
118	H/3427	AMNH	Level 3 SW corner	Gallup B/W	bowl
119	H/3424	AMNH	Level 3 SW corner	Gallup B/W	bowl
120	H/3215	AMNH	Level 3 SW corner	Reserve B/W	bowl
121	H/3216	AMNH	Level 3 SW corner	Gallup B/W	bowl
122	H/3258/52053	NMAI	Level 3 SW corner	Gallup B/W	cylinder jar
123	H/3237	AMNH	Level 3 SW corner	Gallup B/W	cylinder jar
124	H/3257	AMNH	Level 3 SW corner	white ware	cylinder jar
125	H/3255	AMNH	Level 3 SW corner	Gallup B/W	cylinder jar
126	H/3287	AMNH	Level 3 SW corner	Chaco B/W	pitcher
127	H/3285/52097	NMAI	Level 3 SW corner	Gallup B/W	pitcher
128	H/3213/53023	NMAI	Level 3 SW corner	Gallup B/W	bowl
129	H/3275	AMNH	Level 3 SW corner	Chaco B/W	pitcher
130	H/3279	AMNH	Level 3 SW corner	Gallup B/W	pitcher
131	H/3280/ PM 30-18-10/ A6917*	Peabody	Level 3 SW corner	unidentified	pitcher
132	H/3288/52047	NMAI	Level 3 SW corner	white ware	cylinder jar
133	H/3292/52116	NMAI	Level 3 SW corner	white ware	cylinder jar
134	H/3267/52119	NMAI	Level 3 SW corner	Chaco B/W	pitcher
135	H/3290	AMNH	Level 3 SW corner	Gallup B/W	cylinder jar
136	H/3422	AMNH	Level 3 SW corner	Blue Shale Corrugated	corrugated jar
137	H/3246/52107	NMAI	Level 3 SW corner	Chaco B/W	cylinder jar
138	H/3198	AMNH	NE corner by door to 51a	Red Mesa B/W	bowl
139	H/3217	AMNH	NE corner by door to 51a	Red Mesa B/W	bowl
140	H/4154	AMNH	NE corner by door to 51a	Red Mesa B/W	bowl
141	H/3286/52085	NMAI	NE corner by door to 51a	Chaco-McElmo B/W	pitcher
142	H/3194	AMNH	NE corner by door to 51a	Red Mesa B/W	bowl
143	H/3218	AMNH	NE corner by door to 51a	Puerco B/W	bowl
144	H/4149	AMNH	NE corner by door to 51a	Puerco B/W	partial pitcher
145	H/3423	AMNH	on south wall	Chaco B/W	bowl
146	H/3272	AMNH	by south door to West Court	Chaco-McElmo B/W	pitcher
147	H/3244/52056	NMAI	by south door to West Court	white ware	cylinder jar
148			no vessel associated with this number		
149	H/3273/ PM 30-18-10/ A6916*	Peabody	Level 4 SW corner	Chaco B/W	pitcher
150	H/3377	AMNH	Level 4 SW corner	Gallup B/W	cylinder jar
151	H/3381	AMNH	Level 4 SW corner	unknown organic painted type	cylinder jar
152	H/3248	AMNH	Level 4 SW corner	white ware	cylinder jar
153	H/3375	AMNH	Level 4 SW corner	white ware	cylinder jar
154	H/3245	AMNH	Level 4 SW corner	Escavada B/W	cylinder jar
155	H/3247	AMNH	Level 4 SW corner	Gallup B/W	cylinder jar
156	H/3249/52049	NMAI	Level 4 SW corner	Chaco B/W	cylinder jar
157	H/3378	AMNH	Level 4 SW corner	Showlow Red	cylinder jar
158	H/3250	AMNH	Level 4 SW corner	Chaco B/W	cylinder jar
159	H/3384	AMNH	Level 4 SW corner	Escavada B/W	cylinder jar
160	H/3224	AMNH	Level 4 SW corner	Chaco B/W	cylinder jar
161	H/3376	AMNH	Level 4 SW corner	Gallup B/W	cylinder jar
162			no vessel associated with this number		
163			same as vessel 159: H/3384		
164	H/4150	AMNH	Level 5 SW corner	Gallup B/W	cylinder jar
165	H/4151	AMNH	Level 5 SW corner	white ware	cylinder jar
166	H/4152	AMNH	Level 5 SW corner	Gallup B/W	cylinder jar
167	H/4153	AMNH	Level 5 SW corner	Gallup B/W	cylinder jar
168	H/3586	AMNH	Level 5 SW corner	Puerco B/W	cylinder jar
	52575	NMAI	unknown	Puerco B/W	duck effigy

* Vessel not analyzed for this study nor illustrated in appendix A.

AMNH = American Museum of Natural History; B/W = Black-on-white; FN = Field Number; NMAI = National Museum of the American Indian; Peabody = Peabody Museum of Archaeology and Ethnology.

TABLE 3.5. **Ceramic type classifications for whole vessels recovered by the Hyde Exploring Expedition from Room 28 in 1896**

TYPE	BOWL	CYLINDER JAR	PITCHER	CORRUGATED JAR	GOURD EFFIGY	DUCK EFFIGY	TOTAL (%)
Kiatuthlanna B/W	2	—	—	—	—	—	2 (1.1)
Red Mesa B/W	13	—	—	—	1	—	14 (8.0)
Gallup B/W	9	30	9	—	—	—	48 (27.6)
Escavada B/W	1	4	—	—	—	—	5 (2.9)
Puerco B/W	1	5	1	—	—	1	8 (4.6)
Chaco B/W	5	18	7	—	—	—	30 (17.2)
Chaco-McElmo B/W	1	1	5	—	—	—	7 (4.0)
Reserve B/W	1	—	—	—	—	—	1 (0.6)
learner design B/W	1	—	—	—	—	—	1 (0.6)
White ware	—	47	—	—	—	—	47 (27.0)
Naschitti B/W	—	1	—	—	—	—	1 (0.6)
Toadlena B/W	—	1	—	—	—	—	1 (0.6)
Brimhall B/W	—	1	—	—	—	—	1 (0.6)
Nava B/W	—	1	—	—	—	—	1 (0.6)
Blue Shale Corrugated	—	—	—	1	—	—	1 (0.6)
Unknown organic painted type	—	2	—	—	—	—	2 (1.1)
Showlow Red	—	1	—	—	—	—	1 (0.6)
Unidentified	1	—	2	—	—	—	2 (1.1)
GRAND TOTAL (%)	35 (20.1)	112 (64.4)	24 (13.8)	1 (0.6)	1 (0.6)	1 (0.6)	174 (100)

B/W = Black-on-white.

Recovery Contexts and Types

Table 3.4 lists all of the known vessels from Room 28 from the 1896 excavations with their field number, H catalog number, NMAI or Peabody Museum catalog number where relevant, recovery location, my interpretation of type, and the vessel form. I included all possible field numbers (1–168), which were numbers Pepper assigned when he took photographs of the vessels. Appendix A provides thumbnail photographs of all of the vessels I analyzed from Room 28, organized first by vessel form and then in the same order as table 3.4. As noted above, I did not analyze two pitchers curated at the Peabody Museum, and I was unable to locate one bowl (H/3202) and two pitchers (H/3274 and H/4095) from Room 28. There is also one vessel (52575) at NMAI cataloged as coming from Room 28 that I was not able to associate with any missing field numbers; it is a bird effigy vessel and so distinctive and striking that I doubt Pepper would have called it anything else. While the NMAI records indicate that it came from Room 28, I have no corroborating evidence in photographs or notes that it did indeed come from there. I have included it here for completeness, but it probably did not come from Room 28. There is also a partial gourd effigy vessel from Room 28,

but it is not the one that Pepper (1920:figure 47b) illustrated as coming from there. Pepper's published image is a complete vessel that apparently came from a burial mound in the canyon.

As shown in tables 3.4 and 3.6, the excavators first encountered broken vessels in debris about 1 m below the surface on the western end of the room (Pepper 1920:117; on page 122, Pepper stated that the pottery was found 2 feet below the surface rather than 3 feet, but everywhere else indicates 3 feet or 1 m). We do not know where the surface was when they started excavating Room 28, but photographs suggest that the room was entirely filled with dirt and fallen masonry, so 1 m might be as high as the base of the late upper-story wall partitioning Room 28b from Room 55. It is likely then that the vessels were smashed on the upper-story floor. The HEE excavators collected the pieces, and these were cataloged at AMNH as H/4078. The vessels reconstructed from this mass of sherds includes four cylinder jars—two white ware, one Chaco Black-on-white, and one Naschitti Black-on-white (a Chuska White Ware type with mineral paint and all solid designs)—and a partial bowl painted by an unskilled learner that depicts quadrupeds (Pepper 1920:figure 46a). Apparently, a fragmentary pitcher was

TABLE 3.6. **Vessel forms recovered in 1896 by location in Room 28**

LOCATION	BOWL	CORRUGATED JAR	CYLINDER JAR	DUCK EFFIGY	GOURD EFFIGY	PITCHER	TOTAL
Above floor	1	—	10	—	1	1	13
By south door to West Court	—	—	1	—	—	1	2
Level 1 SW corner	—	—	37	—	—	6	43
Level 2 SW corner	2	—	25	—	—	4	31
Level 3 SW corner	6	1	20	—	—	8	35
Level 4 SW corner	—	—	12	—	—	1	13
Level 5 SW corner	—	—	5	—	—	—	5
NE corner in front of door to 51a	25	—	2	—	—	3	30
On south wall	1	—	—	—	—	—	1
Unknown	—	—	—	1	—	—	1
GRAND TOTAL	**35**	**1**	**112**	**1**	**1**	**24**	**174**

also discovered in this area (H/4095), but I have not been able to locate it.

A second group of seven vessels was located "about 3′ above the floor and were partially restored to see if any of the pieces were missing" (AMNH H catalog:72). One meter above the floor would place the vessels approximately 1 m below the group of vessels described above. Pepper (1920:117) stated that a cylinder jar and a partial pitcher were found in the northeast corner of the room at a depth below the group of vessels described previously, and these might be two of the seven vessels found "about 3′ above the floor." From his description, another jar was found about 0.5 m below these vessels, still in the northeastern corner of the room. This group of vessels includes the partial gourd effigy and six cylinder jars: a Puerco Black-on-white and five plain white ware jars. All of these vessels exhibit evidence of exposure to the fire that caused the room to collapse. Three of the white ware jars are incomplete. Given their location, the measurements, and Pepper's description, these seven vessels could have been part of the larger group of vessels found in the northeast corner of the room (described below).

The remaining 160 vessels (minus the bird effigy vessel of questionable provenience) came from several different locations on or near the floor of Room 28, and these were documented with more care. I discuss them in the order they were found. Pepper (1920:117–19) initially found vessels in the northeast corner of the room directly in front of the open door to Room 51a to the north of Room 28. The photographs show that the excavators found fragments of at least two baskets in addition to the vessels. Inside some of the bowls were groups of ornaments, including turquoise and shell beads (see chapter 5). The vessels were excavated and photographed in

two layers, but undoubtedly constituted a single deposit. There are 25 bowls, 3 pitchers, and 2 cylinder jars, for a total of 30 vessels (table 3.7; note that these numbers do not agree with Pepper's [1920:119] vessel counts, but they do match the photographed, cataloged, and curated vessel numbers). The bowls include a wide range of vessel types, but half of them are either Kiatuthlanna Black-on-white or Red Mesa Black-on-white. The pitchers are Puerco Black-on-white (1 vessel) and Chaco-McElmo Black-on-white (2 vessels). The 2 cylinder jars are both plain white ware. The surprising things about this group of vessels are that so many are early types and yet they could not have been placed in this location until around AD 1100, given the latest dated vessels (Chaco-McElmo Black-on-white) and the fact that they blocked a door. The earliest vessels (Kiatuthlanna Black-on-white) date from about AD 850–950, so they would have been 150–250 years old by the time they were placed in this location.

There is no chronological patterning to the placement of the vessels: nested vessels sometimes had later types inside earlier ones, but also sometimes there were earlier vessels inside later ones. From this, I infer that the vessels were placed in this location in a single event, probably as part of the ritual destruction of the room by fire. The vessels blocked the door to Room 51a, with three bowls placed on the sill of that doorway (Pepper 1920:119). While not as effective as the masonry blocking the doorway to Room 32, the ceramics essentially prevented passage from Room 51a into Room 28 or vice versa. While anyone desiring access could have moved the vessels out of the way, their placement on and around the doorsill suggests that they functioned, at least symbolically, to block passage. I have suggested elsewhere that these might have been "guardian" vessels based on their placement (Crown 2018:393). Interestingly, a similar grouping of vessels clustered around the northwest doorway of Room 28, but on the Room 32 side of that door (Pepper 1920:129–40). Historically, the Pueblo peoples do not allow outsiders in rooms where sacred and powerful things are stored; for example, at Zuni "the rooms where sacred things are kept are taboo to outsiders.... if any one crosses the threshold he is 'caught' and must be initiated into the group" or whipped and forced to make payments (Bunzel 1932:502). The vessels may have served as a warning that crossing the threshold into Room 28 was taboo, perhaps as part of preparations to burn the room to the ground.

TABLE 3.7. **Types and forms of vessels found in front of the door to Room 51a**

	BOWL	CYLINDER JAR	PITCHER	TOTAL
Kiatuthlanna B/W	2	—	—	2
Red Mesa B/W	13	—	—	13
Puerco B/W	1	—	1	2
Gallup B/W	4	—	—	4
Escavada B/W	1	—	—	1
Chaco B/W	2	—	—	2
Chaco-McElmo B/W	1	—	2	3
Plain white ware	—	2	—	2
Unidentified	1	—	—	1
GRAND TOTAL	25	2	3	30

B/W = Black-on-white.

After uncovering the vessels by the door to Room 51a, Pepper moved toward the western part of the room. In an area 1.85 m² in the southwestern corner of the room, he found 127 vessels (table 3.8; Pepper [1920:120] gave the total as 136 vessels, but this number is not correct). These were excavated in five levels, each pot numbered sequentially, and each level photographed with the number cards in place. Pepper marked each vessel with its number; between the numbers and the photographs, it is possible to reconstruct which vessel came from which level.

The term "level" is inaccurate though. We reconstructed the levels by matching up witness rocks that appear in multiple photographs (figure 3.4). From this, we discovered that the vessels in Levels 1–3 are superimposed over one another and that Levels 4 and 5 are at the same depths as 1–3, but farther to the west. Pepper had to excavate and remove the first three layers of vessels to reach and uncover the deposit farther west, which lay in debris directly beneath the upper-story wall that partitioned upper Room 28b from Room 55. He and his workers burrowed as deeply under the debris at floor level as was safe. It is possible that additional cylinder jars remain in the debris, but we also found it was not safe to burrow farther into the debris under that wall. On the other hand, as I argued in chapter 2, there was likely a partitioning wall of some kind between lower Room 28 and Room 55 located roughly where the wall of debris and the upper-story partition wall are. If this

TABLE 3.8. **Counts of vessels found in a large pile in the southwestern portion of Room 28**

	BOWL	CORRUGATED JAR	CYLINDER JAR	PITCHER	TOTAL
Puerco B/W	—	—	4	—	4
Gallup B/W	5	—	30	9	44
Escavada B/W	—	—	4	—	4
Chaco B/W	2	—	17	7	26
Reserve B/W	1	—	—	—	1
Chaco-McElmo B/W	—	—	1	2	3
Toadlena B/W	—	—	1	—	1
Brimhall B/W	—	—	1	—	1
Nava B/W	—	—	1	—	1
Unidentified organic B/W	—	—	2	—	2
White ware	—	—	37	—	37
Showlow Red	—	—	1	—	1
Blue Shale Corrugated	—	1	—	—	1
Unidentified	—	—	—	1	1
GRAND TOTAL	8	1	99	19	127

B/W = Black—on—white.

Layer 1
Layer 2
Layer 3
Layer 4
Layer 5
Witness Rocks

FIGURE 3.4. Composite figure showing all five of the excavation "layers" for the vessels found in the western part of Room 28. We used witness rocks that appeared in multiple HEE photographs to match up the photos. Note that Layers 1–3 are atop one another, but Layers 4 and 5 are behind the larger pile and dug deeper into the debris on the west side of the room. Composite created by Patricia Crown.

hypothesized western room wall existed, it would have limited how far to the west the cylinder jars might have fallen. Pepper did not find any cylinder jars in the lower part of Room 55 to the west, although he apparently could not excavate as deeply as he wished to. He stated, "Excavations were carried to a depth of over 4 feet below the old floor beams, but nothing but clean sand was discovered" (Pepper 1920:216). However, the floor beams would be associated with the upper story, and so it is unclear whether they reached the actual floor of lower Room 55. As noted in chapter 2, we could not locate the debris that is visible in photographs on the Room 28 side. We could only surmise that Pepper had excavated the deposits not only from the Room 28 side, but also from the Room 55 side, removing all original deposits from the HEE excavations. We will probably never know if there were other cylinder jars on the Room 55 side, but Pepper did not locate any.

As shown in table 3.8, the 127 vessels found in the southwest corner consist of 99 cylinder jars, 19 pitchers, 8 bowls, and 1 partial corrugated jar. One cylinder jar is red ware, and the remaining vessels are white ware. Eighty-two of the vessels are decorated Cibola White Ware, 3 are decorated Chuska White Ware, 1 is a corrugated Chuska Gray Ware, 2 are unidentified organic paint black-on-white types, 1 is an unidenti-

fiable type, and 37 are unidentified plain white ware. As noted above, identification to ware is difficult for whole vessels because wares in this area are identified by aplastic inclusions, which may not be visible when the vessel is largely complete. The ware identifications thus should be considered tentative. The decorated white ware vessels include primarily Gallup Black-on-white and Chaco Black-on-white (70 vessels). There are no Red Mesa Black-on-white vessels, so this group of vessels does not include the early vessels found in the northeast corner of the room. There are Red Mesa Black-on-white cylinder jars in other southwestern collections, but none from Room 28 (Crown 2018). As described in chapter 2, the evidence indicates that these vessels had been placed on a room-wide shelf that ran north-south on the western end of the room. The fire that destroyed the room was set directly under the shelving, and the shelving collapsed as it burned, first at the southern end, so the vessels tumbled toward that corner of the room, where Pepper found them.

Finally, the HEE excavators found a few vessels located along the south wall. Two of these, a white ware cylinder jar and a Chaco-McElmo Black-on-white pitcher, sat atop a plaster/adobe construction that represents part of the southern doorway that led to the West Court. Although the HEE excavation destroyed the outline of whatever that construction was, it placed the two vessels above the floor at the level of the circular step up to that doorway. A third vessel, a small Chaco Black-on-white bowl, sat near the south wall to the west of that doorway.

Finally, the bird effigy vessel comes from an unknown location in the room. While the NMAI catalogs it as coming from Room 28, there are no other records to show where in the room it came from. I suspect it came from a different room, but I have been unable to track down which room.

Vessel Forms and Wares

Table 3.6 summarizes the vessel forms found in all areas of the room. The three primary forms (cylinder jars, pitchers, and bowls) were found in all parts of the room but were concentrated in different areas. Bowls were primarily found in front of the door to Room 51a, while pitchers and cylinder jars were primarily recovered in the southwest corner of the room in the large pile of vessels. Temporal patterns show the bowls as including more early types than either the pitchers or the cylinder jars. In contrast, the pitchers include five of the seven Chaco-McElmo Black-on-white vessels, the latest Cibola White Ware vessels found in the room. While most vessels are Cibola White Ware and thus locally produced, the cylinder jars and the corrugated jar include vessels from the Chuska and Puerco Valley or Mogollon areas.

CYLINDER JARS Room 28 is best known for the discovery of the first Chacoan cylinder jar and for having the largest assemblage of cylinder jars yet found (see figure A.1). The 112 cylinder jars recovered in Room 28 represent more than half of all known cylinder jars, estimated to be around 200. As shown in table 3.5, most of the cylinder jars from Room 28 appear to be Cibola White Ware (although this is difficult to confirm on whole vessels) with primarily Dogoszhi-style hatched designs (48 vessels or 43%). Other Cibola White Ware types include Puerco Black-on-white, Escavada Black-on-white, and a single Chaco-McElmo Black-on-white vessel. There are 47 (42%) white-slipped vessels, which appear to be unpainted. However, I believe that at least some of these once had designs that were either burned out in the room fire or cleaned off through scrubbing. The latter would have consisted of designs added after the vessels were fired, perhaps using pigments that cannot be fired. Such vessels would have been treated much like kiva walls, with repeated plastering and painting, followed by cleansing (Crown and Wills 2003).

There are only 58 known unpainted white ware cylinder jars in the US Southwest, and all but 2 of these come from one of the rooms in this north-central part of Pueblo Bonito (the northern burial cluster). The remaining Room 28 cylinder jars include 4 different types of Chuska White Ware, 2 organic-painted vessels of unknown ware, and 1 Showlow Red jar from southwest of Chaco Canyon. The Chuska and Showlow vessels are unquestionably from outside the canyon, but other cylinder jars may be intrusive too. This is because it is impossible to discern provenance on many of these whole jars because the aplastic inclusions are not visible. In addition, potters produced Cibola White Ware in Chaco Canyon, but also in a wide area beyond the canyon, so we cannot discern which Cibola White Ware cylinder jars are local and which are intrusive.

The cylinder jars recovered in Room 28 vary in size from 12.4 cm to 36.6 cm in height and from 7.2 cm to 15.5 cm in maximum diameter, with an average ratio of height to base of 2.23:1. The shape profiles of these

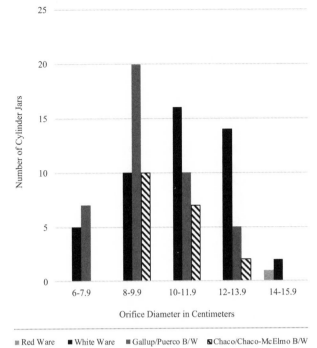

FIGURE 3.5. Orifice diameters for cylinder jars from Room 28.

jars vary from almost straight-walled cylinders to bell-shaped vessels with wider bases than orifices to out-curving forms with wider orifices than bases. I have previously argued (Crown 2018) that cylinder jars tend to get smaller in both diameter and volume over time, and I have suggested that individuals would have needed two hands to hold the larger, earlier vessels, while the later vessels with smaller diameters could have been held in one hand. I interpret this as a change in the etiquette of drinking, from holding the ritual drinking vessel in two hands to holding it in one. But what are the actual measurements of one-handed versus two-handed vessels? Measurements associated with modern glassware and water bottles indicate that 6–7.9 cm is typically considered comfortable for one-handed drinking, although older water bottles were 8.9 cm in diameter. While ceramics provide a surface with greater friction than glass or plastic, any cylinder jar over about 8 cm would likely have been difficult to hold in one hand when filled. Figure 3.5 shows the distribution of diameters for most Room 28 cylinder jars. It can be compared with a published bar chart that shows a larger sample of Chacoan cylinder jars from all sites (Crown 2018:395). Both show that white ware jars are distributed in a fairly normal curve centered on 10–11.9 cm, while Gallup/Puerco and Chaco/Chaco-McElmo jars have a more skewed distribution centered on 8–9.9 cm. The overall distribution indicates that most jars required two hands to hold comfortably, with only 12 jars falling into a size range under 8 cm.

The other aspect of cylinder jar profiles that varies is the presence, direction, and number of lug handles. Of 109 cylinder jars from Room 28 complete enough to determine the presence and number of lugs, 104 had lug handles (table 3.9). Most (80) had four handles placed equidistantly around the vessel, 21 had three handles, and 1 Nava Black-on-white from the Chuska area had two handles; 2 were too fragmentary to determine the number of lugs. Five had no handles, although these included 2 jars with 4 pairs of holes instead of lugs. Lugs varied in shape and direction as well as number. Most (99) were made by taking a single coil of clay and attaching the two ends to the vessel. In some cases, the entire coil was attached to the vessel wall, so there was no opening in the lug; in most, though, the placement of the coil created an open loop of clay. When the lug was not made of a coil/loop of clay, it was made of a round knob (4) or a flattened strap of clay (1). As shown in table 3.9, the majority (42) had horizontal lugs that had a slight Ω shape caused by the two sides being attached to the vessel wall slightly lower than the midpoint of the loop of clay. The second most common lug form (32) is the I-shaped loop, where the coil was attached so that the two sides formed a vertical loop. Horizontally oriented lugs occur on 25 of the cylinder jars from Room 28.

The loop lugs vary in size from tiny, thin coils that Washburn (1980) called "vestigial" to larger and sturdier coils. While some have posited that lugs were used to tie jar lids to the tops of jars or tie hides to vessels to make ceramic drums, many of the lugs would not permit such functions, either because the lugs are completely attached to the vessel wall so that nothing could be tied to them or because the lugs are too fragile to permit attachments that would apply pressure. However, as discussed below, eight of the cylinder jars had cut marks adjacent to the lugs, suggesting that something was tied to them that was sufficiently valuable to merit removal with a sharp object (probably a stone tool). It is interesting that time was taken to remove what was tied on by cutting rather than simply snapping off the lug. This suggests that whoever cut off the object planned to replace it at some time. Most lugs show no wear or polish indicating use (Washburn 1980:79–80). I have suggested (Crown 2018) that lugs may have been purely decora-tive, or perhaps used to attach lightweight ornaments or feathers to the pots, ornaments that would have been valuable enough to warrant cutting off.

Knob-shaped lugs are made of circular blobs of clay with a hole placed through the blob either horizontally (three vessels) or vertically (one vessel). The holes were probably created by piercing the blob with a twig, which would then burn out during firing, leaving the hole.

A single jar has two strap handles attached horizontally with an indentation in the center, creating a W shape. This jar is Nava Black-on-white, a Chuskan white ware.

Two cylinder jars have four sets of two holes, instead of lugs. String could have been threaded through the holes to facilitate carrying the jar, or ornaments could have been hung from the holes. Portions of a cylinder jar with a series of holes around the entire rim was discovered in the backfill from Room 28. Drinking out of such a vessel would obviously be impossible unless the holes were sealed.

As discussed in chapter 4, a large number of sandstone jar lids were recovered in Room 28 in 1896. Pepper (1920:125) stated that 121 came from the room, but he also said (Pepper 1920:122) that 78 came from approximately the floor level and 11 from the "upper deposit," which I take to mean the collapsed upper floor, totaling 89. Yet the material tabulated by B. T. B. Hyde in the back of the volume (Pepper 1920:363, table 3) shows 75 jar covers from Room 28. The H catalog from the expedition lists 89 jar covers, which exactly matches the combined total Pepper provided for the floor and upper floor. I think it is entirely possible that there were originally 121 jar lids, but many were discarded. Pepper (1920:125) stated, "These covers were evidently made to be used in connection with the cylindrical jars and pitchers with which they were found." Other researchers have suggested that this was the case, and in chapter 4 Kocer compares orifice diameters of cylinder jars with jar lid diameters, an exercise that confirms the likelihood that the lids were used with the jars. A cylinder jar at the Museum of Man has a lip just below the orifice, apparently to receive a jar lid. This vessel is not from Room 28, but is mentioned here because it provides additional support for the argument that the lids were used with the cylinder jars. I have previously argued (Crown 2018) that the jar lids suggest that the beverages consumed from cylinder jars were served hot, with the lids promoting heat retention. Experimental work shows that the

TABLE 3.9. **Lugs and straps on cylinder jars from Room 28**

Number of lugs	FORM						TOTAL
	Ω-shaped loop	I-shaped loop	Horizontal loop	Knob with vertical hole	Knob with horizontal hole	W-shaped strap	
2	—	—	—	—	—	1	1
3	6	14	1	—	—	—	21
4	36	18	22	1	3	—	80
Unknown	—	—	2	—	—	—	2
GRAND TOTAL	**42**	**32**	**25**	**1**	**3**	**1**	**104**

TABLE 3.10. **Maker's marks on Room 28 vessels by form**

MAKER'S MARK	CYLINDER JAR	PITCHER	CORRUGATED JAR	BOWL	GOURD EFFIGY	DUCK EFFIGY	TOTAL
None	98	14	1	31	—	1	145
Base missing	4	1	—	1	1	—	7
Line	3	1	—	2	—	—	6
Dot	—	1	—	—	—	—	1
Circle	4	—	—	—	—	—	4
Cross	2	—	—	—	—	—	2
Inside neck and base squiggle	1	—	—	—	—	—	1
Two parallel lines	—	1	—	—	—	—	1
Circle with inner line	—	1	—	—	—	—	1
Cross gurgity/spinning cross	—	1	—	—	—	—	1
GRAND TOTAL	**112**	**20**	**1**	**34**	**1**	**1**	**169**

cylindrical form has superior heat retention properties (Crown 2018).

Potters created many, if not all, cylinder jars as sets that included two or four vessels of identical form (Crown 2018). Sometimes the designs were identical as well, but some sets show identical forms and different designs. In some cases, all of the vessels in a single set were recovered in Room 28. But in other cases, vessels from a set were found in different contexts. Perhaps the most dramatic example of this is the set of four Showlow Red jars: one was found in Room 28, but the other three came from a single room context (Room 15) in Pueblo del Arroyo, a village to the west of Pueblo Bonito. The four vessels are virtually identical and clearly were made by the same potter. I have suggested (Crown 2018) that these sets of cylinder jars were used in drinking rituals involving caffeinated beverages, perhaps for frothing the drinks. This might have involved frothing by pouring the contents from one vessel held horizontally into a vessel set on a surface below. This would have created a waterfall-like effect, with the drink aerating as it fell into the vessel below and creating a froth. This frothing

method is depicted in Maya and Aztec images (Coe and Coe 2007) and so has great time depth that overlaps with the occupation of Pueblo Bonito.

Further evidence that a single potter made all of the cylinder jars in a set comes from 4 identical white ware cylinder jars, each of which has an open-circle maker's mark on the base. While the function of these marks remains unknown, they may be maker's marks placed on vessels to make it easier for a potter to identify their own work in a large-scale firing event. Only 10 of the cylinder jars from Room 28 have maker's marks (table 3.10).

Finally, many of the cylinder jars from Room 28 show evidence of repainting over time. This appears in one of three ways: earlier designs showing through later slip, fireclouds from earlier firing showing through later slip, and ghost designs fired out of vessels.

PITCHERS Twenty-three pitchers were recovered from all parts of Room 28 except above the floor, but most (19) were found in the large pile of vessels in the southwestern portion of the room (figure A.2). I analyzed 20 of the pitchers, and they range in type from Gallup Black-on-white to Chaco-McElmo Black-on-white, therefore dating to between about AD 1000 and the early 1100s. Apart from a single partial Puerco Black-on-white pitcher, the remainder are either Dogoszhi style (all hatched designs) or Sosi style (all solid designs). The 5 Chaco-McElmo Black-on-white pitchers all have Sosi-style designs. As shown in table 3.10, 5 of the pitchers have maker's marks, and each mark is different. Although the sample is small, the high percentage of maker's marks on the pitchers relative to the cylinder jars and bowls is interesting. Twenty-five percent is also higher than the estimates for maker's marks reported in previous studies, which range from 10% to 19% (Neitzel 2008; Trowbridge 2007; Windes 1984), suggesting that the Room 28 sample of pitchers is biased toward those with maker's marks.

The 19 complete pitchers range in height from 13.5 cm to 17.9 cm (with a mean of 15.75 cm) with orifices ranging from 5.2 cm to 8.8 cm (with a mean of 6.9 cm). Unlike the cylinder jars, there is no evidence that Chacoan potters produced pitchers in sets. Each pitcher in this assemblage and in the larger assemblage from Pueblo Bonito is unique.

BOWLS The 35 bowls recovered in Room 28 came from above the floor (1), the large pile in the southwest portion of the room (8), in front of the door to Room 51a (25), and next to the south wall (1) (table 3.6, figure A.3). The high frequency of bowls recovered in front of the door to Room 51a is striking, particularly when we consider the types/wares of these bowls. As noted above, the presence of vessels that are at least 150 years apart in age indicates that heirloom vessels were stored/placed in Room 28 along with what must have been fairly new vessels when the room was burned down, an event that I estimate to have occurred around AD 1100.

The bowls range in size from a minimum of 11.6 cm to a maximum of 32.5 cm in diameter. Figure 3.6 shows the strong correlation between vessel height and rim/orifice diameter in this sample of 33 bowls covering around two centuries of ceramic production (1 of the Room 28 bowls was not located, and another is too fragmentary to measure rim diameter). Although this is a small sample, the distribution of sizes matches the rim diameter analysis for the sample of bowl sherds from the Pueblo Bonito trash mounds (Arazi-Coambs 2016:figure 3.12), with modes around 10–15 cm, 18–24 cm, and more than 30 cm. These groupings likely represent individual eating vessels (12), household serving/eating vessels

(17), and larger group serving/eating vessels (4). The 4 bowls greater than 30 cm in diameter (H/3209, 53023, H/3212, and H/3204) are all Gallup Black-on-white; 2 have squiggle hatch and thus are probably early Gallup. All 4 have two handles located on the exterior; 3 have straps with an indented center, creating a W shape when seen from the top. The final bowl has two strap handles that lack the W indentation. All 4 are undoubtedly serving vessels used in large group events, such as feasts. Two of these large bowls were found in the northeast corner of the room in front of the door to Room 51a. They are clearly visible in Pepper's (1920) figures 42 and 44. One of these large bowls had another bowl and a basket nested inside. The other had seven turquoise and shell ornaments inside, which we reconstructed at AMNH in 2014 (figure 3.7). The other 2 large bowls were found in Layer 3 of the large pile of vessels found in the southwestern area of Room 28. Interestingly, the only other bowl with handles is the smallest, a Chaco Black-on-white bowl with four small Ω-shaped lugs (H/3423). This small bowl was found along the southern wall of the room, one of the few vessels found in this location. One final bowl deserves additional comment. A bowl found by the Room 51a doorway is Red Mesa Black-on-white, but orange pigment was added on half of the vessel. This appears to be an early attempt at a polychrome, showing experimentation with technology to achieve a novel color combination.

OTHER FORMS Three additional vessels from Room 28 have unique forms (figure A.2b). The first is a Blue Shale Corrugated jar, a Chuska Gray Ware vessel. It is 25.6 cm high with an orifice 17.3 cm in diameter. This partial vessel was recovered in Layer 3 in the pile of vessels in the southwest corner of Room 28. The jar shows moderate use wear inside and out, but no soot suggestive of use over a fire. As the only utility ware vessel recovered in Room 28, this jar probably had an important role in the preparation of food or drink to be served in the many serving vessels recovered in the room. But without additional analysis, we likely will not ever know exactly how it was used.

There are two effigy vessels in the assemblage, only one of which definitely came from Room 28. A partial Red Mesa Black-on-white gourd effigy jar (H/3434) was recovered 1 m above the floor, and so probably was on the upper-story floor when the room burned. Only about half of the vessel was recovered, and it was heav-

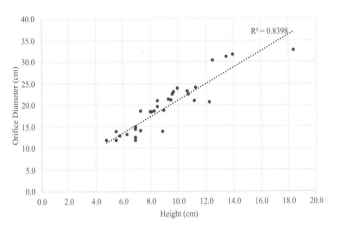

FIGURE 3.6. Scatter plot of bowl rim diameter by height.

FIGURE 3.7. Gallup Black-on-white bowl recovered in the northeast corner of Room 28, which was found with seven turquoise and shell ornaments inside. AMNH H/3212 (bowl) and H/4118 (offering). Courtesy of the Division of Anthropology, American Museum of Natural History. Photograph by Patricia Crown.

ily burned. Shaped like a gourd, with a peduncle handle, the jar orifice is only 1.3 cm in diameter. It may have functioned as a canteen. The exterior shows heavy use wear. Pepper (1920:figure 47) illustrated a completely different gourd effigy jar in his volume and indicated it came from Room 28, but as noted above, that jar actually was recovered from a burial elsewhere in the canyon.

A second effigy vessel (52575) in the collections of the National Museum of the American Indian is listed in its catalog as coming from Room 28. However, Pepper did not mention this vessel in any of his descriptions of the room, and if it came from Pueblo Bonito, it does not have an H catalog number visible anywhere. It also does not appear in any of the room photographs. It is a beautiful and distinctive vessel, and I doubt that Pepper would have left it out of his discussion of the room contents

if it had come from Room 28. So, I do not believe it actually came from Room 28, but I discuss it here because it is possible that it was reconstructed from the broken vessels found on the upper story of the room. The jar is a duck effigy, with a small handle attached to the back of the neck of the jar. The handle was fashioned into an animal head with ears. The vessel is beautifully painted in a complicated decorative style that best fits the Reserve Black-on-white type designation. The jar is 17 cm high and 20.7 cm long with an orifice 8.1 cm in diameter. The base shows moderate use wear.

Vessel Use Wear, Modification, and Residues

The large number of vessels in Room 28 and the placement of most on a room-wide shelf raises the question of whether the vessels were stockpiled in Room 28 pending future use, or made and brought to the room specifically to be sacrificed in the fire, or stored in the room between uses. In other words, were they unused or used? As discussed above, I recorded use wear on both the interior and exterior of the vessels using a qualitative scale from none to heavy use wear. Vessels with no use have no scratches or other marks indicative of use. Vessels with light use may show some abrasion or dulling of slip polish, but very little. Vessels with moderate use wear have slip that has flaked off in places and paint that is partially gone. Heavy use wear is indicated by abrasion that has worn the ceramic paste as well as the slip; the slip is completely gone in patches. Here, I focus first on the results of the analysis of interior use wear (table 3.11).

Most cylinder jar interiors showed no use, probably because they were intended for the consumption of liquids. While Washburn (1980) argued that cylinder jars were used to hold precious items, such as shell or obsidian, that usage would have scratched the interior of the jar. I found only one cylinder jar with scratches that matched her description (H/3403, NMAI 052106.00). This plain white jar also had very heavy exterior use wear. As a group, only 7% of the cylinder jars showed moderate to heavy interior use. Similarly, only 10% of the pitchers showed moderate to heavy use wear. Both drinking vessels contrast with the bowls, where 38% of the sample show moderate to heavy use wear on the interior.

Basal use reflects abrasion due to contact with rough surfaces, such as sand floors during use. As can be seen in table 3.12, 88% of all vessels from Room 28 show some use wear, and 52% show moderate to heavy use wear.

TABLE 3.11. **Interior use wear for vessel forms found in Room 28**

	CYLINDER JAR	PITCHER	CORRUGATED JAR	BOWL	GOURD EFFIGY	DUCK EFFIGY	TOTAL (%)
None	49	8	1	4	1	—	63 (37)
Light	54	10	—	17	—	1	82 (49)
Moderate	6	2	—	7	—	—	15 (9)
Heavy	2	—	—	6	—	—	8 (5)
GRAND TOTAL	**111**	**20**	**1**	**34**	**1**	**1**	**168 (100)**

TABLE 3.12. **Exterior basal use wear for vessel forms found in Room 28**

	CYLINDER JAR	PITCHER	CORRUGATED JAR	BOWL	DUCK EFFIGY	TOTAL (%)
None	7	2	—	10	—	19 (12)
Light	39	6	—	14	—	59 (36)
Moderate	43	8	—	6	—	57 (35)
Heavy	20	3	1	3	1	28 (17)
GRAND TOTAL	**109**	**19**	**1**	**33**	**1**	**163 (100)**

TABLE 3.13. **Room 28 vessels with evidence of reslipping, repainting, and fired-out paint**

	CYLINDER JARS (N = 112)	PITCHERS (N = 20)	BOWLS (N = 35)	TOTAL (N = 167)
Earlier designs under slip	49 (44%)	9 (45%)	2 (6%)	60 (36%)
Earlier fireclouds under slip	40 (36%)	4 (20%)	0	44 (26%)
Ghost designs on white vessels	11 (10%)	0	0	11 (7%)

Fifty-eight percent of the pitchers and cylinder jars show moderate to heavy basal use wear. As a group, the bowls show the least basal use wear. Fully 73% of the 33 bowls have no visible use wear or light use wear. This represents the least use wear of any form category. Most surprisingly, the earliest bowls, which are Kiatuthlanna and Red Mesa Black-on-white, show relatively little use wear. Of the 15 bowls of these two types, only 2 Red Mesa bowls show moderate basal use wear; the remainder show no wear to little wear. Eleven of the 15 bowls of these two early types show little to no wear on the interior as well. The reasons that bowls that were perhaps 250 years old at the time of the destruction of the room would show so little wear include that the bowls were stockpiled for later use but then never used, or that they were removed from non-use contexts, such as burials or abandoned rooms/sites, and placed in Room 28. Otherwise, it is difficult to understand how bowls

kept for centuries could show so little evidence of use. It is possible that they were used only for non-abrasive purposes (such as for drinking), but in an environment made of sand and sandstone, it would be difficult to preserve vessels from abrasion for so long. Heirloom bowls might be used only on special occasions and for display, but they had to have been kept from use when they were made and for some period of time before they would be considered heirlooms. Overall though, the results indicate that the vessels found in Room 28 were in use before their final deposition in Room 28, and they were not created for caching and terminating.

Many of the vessels show modification over time by repainting, reslipping, and/or refiring (Crown and Wills 2003), which also demonstrates that the vessels were in use prior to their final deposition in Room 28. As shown in table 3.13, this modification appears in three ways: 60 vessels, including 49 cylinder jars, have earlier designs visible beneath later slip/paint; 44 vessels, again primarily cylinder jars, have fireclouds clearly visible beneath slip, indicating that the vessels had been fired at least twice; and 11 vessels, all cylinder jars, show faint traces of painting that is no longer present. In the latter case, some of the vessels appear to have matte areas where paint burned out in refiring, possibly due to the burning of Room 28. All of these types of modification show that many vessels were used for some period of time and not placed in Room 28 unused. In other words, the vessels were not stockpiled in Room 28 for future use, but were used prior to placement in the room.

Residues provide additional evidence of use prior to the vessels' placement in Room 28. I recorded residues on each vessel's interior surface and exterior surface separately. Vessels at the NMAI had been cleaned so thoroughly that residues were no longer visible, but those at the AMNH had not been cleaned. Most of the vessels had no clear residues apart from dirt. Nine vessels (2 pitchers and 7 cylinder jars) had material crusted on them that appeared to be charred organic matter. Eleven vessels, including 10 cylinder jars and 1 bowl, had stains penetrating the paste that appeared greasy or oily. The material had soaked into the vessel wall and so did not appear to be drips of resin from the burning ceiling or shelving. These vessels came primarily from the pile of vessels in the western portion of the room and from Levels 1, 2, 4, and 5. Five of the vessels came from the lowest, westernmost levels. As shown in figure 3.8, it is possible that this material represents a greasy substance, such as fat, poured on the vessels to encourage burning.

Taken together, all of these analyses indicate use of the vessels prior to their placement in Room 28. This likely means they were stored in the room at the time it was deliberately set on fire, rather than moved to or created specifically for a termination event in Room 28.

Mutilation and Termination

In addition to use abrasion and refurbishing over time, many of the vessels show other types of modifications, including subtraction of some portion of the vessel or the addition of ocher. As shown in table 3.14, the most common form of subtractive modification involved the removal of parts of the rim. In some cases, it is possible that this was just accidental breakage of the rim. But I report in this table only vessels where portions of the rim appear to have been purposefully "chewed" or snapped off, sometimes in patterns around the vessel. Because 22% of the analyzed vessels (1 bowl and 36 cylinder jars) had such rim subtraction, I believe these were purposefully modified prior to their placement or termination in Room 28.

Eight (5%) of the total vessels had cut marks that were unquestionably culturally formed, and all of these were cylinder jars. The cut marks were typically found adjacent to the lugs of cylinder jars (figure 3.9; H/3397, vessel

left FIGURE 3.8. Cylinder jar with greasy-looking discoloration. AMNH H/3265. Courtesy of the Division of Anthropology, American Museum of Natural History. Photograph by Marianne Tyndall.

right FIGURE 3.9. Cylinder jar with cut marks near lug handles, which were created by a sharp tool. AMNH H/3397. Courtesy of the Division of Anthropology, American Museum of Natural History. Photograph by Patricia Crown.

TABLE 3.14. **Modifications to Room 28 vessels by form and type (some vessels show multiple types of modification)**

	RIM CHEWED	CUT MARKS	PATCH	OCHER	TOTAL VESSELS ANALYZED
Cylinder jars	36	8	14	5	112
Gallup B/W	11	1	1	2	30
Escavada B/W	1	—	—	—	4
Puerco B/W	—	1	—	—	5
Chaco B/W	3	—	2	1	18
Chaco–McElmo B/W	—	—	—	—	1
Naschitti B/W	1	—	—	—	1
Brimhall B/W	1	—	—	—	1
Nava B/W	—	—	—	—	1
Toadlena B/W	—	—	—	—	1
Unknown organic painted type	1	1	—	—	2
White ware	17	5	11	2	47
Showlow Red	1	—	—	—	1
Pitchers	—	—	—	—	20
Chaco B/W	—	—	—	—	6
Chaco–McElmo B/W	—	—	—	—	5
Gallup B/W	—	—	—	—	8
Puerco B/W	—	—	—	—	1
Corrugated jar	—	—	—	—	1
Blue Shale Corrugated	—	—	—	—	1
Bowls	1	—	—	—	34
Kiatuthlanna B/W	—	—	—	—	2
Red Mesa B/W	1	—	—	—	13
Gallup B/W	—	—	—	—	9
Escavada B/W	—	—	—	—	1
Puerco B/W	—	—	—	—	1
Chaco B/W	—	—	—	—	5
Reserve B/W	—	—	—	—	1
Chaco–McElmo B/W	—	—	—	—	1
Other	—	—	—	—	1
Gourd effigy	—	—	—	—	1
Red Mesa B/W	—	—	—	—	1
Duck effigy	—	—	—	—	1
Puerco B/W	—	—	—	—	1
GRAND TOTAL	37 (22%)	8 (5%)	14 (8%)	5 (3%)	169 (100%)

B/W = Black-on-white.

98 from Level 2), as if something that had been tied to or through the lugs was removed. Another 14 vessels, again all cylinder jars, had unusual rectangular patches removed from the wall of the vessel on one side. These patches (figure 3.10) appear to have been created by cutting or grinding an area of the vessel about 1.7 cm wide × 4 cm long. The long side of each patch runs vertically up the jar as it sits on its base. These patches are fairly shallow but are quite distinctive. The sharp edges of most of the patches suggest cutting rather than grinding, but only a very sharp tool, such as an obsidian blade, would create such clean edges. The AMNH staff assured me that these were not sampling areas, and in some cases, the presence of glued breaks that run through a patch confirms that the patches were present when the vessels were reconstructed. These patches are almost certainly prehispanic, although there may never be a way to prove this. Most of the patches occur on undecorated white ware vessels; this selective sample again suggests they were created in the deep past. Five of the cylinder jars have some red ocher applied to the exterior.

The patterns described here indicate that cylinder jars were modified in ways that bowls and pitchers were not. Cylinder jars were subject to cutting, rim chipping (sometimes in patterns), patch removal, and red ocher application. Pitchers do not show any of these modifications, and only one bowl shows rim chipping.

There are two other forms of modification that might be related to these. Nineteen percent of all cylinder jars have one or more lugs missing. While it is possible that this is due to accidental breakage of these fragile appendages, it is also possible that they were purposefully snapped off. Another 7% of cylinder jars have a form of abrasion that I have designated "scrubbing," which is characterized by exterior walls with small vertical abrasion lines. These appear to have been caused by scrubbing the vessels from top to bottom as if to remove something from the exterior wall. I have suggested previously (Crown 2007) that these vessels had plaster or stucco that might have been decorated with post-firing paints, which were then removed by using wet sand to abrade the exterior. Post-firing pigments impart colors that could not be achieved as fired designs in the prehispanic US Southwest, including greens, blues, and turquoises. In removing the stucco coating with abrasive sand or a sandstone abrader, the sand grains created tiny vertical abrasion lines, visible primarily in oblique light and present only on the vessel exteriors

FIGURE 3.10. Cylinder jar with a patch cut or ground from surface. AMNH H/3265. Courtesy of the Division of Anthropology, American Museum of Natural History. Photograph by Marianne Tyndall.

FIGURE 3.11. Abrasion lines on exterior wall of a cylinder jar, possibly caused by scrubbing with sand. AMNH H/4151. Courtesy of the Division of Anthropology, American Museum of Natural History. Photograph by Patricia Crown.

(figure 3.11). These patterns indicate that cylinder jars were viewed as different from both another drinking vessel form (pitchers) and bowl forms that lack such modification.

While red ocher was generally viewed as a powerful substance and perhaps a sign of respect or was used merely in an attempt to change the color of a vessel, the other modifications involved destructive actions that altered the pots. The question then becomes why individuals or groups would alter and sometimes mutilate the cylinder vessels. I believe that the mutilation of these vessels is a sign that they were viewed as powerful objects, and at the end of their use lives, that power had to be removed by actions that destroyed the integrity of their surfaces. As I discuss in the conclusions to this volume (chapter 12), burning the room down with the vessels inside was another way to destroy them and remove their power (Crown 2018). Such termination or retirement practices are typically associated with beliefs surrounding animated objects. The objects take on power when they are made, and this power must be removed from them or they retain power that may be dangerous, particularly for individuals who are not supposed to handle them. In her study of the Pueblo of Zuni, Ruth Bunzel (1932:502) emphasized that "all sacred objects are taboo to all people who do not 'belong' to them." The means of removing power may involve breaking, mutilating, or burning the objects as forms of deanimation (Lucero 2008:191; Mock 1998).

In the case of the cylinder jars, the mutilation of the vessels and burning of the room seem to have coincided with the ending of the ritual associated with the cylinder jars. There are no known cylinder jars in the northern San Juan that postdate this termination event. Indeed, as I have argued elsewhere (Crown 2018), mugs seem to have replaced cylinder jars and pitchers in Chaco as the preferred drinking vessels after about AD 1100. Both pitchers and mugs appear to be individual (rather than group) drinking vessels used and probably owned by individuals; pitchers particularly are common mortuary vessels. In contrast, cylinder jars rarely occur in burials (only one cylinder jar found in Pueblo Bonito was in direct association with a burial: that of an adult female buried in Room 33). Some cylinder jars are so large that they probably were used for group, rather than individual, consumption of the contents. Taken together, these patterns of use and discard suggest that cylinder jars were not the property of individuals. Instead, they probably belonged to one or more corporate groups: either kin groups, such as clans, or sodalities, such as religious groups. Room 28 would then have been the storage room for these objects used for special occasions and ceremonies associated with that group. These interpretations are discussed further in the conclusions.

SHERDS FROM ROOM 28 FILL FOUND IN 2013 EXCAVATIONS

When we opened Room 28 in 2013, we screened all deposits. As discussed in chapter 1, our strategy initially involved screening nine buckets with quarter-inch mesh and the tenth with eighth-inch mesh. However, as we encountered high numbers of minute ornaments, even the eighth-inch mesh was insufficient, and we switched to 100% screening through window-screen mesh until

we reached the level above the floor, when we switched back to the original screening protocol. The resulting ceramics assemblage came from backfill, which reduces its utility for addressing many questions. However, these ceramics turned out to be critical for addressing one of the most important questions we had about our excavations of Room 28: Where did the backfill come from?

The fill assemblage contained 900 sherds of 17 wares and 71 types (table 3.15). Forty-eight percent of the sherds were Cibola White Ware, and another 24% were Cibola Gray Ware and so possibly locally made. Ten percent of the sherds (91) were either Chuska Gray Ware or Chuska White Ware. Other intrusive wares were Mesa Verde Gray Ware (0.1%), Tusayan Gray Ware (0.1%), Little Colorado White Ware (0.3%), Mesa Verde White Ware (1.9%), Tusayan White Ware (1%), Puerco Valley/ Mogollon Brown Ware (2.1%), Aztec Black Ware (0.1%), Chuska Red Ware (0.2%), Puerco Valley/Mogollon Red Ware (9.6%, including Showlow Red types), San Juan Red Ware (0.4%), Tsegi Orange Ware (0.2%), and White Mountain Red Ware (0.7%). These numbers are somewhat deceptive, however, because the sherds reported for some wares came from single broken vessels, a pattern discussed further below.

Fifty-four percent of the assemblage came from jars, 32% from bowls, and 5% from cylinder jars (table 3.15). As is typical in Chaco collections, the gray ware includes only jar sherds. The possibly locally made Cibola White Ware has a roughly equal proportion of bowls and jars; the incidence of cylinder jars as 10% of the Cibola White Ware assemblage is unusual. Among the intrusive wares, bowls represent 59% of intrusive white ware and 66% of intrusive red ware, while jars represent only 30% of intrusive white ware and 2% of intrusive red ware. This indicates that bowls were more commonly imported to Pueblo Bonito than were jars.

However, this assemblage is not typical of room fill generally in Chaco. For instance, comparing the sizes of sherds in the 2013 fill versus the subfloor fill provides an interesting contrast. The mean weight of a sherd from the fill under the floor of Room 28 is 3.3 grams, with a range from 0.1 to 25.7 grams. In contrast, the mean weight of a sherd from the 2013 room fill above the floor is 6.6 grams, with a range from 0.1 to 127.4 grams. In other words, the sherds in the backfill above the floor are, on average, twice the size of the sherds in the intact fill under the floor. And the range indicates that some of the sherds found above the floor are quite large—

TABLE 3.15. **Counts of types and forms recovered in the backfill levels in Room 28 in 2013**

COUNT OF TYPE

Ware	Type	Bird effigy	Bowl	Bowl or cylinder jar	Bowl or ladle	Cylinder jar	Cylinder jar/ pitcher	Effigy	Jar	Mug	Pitcher	Scoop	Unknown	Total (%)
Cibola GW	Lino Gray	—	—	—	—	—	—	—	1	—	—	—	—	1 (0.1)
	Lino Fugitive Red	—	—	—	—	—	—	—	8	—	—	—	—	8 (0.9)
	Plain Gray	—	—	—	—	—	—	—	148	—	—	—	—	148 (16.4)
	Plain Gray with fugitive red	—	—	—	—	—	—	—	1	—	—	—	—	1 (0.1)
	Wide Neckbanded	—	—	—	—	—	—	—	11	—	—	—	—	11 (1.2)
	Narrow Neckbanded	—	—	—	—	—	—	—	6	—	—	—	—	6 (0.7)
	Wide Clapboard Corrugated	—	—	—	—	—	—	—	1	—	—	—	—	1 (0.1)
	Narrow Clapboard Corrugated	—	—	—	—	—	—	—	3	—	—	—	—	3 (0.3)
	Undifferentiated clapboard corrugated	—	—	—	—	—	—	—	4	—	—	—	—	4 (0.4)
	Incised Clapboard Corrugated	—	—	—	—	—	—	—	1	—	—	—	—	1 (.1)
	Wide fillet rim	—	—	—	—	—	—	—	1	—	—	—	—	1 (0.1)
	Indented Corrugated	—	—	—	—	—	—	—	22	—	—	—	—	22 (2.4)
	Exuberant Indented Corrugated	—	—	—	—	—	—	—	1	—	—	—	—	1 (0.1)
	Flattened Indented Corrugated	—	—	—	—	—	—	—	1	—	—	—	—	1 (0.1)
	Indented Zoned Corrugated	—	—	—	—	—	—	—	1	—	—	—	—	1 (0.1)
	Basketry impressed	—	—	—	—	—	—	—	1	—	—	—	—	1 (0.1)
	Obliterated Indented Corrugated	—	—	—	—	—	—	—	6	—	—	—	—	6 (0.7)
	Unidentified	—	—	—	—	—	—	—	1	—	—	—	1	2 (0.2)
Cibola Gray Ware Total		—	—	—	—	—	—	—	218	—	—	—	1	219 (24.3)
Chuska GW	Plain Gray	—	—	—	—	—	—	—	22	—	—	—	—	22 (2.4)
	Clapboard Corrugated	—	—	—	—	—	—	—	3	—	—	—	—	3 (0.3)
	Wide Clapboard Corrugated	—	—	—	—	—	—	—	1	—	—	—	—	1 (0.1)
	Narrow Clapboard Corrugated	—	—	—	—	—	—	—	2	—	—	—	—	2 (0.2)

FORM

TABLE 3.15. *Continued*

COUNT OF TYPE

Ware	Type	Bird effigy	Bowl	Bowl or cylinder jar	Bowl or ladle	Cylinder jar	Cylinder jar/pitcher	Effigy	Jar	Mug	Pitcher	Scoop	Unknown	Total (%)
	Wide Neckbanded	—	—	—	—	—	—	—	1	—	—	—	—	1 (0.1)
	Indented Corrugated	—	—	—	—	—	—	—	18	—	—	—	—	18 (2.0)
	Festoon Indented Corrugated	—	—	—	—	—	—	—	3	—	—	—	—	3 (0.3)
	Indented Obliterated Corrugated	—	—	—	—	—	—	—	1	—	—	—	—	1 (0.1)
	Indented Zoned Corrugated	—	—	—	—	—	—	—	2	—	—	—	—	2 (0.2)
	Patterned Corrugated	—	—	—	—	—	—	—	1	—	—	—	—	1 (0.1)
	Wide fillet rim	—	—	—	—	—	—	—	2	—	—	—	—	2 (0.2)
Chuska Gray Ware Total		—	—	—	—	—	—	—	56	—	—	—	—	56 (6.2)
Mesa Verde GW	Undifferentiated gray ware	—	—	—	—	—	—	—	1	—	—	—	—	1 (0.1)
Mesa Verde Gray Ware Total		—	—	—	—	—	—	—	1	—	—	—	—	1 (0.1)
Tusayan GW	Undifferentiated gray ware	—	—	—	—	—	—	—	1	—	—	—	—	1 (0.1)
Tusayan Gray Ware Total		—	—	—	—	—	—	—	1	—	—	—	—	1 (0.1)
Cibola WW	White Mound B/w	—	1	—	—	—	—	—	—	—	—	—	—	1 (0.1)
	Red Mesa B/w	—	21	—	—	—	2	—	18	—	1	1	—	43 (4.8)
	Red Mesa B/w/ Escavada B/w	—	1	—	—	—	—	—	—	—	—	—	—	1 (0.1)
	Escavada B/w	—	10	—	—	—	—	—	6	—	—	—	—	16 (1.7)
	Gallup B/w	—	18	—	—	12	6	—	22	—	2	—	—	60 (6.7)
	Puerco B/w	—	1	—	—	4	1	—	8	—	1	—	—	14 (1.6)
	Sosi B/w	—	—	—	—	—	1	—	—	—	—	—	—	1 (0.1)
	Chaco B/w	—	2	—	—	—	3	—	5	—	—	—	—	10 (1.1)
	Chaco-McElmo B/w	—	13	—	—	—	—	—	3	1	—	—	1	18 (2.0)
	Reserve B/w	—	1	—	—	—	—	—	3	—	—	—	—	4 (0.4)
	Unidentified	1	65	—	—	—	—	—	56	—	1	—	5	128 (14.2)
	Unidentified polychrome	—	—	—	—	—	—	—	1	—	—	—	—	1 (0.1)
	White ware	—	30	—	—	28	5	—	64	—	2	—	9	139 (15.4)
Cibola White Ware Total		1	163	—	—	44	17	1	186	1	7	1	15	436 (48.4)

FORM

Ware / Type												Total
Chuska WW												
Newcomb B/w	2	—	—	—	—	—	—	1	—	—	—	3 (0.3)
Naschitti B/w	1	—	—	—	—	—	—	—	—	—	—	1 (0.1)
Chuska B/w	1	—	—	—	—	—	—	—	—	—	—	1 (0.1)
Unidentified b/w	10	—	—	—	—	—	—	13	—	—	1	24 (2.7)
White ware	2	—	—	—	—	1	—	3	—	—	—	6 (0.7)
Chuska White Ware Total	**16**	—	—	—	—	**1**	—	**17**	—	—	**1**	**35 (3.9)**
Little Colorado WW												
Walnut A B/w	1	—	—	—	—	—	—	—	—	—	—	1 (0.1)
Walnut B B/w	2	—	—	—	—	—	—	—	—	—	—	2 (0.2)
Little Colorado White Ware Total	**3**	—	—	—	—	—	—	—	—	—	—	**3 (0.3)**
Mesa Verde WW												
Piedra B/w	1	—	—	—	—	—	—	—	—	—	—	1 (0.1)
Mancos B/w	1	—	—	—	—	—	—	—	—	—	—	1 (0.1)
McElmo B/w	8	—	—	—	—	—	—	1	—	—	—	9 (1.0)
Unidentified	4	—	—	—	—	—	—	—	1	—	—	5 (0.6)
White ware	1	—	—	—	—	—	—	—	—	—	—	1 (0.1)
Mesa Verde White Ware Total	**15**	—	—	—	—	—	—	**1**	**1**	—	—	**17 (1.9)**
Tusayan WW												
Kana'a B/w	3	—	—	—	—	—	—	1	—	—	—	4 (0.4)
Black Mesa B/w	—	—	—	—	4	—	—	—	—	—	—	4 (0.4)
Unidentified	1	—	—	—	—	—	—	—	—	—	—	1 (0.1)
Tusayan White Ware Total	**4**	—	—	—	**4**	—	—	**1**	—	—	—	**9 (1.0)**
Puerco Valley/Mogollon Brown Ware												
Unidentified	1	—	—	—	—	—	—	—	—	—	—	1 (0.1)
Woodruff Brown Smudged-Sand	18	—	—	—	—	—	—	—	—	—	—	18 (2.0)
Puerco Valley/Mogollon Brown Ware Total	**19**	—	—	—	—	—	—	—	—	—	—	**19 (2.1)**
Aztec Black Ware												
Aztec Black	—	—	—	—	—	—	—	1	—	—	—	1 (0.1)
Aztec Black Ware Total	—	—	—	—	—	—	—	**1**	—	—	—	**1 (0.1)**
Chuska RW												
Sanostee Orange Plain	1	—	—	—	—	—	—	—	—	—	—	1 (0.1)
Sanostee Red/Orange	1	—	—	—	—	—	—	—	—	—	—	1 (0.1)
Chuska Red Ware Total	**2**	—	—	—	—	—	—	—	—	—	—	**2 (0.2)**
Puerco Valley/Mogollon RW												
Woodruff Red Smudged-Crushed Rock	5	—	—	—	—	—	—	—	—	—	—	5 (0.6)
Woodruff Red Smudged-Sand	37	—	—	—	—	—	—	—	—	—	—	37 (4.1)

TABLE 3.15. *Continued*

COUNT OF TYPE

Ware	Type	Bird effigy	Bowl	Bowl or cylinder jar	Bowl or ladle	Cylinder jar	Cylinder jar/ pitcher	Effigy	Jar	Mug	Pitcher	Scoop	Unknown	Total (%)
													FORM	
	Woodruff Red–Crushed Rock	—	1	6	—	—	—	—	—	—	—	—	—	7 (0.8)
	Woodruff Red–Sand	—	1	—	—	—	—	—	—	—	—	—	—	1 (0.1)
	Showlow B/R	—	1	—	—	—	—	—	—	—	—	—	—	1 (0.1)
	Showlow Red	—	—	25	—	—	—	—	1	—	—	—	—	26 (2.9)
	Showlow Red–Smudged	—	8	—	—	1	—	—	—	—	—	—	—	9 (1.0)
Puerco Valley/Mogollon Red Ware Total		—	53	31	—	1	—	—	1	—	—	—	—	**86 (9.6)**
	San Juan RW	—	3	—	—	—	—	—	1	—	—	—	—	4 (0.4)
San Juan Red Ware Total		—	3	—	—	—	—	—	1	—	—	—	—	**4 (0.4)**
Tsegi Orange Ware	Medicine B/R	—	1	—	—	—	—	—	—	—	—	—	—	1 (0.1)
	Tsegi Orange	—	1	—	—	—	—	—	—	—	—	—	—	1 (0.1)
Tsegi Orange Ware Total		—	2	—	—	—	—	—	—	—	—	—	—	**2 (0.2)**
White Mountain RW	Puerco Black-on-red	—	1	—	—	—	—	—	—	—	—	—	—	1 (0.1)
	St Johns Polychrome	—	2	—	—	—	—	—	—	—	—	—	—	2 (0.2)
	Unidentified	—	3	—	—	—	—	—	—	—	—	—	—	3 (0.3)
White Mountain Red Ware Total		—	6	—	—	—	—	—	—	—	—	—	—	**6 (0.7)**
Unknown RW	Unidentified	—	—	—	—	—	—	1	—	—	—	—	—	1 (0.1)
Unknown RW Total	-	—	—	—	—	—	—	1	—	—	—	—	—	**1 (0.1)**
Unknown	Red on gray	—	—	—	—	—	—	—	1	—	—	—	—	1 (0.1)
	Unidentified	—	—	—	—	—	—	—	1	—	—	—	—	1 (0.1)
Unknown Total		—	—	—	—	—	—	—	2	—	—	—	—	**2 (0.2)**
GRAND TOTAL (%)		1 (0.1)	286 (31.8)	31 (3.4)	1 (0.1)	49 (5.4)	18 (2.0)	1 (0.1)	487 (54.1)	1 (0.1)	7 (0.8)	1 (0.1)	17 (1.9)	900 (100)

B/w = Black-on-white; GW = gray ware; RW = red ware; WW = white ware.

almost five times as large as the largest sherd found under the floor. This alone suggests that they are not normal refuse, and further examination shows that many of the sherds came from reconstructible vessels. By laying out all of the sherds and attempting to refit them into individual vessels, I found that 21% of all sherds found in the 2013 room fill came from 19 partial vessels, with individual sherds from these partial vessels scattered over levels from close to the surface to the floor of Room 28. For instance, virtually all of the Showlow Red and Showlow Red Smudged sherds came from 2 partial vessels. Eight of the 17 Mesa Verde White Ware sherds came from 2 partial bowls. This raised the question of where the rest of these vessels are.

To determine where these partial vessels, and thus the fill, might have originated, I began by comparing the cylinder jar sherds recovered in the fill to photographs of cylinder jars from Pueblo Bonito. By doing so, I discovered that sherds found in Room 28 in 2013 fit onto nearly complete cylinder jars at AMNH and the Robert S. Peabody Museum at Andover that were recovered from Rooms 53 and 56 in 1897 (figure 3.12). I then visited AMNH armed with photographs of the sherds found in the fill of Room 28 and tried to match the sherds in the collections to these photographs. Additional portions of several of the partial vessels from Room 28 were located at AMNH; these came from sherd collections and partial vessels recovered in 1897 from Rooms 39b, 52, 53, and 56.

As discussed in chapter 2, Rooms 53 and 56 were partially "excavated" by Warren Moorehead in April 1897. When the Hyde Exploring Expedition resumed in May 1897, the excavators found the mess created by Moorehead's work and cleaned it up both by throwing his backdirt into the open Room 28 and by excavating the remaining portions of Rooms 53 and 56. The recovery of sherds in the Room 28 fill in 2013 that match partial vessels from Rooms 53 and 56 confirms that at least some of the backdirt from those rooms was thrown into Room 28 in 1897 either by Moorehead or by the HEE. But portions of that backfill had apparently already been tamped down into other rooms surrounding Rooms 53 and 56, including Rooms 39b and Room 52, both also excavated in 1897. These results agree with the results of Kerriann Marden's (2011) reassociation work with the human skeletal material from Rooms 53 and 56, which showed that Moorehead threw portions of skeletons from those rooms into several adjacent rooms (figure 3.13). I am arguing then that the unburned backfill found

FIGURE 3.12. Rejoining sherds recovered in Room 28 with a photograph of a double cylinder vessel from Room 56. R. S. Peabody Museum vessel 90.83.2. Photograph by W. H. Wills.

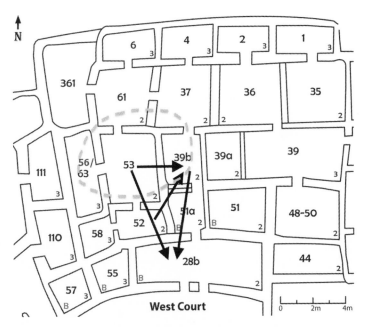

FIGURE 3.13. Map showing upper-story rooms in the northern portion of Pueblo Bonito. Arrows indicate the locations of pottery from Rooms 52, 53, 56, 63, and 39b that were refit with sherds from Room 28 found in 2013. The circled area indicates the rooms where human skeletal remains originally found in Rooms 53 or 56 were recovered and reassociated by Kerriann Marden (2011). A "B" indicates a burned room, and the small numbers indicate the number of stories. Drawing by Drew Wills.

in Room 28 in 2013 came from Rooms 53 and 56, and backfill from those rooms was also tossed into Rooms 52 and 39b. The burned backfill came from the adjacent Room 28a, but I did not find any sherds from the 2013 Room 28 fill that fit onto sherds from Room 28a. As the HEE excavations did not recover any partial vessels from Room 28a, the lack of refits may simply confirm that the Room 28a backfill thrown into Room 28 included only discarded refuse. This contrasts with the large sherds from the unburned fill, which often refit other sherds and probably came from broken but complete vessels that Moorehead shoveled through in Rooms 53 and 56.

Among the material found in Room 28 in 2013 that almost certainly came from Rooms 53 and 56 were portions of at least eleven previously undocumented cylinder jars (figure 3.14). In addition to these jars (which join the three cylinder jars found by Moorehead and Pepper in Rooms 53 and 56), the partial vessels include bowls of Little Colorado White Ware, Mesa Verde White Ware, Woodruff Brown Smudged, and Showlow Red Smudged. In other words, there were many intrusive vessel types, particularly bowls. The partial vessels include types that range in time from Red Mesa Black-on-white (a bowl) to Mesa Verde Black-on-white (a bowl). I believe that Room 53 was once a storage room for ritual materials that included many cylinder jars and bird wing fans (Ainsworth et al. 2018). Room 53 probably functioned much like Room 28, but on the basis of the Mesa Verde Black-on-white bowl, it may have been used for longer than Room 28 was. The interpretation of Rooms 53 and 56 is discussed further in chapter 12.

WORKED SHERDS

We recovered 10 worked sherds in the 2013 Room 28 excavations. All have at least one ground edge, and all are at least vaguely geometric in outline. While it is possible that they were used as scrapers, it is more likely that they were gaming pieces (Riggs 2016). Eight of these came from the fill and probably originated in Rooms 53 and 56. These included 1 unidentified Chuska White Ware, 1 Newcomb Black-on-white (also a Chuska White Ware), 2 Woodruff Red Smudged–Sand (Puerco Valley/Mogollon Red Ware), 1 Red Mesa Black-on-white (Cibola White Ware), 1 Gallup Black-on-white (Cibola White Ware), and 1 unidentified Cibola White Ware. The fact that 5 of the 8 are of nonlocal wares is significant and probably speaks to the value of these foreign wares, particularly for gaming pieces.

FIGURE 3.14. Portions of cylinder jars recovered in backfill in Room 28 in 2013 (believed to have come originally from Rooms 53 and/or 56). Photograph by Patricia Crown.

The remaining two worked sherds came from floor contexts: one Piedra Black-on-white (Mesa Verde White Ware) and one Red Mesa Black-on-white (Cibola White Ware).

SUMMARY AND CONCLUSIONS

Room 28 excavations in 1896 and 2013 produced large and varied assemblages of sherds and whole vessels. The sherds provide critical data for dating the subfloor contexts, demonstrating that the area beneath the room was used between about AD 650 and 850/900. The whole vessels provide evidence of the use of Room 28 from probably the mid-1000s to around AD 1100 as a storage room for ceramics used in ritual activities, including a drinking ritual. Finally, the sherds found in the fill in 2013 demonstrate how the HEE used Room 28 as a convenient place to throw backdirt, primarily from two locales: the adjacent Room 28a and Rooms 53 and 56, located two rooms to the north. The fill assemblage thus provides a critical piece of the Room 28 puzzle while also giving us further information about the rooms looted by Moorehead.

Comparison of the different assemblages provides additional insight into issues of exchange and vessel use. Figure 3.15 shows the relative proportions of red, brown, white, and gray wares in the four assemblages. Of these, the subfloor assemblage is probably the least biased in terms of collection method, having derived from 100% screening. This assemblage shows almost equivalent amounts of utility/gray ware and decorated wares. Al-

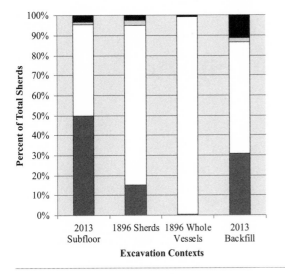

FIGURE 3.15. Proportions of wares found in Room 28 assemblages.

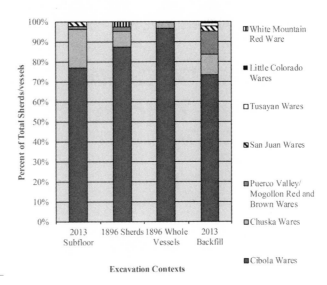

FIGURE 3.16. Proportions of regional wares for different contexts in Room 28.

though dominated by white ware, the assemblage shows 4% red and brown wares, a figure that matches the relative frequency of red and brown wares in the Pueblo Bonito trash mounds (Crown 2016b).

The 1896 fill sherds show the type of bias we might expect when sherds are pulled from fill rather than screened. That is, the gray ware blends in with the matrix and is underrepresented. Contrasting colors, such as white and red, show up better and are consequently more easily noticed and picked up.

The whole vessel assemblage shows that red and gray wares were not considered as important for the ritual activities associated with Room 28 as white ware was. Alternatively, red and gray wares may have been so highly valued that they were removed from the room prior to its burning. One piece of evidence that may support this latter interpretation is the recovery of three Showlow Red cylinder jars in Pueblo del Arroyo Room 15, which are part of a set of four vessels that includes the red ware jar found in Room 28. In other words, the entire set may have been stored in Room 28, but three of the four red jars may have been salvaged and placed in Pueblo del Arroyo prior to the room burning. However, those four jars are the only known red ware cylinder jars, and there are no known brown ware cylinder jars. Painted or unpainted white ware seems to have been the preferred ware for cylinder vessels.

Finally, the fill removed from Room 28 in 2013 shows a high relative frequency of red and brown wares (13%) compared to all other contexts, and a relatively low frequency of gray ware. However, the red and brown wares

primarily consist of sherds from three partial vessels rather than refuse, explaining this high percentage.

Figure 3.16 shows the proportions of specific wares in the four contexts. This chart combines all wares from each region; for instance, the Chuska numbers include gray, white, and orange wares. The patterns here show that the subfloor, the HEE fill excavation, and the whole vessel assemblages all include three to four wares. Most sherds or vessels are Cibola White or Gray Wares; Chuska White, Gray, or Orange Wares are the second most common; and Puerco Valley/Mogollon Red or Brown Wares are present in small numbers. San Juan Red Ware occurs under the floor and White Mountain Red Ware in the 1896 fill material. This fairly consistent pattern contrasts with the 2013 fill, which includes wares from seven different areas. As discussed, this material derives primarily from Rooms 53 and 56 and confirms the wide array of intrusive wares that were present in those special rooms.

Room 28 held one of the most important ceramic assemblages in Pueblo Bonito and perhaps even in Chaco Canyon. The subfloor sherds demonstrate the longevity of the use of this space prior to construction of the room. The whole vessel assemblage includes a majority of all cylinder jars in the US Southwest, distributed in patterns around the room that speak to the importance of these vessels and the power they once held. The 2013 fill material provides critical new information about the assemblages once stored in Rooms 53 and 56. All of these together provide information on production, exchange, ritual, and discard pathways, which are discussed further in chapter 12.

JACQUELINE M. KOCER

CHAPTER FOUR

Chipped and Ground Stone from Room 28

In this chapter I describe the general types of stone tools and debitage unearthed from the 1896 Hyde Exploring Expedition (HEE) excavations and the 2013 University of New Mexico (UNM) reexcavation of Room 28. I discuss the technological style of both flaked and ground stone objects, addressing a variety of questions: How do materials from Room 28 excavations compare to other contexts in Chaco Canyon? Are there differences in the artifacts from backfill versus intact portions of the room? Is there evidence of special or unusual materials with unique use or discard? The discussion is based on my analysis of the 2013 material and Hannah Mattson's analysis of the 1896 material at the American Museum of Natural History, which included only projectile points and ground stone.

FLAKED STONE

Methods

We conducted the analyses using a caliper for linear measurements, a digital scale for weight, and a hand lens to examine debitage and tool edges. The flaked stone analysis included all debitage, including utilized flakes, retouched flakes, and non-utilized flakes, as well as cores and unifacial and bifacial tools. We recorded the following attributes:

LITHIC TYPE: TOOL/NON-TOOL We identified tools based on evidence of edge damage from use or intentional retouch. Non-tools were classified as either debitage or cores.

TOOL TYPE Tool categories included mainly utilized and/or retouched flakes. Utilized flakes had some apparent edge damage with minimally intrusive overlapping flakes at a length of at least 1 mm. Retouched flakes were those that had clearly been modified, which was evident in intrusive flake scars from the edge to achieve a more desirable edge angle. A marginal flake-scarring length of at least 3 mm defined "retouch" (Sullivan and Rozen 1985). Retouched flakes were present in only low proportions and were analyzed together at the end of the analysis for consistency in classification. Other categories were bifaces, unifaces, drills, preforms, and scrapers. However, no non–projectile point bifaces, preforms, or scrapers were present in the assemblage.

FLAKE TOOL COMPLETENESS We recorded completeness using categories of complete, distal fragment, medial fragment, proximal fragment, longitudinal fragment, angular debris, and unidentifiable fragment (Andrefsky 2005; Crabtree 1972).

SULLIVAN AND ROZEN SYSTEM Classification types per Sullivan and Rozen (1985) included complete flakes, F+ (broken flake with platform), F– (flake fragment without platform), longitudinal fragment, and angular debris. Although similar to the "Flake Tool Completeness" category, the Sullivan and Rozen system types were recorded for ease of comparing these data to those that use different systems.

PLATFORM TYPE AND TERMINATION TYPE Platform type was noted on proximal and complete flakes. If flakes were complete or distal, termination type was noted. Platform types included cortical, plain, dihedral, and faceted. Termination types included feather, hinge, step, plunging, and axial.

METRIC DATA Weight was recorded in grams. If complete, length and width measurements were recorded with the width measurement taken at the midpoint perpendicular to the length. Maximum width was also recorded. If a flake was incomplete, the maximum dimension was taken in line with the direction of the bulb and termination. If a flake was incomplete, only a maximum width measurement was taken perpendicular to that line. For angular debris, the maximum dimension was the length, and the second longest measurement was the width, followed by the smallest measurement, thickness. Thickness measurements on all flakes, flake fragments, and angular debris were taken at the thickest point.

RAW MATERIAL Materials included silicified wood varying in color: white, red, brown, or translucent. Cherts included apparent Morrison Formation cherts in the pale blue and green colors; due to the range of possible colors, we recorded chert color. Quartzite appeared in a few different colors, including brown, tan, white, pink, and red varieties. Igneous materials consisted of dacite and obsidian. Nonlocal materials included Pedernal chert, Washington Pass/Narbona Pass chert, and obsidian.

FLAKED STONE UTILIZATION AND RETOUCH The number of utilized margins and the number of retouched margins were recorded. Flake tools were carefully examined for edge damage. Edge damage included utilization and/or retouch (as described in "Tool Type" above), and the number of margins with the specific damage was recorded. Shape (concave, convex, or straight) and length of each utilized edge was recorded. Edge angle was recorded on each edge, and if debitage was classified as a non-tool, then the angle of the most prominent flake edge was measured. Edge angle was calculated using the caliper method based on Dibble and Bernard (1980), since their study showed it is the most replicable method within a given analysis. A fixed vertical bar is attached to the calipers directly behind the needle. This way, each flake thickness is measured from the same point. The edge thickness of each flake being measured rests on this bar, and in my analysis this distance was 3 mm. Using the thickness measure and the known constant value for the distance from the bar to the end of the needle point, a simple trigonometric equation was used to compute the edge angle (Dibble and Bernard 1980:861). The formula is $\Theta = 2[Tan-1 (.5T/D)]$, where D is the distance from a known point on the caliper to the edge of the needle and T is the thickness of the edge.

BURNING For each specimen, the presence or absence of burning was recorded. The level of burning, including spalling and crazing, was also recorded. Much of the flaked stone, tools or otherwise, exhibited heat-induced spall fractures with a prominent arching curvature. Other information about burning and/or other unusual morphological/technological attributes was added in the comments section of the database.

Assemblage Overview

The 2013 reexcavation of Room 28 yielded 323 pieces of flaked stone, and 47 pieces of unmodified lithic material, 111 gullet stones, 4 hammerstones, and 1 chopper were also measured and analyzed. Some of the gullet stones (Conrad, this volume) appear to have been swallowed debitage with smoothed and polished edges from the turkey gizzards. The most prevalent nonflaked, natural materials in the assemblage were gypsum (68%) and iron concretions (8.5%).

In terms of context, 77.7% of the entire assemblage was from the fill (Levels 1–12), 5.9% from the floor (Level 13), and 16.4% from subfloor contexts. The subfloor material suggests that lithic reduction activities took place in the area before Room 28 was constructed. In terms of formal tools, five projectile points were recovered from the floor during the 1896 excavations, and seven projectile points were recovered from the fill during the 2013 reexcavations. There were no formal tools in subfloor contexts.

The majority of the flaked stone (81.3%) is non-utilized debitage. Utilized flakes were the most prominent tool type, comprising about 10.3% of the assemblage. Tools included 12 projectile points, 1 drill, 6 cores, 5 retouched flakes, and 1 uniface (figure 4.1). The assemblage reflects expedient production, but with a relatively high percentage of formal tools (projectile points and drills), which make up about 4% of the entire assemblage. In comparison, the proportion of formal tools at Pueblo Alto was 1.5% (Cameron 1997a:561) and in the Pueblo Bonito mounds was 1.1% (Wills and Okun 2016) of the total assemblage. The higher proportion of formal tools in Room 28 is probably due to the purposeful placement of tools in the room (and the adjacent rooms that made up the backfill) as well as the relative lack of trash discard in the rooms. The proportions of flaked stone technologies in Room 28 are in line with expectations for the sedentary nature of the Chacoan lifeway (Kelly 1988; Kelly and Todd 1988; Parry and Kelly 1987).

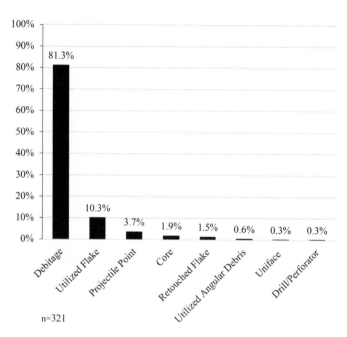

FIGURE 4.1. Frequencies of flaked stone by type.

n=321

Material Frequencies: Tool versus Non-Tool Debitage

Utilized flakes represent 10.3% of the entire assemblage while formal tools, including retouched flakes, projectile points, and drills, comprise 5.5% of the entire assemblage. Tools were produced on a narrower range of materials than non-utilized debitage (table 4.1). Most of the flaked stone, tool or otherwise, was produced on various chert and chalcedonies as well as silicified wood, an abundant source in and around Chaco Canyon. Obsidian was present in small proportions (2.8%) in Room 28. In comparison, the Chaco Project materials exhibit frequencies of no more than 2% obsidian in assemblages dating from AD 820 to 1320, with the exception of the period AD 1120–1220, which yielded 7% obsidian for all flaked stone (Cameron 1997a). Although Chacoans primarily used Mount Taylor obsidian, the use of Jemez obsidian increased during the Pueblo II period (Duff et al. 2012). X-ray fluorescence analysis was not conducted on the nine specimens of obsidian excavated from Room 28.

The most prominent identifiable exotic material is Narbona Pass chert at 5.3%. For the Chaco Project, Narbona Pass chert made up more than 20% of the entire assemblage from AD 1020 to 1120 (Cameron 1997a:546). For the Pueblo Bonito trash mound trenches, Narbona Pass chert represents about 42% of the assemblage (Wills

and Okun 2016:table 6.3). The low percentage of Narbona Pass chert from the 2013 Room 28 excavations suggests several possible interpretations: the material may be relatively early, Narbona Pass material was differentially disposed of in the trash mounds, or little primary reduction took place in room contexts. Unfortunately, the HEE did not screen systematically or collect non-tool material, so it is difficult to put the tools in the room into context.

Formal Tools

PROJECTILE POINTS Of the 12 projectile points, 7 points came from the 2013 reexcavation (recovered from Levels 4, 7, 10a, and 12), and 5 points came from the 1896 excavation materials housed at AMNH. All measurements and qualitative assignments were based on Andrefsky (2005). The Room 28 points fall within the morphological categories found elsewhere in Pueblo Bonito (table 4.2; Justice 2002). Two points were made of silicified wood, 1 of the points was made of Pedernal chert, and 2 were made of obsidian. Chacoan knappers used red, white, brown, and light gray chert as well as chalcedonies to produce the others. Six of the 12 points were complete or near complete.

Eleven of the 12 projectile point/point fragments unearthed from Room 28 had notch or basal attributes present, which are used here for general typological classification. These types consisted of 5 corner-notched, 5 side-notched, and 1 basal-tanged point. Replacing stemmed points, corner-notched and side-notched points most commonly occur at Chaco from AD 920 to 1120 (Cameron 1997a). These corner- and side-notched points appear to fall within the Justice (2002:249–54) Bonito Notched varieties dating from AD 950 to 1150.

Bonito Notched points have narrow notchings and occur in both corner- and side-notched varieties. Basal morphology for Bonito Notched points may be straight or convex with either an expanding or completely expanded stem parallel with the shoulders as a result of side-notching. One unique variety, the basal-tanged or basal-notched point, was recovered in Room 28 backfill (figure 4.2a). Basal-tanged points have been found elsewhere in Pueblo Bonito, including two from Burial 10 in Room 330 (Judd 1954:plate 98). It is possible that this point style represents a corner-notched point that broke at the neck and was reworked. Another identifiable point morphology is a long-barbed, corner-notched variety

TABLE 4.1. **Tools versus non-tools by material (count and percentage)**

MATERIAL	NON-TOOL		TOOL		TOTAL	
	Count	% within type	Count	% within type	Count	%
Silicified wood	129	47.8	28	52.8	157	48.6
Chalcedony	47	17.4	4	7.5	51	15.8
Other chert	37	13.7	13	24.5	50	15.5
Quartzite	16	5.9	1	1.9	17	5.3
Narbona Pass chert	16	5.9	1	1.9	17	5.3
Obsidian	5	1.9	4	7.5	9	2.8
Pedernal chert	4	1.5	1	1.9	5	1.5
Quartz	4	1.5	0	0	4	1.2
Iron concretion	2	0.7	1	1.9	3	0.9
Sandstone	3	1.1	0	0	3	0.9
Dacite	1	0.4	0	0	1	0.3
Shale	1	0.4	0	0	1	0.3
Unidentified sedimentary	4	1.5	0	0	4	1.2
Unidentified igneous	1	0.4	0	0	1	0.3
Total	**270**	**100**	**53**	**100**	**323**	**100**

TABLE 4.2. **Morphological description of projectile points found in Room 28**

ID	EXCAVATOR	LEVEL	RAW MATERIAL	COMPLETENESS	GENERAL TYPE	WEIGHT (GRAMS)	MAX LENGTH (MM)	BLADE LENGTH (MM)	SHOULDER WIDTH (MM)	NECK WIDTH (MM)	HAFT THICKNESS (MM)	BASE WIDTH (MM)	BASE SHAPE
a	UNM	4	other chert (white)	nearly complete (missing distal tip)	basal—notched	1.18	41.88	40.62	14.66	—	2.39	14.66	—
b	UNM	4	chalcedony	distal fragment	corner—notched	0.87	26.05	25.07	11.65	6.59	3.74	—	—
c	UNM	7	Pedernal chert	proximal fragment	side—notched	0.64	16.19	—	10.72	7.33	3.05	10.71	straight
d	UNM	10a	silicified wood	distal fragment	corner—notched	0.55	20.42	6.46	12.44	5.93	2.22	—	convex
e	UNM	10a	other chert (red)	complete	corner—notched	1.37	38.45	34.25	13.44	7.26	1.85	11.86	convex
f	UNM	12	other chert	medial fragment	unknown	0.44	14.82	—	—	—	—	—	—
g	UNM	12	silicified wood	complete	side—notched	1.24	29.34	24.66	14.58	7.55	3.14	15.04	convex
h	HEE	?	obsidian	nearly complete, missing shoulder	side—notched	1.45	36.33	32.17	12.10	7.92	2.71	10.74	convex
i	HEE	?	other chert	nearly complete, missing shoulder	corner—notched	1.20	30.64	24.10	15.78	4.65	2.83	7.17	convex
j	HEE	?	other chert	complete	side—notched	0.74	23.18	17.42	10.68	7.13	2.52	11.67	straight
k	HEE	?	chalcedony	proximal fragment	side—notched	0.78	26.97	23.53	9.64	6.79	2.29	9.70	straight
l	HEE	?	obsidian	distal fragment	corner—notched	1.26	27.07	28.25	14.34	6.38	2.80	—	—

HEE = Hyde Exploring Expedition; UNM = University of New Mexico.

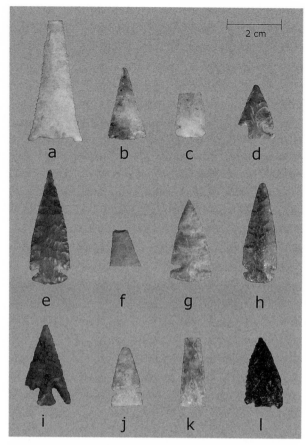

FIGURE 4.2. Projectile points from Room 28 excavations. (*a–g*) National Park Service catalog numbers CHCU 121119–121125 (photos by Jacqueline Kocer from the 2013 excavation); (*h–l*) AMNH catalog numbers H/4104, H/4105, H/4106, H/4107, and H/12772 (photos by Hannah Mattson). Courtesy of the Division of Anthropology, American Museum of Natural History.

(figure 4.2i), a type also found with Burial 9 in Room 330. Basal-notched points were also found in Burial 10 in Room 330: eight were beneath the knees of a headless individual, and four more were in the quiver context.

DRILL AND CORES A single drill recovered from Room 28 was made on the proximal end of a brownish yellow chert flake. The six cores were all irregular in form and exhibited less than 50% cortex. Two cores were produced on Washington Pass/Narbona Pass chert with evidence of bipolar reduction. The other four cores were made on silicified wood (*n* = 2) and chalcedony (*n* = 2). The Washington Pass/Narbona Pass chert cores are 3.2 cm and 4.5 cm in maximum dimension; the silicified wood cores are 3.1 cm and 3.6 cm; and the chalcedony cores are 3.9 cm and 12.5 cm. The sample size is small, making it difficult to draw comparisons to other core assemblages in Chaco. However, similar to this assemblage, 29% of cores

at the Pueblo Bonito trash mounds exhibited evidence of bipolar reduction with about one-third (31.5%) on Washington Pass/Narbona Pass chert (Wills and Okun 2016:table 6.10).

BURNING Twenty-three percent of all flaked stone recovered from Room 28 exhibited burning. During the reexcavation of Room 28, most levels included at least some heavily burned material, including charred roofing beams. As discussed in chapter 2, it is thought that this material was backfill thrown into the room in 1897 when the adjacent Room 28a was excavated. This room also burned, so any burned material in the fill of Room 28 could be from Room 28a. However, the excavations also revealed that at many of the same levels, some of the backfill was unburned; the unburned matrix was designated Levels 7a, 8a, 9a, and 10a. This material probably came from Room 53 and/or Room 56, based on refitting of ceramics from that room. As expected, in examination of the evidence of burned/heat-treated flaked stone by level, the most evidence of burning does not come from the "a" levels (figure 4.3). It is possible that at least some of the debitage was heat-treated flaked stone, rather than flaked stone that burned when the room burned. Of the flaked stone that burned, 70% exhibited evidence of thermal spalling, and 36% exhibited evidence of crazing. Crazing was most common in Levels 6, 5, and 3.

In examination of tools by level with evidence of burning, 35% (*n* = 19) were burned, and all occurred in Levels 7 and deeper. For non-tools, 33.7% (*n* = 91) were burned, and they were located in all levels except for Levels 2, 7a, 9a, 10a, and 14. In terms of special placement of tools or exotic materials, such as Narbona Pass chert, there were no apparent offerings (burned or unburned) in any of the floor/subfloor features.

Completeness and Metric Data Summaries

Length, width, and thickness of complete flakes (*n* = 299) varies between utilized flakes, non-utilized, and retouched types. Utilized and retouched flakes tend to be longer than non-utilized flakes with median values of 33 mm and 32 mm, respectively, versus 13 mm for non-utilized flakes. Median width values are similar for both utilized and retouched flakes at about 25 mm, versus only 11 mm for non-utilized flakes. Retouched flakes tend to be thicker than both non-utilized and utilized flakes with a median value of about 12 mm, twice as thick as the median value for utilized flakes and four times the

FIGURE 4.3. Flaked stone with evidence of burning by level.

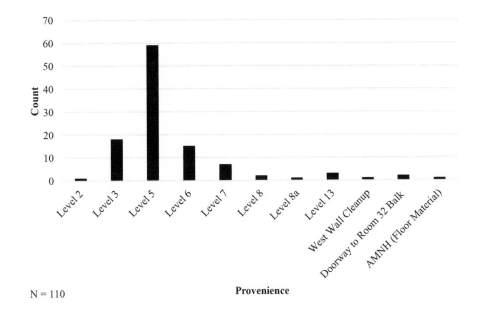

N = 110

median value for non-utilized flakes. Finally, in terms of weight, retouched flakes have the heaviest median value of 8 grams, followed by utilized flakes at 4.7 grams and non-utilized flakes at less than a gram.

Past researchers have not published metric data on complete flakes, so it is not possible to compare these results to other contexts. Some of the comparison issues relate to sampling protocols: size classes and measurements of debitage are directly related to the size of the screens used during recovery and post-depositional processes. Since the excavation methods in this study incorporated eighth-inch screens and flotation, the data presented here may be useful to future researchers.

Description of Utilized Edges
Utilized flakes exhibit mainly convex (42.4%) and straight (54.6%) margins for the first utilized margins (n = 33). Retouched flakes also exhibit some utilization overlapping the retouch, and those edges are either convex (40%) or straight (60%), though the sample size is small (n = 5). Although it is difficult to definitively tie edge shape to specific tasks (Tainter 1979), straight and convex edge shapes are more suitable for butchering, and concave shapes are best for woodworking (Gould et al. 1971). Only about 3% of utilized flakes are concave in shape. Based on this interpretation, most activities for the Room 28 assemblage included cutting or slicing.

General functional types can be associated with different edge angle ranges, with those above 45 degrees used for scraping and those below 45 degrees used for

cutting; tools with edge angles in the 70-degree range would be used for more intense shredding of bone or wood (Wilmsen 1970). Thomas (1971a) suggested that flakes with edge angles under 20 degrees might have been used for whittling wood. Based on these interpretations and the distribution of edge angle ranges for utilized and retouched flakes, it appears that these tools were used mainly for cutting and scraping (the proportions are almost evenly split). Most edge angles on both utilized and retouched flakes fell within the 30–45 or 45–60 degree range (80% and 91%). A total of 6% of utilized flakes fell into the 60–75 degree range, indicative of tasks requiring a more robust edge angle. Only 3% of utilized flakes had an edge angle of less than 30 degrees, which would include those that may have been used for wood whittling.

Choppers and Hammerstones
Four complete hammerstones and one chopper were recovered from Room 28 backfill in 2013. Following Wills (1997), the variables measured were the tool type, raw material, metric data, and parent state (table 4.3). As Wills (1997:947) noted, unlike other artifact classes, hammerstones are difficult to assign to typological or functional classes. As he described it, a hammerstone can be defined as a "modified or unmodified pieces of stone showing evidence of percussion." Choppers have a more acute edge angle and often had been exhausted from use as a hammerstone (Wills 1997:949).

The four hammerstones and one chopper exhibit some

TABLE 4.3. **Hammerstones and chopper by raw material, metric data, and parent state**

FS	LEVEL	TOOL TYPE	RAW MATERIAL	LENGTH (MM)	WIDTH (MM)	THICKNESS (MM)	MAXIMUM DIMENSION (MM)	MASS (COMPLETE) (GRAMS)	MASS (FRAGMENTARY) (GRAMS)	MORPHOLOGY (HAMMERSTONE)	PARENT STATE
144	9a	hammerstone	quartzite	7.80	6.60	3.10	7.80	231.6	—	discoidal	cobble
180	10a	hammerstone	quartzite	7.45	6.50	4.40	7.45	232.2	—	angular	cobble
298	13	hammerstone	sandstone	13.91	10.02	4.40	13.91	1472.6	—	tabular	tabular
504	6	hammerstone	sandstone	9.80	9.40	5.30	9.80	646.5	—	discoidal	tabular
146	9	chopper	sandstone	8.95	9.50	1.05	10.41	—	105.2	tabular	tabular

differences compared to others found in Chaco. As the sample size is small, only general comparisons can be made on a few of the variables. For the hammerstones, most of the specimens from Wills's eight-site analysis (1997:table 6.11) are angular in shape (57%–95%). Only one of the four Room 28 hammerstones is angular, while two are discoidal and one is of the tabular variety. Two of the four Room 28 hammerstones are made of sandstone, while only 25% or less of the hammerstones were made of sandstone at each of Wills's eight sites. In terms of weight, the majority (81%) of hammerstones weighed 200 grams or less at Wills's sites, but for Room 28 all were more than 200 grams.

Summary and Conclusions

The flaked stone assemblage from Room 28 reflects the expedient nature of technology typically associated with sedentary groups, consisting of low proportions of formal tools and higher frequencies of utilized flakes. General activities of cutting and scraping are evident in edge angle frequencies and, to some extent, shape. Most material proportions fall within the range of those in other Chaco Canyon assemblages with a high frequency of silicified wood and low frequencies of both obsidian and Pedernal chert. However, there is an absence of Zuni Spotted chert and a lower frequency of Narbona Pass chert than in other Chaco assemblages. Projectile point types include the corner-notched and side-notched varieties of the Bonito Notched type. However, some basal-tanged and long-tanged corner-notched points appear to be more carefully manufactured and are similar to those types found in Burial 10 in Room 330. Finally, the small sample of hammerstones indicates that Room 28 had a higher proportion made of sandstone.

GROUND STONE

Here I summarize the ground stone recovered from the reexcavation of Room 28 in Pueblo Bonito in 2013 and the ground stone recovered by the HEE in 1896. As discussed, due to the commingling of backdirt from Room 28 and adjacent rooms during previous excavations, we cannot assume that all materials were from Room 28. Nonetheless, the frequencies of types lend insight into the kinds of activities associated with Room 28 and neighboring rooms.

Room 28 yielded 165 pieces of ground or worked stone, 89 recovered from the 2013 reexcavation and 76 from the 1896 excavations housed at AMNH. Undergraduate student Curtis Randolph collected data on the ground stone under my supervision at the University of New Mexico. Hannah Mattson measured the jar lids housed at AMNH. The analysis used the procedures and methods from Hegberg and Crown (2016). Table 4.4 illustrates the ground stone types unearthed in Room 28.

Following Adams (2002:142–43), in this ground stone analysis I discuss netherstones, handstones, and jar lids. Netherstones include all ground stone with passive grinding surfaces on top of which an active abrader or a handstone made contact: metates, mortars, anvils, lapidaries, and unidentifiable base stones or grinding stones. Grinding stones or grinding slabs are usually of natural shape and too large to be handheld (Adams 2002:145). Adams (2002) acknowledges the ambiguity in the classification of grinding stones since some could be lapidary stones or other netherstones. All three of these categories—grinding stones, lapidary stones, and netherstones—are passive base stones used for pecking and grinding motions. Some grinding stones may have been

TABLE 4.4. **Frequency of ground stone types from Room 28**

	COUNT	% OF TOTAL
Jar lid	86	52.1
Pecked stone	28	17.0
Grinding stone	13	7.9
Indeterminate	13	7.9
Metate	8	4.8
Polishing stone	7	4.2
Mano	6	3.6
Lapidary	3	1.8
Tabular tool	1	0.6
TOTAL	**165**	**100**

used as shallow mortars. Lapidary stones differ because they are small enough to be handheld or held in the lap. Those tools that were too large and could not confidently be identified as lapidary stones were assigned to the grinding stone category. Handstones include manos, polishing stones, pestles, and other handheld abraders. The following sections describe the frequency and characteristics of each type of ground stone unearthed from Room 28.

Passive Abraders

GRINDING STONES/SLABS All 13 pieces of grinding stones are made of sandstone. Seven are fine-grained, five are medium-grained, and one is coarse-grained. Only one grinding stone was determined to be complete while the rest were indeterminate. The functions of grinding stone fragments include door hatches, slabs for lining posts and fire pits, and possibly mortars. The grinding stone fragments from Room 28 (n = 12) average 15.7 cm in length by 11.6 cm in width by 2.94 cm in thickness. The average weight is 1,007 grams. The one complete grinding stone measures 46.2 cm in length by 27.8 cm in width by 3.7 cm in thickness and weighs 10,450 grams. Although the sample size is also small (n = 13), the grinding stone fragments in the Pueblo Bonito trash mounds were smaller, averaging 11.8 cm in length by 9.2 cm in width by 2.8 cm in thickness and 641 grams in weight (Hegberg and Crown 2016). Finally, one tabular tool made of shale measures 4 cm in length by 2.7 cm in width by 3 cm in thickness; it has a very fine texture.

METATES Metates are the base stones for specialized subsistence activities, and in the Southwest the main use

is for grinding corn. All eight metates from Room 28 are made of sandstone. Three of the eight are open trough metates, four are indeterminate trough metates, and one is an indeterminate metate. Two of the open trough metates are complete, three metates are less than half complete, and three are too fragmentary to determine completeness. For those that are complete, base shape includes four with very concave trough bases and one with a flat bottom. All were ground, pecked, and shaped, rectilinear in plan view, and rectangular in cross section. Soot residues were present on five of the metates/metate fragments, with all but one exhibiting heavy use. The two complete metates exhibit fine and medium texture. The largest of the two complete metates is 39 cm in length by 25.6 cm in width by 13.4 cm in thickness, weighing 19,005 grams. In contrast to the trash mounds, where most metates were of the basin variety (Hegberg and Crown 2016), Room 28 follows the patterns described by Judd (1954:135) and Schelberg (1997:table 9.8), where only trough forms were recovered.

LAPIDARY STONES Lapidary stones are base stones on which other materials are abraded; they were most often used for bead manufacture and pigment processing (Adams 2002:143–46). Room 28 excavations yielded three lapidary stones, all of which are fine-textured sandstone. All three are fragmented, and one has two opposing working sides. One has four different working surfaces, and the other two have three and two working surfaces, respectively. In plan view, two lapidary stones are rectilinear, and one is trapezoidal. In cross section, two are rectangular, and one is tabular. All lapidary stone fragments were ground, pecked, and shaped in manufacture and were modified with roughing/abrasion wear. All exhibit heavy use wear, and one has red ocher staining.

The largest lapidary stone fragment measures 24 cm in length by 21.5 cm in width by 4 cm in thickness and weighs 3,605 grams. The other two are much smaller and weigh about 190 and 9 grams, respectively. Windes (1993:225) suggested that passive lapidary stones should be grouped into three categories, averaging 1,325 grams, 852 grams, and 300 grams. The three lapidary stones excavated from Room 28 are fragments: the largest one is greater than half complete, but the other two are less than half complete and indeterminate. It is thus difficult to discern which group the three lapidary stones might have fallen under; however, if the largest one was greater than half complete, then it would be well over Windes's

(1993) largest cluster average. In terms of those that might have been used for bead production, one lapidary stone is only 0.7 cm in thickness, and the other two are 4 cm and 3.5 cm thick. This finer lapidary stone could have been used for more delicate tasks in the sequence of bead production since extreme thinness is an attribute of lapidary stones found in context with turquoise (Windes 1993).

In comparison to other lapidary stone attributes from other Chaco excavations, the Pueblo Bonito trench project yielded 102 lapidary abraders, none of which were complete (Hegberg and Crown 2016). The Chaco Project yielded a sample of 22 lapidary stones, which were all complete and found in association with turquoise at small site 29SJ629 (Windes 1993). The small sample of lapidary stones from Room 28 is consistent with the fragmented nature seen elsewhere in Pueblo Bonito. Some bead production likely took place nearby since more than 3,600 specimens of raw turquoise, beads, and shell were unearthed in Room 28 backdirt (see Mattson and Kocer, this volume).

Active Abraders

MANOS Manos are the active abraders used in corn/seed grinding activities. The mano form can be indicative of use in either a basin or trough mano-metate set. Room 28 yielded six manos, which complement the trough metates discussed above. Five of the six manos are sandstone, and one is made of quartzite. Four are trough manos, one is flat, and one is indeterminate. Only two of the six are complete. Four have fine texture, and the other two are medium- and coarse-grained, respectively. Two manos each fit heavy, moderate, and light surface wear categories. For complete manos, the dimensions are quite similar with a less than 8 mm difference in both length and width, averaging 9.6 cm in length and 7.1 cm in width. The complete quartzite mano measures 5.1 cm in thickness, and the complete sandstone mano measures 3.8 cm in thickness.

For manos, plan-view and cross-section types can indicate differences in use and tool exhaustion. Four of the six manos are rectangular in cross section, one is diamond-shaped, and one is wedge-shaped. Five of the manos are rectilinear in plan view, and one is oval. Mano profiles can serve as correlates for stroke and wear-management strategies. According to Adams (2002:112), a wedge-shaped cross section is less balanced because

the user did not rotate the mano 180 degrees to even out the use wear. It follows that a wedge-shaped cross section is indicative of less use than one with a rectangular or diamond shape since the latter two are signatures of intense use on both ends for balance. But in opposing perspectives (Cameron 1997b; Windes 1987a), the use wear signatures depend on the hardness of the material, and a wedge-shaped profile is indicative of exhausting a once rectangular profile. In the Room 28 assemblage, the mano with the wedge-shaped profile and one rectangular mano exhibit heavy use while the diamond-shaped mano and the other two rectangular manos exhibit light or moderate use wear on the primary grinding surface. In terms of residue, two of the manos are sooted, and one mano has red ocher staining. One rectangular mano was also used as a hammerstone.

Compared to other mano assemblages from Chaco Canyon, the Room 28 mano assemblage is similar in the dominance of the trough variety. All manos recovered from Pueblo Alto (Windes 1987a) and 96% of those recovered from 29SJ629 were for trough metates (Windes 1993). For the Chaco Project, Cameron (1997b) stated that almost 70% of manos were of the trough variety. For the Pueblo Bonito trash mounds (Hegberg and Crown 2016), there were no complete manos, so identification to type was difficult. However, most manos (54%) had wedge-shaped cross sections. In contrast to one-handed manos, the two-handed trough-variety manos from Room 28 conform to the specialized maize-processing tasks associated with increased reliance on agriculture after AD 1000 in Chaco Canyon.

POLISHING STONES Polishing stones alter the surface of another object by creating a sheen or polish from abrasive activities (Adams 1993, 2002). All seven polishing stones from the 2013 Room 28 excavations are made of quartzite, and four are complete. All are ovoid in cross section except for one wedge-shaped specimen. In plan view, polishing stones are either irregular ($n = 1$), oval ($n = 2$), rectilinear ($n = 1$), or circular ($n = 3$). For the complete polishing stones, dimensions average 6.9 cm in length by 4.9 cm in width by 1.9 cm in thickness, and they weigh an average of 116 grams. Two of the polishing stones are burned.

Potters use small polishing stones in ceramic production; they often choose river cobbles or pebbles because they do not scratch the pot surface (Adams 2002). Four of these polishing stones are ceramic polishing stones made from quartzite river pebbles. One is of tabular morphology. Two polishing stone fragments are larger than most and have a distinct morphology. These appear to be what Adams (2002:94) and Judd (1954:125, plate 25g) described as "floor polishers." Although their intended use or function is still unknown, both of the specimens from Room 28 are circular/disk-shaped in plan view. They would have been considerably larger than the other polishing stones at about 12–14 cm in diameter and a thickness of 3-4 cm; they exhibit linear striations.

Nancy Akins (1997:812–13) summarized polishing stone categories for the Chaco Project, assigning function based on size classes. Pot polishing stones averaged 5.1 cm in length by 3.9 cm in width by 1.8 cm in thickness. Pot polishers were the most numerous: 51% of the identifiable polishers recovered in the Chaco Project. Floor polishers were the next most abundant, making up 43% of the identifiable polishers and averaging 11.5 cm in length by 8.7 cm in width by 5.1 cm in thickness. From Room 28, the four smaller (5–6 cm) polishing stones fall within Akins's pot polisher category, and the two larger polishing stones fall within the shape and size class of floor/wall polishing stones (Akins 1997:figure 5.46b).

Pecked Stone

Some sandstone is shaped with flake removal or pecking. Room 28 excavations yielded 28 pieces of sandstone, all coarse-grained, with pecking along the edges. These thin sandstone pieces are probably architectural materials: they are rectangular in cross section and rectilinear, trapezoidal, or irregular in plan view. Average dimensions for the fragments are 18.2 cm in length by 12.6 cm wide by 3.6 cm in thickness; and they weigh on average 1,696 grams. Four complete pieces of pecked stone average 14.5 cm in length by 27.9 cm in width by 4.7 cm in thickness; and they average 7,944 grams in weight. Six of the 28 pieces have soot. Finally, one of the complete rectilinear pieces is a likely door hatch; it measures 51 cm in length by 41.7 cm in width by 2.7 cm in thickness and is 7,165 grams in weight with heavy sooting residue.

Jar Lids

A total of 86 jar lids were analyzed from Room 28: 12 were recovered from the 2013 reexcavation of the room, and 74 were at AMNH from the 1896 excavations. Many of the jar lids originally excavated in 1896 had been dis-

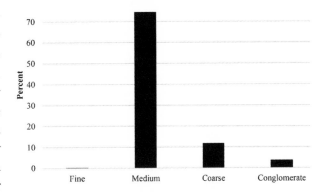

FIGURE 4.4. Percentage of jar lids and fragments by texture.

carded over the last century and were no longer available for analysis. All of the extant jar lids are made of sandstone pecked and/or ground into a roughly circular shape. Of the 86 jar lids, 9 have soot residue, 2 have ocher, and 3 have organics. The majority of jar lid/lid fragments are medium in texture (74%, n = 64) (figure 4.4). Seventy-seven of the 86 jar lids are complete. Their mean dimensions are 9.6 cm in length by 9.1 cm in width by 0.89 cm in thickness.

Some scholars have suggested that the jar lids were made to cover cylinder jars (Crown 2008; Toll 1990). To examine this, I compared the sizes of jar lids with the sizes of the cylinder jars from Room 28. Orifice diameters from Room 28 average 10.3 cm. Crown (2008) examined 140 vessels from Pueblo Bonito and Pueblo del Arroyo. Crown's (2008:5) data show cylinder jar orifices averaging 10.4 cm as a whole for the assemblage. Length and width measurements of the jar lids averaged 9.6 and 9.1 cm, respectively. Length, width, mean values, and coefficient of variation (CV) values for jar lids as well as jar orifice diameters are in table 4.5. The data fit well with the mean values and CV values of the entire cylinder jar assemblage. However, there are not complete jar lids that would cover the largest cylinder jars.

Most of the ground stone (95.2%, n = 157) is unburned and consists mainly of jar lids (n = 72). Aside from the ground stone analyzed at AMNH, the majority (14.5%, n = 24) of the ground stone came from Level 5 and consists of 9 pecked pieces, 1 lapidary stone, 2 jar lids, 7 grinding stones, and 5 indeterminate pieces. Two manos each were recovered from Levels 6 and 11 and 1 each from Levels 8 and 12. For metates, 1 was found in Level 8, 2 in Level 9a, and 1 each in Levels 11–14. Although traces of soot were found on 5 metates, only 1 metate

TABLE 4.5. **Orifice diameter and coefficient of variation values for cylinder jars (Crown 2008) compared to dimensions and CV values for cylinder jars and jar lids analyzed in this study**

JAR/LID SAMPLE	N	MEAN (CM)	CV (%)
Orifice diameter: cylinder jars (Crown 2008)	140	10.4	20.4
Orifice diameter: cylinder jars from Room 28 (this study)	109	10.3	18.9
Complete jar lids: length (this study)	77	9.6	15.0
Complete jar lids: width (this study)	77	9.1	15.9

TABLE 4.6. **Ground stone types by level**

LEVEL	GRINDING STONE	INDETERMINATE	JAR LID	LAPIDARY STONE	MANO	METATE	POLISHING STONE	TABULAR TOOL	PECKED PIECES	TOTAL
3	2	0	1	0	0	0	0	0	1	4
5	7	5	2	1	0	0	0	0	9	24
6	1	3	0	1	2	0	0	0	5	12
7	0	0	1	0	0	0	0	0	0	1
7a	0	0	0	1	0	0	0	0	0	1
8	0	1	2	0	1	1	1	0	0	6
8a	0	1	0	0	0	0	0	0	0	1
9a	0	1	1	0	0	2	1	0	0	5
10a	0	0	0	0	0	0	0	0	1	1
11	1	0	0	0	2	1	1	0	3	8
12	0	0	3	0	1	1	1	0	1	7
13	0	2	2	0	0	1	2	0	3	10
14 SEQ	2	0	0	0	0	1	0	0	3	6
AMNH NP	0	0	74	0	0	1	0	1	0	76
HEE excavation	0	0	0	0	0	0	1	0	0	1
PH 24	0	0	0	0	0	0	0	0	1	1
PH 4 and 5	0	0	0	0	0	0	0	0	1	1
Total	13	13	86	3	6	8	7	1	28	165

AMNH = American Museum of Natural History; HEE = Hyde Exploring Expedition;
NP = no provenience; PH = posthole; SEQ = southeast quadrant.

(the trough metate analyzed at AMNH) exhibits evidence of burning. Two burned polishing stones were found in Level 13, and the other 5 were unburned in Levels 8, 9a, 11, and 12 (table 4.6).

CONCLUSIONS

The majority (52%) of ground stone from Room 28 consists of jar lids. Jar lid dimension distributions suggest that many jar lids were manufactured specifically for the cylinder jars from Room 28. However, the jar lids recovered in the 2013 excavations likely came from Rooms 53 and 56, so these jar lids may match cylinder jars from those rooms. Manos and metates are of the trough varieties and are consistent with those found at other places besides the Pueblo Bonito trash mounds, where the basin metate was the dominant form (Hegberg and Crown 2016). Polishing stones fall within the pot polishing and floor polishing functional classes and are consistent in size and shape with others found at Chaco sites. Finally, the lapidary stone fragments suggest that activities in Room 28 and adjacent rooms included some bead production tasks.

Overall, the ground stone assemblage for Room 28 is not unusual when compared to others from Chaco. While some of the material was clearly discarded when exhausted, other tools were still usable and may represent artifacts abandoned in place. The HEE may have left the metates in backfill rather than ship these large, heavy objects back to New York. Much of the material represents food production and crafting activities, while the jar lids may be related to whatever ritual involved the cylinder jars (Crown 2018, and chapter 3, this volume).

ACKNOWLEDGMENTS

Thank you to the people who lived in Pueblo Bonito (and who live in descendant Puebloan communities) for these amazing cultural materials, which enrich our knowledge of Ancestral practices in a very special room in Pueblo Bonito. Thank you to Patricia Crown for allowing me to contribute to this research and learn a great deal from this analysis. I would also like to thank Bruce Huckell for guidance on some of the data collection methods and questions I had about flaked stone. I am thankful for Wendy Bustard's help in providing access to collections at the Chaco Culture National Historical Park. Thank you to David Hurst Thomas at the American Museum of Natural History for access to the projectile points curated there and to Hannah Mattson for taking the photos. Finally, thank you to the two anonymous reviewers for their input on the chapter.

HANNAH V. MATTSON AND JACQUELINE M. KOCER

CHAPTER FIVE

Ornaments, Mineral Specimens, and Shell Specimens from Room 28

In this chapter we summarize the analyses of personal ornaments, mineral specimens, and shell specimens from Room 28 of Pueblo Bonito, both those excavated during the Hyde Exploring Expedition (HEE) (1896–1900) and those recovered during the University of New Mexico's 2013 reexcavation of the room. Supervised by George Pepper, the initial excavation of Room 28 yielded at least 650 finished ornaments, 128 unfinished ornaments and pieces of lapidary debris, and 26 mineral and shell specimens and manuports; these are housed at the American Museum of Natural History and the National Museum of the American Indian (Mattson 2016b; Pepper 1920). The 2013 investigation, which included both a reexcavation of fill composed of mixed backdirt from adjacent rooms and an excavation of intact floor and subfloor deposits, produced an additional 2,777 finished ornaments, 863 unfinished ornaments and pieces of production debris, 55 shell specimens, and 82 mineral specimens and manuports. Overall, the combined ornament assemblage (N = 4,581) is dominated by turquoise and shell disc (discoidal) beads, shell bilobe beads, *Olivella* shell beads, turquoise tesserae, and turquoise production debris. These artifacts are comparable to those found in other specialized depositional contexts at Pueblo Bonito, such as the rooms comprising the northern burial cluster, ritual storage rooms, and kivas.

After a summary of previous research on ornaments from both Chaco Canyon in general and Pueblo Bonito specifically, we describe the methods of analysis, including the attributes recorded and the ornament typology used. We then present the results of the analyses, first for the assemblage as a whole and then by individual ornament type. For each ornament type, our discussion focuses on variation in form/shape, patterns in dimensional attributes, and distribution by intramural provenience. We then examine these results in the con-

text of previously documented ornaments from adjacent rooms, the fill of which likely contributed to the material recovered from Room 28, and ornaments recovered from all depositional contexts at Pueblo Bonito during the Hyde and National Geographic Society expeditions and the more recent Chaco Stratigraphy Project (Crown, ed. 2016; Judd 1954; Mattson 2016b, 2016c; Pepper 1920; Wills et al. 2016).

PREVIOUS RESEARCH

The large excavation projects of the late nineteenth and early twentieth centuries collected more than 100,000 personal ornaments and pieces of turquoise lapidary debris from Pueblo Bonito (Crown, ed. 2016; Neitzel 2003b; Judd 1954; Pepper 1909, 1920). These were concentrated in mortuary contexts, particularly the northern (Rooms 32, 33, 53, and 56) and western (Rooms 320, 326, 329, and 330) burial crypts, in addition to kiva offerings and ceremonial rooms. Room 33, containing the lavish Burials 13 and 14, alone produced more than 37,000 ornaments (Mattson 2015; Neitzel 2003b; Pepper 1909, 1920), and the western burial rooms together contained almost 5,000 ornaments (Judd 1954; Mattson 2015). Approximately 6,000 ornaments were found in kiva offerings, particularly in association with pilasters, and nearly 5,000 were recovered from rooms interpreted as ritual storage facilities (particularly Rooms 28, 38, and 39). Pepper (1909, 1920) and Judd (1954) provided general summaries of these objects in their excavation monographs.

Pepper (1920:117–24) reported numerous mineral specimens and manuports, along with a piece of hammered copper, in the fill of Room 28 and abundant finished ornaments on or just above the floor (table 5.1). Specifically, he described turquoise and shell beads, pendants, inlays, and bracelets scattered among the ceramic vessels on the floor, as well as beads intentionally placed inside five pottery bowls in the northeast corner of the room. Based on Pepper's (1920) counts, the room yielded a minimum of 650 finished ornaments. Of these, Mattson (2015, 2016b) analyzed 564 finished ornaments.

Much of the research on Chacoan jewelry conducted since the 1980s has centered on either material from the National Park Service's Chaco Project or the sourcing of turquoise artifacts. The Chaco Project investigated more than 20 sites, including the Pueblo Alto great house and 10 small house sites (Mathien 1987, 1988, 1992, 1993, 1997; McKenna 1984). These investigations yielded approximately 5,000 ornaments, which were analyzed and summarized by Mathien (1997). Of these, more than 80% were recovered from two small house sites: 29SJ1360 and 29SJ629. These sites also produced abundant ornament production debris, unfinished ornaments, and lapidary tools, such as lithic microdrills and abraders, indicating that they had contained household jewelry workshops (Mathien 2001:108; Windes 1992). Although ornament production appears to have been more concentrated at these two sites compared to other small house sites, evidence of small-scale turquoise ornament production is widespread throughout the canyon (Hagstrum 2001; Mathien 2001). Since finished ornaments, particularly those made from turquoise, are more abundant at great houses than at small houses, it has been suggested that they were part of a corporate political strategy wherein goods produced in surrounding small houses were used to sustain communal events related to construction activities and ritual performances (Earle 2001; Peregrine 2001; Saitta 1997; Toll 2006). Research conducted by Mattson (2015, 2016b) suggests that significant ornament production likely also occurred on-site at Pueblo Bonito.

Pueblo Bonito is notable for its extremely high concentration of turquoise, which occurs in the form of finished and unfinished ornaments, lapidary debris, and unmodified mineral specimens. Just one room from the site (Room 33) contains more turquoise artifacts than all other known archaeological sites in the US Southwest put together (Plog and Heitman 2010; Snow 1973). Turquoise, along with imported timbers and ceramics, is thus a major focus of Chacoan resource procurement studies. Various geochemical signatures have been used to source turquoise specimens, including trace and rare earth element concentrations, lead isotopes, ratios of

TABLE 5.1. **Ornaments, mineral specimens, and shell specimens from Room 28 as reported by Pepper**

CONTEXT	ARTIFACT DESCRIPTION
"Upper layer of room"	worked turquoise
	turquoise matrix
	hammered copper
	Glycymeris sp. shell bracelet
General debris	jet inlay
	limonite
	red and yellow ocher
	crinoid stems
	7 fossil shells
	shark's tooth
	sulphur
	calcite crystal
	"silica of iron"
	mica
General debris above the pottery vessels	burned *Murex* sp. shell
	16 turquoise beads
Among bowls and jars on the floor	93 turquoise disc beads
	12 turquoise pendants and broken beads
	turquoise inlays
	turquoise matrix
	69 shell bilobe beads
	43 *Olivella* sp. beads
	fragments of shell
	9 *Glycymeris* sp. shell bracelet fragments
Associated directly with pottery vessels	400 shell beads, including 105 *Olivella* sp. beads and 130 shell bilobe beads
"In bowls on the floor"	Bowl 11: 1 *Glycymeris* sp. shell bracelet
	Bowl 13: 1 turquoise disc bead
	Bowl 4?: 2 shell bilobe beads, 1 *Olivella* sp. bead
	Bowl 1: 4 shell bilobe beads, 1 circular shell bead, 1 turquoise disc bead, 1 carved *Olivella* sp. bead
	Bowl 12?: 2 shell bilobe bead, 1 *Olivella* sp. bead, 1 turquoise bead

Source: Pepper 1920:117–24.

lead and strontium isotopes, and ratios of hydrogen and copper isotopes (Harbottle and Weigand 1992; Hull et al. 2008; Hull et al. 2014; Kim et al. 2003; Mathien 2001; Ruppert 1982, 1983; Thibodeau et al. 2012; Thibodeau et al. 2015; Weigand and Harbottle 1993; Weigand et al. 1977; Young et al. 1994). A 2014 sourcing study, which includes two artifacts from Room 28, demonstrates that Chacoan turquoise originated from all over the Southwest, with sources to the west being most common (Hull et al. 2014). One of the Room 28 samples was identified as coming from the Crescent Peak geologic source in southern Nevada, and the other could not be tied to a specific source (Hull et al. 2014:table 2). Nineteen samples from Room 33, located immediately to the northwest of Room 28, were also tested. Of the 11 samples for which a source area could be identified, 5 are from the Cerrillos Hills (near Santa Fe, New Mexico), 3 are from Villa Grove (south-central Colorado), 2 are from Orogrande (southern New Mexico), and 1 is from Crescent Peak (Hull et al. 2014:192).

As turquoise ornaments at Pueblo Bonito are concentrated in rich interments, kiva offerings, and rooms that contain other exotic goods and unique ceremonial items, their meanings have been variously interpreted as relating to status, ritual practice, social memory, lineage affiliation, and social group membership (Lewis 2002; Mathien 2001; Mattson 2016b; Mills 2004, 2008; Neitzel 1995, 2003a; Plog 2003; Saitta 1997; Toll 2006). Neitzel (1995) suggested that turquoise, along with the Gallup-Dogoszhi style of decoration applied to cylinder vessels, may have been an important ceremonial and status symbol of Chacoan society, perhaps even serving as a badge of office. Following Brody (1991), Plog (2003) also notes an association between turquoise and hatchured Dogoszhi decoration at Pueblo Bonito, suggesting that the style may symbolize the color blue-green, a color of ritual importance throughout the prehispanic Southwest. In her study of the distribution of blue-green pigments (azurite and malachite) and painted artifacts in Chaco Canyon, Lewis (2002) concludes that these colors were specifically associated with ritual leadership and ceremonies performed at great houses. Mills (2008) suggests that the deposition of ornaments among other valuable and inalienable objects in specialized contexts at Pueblo Bonito and Chetro Ketl is associated with the dedication and memorialization of ritual structures, ceremonial retirements of powerful objects, and practices of renewal. She refers to these deposits as archives of

social memory, which would have been remembered by residents and visitors even when they were no longer visible once sealed away (Mills 2015:263).

In a large-scale contextual study of personal ornaments from Pueblo Bonito, Mattson (2015, 2016b) proposes that shell and shale discoidal beads and shell bracelets referenced large-scale elements of group identity, such as ethnicity or tribal membership; turquoise discoidal beads, circular abalone pendants, shell zoomorphic pendants, and *Spondylus* shell dentate beads indicated differences in vertical (hierarchical) social status; and *Olivella* shell beads, bilobe shell beads, and beads of specialized shapes (tadpole/frog, bifurcated, and feet/shoes) were used in ritual practices associated with kivas (Mattson 2016b:128–32). A study by Crown, Marden, and Mattson (2016) finds that both turquoise foot/footwear-shaped ornaments and foot-related images produced in other media (ceramic effigies and rock art) are associated with highly ritualized and structured contexts at Pueblo Bonito. Furthermore, this imagery appears to be associated with the condition of polydactyly, the burials in Room 33, and elevated or special social status (Crown et al. 2016).

METHODOLOGY

The Room 28 ornament assemblage was analyzed in three main stages. In 2008, as part of her dissertation research, Mattson individually analyzed 248 ornaments and related materials from the room that are housed at AMNH. This included all unique and singular items; a 20% sample of redundant objects, such as lots of beads of the same form and material; and turquoise chips/flakes. In 2011, Mattson analyzed the only ornament from Room 28 at NMAI: a shell bracelet found in a pottery bowl on the floor. In 2014, she returned to AMNH with Crown and analyzed 449 ornaments and pieces of production debris that had been previously sampled, thereby completing a 100% analysis of the previously excavated material from the room (N = 698). From 2013 to 2014, Jacqueline Kocer conducted a 100% analysis of the ornaments, mineral specimens, and shell specimens recovered from the room during UNM's 2013 excavation (N = 3,777). Thus, the analyzed Room 28 assemblage totals 4,475 items (table 5.2).

Based on the written descriptions provided by Pepper (1920:117–24), approximately 106 additional objects from the room were not identified during our visits to

TABLE 5.2. Room 28 assemblage by project

ARTIFACT TYPE	HYDE EXPLORING EXPEDITION (AMNH/NMAI)		UNIVERSITY OF NEW MEXICO	TOTAL ANALYZED	TOTAL ARTIFACTS
	Analyzed 2007–2013	*Additional items reported by Pepper (1920:125–26)*	*Analyzed 2013–2014*		
Bead	544	83+	2,608	3,152	3,235+
Bead blank	7	—	81	88	88
Bracelet	8	1	4	12	13
Disk	1	—	—	1	1
Lapidary debris	120	—	782	902	902
Manuport	1	11+	9	10	21+
Mineral specimen	5	6+	73	78	84+
Mosaic piece	1	—	147	148	148
Pendant	10	2	17	27	29
Shell specimen	—	3+	55	55	58+
Unknown ornament	—	—	1	1	1
Worked piece	1	—	—	1	1
Grand Total	**698**	**106+**	**3,777**	**4,475**	**4,581+**

AMNH = American Museum of Natural History; NMAI = National Museum of the American Indian.

AMNH: 83 beads, 1 shell bracelet, 11 manuports, 6 mineral specimens, 2 pendants, and at least 3 shell specimens. In the case of the finished ornaments, these items were likely disassociated from their original provenience information, while the unmodified mineral and shell specimens may not have been curated.

In our analyses we measured 18 qualitative and quantitative attributes, which were entered into a Microsoft Excel database (table 5.3). We recorded dimensions to the nearest hundredth of a millimeter using electronic calipers, and we recorded weight to the nearest hundredth of a gram utilizing an electronic scale. Below we discuss some of the major attributes related to artifact classification (type, form/style, and shape) and raw material.

Classification

The classification scheme employed for this study follows that outlined by Mattson (2015, 2016c), which incorporates attributes presented by Adams (1996), Jernigan (1978), and Mathien (1997). The major ornament types documented in the assemblage are beads, bead blanks, pendants, mosaics, and bracelets (figure 5.1). Other artifact types analyzed include lapidary debris, mineral and shell specimens, and manuports. These artifact types,

TABLE 5.3. Attributes recorded during ornament analyses

QUALITATIVE ATTRIBUTES	QUANTITATIVE ATTRIBUTES
artifact type (e.g., bead, pendant, mineral specimen)	maximum length (mm)
	maximum width (mm)
form/style (e.g., discoidal, tabular)	thickness (mm)
	diameter (mm)
shape (e.g., circular, bilobe)	weight (grams)
hole type (cylindrical, conical, biconical)	number of complete holes
	number of incomplete holes
material type	number of worked edges
shell species (if applicable)	number of worked surfaces
color	
condition (complete, broken, broken in manufacture)	
presence of polishing	

FIGURE 5.1. Common ornament types from Room 28. *Top row, left to right*: turquoise disc beads, shell disc beads, jet disc beads, and turquoise tesserae; *second row, left to right*: *Olivella* truncated barrel beads, *Olivella* spire-lopped beads, shell bilobe beads, and jet tesserae; *third row, left to right*: turquoise pendant and pendant beads, turquoise lapidary debris; *bottom row, left to right*: *Glycymeris* shell bracelet fragments and hematite cylinders. Photographs by Jacqueline Kocer.

along with the range of forms and shapes documented for each, are discussed individually below.

Beads are generally perforated so that the outer perimeter of the piece is most visible when strung. The documented bead forms are discoidal, pendant, dentate, spherical, barrel, and tubular. Discoidal (disc) beads are circular in shape, have two flat opposing surfaces, and are perforated centrally. In addition, the thickness of a discoidal bead is less than its circumference. Pendant beads include holes offset from their centers like pendants, though their edges are still most visible when strung, and they are typically tabular in cross section. Common tabular pendant bead shapes in the assemblage are bilobe (shaped like two conjoined discoidal beads or a figure eight) and ovoid. Dentate beads also have offset holes, but they are three-dimensional and tooth-shaped, rather than tabular or flat, when strung. These types of beads are usually produced from min-

imally worked, irregularly shaped shell that is pink/red to purple in color, such as that of the *Spondylus* or *Chama* genera.

Spherical beads are globe-shaped with equal dimensions. Barrel beads have central holes, but they are tube-shaped with thicknesses greater than their circumferences. Barrel beads, such as spire-lopped *Olivella* shell beads, have convex edges, whereas tubular beads have straight edges. Truncated barrel beads are *Olivella* shell beads in which the tapered ends have been removed. Bead blanks were identified based on similarity in size and shape to finished beads and pendants, the presence of shaping and/or grinding, and a lack of completed perforations.

A pendant is generally larger than a bead and has an offset hole that allows for greatest visibility of the surface, rather than the perimeter, of the piece when it is suspended. Pendant styles represented in the assemblage are tabular and dentate. Tabular pendants vary widely in shape, although they occur most commonly as circular, ovoid, rectangular, trapezoidal, and teardrop in outline. Dentate pendants are the same as dentate beads, only larger in size.

Mosaic pieces, also known as tesserae or inlay, are thin and tabular pieces designed for attachment to a backing material with an adhesive, such as pitch or resin. These items are often of geometric shapes, particularly rectangles and squares. However, broken and unfinished ornaments were also used as makeshift inlays, particularly on large pieces.

The bracelets in the assemblages are all bands fashioned from the outer perimeter of large *Glycymeris* shells. These are identical to those common in the Hohokam area and consistent with those found in other portions of Pueblo Bonito.

Mineral specimens include both modified and unmodified mineral and stone objects. This category typically excludes raw materials used for lithic tools, such as chert, obsidian, chalcedony, petrified wood, quartzite, and basalt. Thus, the mineral specimen category is composed primarily of soft minerals that could be used, or have evidence of use, as pigments. Turquoise flakes/chips, ground/worked turquoise pieces without a specific form, and pieces of matrix were recorded as lapidary debris. Shell specimens are unmodified faunal specimens, flakes of shell too small to determine level of modification, and shaped shell without clear evidence of use as personal adornment.

Raw Material

The Room 28 ornament assemblage is dominated by turquoise, marine shell, and jet, while the mineral specimen assemblage is predominantly composed of muscovite mica, concretions, fossils, and pigments—particularly limonite (yellow ocher, as reported by Pepper 1920), hematite, and azurite. Other material types present, but only in small quantities, are shale, argillite, copper, biotite, quartz crystal, and micaceous schist. Likely source areas for these raw materials are discussed briefly below. For additional information on possible local sources of materials, see Mathien (1997) and Northrup (1959).

Turquoise is a hydrous phosphate mineral of copper and aluminum and can vary widely in chemical composition, both between and within sources. The closest source of turquoise to Chaco Canyon is the Cerrillos Hills area southeast of Santa Fe, located 185 km to the

east. Before the initiation of geochemical provenance studies, this was assumed to be the primary source of Chacoan turquoise. As discussed above under "Previous Research," these studies demonstrate that sources in Arizona, Colorado, Nevada, and New Mexico are all represented in the Pueblo Bonito assemblage (e.g., Hull et al. 2008; Hull et al. 2014; Thibodeau et al. 2012; Thibodeau et al. 2015).

Shale is a type of sedimentary rock composed of consolidated and compacted silts and clays. Sometimes known as red claystone or red dog shale, argillite is a reddish orange shale that occurs naturally over much of New Mexico. It has been reported from the Zuni, Nacimiento, and San Juan Mountains, as well as in Chaco Canyon, on the western talus of Chacra Mesa, and along the southern and southwestern flanks of West Mesa, which encompasses the undated quarry site 29SJ1825 (Thomas Windes, personal communication, 2004; Mathien 1997:1124). Similar to argillaceous shale, black and gray carbonaceous shale is also a commonly occurring material in the San Juan Basin, particularly within outcrops of Mancos shale (Mathien 1997; Jernigan 1978). Jet, also known as lignite, is a mineraloid formed from metamorphosed wood. According to Mathien (1997:1121), jet was likely available within coal seams in Chaco Canyon and in the Fruitland Formation on the western margins of the San Juan Basin.

Hematite, a red iron oxide mineral that comprises the majority of the paint stones found at Chaco Canyon, has been reported from the Cliff House formation and is found in all portions of New Mexico (Mathien 1997:table 10.1; Northrup 1959:282–86; Warren 1967). Limonite is a mixture of various hydrated iron oxide minerals, which may also occur in the form of goethite or jarosite, a type of hematite. It is yellowish orange to yellowish brown in color and is widespread in New Mexico, occurring in 26 different counties (Brand 1937; Mathien 1997; Northrup 1959).

Azurite is a bright blue mineral resulting from the weathering of copper ore deposits. Similar to this, and often found together with azurite, is malachite, a bright green copper mineral. Reported sources of both of these minerals are the Zuni, Nacimiento, and San Juan Mountains (Brand 1937; Mathien 1997; Northrup 1959). Mathien (1997:1124) noted that McKinley County and the Haystack area are two other possible source areas. Although these native copper sources are not far from the canyon, there is as yet no evidence of prehistoric mining in these locales (Brand 1937; Mathien 1997; Northrup 1959).

To date, sourcing studies of copper bells recovered from Pueblo Bonito have yielded inconclusive results (Judd 1954; Palmer et al. 1998; Root 1937). The first study was conducted by W. C. Root of the Peabody Museum in 1928 (Root 1937; also cited in Judd 1954:110–11). He analyzed 5 copper bells from Pueblo Bonito and 3 from Pueblo del Arroyo using spectrographic techniques and concluded that native ores from Chihuahua (Mexico), Arizona, or New Mexico were used. Judd (1954) remained unconvinced given the lack of supporting evidence for local metallurgy in these locations during the occupation of Pueblo Bonito, and he submitted the same samples for spectrochemical analysis to William Meggers at the National Bureau of Standards ten years later (Judd 1954:111–15). In addition to the Chacoan specimens, the study included other prehistoric copper bells from Honduras, Mexico, Arizona, and New Mexico, as well as native ore samples (Judd 1954:111). In a personal letter to Judd (1954) in 1938, Meggers reported finding significant differences between the relative composition of native copper ores from New Mexico (Fort Bayard and Santa Rita in southwestern New Mexico) and Mexico, but he could not link any of the copper artifacts either to the sampled source areas or to one another. Almost 60 years later, Palmer and colleagues (1998) reevaluated 6 of the copper bells included in the original studies—5 bells from Pueblo Bonito and 1 from Pueblo del Arroyo—and compared them to specimens from other archaeological sites in the greater Southwest using particle-induced X-ray emission and scanning electron microscope analyses. The samples from Chaco did not yield any measurable trace elements, though the studies reported by Judd (1954) had noted very small amounts of arsenic, lead, gallium, and antimony. Palmer and colleagues (1998) suggested that the relative purity of the copper may be the result of using local cuprite sources, since West Mexican bells contain more contaminants (Hosler 1994). However, in her study of 622 copper bells from the greater Southwest, Vargas (1995:tables 4.1 and 4.2) found that the 18 bells from Pueblo Bonito are clearly West Mexican in style (Hosler 1986). Based on the distribution and quantity of copper bells of different styles across the US Southwest and northwestern Mexico, she suggested that the bells found at Chaco Canyon were dispensed by "emerging elites in the Hohokam region" (Vargas 1995:70).

The majority of the marine mollusk genera represented in the assemblage are native to the Gulf of California and the vicinity of the Baja Peninsula, including *Olivella*, *Conus*, *Strombus*, *Glycymeris*, *Spondylus*, and *Chama*. Two others, *Haliotis* and *Murex*, are found only along the Pacific coast. *Olivella dama*, known as the dwarf olive, is a small marine gastropod found along the southern California coast and in the upper Gulf of California. *Olivella* beads were formed by the simple removal of the spire (spire lopping) or by sawing either end (truncation). *Conus* is a genus of large marine sea snails with cone-shaped shells typically used for tinklers (a type of pendant sewn to clothing). The most commonly used *Conus* species for ornaments in the Southwest, *Conus perplexus*, is native to the Gulf of California. *Strombus* is a large marine conch found in the Gulf of California and is notable for its thick and durable shell. It was used for both ornaments and shell trumpets at Pueblo Bonito. *Murex*, a large gastropod found along the Pacific coast, was also used for shell trumpets. Pepper (1920:125) reported burned fragments found above the floor of Room 28, but we were not able to locate them. *Glycymeris* is a genus of large marine pelecypodae (clams) found in the Gulf of California and in Baja California Sur. *Glycymeris gigantea* was used widely for bracelets, particularly in the Hohokam area. *Spondylus*, also known as a spiny oyster, is a bivalve mollusk genus found in the northern Gulf of California and along the Pacific coast of Baja California. Based on their geographic distributions, three *Spondylus* species—*S. limbatus*, *S. crassisquama*, and *S. leucanthus*—were primarily used by prehispanic populations in the greater Southwest (Lodeiros et al. 2016). *Chama*, or jewel box clam, is a genus of marine bivalve found in the southern Gulf of California. The species of *Spondylus* and *Chama* utilized in Chacoan assemblages are red to pink in color. *Haliotis* (abalone) is a large marine gastropod found on the Pacific coast from Oregon to Baja with an iridescent (mother-of-pearl) inner shell. The shell of *Haliotis cracherodii*, in particular, was commonly used for pendants in Chaco Canyon.

ASSEMBLAGE SUMMARY

Of the 4,475 artifacts analyzed, the HEE (Pepper 1920) recovered 15.6% (*n* = 698) and UNM (this volume) recovered 84.4% (*n* = 3,777). Just over 40% of the assemblage (*n* = 1,812) was found within intact floor deposits (UNM's Level 13 and Pepper's "floor" and "among vessel"

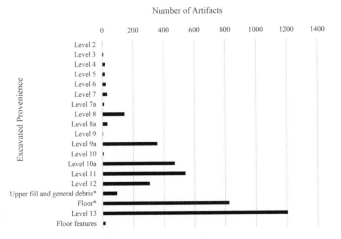

FIGURE 5.2. Frequency of ornaments and related items by excavated context, organized by relative depth. * = contexts excavated by Pepper; "a" levels are burned.

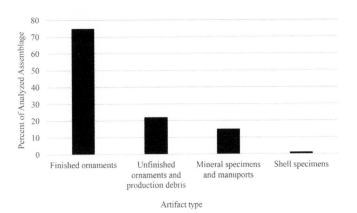

FIGURE 5.3. Artifact categories in the analyzed Room 28 ornament, mineral, and shell assemblage.

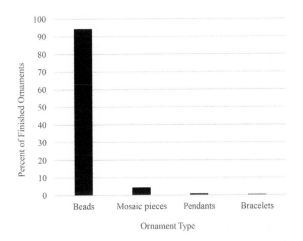

FIGURE 5.4. Finished ornament types from Room 28.

contexts) (figure 5.2 and table 5.4). Of the backdirt levels excavated in 2013, Levels 9–12 (including a hole in the floor filled with backdirt) yielded 2,000 ornaments and related items, accounting for another 45% of the assemblage.

The assemblage is dominated by finished ornaments (*n* = 3,341; 74.7%) and items related to ornament production (turquoise lapidary debris, worked pieces, and blanks) (*n* = 991; 22.1%). Mineral specimens/manuports (*n* = 88; 2%) and shell specimens (*n* = 55; 1.2%) comprise only minor portions of the entire assemblage (figure 5.3). The majority of the finished ornaments are beads (*n* = 3,152; 94.3%), followed by mosaic tesserae (*n* = 148; 4.4%), pendants (*n* = 27; 0.8%), and bracelets (*n* = 12; 0.4%) (figure 5.4).

Turquoise is the dominant material type, representing 77.1% of the total assemblage. Of the turquoise objects, 71.4% are finished ornaments, and 28.6% are either ornaments in the process of manufacture or production debris (table 5.5 and figure 5.5). Shell is the second most common material type, comprising 20% of the assemblage; the majority of the shell artifacts are finished ornaments (93.5%). While most of the shell artifacts do not retain diagnostic morphological characteristics (*n* = 553; 61.7%), of the identifiable genera, the most common are *Olivella* (*n* = 314; 35%) and *Glycymeris* (*n* = 16; 1.8%). *Spondylus*, *Conus*, *Murex*, and *Strombus* each account for less than 0.5% of the shell assemblage (table 5.6).

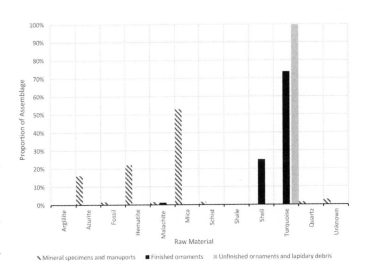

FIGURE 5.5. Raw material by major artifact type, Room 28.

TABLE 5.4. **Artifact types by provenience**

PROVENIENCE		BEAD	BEAD BLANK	BRACELET	DISC	LAPIDARY DEBRIS	MANUPORT	MINERAL SPECIMEN	MOSAIC PIECE	PENDANT	SHELL SPECIMEN	UNKNOWN ORNAMENT	WORKED PIECE	TOTAL
Refuse/fill*	general debris	—	—	—	—	—	1	4	—	—	—	—	—	5
	upper fill	23	1	—	—	61	—	—	—	—	—	—	1	86
Level 2		—	—	—	—	—	—	3	—	—	—	—	—	3
Level 3		1	—	—	—	—	—	6	—	—	—	—	—	7
Level 4		6	1	—	—	4	1	7	—	—	—	1	—	20
Level 5		6	—	3	—	1	1	4	—	1	2	—	—	18
Level 6		9	1	—	—	6	3	3	1	—	3	—	—	26
Level 7		25	—	—	—	—	3	3	—	2	1	—	—	34
Level 7a	(burned)	4	—	—	—	6	—	1	—	—	—	—	—	11
Level 8		97	2	—	—	28	—	7	2	2	5	—	—	143
Level 8a	(burned)	17	—	—	—	12	—	—	2	—	1	—	—	32
Level 9		3	—	—	—	—	1	—	—	—	1	—	—	5
Level 9a	(burned)	247	8	—	—	74	—	5	14	1	6	—	—	355
Level 10		3	—	—	—	4	—	—	—	—	—	—	—	7
Level 10a	(burned)	310	7	—	—	126	—	10	16	—	6	—	—	475
Level 11		376	8	—	—	124	—	4	23	—	6	—	—	541
Level 12		216	5	—	—	63	—	5	14	2	2	—	—	307
Hole in front of door to Room 32		257	3	—	—	52	—	—	9	2	—	—	—	323
Level 13	general level	770	27	1	—	199	—	6	53	5	19	—	—	1,080
	southwest corner	2	—	—	—	3	—	—	—	—	—	—	—	5
	below burned area east of posthole 7	77	5	—	—	—	—	2	—	2	—	—	—	86
	below burned area east of ph 2	6	—	—	—	25	—	—	3	—	1	—	—	35
	TOTAL LEVEL 13	855	32	1	—	227	—	8	56	7	20	—	—	1,206
Ashpit		2	—	—	—	—	—	—	—	—	—	—	—	2
Floor	floor*	137	6	1	1	58	—	—	1	10	—	—	—	215
	among vessels*	361	—	6**	—	—	—	—	—	—	—	—	—	367
	general debris, floor level*	9	—	—	—	—	—	—	—	—	—	—	—	9
	Bowl 1*	7	—	—	—	—	—	—	—	—	—	—	—	7
	Bowl 3*	3	—	—	—	—	—	—	—	—	—	—	—	3
	Bowl 4*	2	—	—	—	—	—	—	—	—	—	—	—	2
	Bowl 11*	—	—	1	—	—	—	—	—	—	—	—	—	1
	Bowl 12*	1	—	—	—	—	—	—	—	—	—	—	—	1
	Bowl 13*	1	—	—	—	—	—	—	—	—	—	—	—	1
	TOTAL	521	6	8	1	58	—	—	1	10	—	—	—	606
Surface 1 sweeping		5	—	—	—	—	—	1	1	—	—	—	—	7
Sweeping from step		1	—	—	—	—	—	—	—	—	—	—	—	1
Posthole 1		1	—	—	—	—	—	—	—	—	—	—	—	1
Posthole 2		2	—	—	—	—	—	—	—	—	—	—	—	2

PROVENIENCE		BEAD	BEAD BLANK	BRACELET	DISC	LAPIDARY DEBRIS	MANUPORT	MINERAL SPECIMEN	MOSAIC PIECE	PENDANT	SHELL SPECIMEN	UNKNOWN ORNAMENT	WORKED PIECE	TOTAL
Posthole 7		4	—	—	—	2	—	—	—	—	—	—	—	6
Posthole 22		3	—	—	—	—	—	—	—	—	—	—	—	3
Thermal feature		6	—	—	—	2	—	—	—	—	—	—	—	8
Level 14	southeast quadrant	1	—	—	—	—	—	1	—	—	—	—	—	2
Level 15	general level	—	—	—	—	—	—	1	—	—	—	—	—	1
	southeast quadrant	—	—	—	—	2	—	—	1	—	—	—	—	3
Level 16		—	—	—	—	—	—	1	—	—	—	—	—	1
East wall cleaning		11	8	—	—	4	—	—	2	—	—	—	—	25
North wall cleaning		10	1	—	—	—	—	—	—	—	—	—	—	11
Slit trench, north wall		—	—	—	—	1	—	—	—	—	—	—	—	1
South wall cleaning		4	—	—	—	—	—	—	1	—	—	—	—	5
West wall Cleaning		1	—	—	—	—	—	1	—	—	—	—	—	2
Southeast door cleaning		103	3	—	—	39	—	3	3	—	—	—	—	151
North door fill		—	1	—	—	—	—	—	—	—	—	—	—	1
Northeast balk cleaning		6	—	—	—	1	—	—	—	—	—	—	—	7
West profile		1	—	—	—	—	—	—	—	—	—	—	—	1
Backdirt		15	1	—	—	4	—	—	2	—	2	—	—	24
TOTAL		3,152	88	12	1	902	10	78	148	27	55	1	1	4,475

* Object excavated by the Hyde Exploring Expedition.

** Includes two refits for a total of eight fragments.

TABLE 5.5. **Artifact types by raw material, Room 28**

MATERIAL	BEAD	BEAD BLANK	BRACELET	DISC	LAPIDARY DEBRIS	MANUPORT	MINERAL SPECIMEN	MOSAIC PIECE	PENDANT	SHELL SPECIMEN	UNKNOWN ORNAMENT	WORKED PIECE	TOTAL
Argillite	1	—	—	—	—	—	—	2	—	—	—	—	3
Azurite	—	—	—	—	—	—	11	—	—	—	—	—	11
Biotite	—	—	—	—	—	—	1	—	—	—	—	—	1
Chalcedony	—	—	—	—	—	—	1	—	—	—	—	—	1
Concretion	—	—	—	—	—	—	9	—	—	—	—	—	9
Copper	—	—	—	—	—	—	—	—	—	—	—	1	1
Fossil	—	—	—	—	—	8	—	—	—	—	—	—	8
Hematite	—	—	—	—	—	—	15	—	—	—	—	—	15
Jet	22	—	—	1	—	—	—	12	—	—	—	—	35
Malachite	—	—	—	—	—	—	1	—	—	—	—	—	1
Micaceous schist	—	—	—	—	—	—	1	—	—	—	—	—	1
Muscovite	—	—	—	—	—	—	35	—	—	—	—	—	35
Petrified wood	—	—	—	—	—	—	1	—	—	—	—	—	1
Quartz crystal	—	—	—	—	—	2	—	—	—	—	—	—	2
Shale	1	—	—	—	—	—	—	—	—	—	—	—	1
Shell	818	3	12	—	—	—	—	—	5	55	—	—	893
Turquoise	2,308	85	—	—	902	—	—	134	22	—	—	—	3,451
Unknown stone	2	—	—	—	—	3	—	—	—	—	1	—	6
Total	3,152	88	12	1	902	10	78	148	27	55	1	1	4,475

TABLE 5.6. **Genera represented by shell artifacts, Room 28**

	Conus	Glycymeris	Haliotis	Olivella	Spondylus/ Chama	Strombus	Murex	Unknown	TOTAL
Bead	1	4	—	310	1	—	—	502	818
Bead blank	—	—	—	—	—	—	—	3	3
Bracelet	—	12	—	—	—	—	—	—	12
Pendant	—	—	1	—	1	—	—	3	5
Shell specimen	—	—	1	4	1	4	≥ 3	45	55+
TOTAL	1	16	2	314	3	4	≥ 3	553	893+*

* Includes several burned *Murex* sp. fragments reported by Pepper 1920:125.

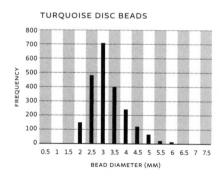

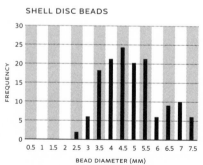

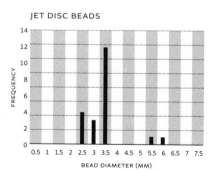

FIGURE 5.6. Diameters of complete disc beads by material type, Room 28.

TABLE 5.7. **Bead types by raw material**

BEAD FORM	BEAD SHAPE	ARGILLITE	JET	SHALE	SHELL	TURQUOISE	UNKNOWN	TOTAL
Barrel	spire-lopped	—	—	—	186	—	—	186
	truncated	—	—	—	124	—	—	124
Dentate	irregular	—	—	—	10	—	—	10
Discoidal	circular	1	21	1	159	2,305	1	2,488
Pendant	bilobe	—	—	—	281	—	—	281
	curved rectangular	—	—	—	1	1	—	2
	ovoid	—	—	—	43	2	—	45
	rounded rectangle	—	—	—	3	—	—	3
	teardrop	—	—	—	1	—	—	1
Spherical	spherical	—	—	—	—	—	1	1
Tubular	tubular	—	1	—	6	—	—	7
Unknown	other	—	—	—	4	—	—	4
TOTAL		1	22	1	818	2,308	2	3,152

BEADS

Disc Beads

Disc beads are the most common bead type in the Room 28 assemblage (n = 2,488; 78.9%) and in the Pueblo Bonito ornament assemblage as a whole (Mattson 2016c; table 5.7). Most of these were produced from turquoise (92.6%) or shell (6.4%) and were found in association with the floor (Level 13). A large number was also recovered from four of the backdirt levels above the floor (Levels 9–12). Complete disc beads average 3.09 mm in diameter and 1.21 mm in thickness. Turquoise and jet disc beads are smaller (mean diameters of 2.96 mm and 3.2 mm, respectively) than shell disc beads (mean diameter of 4.75 mm). As determined by a one-way analysis of variance, these differences are statistically significant ($F[2, 2369] = 329.68$, $p = 0.000$) (figure 5.6). While the distributions of turquoise and jet disc bead diameters do not support the presence of distinct size classes or

gauges of beads, the diameters of shell disc beads are bimodally distributed, with peaks at 4.2 mm and 6.4 mm. There are no significant differences between the mean diameters of turquoise disc beads from backfill and floor contexts, although shell disc beads from backfill levels are significantly smaller than those from intact floor deposits ($F[1, 81] = 16.19$, $p = 0.000$) (figure 5.7). It appears that only the smaller size class of shell disc beads is represented in backdirt contexts, while both size classes are present in intact fill and floor deposits.

It is likely that the disc beads from the backdirt levels of Room 28 originated in nearby rooms, particularly Rooms 33 and 53. As discussed in chapters 1 and 2, records indicate that all of the fill of Rooms 32 and 33 passed through Room 28 for inspection prior to discard. The backfill from Room 28a was also thrown into Room 28 during excavation in 1897. Furthermore, ceramic refitting shows that parts of vessels found in Room 28 in 2013 fit onto vessels recovered from Rooms 53 and 56 in 1897 (Crown, chapter 3, this volume), making it likely that the HEE excavations threw the backdirt from these rooms into the open Room 28 when they cleaned them out. There are no ceramic sherds from Room 28 that match ceramics from Rooms 32 or 33. Ornaments provide another way to consider the origin of the Room 28 backdirt. Room 53 contained quantities of ornaments, including more than 4,000 turquoise beads thought to be part of a necklace (Pepper 1920:210–13). Room 33 contained more than 30,000 turquoise disc beads. However, Room 32 contained very few ornaments, none of which are beads, and ornaments were not reported from either Room 28a or Room 56.

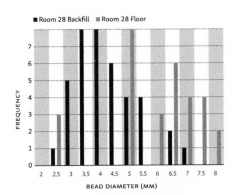

FIGURE 5.7. Diameters of complete shell disc beads from Room 28 by major provenience.

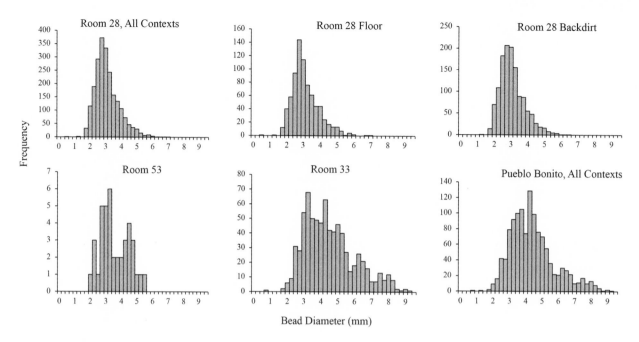

FIGURE 5.8. Distribution of turquoise disc bead diameters by provenience.

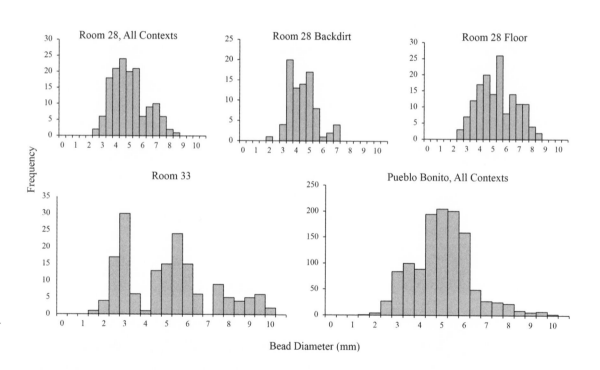

FIGURE 5.9. Distribution of complete shell disc bead diameters by provenience.

Turquoise disc beads from Levels 1–12 (backdirt levels) of Room 28 are significantly smaller in mean diameter than those from Room 53, Room 33, and intact deposits from all combined contexts at Pueblo Bonito (figure 5.8). In comparing the size distributions of these assemblages, it appears that turquoise beads more than 4 mm in diameter are underrepresented in the Room 28 assemblage, in both floor and backdirt contexts. Shell disc beads from Room 28, in both backdirt and floor contexts, also have a smaller mean diameter than those from Rooms 33 and 53. Relatively few shell disc beads were recovered from Room 53, and most of the shell disc beads from Room 33 are either smaller or larger in size (figure 5.9).

The predominance of smaller disc beads in the backdirt levels of Room 28 compared to the disc beads from surrounding rooms and the site as a whole likely relates to the low visibility of these items and the lack of methodical screening by the HEE. However, there are also significant differences in the size distributions of disc beads from the intact Room 28 floor and from nearby rooms, perhaps resulting from differences in room function. It is perhaps not surprising that elite burial contexts contain larger beads of valuable materials, such as turquoise and marine shell, in addition to very small beads representing exceptional craftsmanship. Interestingly, turquoise disc beads from the floor of Room 28 are significantly smaller in diameter than those in other room and kiva offering contexts at Pueblo Bonito ($F[1, 903] = 330.24$, $p = 0.000$).

Pendant Beads

Pendant beads ($N = 332$) comprise 10.5% of the Room 28 bead assemblage and 9.9% of the finished ornaments. The majority of these are bilobe ($n = 281$) or ovoid ($n = 45$) in form and produced from unidentified shell (99%). Other shapes documented are rectangular ($n = 5$) and teardrop ($n = 1$). At Pueblo Bonito, bilobe beads are predominantly associated with kiva offerings, particularly those in court kivas, and Room 33 (Burial 14 and offerings associated with the room) (Mattson 2015). Even excluding items recovered from mixed or backfill contexts, Room 28 contained eight times more bilobe beads than any other non-kiva or non-burial room at the site (followed distantly by Room 186 [$n = 34$], Room 40 [$n = 18$], Room 310 [$n = 11$], and Room 39 [$n = 8$]).

More than 82% of the bilobe beads and 66% of the ovoid pendant beads from Room 28 were recovered from intact floor deposits. The bilobe beads average 7.91 mm in length, 4.48 in width, and 2.56 mm in thickness. Those from floor contexts are slightly shorter than those from backdirt contexts (7.92 mm versus 8.01 mm in mean length, respectively), but this difference is not statistically significant. Ovoid pendant beads average 6.48 mm in length, 3.5 mm in width, and 2.1 mm in thickness. Similar to bilobe beads, there is no significant difference in the length of beads from floor and backdirt contexts.

Both bilobe beads and *Olivella* beads (see below) at Pueblo Bonito have lower coefficients of variation (CVs) than other ornament types do, suggesting greater degrees of standardization (Longacre et al. 1988:103), a possible indicator of manufacture by specialists. Whereas the CVs of disc beads range from 24% to 44%, the CVs of bilobe beads are under 15% (figure 5.10). Bilobe beads from the Room 28 floor have a CV of 12%, compared to 13.76% from kivas, and 7.08%–9.72% from Room 33 (the Room 33 bilobe beads include two distinct size classes; see figure 5.11). This indicates that fewer producers made the bilobe shell beads found at Pueblo Bonito, particularly those included in Room 33, than the disc beads. As there is little evidence of the local production of bilobe beads, this specialization likely occurred closer to sources of marine shell and may indicate that Pueblo Bonito residents obtained these beads from a narrow range of traders or in a small number of transactions.

Barrel Beads

Barrel beads fashioned from *Olivella* shells ($N = 310$) are another common ornament type in the Room 28 assemblage, comprising 9.3% of the finished ornaments and 9.8% of the beads. Most of these ($n = 176$) were found on or near the floor, particularly in association with ceramic vessels. Similar to disc beads, most of the barrel beads from above the floor were recovered from backfill: Levels 9a, 10, 11, and 12. Like bilobe beads, *Olivella* beads—both spire-lopped and truncated—are most concentrated in the two burial clusters (particularly, offerings within Room 33) and kiva offerings at Pueblo Bonito. The intact deposits of Room 28 contained more spire-lopped beads than all other non-burial and non-kiva contexts at the site combined. In addition, Room 28 is one of only three non-burial, non-kiva rooms to contain truncated *Olivella* shell beads (74 were found in Room 310, and 2 were recovered from Room 163).

Complete spire-lopped beads ($n = 128$) average 6.25 mm in diameter and 13 mm in length; whole truncated beads

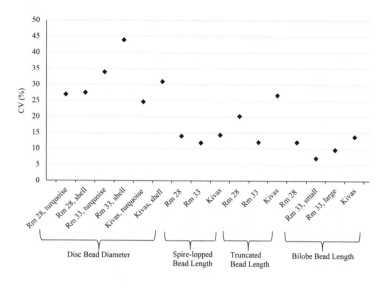

FIGURE 5.10. Coefficients of variation (cv) of bead dimensions by context.

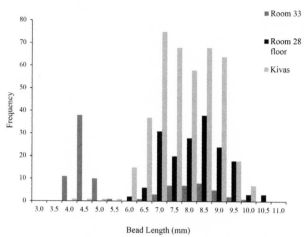

FIGURE 5.11. Distribution of bilobe bead lengths from Room 28, Room 33, and kivas.

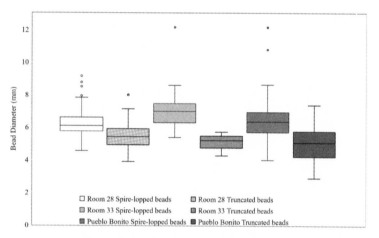

FIGURE 5.12. Diameters of complete spire-lopped and truncated *Olivella* beads from Room 28, Room 33, and all of Pueblo Bonito.

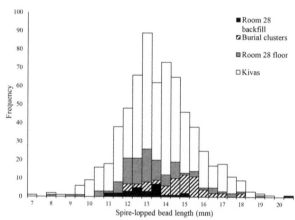

FIGURE 5.13. Distribution of *Olivella* spire-lopped bead lengths from Room 28, kiva offerings, and northern and western burial clusters.

(*n* = 122) have a mean diameter and length of 5.45 mm and 5.93 mm, respectively. Thus, truncated beads are significantly smaller in diameter than spire-lopped beads ($F[1, 249] = 67.01, p = 0.000$). This is also the case for the *Olivella* beads from Room 33 and from Pueblo Bonito as a whole (Mattson 2015), indicating that different sizes of shells were preferred for these different bead types and that truncated beads do not simply represent broken and refurbished spire-lopped beads (figure 5.12). As with bilobe beads, there is no clear evidence of the local manufacture of *Olivella* beads at Pueblo Bonito. Thus,

the sizes likely represent a choice among the original producers, perhaps Hohokam groups located closer to the Gulf of California.

Although truncated beads from all proveniences in Room 28 are similar in size, spire-lopped beads from floor contexts are significantly smaller in diameter, but not length, compared to those from secondary contexts ($F[1, 124] = 5.80, p = 0.017$). If the barrel beads from the Room 28 backdirt originated in Room 33 (no *Olivella* beads were recovered from Rooms 32, 53, or 56 in the northern burial cluster), they may be expected to be of similar size. While there is no significant difference in truncated or spire-lopped bead diameters between the Room 33 assemblage and the Room 28 backfill, spire-lopped beads from Room 33 are significantly longer. The distributions of spire-lopped bead length by context in Pueblo Bonito make it clear that the Room 28 assemblage departs significantly from those of the northern and western burial clusters. Interestingly, spire-lopped beads from kiva offerings encompass the size distributions of both Room 28 and the burial clusters (figure 5.13). This finding may help confirm that the backdirt in Room 28 came from rooms other than Room 33.

Similar to bilobe shell beads, *Olivella* beads have relatively low CVs in both diameter and length compared to other ornaments from Pueblo Bonito (figure 5.10). The CVs of the lengths of spire-lopped and truncated beads from Room 28 are somewhat higher (13.96% and 20.17%, respectively) than those from Room 33 (11.80% and 12.02%, respectively). While the CV of spire-lopped bead lengths from Room 28 is comparable to those from kiva offerings (14.32%), truncated beads from kivas have a much higher CV (26.68%) than those from Room 28 (20.17%).

Other Beads

Several bead types were found in lower frequencies in Room 28: 10 shell dentate beads among the vessels on the floor, 7 tubular beads (1 shell bead from Level 4, 1 shell bead from Level 9a, 4 shell beads from Level 11, and 1 jet bead below the floor in Level 14), 1 spherical bead of unknown material in Level 5, and 4 shell beads of unknown form from Level 13 (floor). Dentate beads are relatively rare at Pueblo Bonito, with only a few hundred recovered from the site. They were concentrated in Room 33 and kiva offerings, but were also found in smaller quantities in domestic rooms and refuse contexts. Room 28 contained more dentate beads than any other non-burial room in the structure. Because the HEE recovered these, they are undoubtedly associated with the room.

Tubular beads are also relatively rare in the Pueblo Bonito ornament assemblage. While tubular beads produced from sections of bird bone are associated with both domestic rooms and kiva offerings, those of stone and shell are virtually restricted to Room 33, particularly Burial 14. Although the sample size is small (*n* = 7), the Room 28 assemblage includes more tubular beads than any other room with the exception of Room 33. All but

one of these came from backfill, however, and thus probably originated in Room 53.

Bead Blanks

Eighty-eight bead blanks were recovered from Room 28, most of which are consistent in size and shape with disc beads in the early stages of manufacture. Of these, all but three are turquoise. Floor contexts contained the highest concentration of blanks (43% of the total), although Level 10a, Level 11, and the cleaning of the east wall also produced numerous examples. In Pueblo Bonito, bead blanks were found in the highest frequencies in kiva offerings, Room 33, and Room 28. The inclusion of unfinished and broken turquoise ornaments along with turquoise lapidary production debris in ritual and highly structured contexts suggests that turquoise was valued and meaningful regardless of form, shape, or size. Turquoise blanks were also found in possible lapidary production areas (particularly Rooms 13 and 40), in the two trash mounds, and in small numbers in numerous domestic rooms. This suggests that while disc bead manufacture may have been concentrated in a few portions of the structure, it was also fairly widespread across the site (Mattson 2015).

PENDANTS

Twenty-seven pendants were collected from Room 28, 17 from intact floor contexts and 10 from redeposited fill (table 5.8). Of these, 22 (81.5%) are turquoise and 5 (18.5%) are shell. Identifiable shell genera are *Spondylus* (*n* = 1) and *Haliotis* (*n* = 1). Tabular forms (*n* = 23) are most common, particularly those of ovoid and rectangular shapes. Complete pendants vary greatly in size, ranging from 3.41 mm to 21.02 mm in maximum dimension. Although small, the pendant assemblage from Room 28 is more similar to that of the northern burial cluster than to other contexts in Pueblo Bonito. Both are dominated by turquoise and lack pendants made from materials other than turquoise or shell (e.g., argillite, jet, selenite). In addition, more than half of each assemblage is composed of ovoid/circular and rectangular forms.

MOSAICS

A large number of mosaic tesserae (*N* = 148) were recovered from Room 28, primarily during UNM's reexcavation of the room. Of these, more than half (61%) were found

TABLE 5.8. **Pendant types from Room 28 by context and material**

CONTEXT	TYPE	SHAPE	TURQUOISE	SHELL	TOTAL
Floor	3-dimensional	rectangular	1		17
	tabular	ovoid	7		
		rectangular	2		
		curved rectangular	1		
		teardrop	3		
		inverted teardrop	1		
		trapezoidal	2		
Level 5	tabular	rectangular	1		1
Level 7		dentate		1	2
	tabular	irregular	1		
Level 8		dentate		2	2
Level 9a	tabular	ovoid		1	1
Level 12	tabular	curved rectangular	2		2
Door to Room 32	tabular	curved rectangular		1	2
		inverted teardrop	1		
TOTAL			22	5	27

in redeposited fill levels. The majority are rectangular in shape (98%) and made from turquoise (91%), followed by jet (8%) and argillite (1%). The maximum dimension of complete items ranges from 2.3 mm to 15.86 mm, with a mean of 5.81 mm. The average size appears to vary by material type: argillite inlays are the largest (13.22 mm), followed by jet (9.65 mm) and turquoise (5.28 mm).

Given that Room 33 contained hundreds of inlays, including the remains of a decayed cylindrical basket surrounded by more than 1,200 turquoise tesserae, it is possible that the inlays found in the Room 28 fill originated in Room 33. In terms of maximum dimension, however, complete turquoise tesserae from the Room 28 backdirt are significantly smaller ($t[83]$ = 3.18, p = 0.002) than those from Room 33. This may indicate another source for these artifacts, such as Rooms 53 and 56. Although no inlays have been documented in these rooms, it is possible that excavators missed an inlaid perishable item similar to the cylindrical basket.

BRACELETS

Twelve *Glycymeris* shell bracelets or bracelet fragments were analyzed from Room 28, nine from the floor (one bracelet portion composed of two refit pieces associated with the general floor area, one from Bowl 11, one from Level 13, and six found among the ceramic vessels on the floor) and three from Level 5 of the redeposited fill. Pepper (1920) reported three additional fragments from the floor, although these could not be located. Several of the bracelets from the room exhibit unique features: one is incised to receive a rectangular inlay, one has a square-notched top (versus a naturally rounded umbo), and one has a perforated umbo.

As measured on three sufficiently complete specimens from Room 28, maximum bracelet diameters range from 67.03 mm to 79.17 mm. When all Pueblo Bonito complete bracelet diameters are plotted, they display two peaks, one from 50 to 56 mm and one from 69 to 78 mm. Thus, at least three of the Room 28 bracelets fall into the larger size category. The sizes may correspond to the manner in which these items were intended to be worn—either around the wrist as bracelets or around the upper arm as armlets—or to the gender of the wearer.

SHELL SPECIMENS

Fifty-five unworked shell specimens were collected from Room 28 during UNM's investigation. Most of these (60%) are from backdirt levels, more than one-third are from floor contexts (Level 13), and two items are unprovenienced. Only 10 of the specimens could be identified to the genus level: 4 *Olivella* (Level 13), 4 *Strombus* (Levels 6 and 8), 1 *Haliotis* (Level 12), and 1 *Spondylus* or *Chama* (Level 5). According to Pepper (1920), fragments of burned *Murex* shell were found in the debris above the pottery vessels on the floor, and fragments of unidentified shell were noted among the bowls and jars on the floor. The *Murex* and *Strombus* fragments likely represent the remains of shell trumpets. Pepper (1920) and Judd (1954) collected at least 15 shell trumpets made from *Strombus* and *Murex* shell during their excavations of Pueblo Bonito. Mills and Ferguson (2008:346) note that these trumpets are associated with specialized contexts, such as ceremonial storage rooms, ritual caches, and high-status burials. Although only one complete specimen was found in the northern burial cluster (*Strombus* in Room 33), the presence of additional trumpets would not be surprising, given the abundance of other socially valuable objects, such as cylinder vessels, ceremonial sticks, and objects of turquoise.

MINERAL SPECIMENS AND MANUPORTS

Eighty-eight mineral specimens and manuports were analyzed from Room 28: 9 from the floor, 3 from subfloor contexts, 5 from intact fill, and 71 from redeposited fill (table 5.9). Muscovite mica is the most common material type, followed by hematite, azurite, iron concretion, fossil shell (crinoid stems and small bivalves), unidentified stone, and quartz crystal. Pepper (1920:117–24) reported the recovery of at least 17 additional items in the upper fill and general debris, including limonite, red and yellow ocher, crinoid stems, fossil shells, a shark's tooth, sulphur, calcite, mica, and "silica of iron."

Items found on the floor and subfloor, likely associated with activities occurring in the room, include seven unworked hematite nodules, one iron concretion, and four fragments of muscovite mica. Numerous hematite paint stones (typically, cylindrical pieces with multiple ground surfaces/facets) have been recovered from various contexts at Pueblo Bonito, indicating that the mineral was used for red pigment. Iron concretions form naturally in the sandstone formations of the canyon and were sometimes collected, presumably for their unique shapes. Portions of larger concretions were occasionally used as small vessels. The function of objects made from mica is unknown, although the presence of galena, quartz crystal, selenite, iron pyrite, and abalone shell in ritual deposits in kivas at the site suggest that brilliant materials were valuable and held special meaning (Mattson 2015, 2016b). In prehispanic Mesoamerica, mirrors were fashioned from polished reflective stone—typically, iron pyrite, obsidian, or hematite—and used as prestige items and/or as "divinatory or magical portals to communicate between parallel dimensions, worlds, or realities" (Gallaga 2016:4; Miller and Taube 2003; Taube

TABLE 5.9. **Mineral specimens and manuports from Room 28 by material type and general context**

	FLOOR	SUBFLOOR	INTACT FILL	REDEPOSITED FILL	TOTAL
Azurite				11	11
Biotite				1	1
Chalcedony				1	1
Concretion	1			8	9
Fossil				8	8
Hematite	4	3		8	15
Malachite				1	1
Muscovite	4		4	27	35
Petrified wood				1	1
Purple micaceous schist				1	1
Quartz crystal			1	1	2
Unidentified stone				3	3
TOTAL	9	3	5	71	88

	NORTHERN BURIAL CLUSTER	WESTERN BURIAL CLUSTER	ROOM 28	ROOM 38	ROOM 39	KIVA OFFERINGS	DOMESTIC ROOMS COMBINED	MIDDENS
Turquoise disc beads	31,055	402	2,305	105	20	818	15	19
Shell disc beads	1,783	888	159	181	5	924	2,496	79
Spire-lopped *Olivella* sp. Beads	243	58	186	—	17	1,386	13	—
Truncated *Olivella* sp. Beads	131	—	124	—	—	238	2	—
Bilobe shell beads	738	47	281	—	8	1,465	52	6
Dentate beads and pendants	62	4	10	—	—	103	4	5
Mosaic tesserae	1,483	263	148	49	9	107	44	9

2016). Among the Woodland and Mississippian cultures of what is now the southeastern United States, mica was a highly prized material associated with high-status mortuary contexts. Mica sheets were used to produce mirrors, clothing attachments, and zoomorphic and anthropomorphic effigy cutouts (Carr and Case 2005).

DISCUSSION

More than 60% of the Room 28 ornament and mineral assemblage is from redeposited fill contexts, primarily Levels 9–12. These artifacts are predominantly beads (67%) and pieces of lapidary debris (23%), followed by mosaic tesserae (4%) and bead blanks (2%). Turquoise disc beads, turquoise inlays, spire-lopped *Olivella* beads, and shell bilobe beads comprise the majority of the finished ornaments from these levels. In an attempt to identify the original provenience of these materials, they were compared to those excavated from both the Room 28 floor and surrounding rooms (Rooms 32, 33, 53, and 56). Spire-lopped *Olivella* beads and both turquoise and shell disc beads from the Room 28 backfill are significantly smaller ($p = < 0.05$) in diameter than those from nearby rooms. Thus, these items may have simply been overlooked during the HEE excavations, perhaps as a result of the recovery techniques of the time (i.e., lack of screening). However, the beads from the Room 28 floor are also small in size compared to other rooms. Although fill strata with evidence of burning (designated with the letter *a*) likely originated in Room 28a, no significant differences were found in bead dimensions from burned versus unburned levels, perhaps a result of mixing due to the significant rodent activity in the room (Ainsworth et al., this volume). Thus, the ornament attributes from the Room 28 backfill do not clearly demonstrate the origin of these deposits, except that the nature of the assemblage indicates that the backfill came from a special context. Based on the ceramic refits between sherds found in the backfill of Room 28 and partial vessels recovered in Rooms 53 and 56, the original contexts for many or all of these unusual items may have been these two rooms (Crown, chapter 3, this volume). If so, this emphasizes the variety of items missed in the Moorehead "excavations" of those rooms and the later cleanup of the rooms by Pepper.

Ornaments from intact floor contexts—collected during Pepper's original excavation of the room ("floor" and "among vessels") and during UNM's investigation of previously unexcavated deposits (Level 13)—are composed primarily of turquoise disc beads (46%), turquoise lapidary debris (13%), shell bilobe beads (11%), *Olivella* spire-lopped (7%) and truncated beads (5%), and turquoise mosaic pieces (3%). These items occurred in greater quantities in Room 28 than in any other room (non-burial and non-kiva) in Pueblo Bonito (table 5.10). This includes other northern non-burial rooms, such as Rooms 38 and 39, which contained concentrations of "fancy" objects (Neitzel 2003b), including macaw skeletons, ceremonial sticks, inlaid scrapers, projectile points, pipes, and objects made from turquoise and shell. Perhaps even more important than the high frequencies of valuable ornaments in Room 28 is the co-occurrence of specific ornament forms and materials that mirror the ornament assemblages from high-status burials (particularly Room 33) and kiva offerings. Not only did the room contain spire-lopped *Olivella* beads, truncated *Olivella* beads, and shell bilobe beads—all three of which are commonly found together in kiva pilaster offerings—but it also included the only bifurcated bilobe bead found in a non-kiva context at Pueblo Bonito (Mattson 2016b). Bifurcated bilobe beads resemble bifurcated baskets and at least one bifurcated ceramic effigy from Pueblo Bonito, the shapes of which may represent ears of corn. The similarity between the ornaments in Room 28 and those in kiva deposits also extends to what are interpreted as offerings of ornaments in five ceramic bowls on the floor, which contained spire-lopped *Olivella* beads, bilobe shell beads, shell disc beads, tabular shell pendant beads, a *Glycymeris* shell bracelet, and turquoise disc beads.

In conclusion, the portion of the ornament assemblage that can be confidently associated with Room 28 is consistent with previous interpretations of the room as a ritual storage area. However, our analysis also suggests that the function and significance of the room and its original contents may have extended beyond the northern burial cluster in referencing collections of objects found in kiva offerings of different sizes across the site, as well as those in the western burial cluster. This implies that the items deliberately deposited and arranged in the room were associated not solely with elevated social status, but also with larger-scale aspects of social identity and ritual practice at Pueblo Bonito.

ACKNOWLEDGMENTS

We would like to thank Patricia Crown for the invitation to participate in the project and two reviewers for their helpful feedback on an earlier version of this chapter. Thanks are due to David Hurst Thomas and Anibal Rodriguez of the American Museum of Natural History for facilitating access to the remarkable Room 28 collections and to Wendy Bustard of the Chaco Culture National Historical Park's collections for allowing access to curated material and providing laboratory space. We are also grateful to Shannon David for assisting with photography and cataloging.

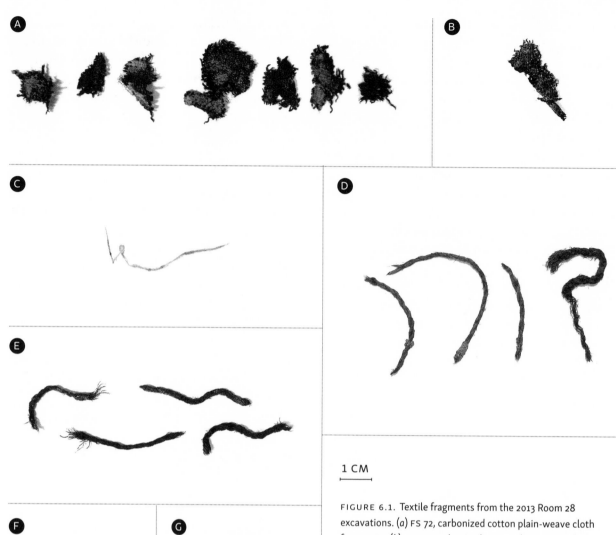

1 CM

FIGURE 6.1. Textile fragments from the 2013 Room 28 excavations. (*a*) FS 72, carbonized cotton plain-weave cloth fragments; (*b*) FS 112, carbonized cotton plain-weave cloth fragment; (*c*) FS 129, strand of unburned cotton yarn; (*d*) FS 178, carbonized yucca cordage fragments, three wrapped with feather quills; (*e*) FS 240, carbonized yucca cordage fragments; (*f*) FS 247, carbonized yucca cordage fragment; (*g*) FS 28, wad of red and yellow wool fiber and commercial knit fabric. Photos by Laurie D. Webster.

LAURIE D. WEBSTER

CHAPTER SIX

Textiles from Room 28 at Pueblo Bonito

The 2013 excavations in Room 28 yielded the remains of cotton plain-weave cloth, cotton and yucca cordage, feather-wrapped yucca cordage, and modern commercial wool yarn and fabric (table 6.1). All specimens are fragmentary, two are unburned, and the rest are carbonized. Most of the nonwrapped yucca cordage probably originated in Room 28, but the cotton cloth and feather-wrapped cordage could be from backdirt cleared from Rooms 28a, 32, 33, 53, or 56. The historic wool yarn and fabric may have been left by one or more members of the Hyde expedition.

COTTON PLAIN-WEAVE CLOTH

Eight small fragments of finely woven, carbonized cotton plain-weave cloth were recovered from Levels 7 and 8 during the 2013 excavations (figures 6.1a and 6.1b). They probably date to the Pueblo II period. Field specimen (FS) 72 consists of seven fragments, and FS 112 contains one. All are woven in 1/1 (over one, under one) warp-dominant plain-weave with single-ply z-spun cotton warps and weft elements. Selvages are missing.

The seven fragments of FS 72 appear to be pieces of the same fabric. The fine warp elements are 0.5–0.6 mm in diameter, and the thicker wefts are 1 mm in diameter.

Thread counts are 24 warps and 8–9 wefts per cm. The single fragment of FS 112 has the same element counts as the fragments in FS 72, but its thread counts are 16 warps and 10 wefts per cm. That all fragments share the same warp and weft diameters and were recovered from adjacent levels suggests that FS 72 and FS 112 could be the remains of the same plain-weave fabric, the discrepancy in thread counts explained by their burned condition. Because all fragments are carbonized black, it is unknown whether any were decorated. They probably represent the remains of one or more cotton blankets or some type of garment.

COTTON YARN

An unburned strand of fine, single-ply z-spun cotton yarn (FS 129), recovered from Level 9, probably also dates to the Pueblo II period (figure 6.1c). The slightly pink color probably represents staining from the soil. The strand is 7 cm long and 0.9 mm in diameter. Its tight spin and slightly kinked form suggest that it is a detached warp strand from a woven cotton fabric. The yarn was probably spun on a supported spindle.

TABLE 6.1. **Textiles from Room 28**

FS	PROVENIENCE	DESCRIPTION
28	Level 4: 99.02–98.82 m	unburned modern wool fiber and commercial knit fabric
72	Level 7: 98.42–98.22 m	carbonized cotton plain-weave cloth
112	Level 8: 98.22–98.02 m	carbonized cotton plain-weave cloth
129	Level 9: 98.02–97.82 m	unburned strand of cotton yarn
178	Level 10a: 97.82–97.62 m	carbonized yucca cordage, some with quill wrapping
240	Level 13: 97.32 m (floor and below)	carbonized yucca cordage
247	Posthole 2, southwest corner	carbonized yucca cordage

YUCCA CORDAGE

Three field specimens (178, 240, and 247) contain fragments of carbonized 2-ply s-spun Z-twist (2s-Z) yucca cordage dating to the Pueblo I and Pueblo II periods. FS 178 from Level 10a consists of four fragments, three bearing the remains of feather quill wrapping (figure 6.1d). The wrapping on each fragment is incomplete and confined to one area of the cord. One cord retains four circuits of wrapping, the other two retain one. The burnt quill strips are 1.0–1.5 mm wide. They seem very fine for turkey quills, but the carbonization process may have shrunk them. The fragments could represent the remains of feather-wrapped cordage or a twined feather blanket. The nonwrapped yucca cordage fragment in FS 178 is 6 cm long, 2 mm in diameter, and slightly bent as if formerly wrapped around another object. The cordage from FS 178 probably dates to the Pueblo II period.

The four fragments of FS 240 in Level 13 were recovered on or below the floor (figure 6.1e). They range from 1.8 mm to 2 mm in diameter and from 3 to 4 cm in length. Three have an undulating form as if formerly wrapped around another object. The single fragment of FS 247 is 3 cm long and 1.8 mm in diameter (figure 6.1f) and was associated with Posthole 2 in the southwest corner of the room. Wood removed from the posthole produced a Pueblo I AMS (accelerator mass spectrometry) date of cal AD 769–893. Like other yucca cordage in the Southwest with a 2s-Z structure, all of the yucca cordage from Room 28 was probably spun by twisting and plying it on the thigh, rather than with the aid of a spindle.

COMMERCIAL WOOL YARN AND FABRIC

Field specimen 28 from Level 4 is a small wad of red and yellow wool fiber adhering to a small piece of commercial knit fabric (figure 6.1g). The mass may represent packrat debris. The wool fibers could be the remains of a sock or sweater, and the knit fabric could be a fragment of hosiery or the lining (interfacing) from a shirt collar or other garment. Assuming that no archaeological work was done in this room prior to 1890, the red and yellow wool fibers were probably colored with synthetic aniline dyes, and the lining was machine-woven. It is tempting to associate these remains with George Pepper, Richard Wetherill, Warren K. Moorehead, or members of their excavation parties. Reexcavations at Turkey Pen Ruin in Grand Gulch, Utah, also yielded fragments of commercial fabrics possibly related to the Wetherill excavations, which are now at the Edge of the Cedars State Park Museum.

DISCUSSION

More than 900 worked-fiber artifacts were recovered during excavations at Pueblo Bonito (Webster 2008:168). George Pepper (1909, 1920) and Neil Judd (1954) briefly described and illustrated some of the more spectacular examples, but most of the worked-fiber assemblage is still unpublished and unstudied. In 2006, I photographed and briefly surveyed the worked-fiber artifacts from Pueblo Bonito at the American Museum of Natural History, the National Museum of the American Indian, and the National Museum of Natural History. They include a diverse array of cordage, twined and plaited sandals, hide moccasins, woven cotton fabrics, feather blankets, plaited mats, coiled and plaited baskets, feather artifacts, and other fiber-related articles (Webster 2006, 2008). The only perishable artifacts from Pueblo Bonito that have been studied in depth are the baskets and mats (Jolie 2018) and some of the painted wood (Webster 2011).

The small amount of textile material recovered from Room 28 during the 2013 excavations appears to have originated there and in backfill thrown in from Rooms 28a, 53, and 56. As discussed in chapters 2 and 12, during the 1896 excavations the HEE (Hyde Exploring Expedition) crew moved backdirt from the unburned Rooms 32 and 33 into Room 28 and later removed at least some of it to behind Pueblo Bonito. After the HEE left for the season, a party led by Warren Moorehead excavated the unburned Rooms 53 and 56, directly north of Rooms 32 and 33, generating backdirt that apparently ended up in Room 28 and Kiva 16. During the 1897 excavation of the heavily burned Room 28a, directly east of Room 28, the burned fill from that room was moved into Room 28 as well.

In his monograph, Pepper (1920:126) mentioned only one worked-fiber artifact from Room 28: a piece of knotted yucca cordage that was cataloged together with some charcoal and a human tooth from this room as H/12775, all of which was later discarded by the museum (AMNH Hyde catalog). He did not note any worked-fiber artifacts from Room 28a (Pepper 1920:128). Likewise, the Hyde catalog does not list any worked-fiber artifacts from these two rooms. However, HEE excavation photographs of Room 28 show two well-preserved baskets in the northeastern doorway of that room (figure 3.3), and the 2013 excavations of Room 28 encountered large quantities of carbonized perishable material (wood, botanical remains) that apparently originated in Room 28a backfill. Thus, the unburned textile artifacts (commercial wool fiber and fabric, unburned cotton yarn) recovered from Room 28 in 2013 most likely originated in the backfill of Rooms 53 and 56, and the carbonized artifacts

(cotton cloth, yucca cordage, some quill-wrapped) from Levels 7, 8, and 10a probably originated in the burned Room 28a. Only the yucca cordage from the floor area and Posthole 2 were apparently deposited in Room 28 while the great house was in use.

As a final note for readers interested in Chaco textiles, I highly recommend two recent excellent sandal studies: Edward Jolie's (2018) analyses of the twill-plaited sandals, and Benjamin Bellorado's study of the twined sandals in his forthcoming University of Arizona dissertation, "Leaving Footprints in the Ancient Southwest."

CAITLIN S. AINSWORTH, STEPHANIE E. FRANKLIN,
AND EMILY LENA JONES

CHAPTER SEVEN

Fauna from Room 28

The faunal assemblage from the 2013 reexcavation of Room 28 contains a total of 7,439 specimens of animal bone (table 7.1). This is a surprisingly large assemblage given the limited scope of the excavation. In fact, the Room 28 assemblage ranks among the larger reported faunal collections from the San Juan Basin: fewer than 10% of reported assemblages from this region contain more than 3,000 specimens (Badenhorst and Driver 2009). Within Chaco Canyon, only the excavations at Pueblo Alto and the 2004–2007 reexcavation of the Pueblo Bonito mounds yielded larger faunal collections (Akins 1985, 1987; Badenhorst et al. 2016).

The unusual size of the assemblage likely relates in part to Room 28's depositional history. The prehispanic inhabitants of Chaco Canyon were the primary creators of the zooarchaeological record of this room. However, the original excavators, George Pepper and Richard Wetherill, also introduced historical material into Room 28 (Crown, chapter 2, this volume), a fact confirmed by our identification in this collection of a piece of bone with cut marks from a metal saw. In addition, the actions of nonhuman agents, such as carnivores and small burrowing animals, also likely contributed material to the Room 28 assemblage. Together, these three depositional pathways created a large and somewhat unusual faunal assemblage.

TABLE 7.1. **Number of faunal specimens from primary (subfloor) and secondary (backdirt) contexts in Room 28**

PROVENIENCE	NSP	% OF TOTAL NSP
Backdirt	6,132	82.43
Subfloor	1,307	17.57
Total	7,439	100

The recovery methods also played an important role in the size of this collection. Screening protocols have tremendous influence on the size and number of specimens recovered for analysis (e.g., Jones and Gabe 2015; Nagaoka 2005; Quitmyer 2004). The 2013 reexcavation of Room 28 incorporated a combination of quarter-inch, eighth-inch, and sixteenth-inch mesh screening (Crown, chapter 2, this volume). The high level of fine screening increased the number of specimens collected.

These factors shaped our analytical decisions. We were naturally interested in comparing the Room 28 faunal assemblage to archaeofaunas from other Chacoan sites. However, many of these sites were excavated early in the history of southwestern archaeology and used different methods than those employed during this project (see Akins 1985 for a discussion of early methods). This limited our ability to make intersite comparisons. As the 2004–2007 excavation of the Pueblo Bonito mounds was codirected by Crown and used similar methods to the Room 28 excavation (Badenhorst et al. 2016), we chose to use that faunal assemblage as our primary comparative assemblage. We also reference other Chacoan faunal collections.

In addition to describing the Room 28 faunal assemblage as a whole and comparing it to that from the Pueblo Bonito mounds, we explore two specific topics of interest informed by the depositional history of this site. First, we evaluate the portion of the assemblage from the backdirt for evidence of modification by nonhuman agents, including physical disturbance and the incorporation of additional faunal material. As discussed earlier in this volume, the backdirt removed from the room in 2013 probably derived from Rooms 28a, 53, and 56 (Crown, chapter 2, this volume). Second, we examine the in situ material recovered from the subfloor levels for information on the diet and subsistence practices of the early occupants of Pueblo Bonito.

METHODS

Ainsworth and Franklin identified all specimens using comparative collections at the University of New Mexico's Zooarchaeology Laboratory and at the Museum of Southwestern Biology. Specimens were considered "identifiable" only if they could be assigned to a taxonomic class, size class, and skeletal element. The identification and recording process followed, with a few alterations, the guidelines outlined in Driver (2005). For each identified specimen, we recorded the following information: provenience, taxon, size class, element, portion (for incomplete elements), side (when applicable), degree of epiphyseal union, breakage, and surface modifications, including burning, gnawing, cut marks, root etching, and digestive corrosion.

We counted and weighed all specimens by level. Articulated elements, refittable specimens, and teeth remaining in the mandible/maxilla were counted as one specimen. We did not record loose teeth if a mandible or maxilla of the same taxon was identified in the same provenience; when no corresponding mandible or maxilla was present, the tooth was recorded but not included in counts or—unless otherwise specified—in any subsequent analysis. The identifications of loose teeth did not lead to any increase in the number of taxa identified in the Room 28 assemblage. Unidentified specimens larger than 2 mm were counted, weighed, and assessed for evidence of burning. No further information was recorded for these specimens. Unidentified specimens smaller than 2 mm were not analyzed.

Since the majority of the Room 28 assemblage is from mixed and uncertain provenience, the aggregation effects associated with derived measures would be particularly severe (see discussions in Grayson 1984 and Lyman 2008). For this reason, we avoided derived measures, such as the minimum number of individuals (MNI) and the minimum number of elements (MNE), and instead used the number of identified specimens (NISP) as the basis for all analyses.

ASSEMBLAGE SUMMARY

We identified 4,093 specimens (55.02% of the total assemblage) to at least the class level (table 7.2). Of these,

3,677 (89.84% of total NISP) are from the backdirt, and 416 (10.16% of total NISP) are from the in situ subfloor assemblage. The vast majority (95.28%) of the identified specimens are mammals; birds comprise 2.81%, reptiles 1.86%, and amphibians 0.49% of total NISP. In addition, there are numerous eggshell fragments (see Conrad, this volume) and a single bone tool in this assemblage.

Class Mammalia

ORDER LAGOMORPHA (RABBITS AND HARES) Rabbits were an important part of the diet for many prehispanic southwestern groups, including the residents of Chaco Canyon (Akins 1985; Badenhorst and Driver 2009; Dean 2007a, 2007b; Grimstead, Quade, et al. 2016; Lightfoot et al. 2013; Speth 2013). Accordingly, it is no surprise that lagomorphs (rabbits and hares) are by far the most abundant order in the Room 28 assemblage, comprising 43.08% of mammal NISP and 41.04% of total NISP (table 7.2). They are abundant in both the backdirt and subfloor assemblages and likely were a substantial dietary component. Lagomorphs are also the most abundant mammalian order in the Pueblo Bonito mounds assemblage (Badenhorst et al. 2016) and in collections from many other Chacoan sites (figure 7.1; Akins 1985).

ORDER RODENTIA (RODENTS) Rodents are the second most abundant order in the Room 28 assemblage, comprising 37.56% of mammal NISP and 35.79% of total NISP (table 7.2). Rodents identified include kangaroo rats, pocket gophers, prairie dogs, mice, voles, and woodrats. These taxa occur in other Chacoan assemblages (Akins 1985). However, compared to the Pueblo Bonito

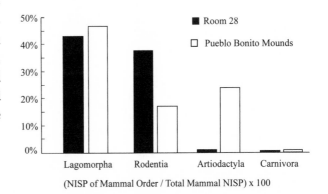

FIGURE 7.1. Relative abundance of mammalian orders for Room 28 and the Pueblo Bonito mounds assemblages.

TABLE 7.2. **Species identified in the Room 28 assemblage**

SCIENTIFIC NAME	COMMON NAME	BACKDIRT	SUBFLOOR	TOTAL	% CLASS TOTAL	% SITE TOTAL
Class Mammalia	**Mammals**					
Family Leporidae	rabbits, hares	442	71	513	13.15	12.53
Sylvilagus spp.	cottontails	628	114	742	19.03	18.13
Lepus spp.	jackrabbit, hare	358	67	425	10.90	10.38
Family Cricetidae	mice, voles	742	5	747	19.15	18.25
Neotoma spp.	woodrat	36	0	36	0.92	0.88
Neotoma albigula	white-throated woodrat	0	1	1	0.03	0.02
Neotoma mexicana	Mexican woodrat	3	0	3	0.08	0.07
Neotoma stephensi	Stephen's woodrat	3	0	3	0.08	0.07
Microtus sp.	vole	1	0	1	0.03	0.02
Peromyscus sp.	mouse	276	5	281	7.21	6.87
Reithrodontomys megalotis	western harvest mouse	2	0	2	0.05	0.05
Family Geomyidae	pocket gophers					
Thomomys sp.	pocket gopher	14	0	14	0.36	0.34
Family Heteromyidae	kangaroo rats, pocket mice	4	0	4	0.10	0.10
Perognathus sp.	pocket mouse	2	0	2	0.05	0.05
Dipodomys sp.	kangaroo rat	3	0	3	0.08	0.07
Family Sciuridae	squirrels, prairie dogs	60	1	61	1.56	1.49
Cynomys sp.	prairie dog	96	2	98	2.51	2.39
Cynomys gunnisoni	Gunnison's prairie dog	10	1	11	0.28	0.27
Small rodent, indeterminate	indeterminate small rodent	95	23	118	3.03	2.88
Large rodent, indeterminate	indeterminate large rodent	62	4	66	1.69	1.61
Rodent, indeterminate	indeterminate rodent	13	1	14	0.36	0.34
Family Antilocapridae	pronghorn antelopes					
Antilocapra americana	pronghorn	2	0	2	0.05	0.05
Family Bovidae	cattle, sheep, goats					
Ovis canadensis	bighorn sheep	8	0	8	0.21	0.20
Family Cervidae	deer, elk					
Cervus elaphus	elk (wapiti)	1	0	1	0.03	0.02
Odocoileus spp.	deer	4	0	4	0.10	0.10
Medium artiodactyl	medium artiodactyl	17	3	20	0.51	0.49
Family Canidae	foxes, wolves, coyotes, dogs	1	0	1	0.03	0.02
Canis spp.	wolf, coyote, dog	3	0	3	0.08	0.07
Canis familiaris	domestic dog	2	0	2	0.05	0.05
Family Felidae	cats	2	0	2	0.05	0.05
Lynx rufus	bobcat	1	0	1	0.03	0.02
Family Mephitidae	skunks, stink badgers					
Spilogale spp.	spotted skunk	1	0	1	0.03	0.02
Medium carnivore	medium carnivore	3	0	3	0.08	0.07
Order Chiroptera	bats	1	0	1	0.03	0.02
small mammal, indeterminate	indeterminate small mammal	554	105	659	16.90	16.10
medium mammal, indeterminate	indeterminate medium mammal	14	1	15	0.38	0.37
large mammal, indeterminate	indeterminate large mammal	29	3	32	0.82	0.78
Class Aves	**Birds**					
Order Passeriformes	perching birds	8	0	8	6.96	0.20
Family Cardinalidae	cardinals, grosbeaks					
Pheucticus melanocephalus	black-headed grosbeak	1	0	1	0.87	0.02
Family Corvidae	jays, crows, magpies	5	0	5	4.35	0.12
Corvus corax	raven	5	0	5	4.35	0.12
Cyanocitta stelleri	Steller's jay	2	0	2	1.74	0.05
Pica hudsonia	magpie	20	0	20	17.39	0.49
Family Fringillidae	grosbeaks, finches	2	0	2	1.74	0.05
Family Icteridae	blackbirds, orioles					
Icterus bullockii	Bullock's oriole	1	0	1	0.87	0.02
Quiscalus mexicanus	great-tailed grackle	1	0	1	0.87	0.02
Family Turdidae	thrushes, robins					
Catharus sp.	nightingale-thrush	1	0	1	0.87	0.02
Family Tyrannidae	New World flycatchers	1	0	1	0.87	0.02
Order Falconiformes	eagles, hawks, falcons	1	0	1	0.87	0.02
Family Accipitridae	eagles, hawks	1	0	1	0.87	0.02
Aquila chrysaetos	golden eagle	2	0	2	1.74	0.05
Haliaeetus leucocephalus	bald eagle	2	0	2	1.74	0.05
Buteo sp.	hawk	2	0	2	1.74	0.05
Buteo jamaicensis	red-tailed hawk	1	0	1	0.87	0.02

SCIENTIFIC NAME	COMMON NAME	BACKDIRT	SUBFLOOR	TOTAL	% CLASS TOTAL	% SITE TOTAL
Family Falconidae	falcons					
Falco sparverius	sparrow hawk	1	0	1	0.87	0.02
Family Phasianidae	turkeys, grouse, pheasants					
Meleagris gallopavo	turkey	6	0	6	5.22	0.15
Family Caprimulgidae	nighhawks, nightjars, etc.					
Phalaenoptilus nuttallii	common poor-will	1	0	1	0.87	0.02
Order Charadriiformes	shorebirds, gulls	2	0	2	1.74	0.05
Family Columbidae	doves, pigeons					
Zenaida macroura	mourning dove	2	0	2	1.74	0.05
Family Gruidae	cranes					
Grus canadensis	sandhill crane	2	0	2	1.74	0.05
Family Picidae	woodpeckers					
Colaptes auratus	common flicker	1	0	1	0.87	0.02
Order Strigiformes	owls	1	0	1	0.87	0.02
Small bird, indeterminate	indeterminate small bird	22	0	22	19.13	0.54
Medium bird, indeterminate	indeterminate medium bird	11	3	14	12.17	0.34
Large bird, indeterminate	indeterminate large bird	4	3	7	6.09	0.17
Class Reptilia	**Turtles, Snakes, Lizards**					
Order Squamata	snakes, lizards	6	0	6	7.89	0.15
Family Colubridae	colubrid snakes	52	3	55	72.37	1.34
Reptile, indeterminate	indeterminate reptile	15	0	15	19.74	0.37
Class Amphibia	**Amphibians**					
Family Bufonidae	true toads					
Bufo sp.	toad	2	0	2	100	0.05
TOTAL		3,677	416	4,093	100	100

mounds fauna, the rank-order abundance of rodents in the Room 28 assemblage is unusually high. Of the four mammalian orders present at Pueblo Bonito mounds, rodents comprise only 17.16% of mammal NISP and are third in rank-order abundance (figure 7.1; Badenhorst et al. 2016). This suggests that some other factor—for instance, the activity of nonhuman foragers—may be responsible for the rodents in the Room 28 assemblage. We explore this hypothesis further in the intrusive rodents section of this chapter.

ORDER ARTIODACTYLA (ARTIODACTYLS) Artiodactyls, including elk (*Cervus elaphus*), deer (*Odocoileus* spp.), pronghorn (*Antilocapra americana*), and bighorn sheep (*Ovis canadensis*), comprise 0.9% of mammal NISP and 0.86% of total NISP in the Room 28 assemblage (table 7.2). Artiodactyls would have been a potentially valuable source of fat and protein to prehispanic people, and archaeologists have a long history of interest in how these resources were obtained and used. Measures of the relative abundance of artiodactyls in archaeofaunal assemblages can be used to make inferences about past usage of these taxa. One such measure is known as the artiodactyl index (Badenhorst 2008; Bayham 1977; Broughton and Bayham 2003; Broughton et al. 2011;

Driver 2002), which compares the proportion of artiodactyl specimens to those from lagomorphs (rabbits and hares) and has been used to evaluate the importance of big game hunting (e.g., Badenhorst and Driver 2009; Broughton 1994, 1999; Byers and Broughton 2004; Byers et al. 2005; Hildebrandt and McGuire 2002). The artiodactyl index is calculated using the following equation:

Artiodactyl NISP/(Artiodactyl NISP + Lagomorph NISP)

Not surprisingly, considering the low number of artiodactyl remains identified in this assemblage, the artiodactyl index value for the Room 28 assemblage is quite low: only 0.02. By comparison, in the Pueblo Bonito mounds assemblage, artiodactyls make up 23.77% of identified mammals and 22.52% of total NISP (Badenhorst et al. 2016). The artiodactyl index value for that assemblage is an order of magnitude higher at 0.40.

The distribution of artiodactyls between rooms and trash mounds at Pueblo Alto provides a useful point of comparison to that at Pueblo Bonito. Like Pueblo Bonito, Pueblo Alto is a Chacoan great house located in the canyon proper, although material from this site may date to a slightly later period than the material recovered from Room 28 (see Windes 1987b:205–70 for the dating of Pueblo Alto). Excavations at Pueblo Alto in the 1970s and 1980s yielded a large faunal assemblage of approximately 50,000 specimens, of which 30,509 were analyzed and published (Akins 1987:445). While the use of only published data constrains the types of comparisons that we can make, some of the Pueblo Alto data are listed by provenience. For example, in Pueblo Alto rooms with a NISP greater than 100, artiodactyls comprise between 1.3% and 16.96% of total NISP, and the artiodactyl index values range from 0.03 to 0.37. In the Pueblo Alto trash mounds, artiodactyls comprise 7.66% of total NISP, and the artiodactyl index value is 0.09—that is, within the range of the artiodactyl index values for the Pueblo Alto rooms (Akins 1987:tables 8.30, 8.34, 8.43, 8.53, 8.60, 8.63, 8.70, 8.92).

These data highlight the dissimilarity in artiodactyl index values between the Room 28 and Pueblo Bonito mounds assemblages, with Room 28 standing out as unusually low and the Pueblo Bonito mounds as unusually high. The dissimilarity does not stem from variation in the abundance of lagomorphs, since in all of these assemblages lagomorphs are the most abundant taxon. Instead, the difference in index values results from variation in the number of artiodactyl remains. In terms of rank order, artiodactyls were the second most abundant mammalian order in the Pueblo Bonito mounds assemblage but are only the third most abundant order from Room 28 (figure 7.1).

One possible explanation for the low relative abundance of artiodactyls in the Room 28 assemblage compared to that in the Pueblo Bonito mounds is differential fragmentation. A number of processes can result in the fragmentation of animal bone. In particular, butchery practices, including the removal of flesh from bones and the extraction of grease and marrow, often fracture the remains (e.g., Binford 1978; Manne et al. 2012). This fact has crucial implications for zooarchaeological analysis because there is an inverse relationship between fragmentation and identifiability. The more fragmentary the remains, the less likely they will be identifiable to taxon; for this reason, differential fragmentation can pose problems in the interpretation of zooarchaeological data (Cannon 2013; Grayson 1984; Lyman 1994, 2008).

In our analysis, highly fragmented and thus unidentifiable artiodactyl remains were classified as either large mammal or unidentified large mammal. Therefore, if differential fragmentation is driving the low abundance of artiodactyls in Room 28, we would expect to see the low number of artiodactyl specimens accompanied by a

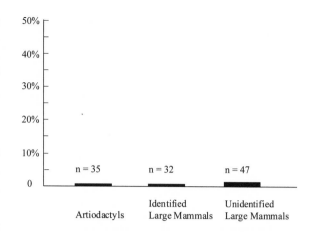

FIGURE 7.2. Relative abundance of large mammal remains in the Room 28 assemblage. Identified specimens are presented as a percentage of the identified assemblage. Unidentified specimens are presented as a percentage of the unidentified assemblage.

large number of specimens classified as large mammal or unidentified large mammal. However, this is not the case. In the Room 28 assemblage, both unidentified and identified large mammals are infrequent; identified large mammal specimens make up only 0.78% of NISP, while unidentified large mammal remains account for 1.41% of all unidentified specimens (figure 7.2). Thus, the low abundance of artiodactyl remains in this assemblage is not related to fragmentation.

This finding leaves two other non–mutually exclusive explanations for the low frequency of artiodactyls in Room 28. First, the previous excavators may have either moved or entirely removed some artiodactyl remains. There is no direct evidence supporting this scenario. However, animal bone was rarely mentioned by late nineteenth-century archaeologists (Jones and Gabe 2015), and there are few records available from Pepper's excavation. The records we do have show that Pepper removed some faunal remains from Pueblo Bonito, and antler fragments from Room 28 in particular (Pepper 1920; artifact catalog, American Museum of Natural History). Unfortunately, museum records also indicate that some of these specimens were later discarded by the museum staff. It is therefore highly unlikely that we will ever conclusively determine whether or not Pepper removed additional faunal remains from Room 28.

However, this explanation (removal by excavators) is only applicable to the backdirt assemblage. Artiodactyl remains are also rare in the subfloor assemblage (artiodactyl index value: 0.01), suggesting that at least one additional factor is at play. One possibility is that large mammal remains were not commonly discarded in this area. Other evidence suggests that Room 28 and several of the rooms around it were special purpose spaces (Ainsworth et al. 2018; Bishop and Fladd 2018; Crown, chapter 2, this volume; Neitzel, ed. 2003; Plog and Heitman 2010). Possibly the lack of artiodactyls in the material recovered from this room reflects depositional practices specific to this area of the site. While there is some spatial variation in both the amount of recovered faunal material and the relative abundance of artiodactyls at Pueblo Alto (Akins 1987), the Room 28 assemblage has a smaller percentage of artiodactyl remains than any of the rooms of Pueblo Alto (with the exception of Room 138, which has a NISP of only 12 and is therefore not comparable to the Pueblo Bonito assemblages; Akins 1987:table 8.52).

In short, while differential deposition likely contributed to differences in artiodactyl representation between Room 28 and the Pueblo Bonito mounds, this explanation in and of itself is insufficient to explain the magnitude of the differences. Some combination of differential deposition and removal by previous excavators may be involved, but the nature of the Room 28 assemblage constrains our ability to draw definitive conclusions as to why it contains so few artiodactyls.

ORDER CARNIVORA (CARNIVORES) Carnivores are among the least abundant orders in the assemblage, making up only 0.34% of mammals and 0.31% of total NISP (table 7.2). A low abundance of carnivore remains is a consistent pattern found in other Chacoan assemblages, including the Pueblo Bonito mounds (figure 7.1; Badenhorst et al. 2016). Felids, including bobcat (*Lynx rufus*), and canids, including domestic dog (*Canis familiaris*), have been identified at numerous other sites in Chaco Canyon (Akins 1985). Spotted skunk (*Spilogale* spp.) has not been previously identified in Chacoan faunal assemblages, but since the spotted skunk is native to New Mexico (Alden and Friederici 1999), its presence is not entirely surprising.

ORDER CHIROPTERA (BATS) Only a single specimen, 0.03% of class Mammalia and 0.02% of total NISP, is from the order Chiroptera (table 7.2). Bats have not been frequently recovered from other sites in the canyon, but the California myotis (*Myotis californicus*) and the pallid bat (*Antrozous pallidus*) have occasionally been identified in Chacoan assemblages. Their presence is likely related to their tendency to roost in abandoned buildings and ruins (Akins 1985).

Class Aves

The overall proportion of avian remains in the Room 28 assemblage is relatively small (2.81% of NISP), yet the number of taxa is surprisingly high (Ainsworth et al. 2018). Although only 72 avian specimens (62.61% of class NISP) were identified to at least the level of order, 9 orders and 13 families are represented in this assemblage (table 7.2). All of these have been found at other sites in Chaco Canyon (Akins 1985) except for order Charadriiformes (shorebirds and gulls).

MELEAGRIS GALLOPAVO (COMMON TURKEY) The proportion of turkey remains in this assemblage is low; turkeys comprise only 5.22% of class Aves and 0.15% of total NISP (table 7.2). Turkey remains were also scarce in the Pueblo Bonito mounds assemblage, making up only 3.5% of class NISP (Badenhorst et al. 2016). This is surprising since turkeys are abundant in avifaunal assemblages from other Chacoan sites (e.g., Grimstead, Reynolds, et al. 2016). At Pueblo Alto, for instance, turkeys make up 67.7% of avian remains (Akins 1987). The low proportion of turkey remains in the Room 28 assemblage does not appear to be the result of differential fragmentation; if it were, we would expect to see a higher proportion of large bird and unidentified avian remains. Instead, large birds comprise only 6.09% of class NISP (0.17% of total NISP) in the Room 28 assemblage, and there are only 12 specimens (0.36% of all unidentified

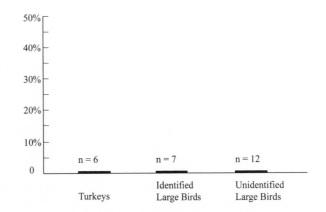

FIGURE 7.3. Relative abundance of large bird remains in the Room 28 assemblage. Identified specimens are presented as a percentage of the identified assemblage. Unidentified specimens are presented as a percentage of the unidentified assemblage.

specimens) of unidentified avian bone in this assemblage (figure 7.3).

As with the artiodactyls, there are at least three viable explanations for the low abundance of turkey remains in the Room 28 fauna. First, the rarity of turkey remains at this site in general may indicate that turkeys were not raised at Pueblo Bonito—or at least not in quantity. The idea that turkeys may have been imported to some Chacoan sites from the northern San Juan Basin is raised by Vivian and colleagues (2006:64); however, it is important to note that they suggest importation for periods later than that of the Room 28 deposits. In addition, Grimstead and colleagues (Grimstead et al. 2015; Grimstead, Quade, et al. 2016) discuss the possible importation of animal remains (though not turkeys) into Chaco Canyon. However, the frequency of turkey eggshell in the Room 28 deposits, along with associated analyses, make this hypothesis less likely (Conrad, this volume). Second, the low frequency of turkeys in the Room 28 assemblage may reflect the relatively early occupation of this room since the turkey-human relationship in the Puebloan Southwest seems to have changed between the Basketmaker/Pueblo I and the mid- to late Pueblo II periods (Badenhorst and Driver 2009; Beacham and Durand 2007). Finally, as with artiodactyl remains, turkey bones may have been deposited elsewhere—either because they had value as a raw material to the inhabitants of Pueblo Bonito or because they were removed by the original excavators. An analysis of excavation notes at the Chaco Research Archive (Conrad, this volume) lends some weight to this idea (see also Bishop and Fladd 2018). While formal evaluation of these three hypotheses is beyond the scope of this chapter, the low abundance of turkey remains in this assemblage does raise questions about the human-turkey relationship at Pueblo Bonito.

Class Reptilia and Class Amphibia

A small number of reptile and amphibian remains were recovered from Room 28. Together, these make up 1.91% of the assemblage (table 7.2). These specimens include snake, lizard, and toad. All these taxa have been found at other sites in Chaco, but they are generally considered to be intrusive rather than subsistence items. Snakes, for example, sometimes occupy the burrows of other animals. The fact that an entire articulated snake skeleton was recovered during the excavation of Room 28 (Crown, chapter 2, this volume) supports the interpretation that the specimens in this assemblage are intrusive as well.

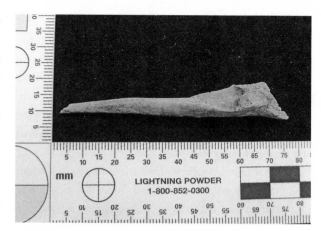

FIGURE 7.4. Bone tool made from a pronghorn ulna.

Bone Tools

Pepper identified "very few" examples of modified bone in Room 28; he recorded two awls purportedly made of deer bone, one unspecified bone implement, and "fifteen fragments of deer antler, cut into lengths averaging 7 cms" (Pepper 1920:126). It is thus not surprising that only one modified bone object was recovered during the 2013 reexcavation (figure 7.4). This specimen, a modified pronghorn ulna, appears to be an awl. It was recovered from the charcoal-rich sediments argued to be the fill from Room 28a (Crown, chapter 2, this volume).

Taphonomy

The term "taphonomy" refers to the study of actions and processes that influence the quantity and condition of artifacts that remain present in the archaeological record (Lyman 1994). These factors have the potential to bias the material record and limit our ability to learn about the past. Understanding the forces that have impacted an assemblage allows us to better comprehend the constraints on our data. At the same time, a better understanding of how an assemblage was formed can provide insight into past human behavior. For these reasons, evaluating the effects of taphonomic processes, including fragmentation and surface modifications, is a key component of zooarchaeological analysis.

EXPOSURE AND TURBATION As highlighted throughout this volume, Room 28 has a complex history involving episodes of exposure, burial, reexposure, turbation, and redeposition. Beginning in 1896, Pepper and Wetherill excavated the room down to floor level. The room then sat open with little backfill from late in

AINSWORTH | FRANKLIN | JONES

the summer of 1896 until the late spring of 1897. At that time the room was backfilled with a mixture of material from Rooms 28a, 53, and 56. The reexcavation of the room in 2013 involved excavation of 2.5 m of fill to return the room to floor level. Additional excavation of in situ deposits lying below the floor yielded material relating to trash disposal and construction activities during the late Basketmaker III/Pueblo I time period.

This history has implications for the composition and condition of the faunal assemblage, particularly material recovered from the backdirt. Actions of the early excavators resulted in the exposure and mechanical mixture of faunal specimens. These processes may have caused the deterioration and further fragmentation of remains (see discussions in, for example, Lyman 1994). Furthermore, both the exposure of the room and its subsequent infilling with an aerated matrix may have, at different times, made the room more attractive to intrusive fauna, particularly burrowing rodents (e.g., Hovezak and Schniebs 2002; Miksicek 1987:232). These issues are discussed in more detail later in this chapter.

FRAGMENTATION As discussed earlier, processing behavior by human agents often results in fragmentation of faunal remains. Other processes, including the actions of living animals, site disturbance (e.g., turbation), and/or archaeological excavation, may further fragment faunal specimens. Differences in the degree of fragmentation, either within or between assemblages, have significant implications for the analysis and interpretation of zooarchaeological data. A slight increase in the fragmentation of a particular taxon will increase its NISP and cause it to appear overrepresented. A more severe increase in fragmentation, relative to other taxa in an assemblage, will reduce identifiability and result in a taxon appearing to be underrepresented. Because of the relationship between NISP and fragmentation, caution must be used in making comparisons between taxa or assemblages that vary in their degree of fragmentation (Lyman 2008).

The degree of fragmentation in an assemblage can be assessed in a number of ways. One commonly used method is the ratio of total number of specimens (NSP) to NISP (Grayson 1991; Wolverton 2002; Wolverton et al. 2008). This proportion increases in a roughly linear fashion with increasing levels of fragmentation (Cannon 2013). Fragmentation can also be presented as a percentage using the following equation (Lyman 2008):

$$(\text{Number of Fragmentary Identified Specimens} / \text{Total NISP}) \times 100 = \% \text{ Fragmentary}$$

We use both metrics to assess fragmentation in the Room 28 assemblage as a whole, in the backdirt assemblage, and in the subfloor assemblage (table 7.3).

As a whole, the Room 28 assemblage has a much lower degree of fragmentation than the assemblage from the mounds (table 7.3). However, the backdirt assemblage is far less fragmentary than the in situ material. This likely reflects differences in depositional processes between the two assemblages. The backdirt assemblage, which derives from at least two different rooms, is composed of a mixture of remains from subsistence activities, ritual deposits (Ainsworth et al. 2018), and remains associated with post-depositional disturbance of the site. In contrast, the subfloor material has a very different depositional history, in large part because it had not been subject to the level of disturbance affecting the backdirt assemblage. The differences in depositional history make it likely that these two assemblages have been differentially impacted by taphonomic processes, including those that would result in fragmentation.

SURFACE MODIFICATIONS Examples of common surface modifications on bone include cut marks, burning, digestive corrosion, gnaw marks, and root etching. These may result from multiple causes, including human

TABLE 7.3. **Fragmentation data for the faunal assemblages of Room 28 and the Pueblo Bonito mounds**

PROVENIENCE	NSP	NISP	NSP/NISP	NISP FRAGMENTARY	% FRAGMENTARY
Room 28 backdirt	6,132	3,677	1.67	1,966	53.47
Room 28 subfloor	1,307	416	3.14	318	76.44
Room 28 Total	**7,439**	**4,093**	**1.82**	**2,284**	**55.80**
Pueblo Bonito mounds	34,720	7,788	4.46	6,310	81.0

TABLE 7.4. **Frequency (%) of five types of surface modification in the faunal assemblages of Room 28 and the Pueblo Bonito mounds**

PROVENIENCE	CUT MARKS	BURNING	ROOT ETCHING	GNAWING	DIGESTIVE CORROSION
Room 28 backdirt	0.84	1.85	1.90	7.59	4.62
Room 28 subfloor	0.72	0.72	0.48	2.16	40.87
Room 28 Total	**0.83**	**1.73**	**1.76**	**7.04**	**8.31**
Pueblo Bonito mounds	0.40	8.03	not recorded	0.80	3.47

actions, the actions of other animals, and landscape-level processes, such as wildfires. The frequency of particular types of surface modifications may be used to make inferences about the depositional and post-depositional history of an assemblage. However, identifying a specific action or agent can be difficult. For example, digestive corrosion can result from either human or animal consumption of bone. Likewise, although cut marks and burning are commonly interpreted as evidence of human consumption, it should be kept in mind that the butchering process may not leave cut marks (Stahl 1996). Similarly, some cooking techniques may produce little or no burned bone (Medina et al. 2012). Burning may also be the result of human activity unrelated to cooking or to nonhuman activity (Clark and Ligouis 2010; Lyman 1994; Stiner 2005). Caution must therefore be used in interpreting the presence or absence of surface modifications.

Cut mark data can be useful for addressing questions about hunting (e.g., Lupo 1994; Shipman and Rose 1983; Stiner et al. 2009), butchery practices (e.g., Binford 1981; Egeland et al. 2014), trade (e.g., Ainsworth 2017), tool technology (e.g., Greenfield 2013; Lewis 2008), and craft production (e.g., Campana 1989; Emery 2008, 2009). In the Chaco system, there has been particular interest in cut marks on avian remains, which may provide evidence of ritual activity and/or craft production (e.g., Akins 1985, 1987; Watson 2012, 2015).

In the Room 28 assemblage, we identified cut marks on 0.83% of identified specimens (table 7.4). A low proportion of cut bone is not uncommon in prehispanic faunal assemblages, including the Pueblo Bonito mounds (Badenhorst et al. 2016). In many cases, this is likely to be at least partially attributable to a tradition of analyzing and reporting modified bone separately from other faunal specimens. In the case of the Room 28 assemblage, the number of cut bones may be underrepresented because we primarily relied on the naked eye to identify such marks. Of the 34 specimens of cut bone identified in this assemblage, 4 are artiodactyls, 18 are lagomorphs, 6 are rodents, 1 is an indeterminate small mammal, 1 is an indeterminate medium mammal, 2 are indeterminate large mammals, and only 2 are pieces of avian bone (one passerine and one indeterminate small bird). Given this small sample size, it is not possible to make inferences based on cut mark data from this assemblage.

Evidence of burning was present on only 1.73% of identified specimens from Room 28. This is a much smaller proportion than what was identified in the mounds assemblage (8.03% of NISP; Badenhorst et al. 2016). This is somewhat surprising, given that Rooms 28 and 28a (a source of some of the backfill) were destroyed by fire around AD 1100. However, not all specimens in this assemblage originate from these rooms: much of the backfill came from Rooms 53 and 56, which did not burn (Crown, chapter 2, this volume). Also, heavily burned bone is both fragile and difficult to identify to taxon (Stiner et al. 1995), and the intense heat created by the fires in Rooms 28 and 28a likely would have created calcined bone. There are 204 specimens of unidentifiable calcined bone in this assemblage (2.74% of the total assemblage and 6.10% of unidentified specimens).

Digestive corrosion is the most common surface modification identified in this assemblage, affecting 8.31% of total NISP. Digestive corrosion is particularly common in the subfloor assemblage (40.87% of NISP). Because corroded bones were not scored for any other form of modification, the low proportions of other types of modification, particularly in the subfloor assemblage, may in part be related to the high frequency of digested bone.

Gnawing, a term that includes both rodent gnawing and puncture marks left by carnivores, is the second most common form of modification overall (7.04% of NISP) and the most common in the backdirt assemblage

(7.59% of NISP). This contrasts sharply with the Pueblo Bonito mounds assemblage, in which evidence of animal gnawing is rare (less than 1% of specimens; Badenhorst et al. 2016).

Diversity

In zooarchaeological analysis, measures of diversity are commonly used to understand past human behavior by examining the range and relative importance of taxa obtained for dietary or other purposes. This information can be used to explore research topics, including changes in diet breadth, resource depression, feasting, and ritual (e.g., Ainsworth et al. 2018; Broughton 1997; Broughton et al. 2011; Grimstead and Bayham 2010; Jones 2004, 2016; Nagaoka 2001; Wolverton et al. 2015). The term "diversity" can refer to a variety of assemblage characteristics (Magurran and McGill 2011); two commonly measured aspects of diversity are richness and evenness (Magurran 2004). For the Room 28 assemblage, we calculated both of these measures at the level of taxonomic order.

RICHNESS Richness is the number of types in a set; in zooarchaeological assemblages, it is measured as the number of identified taxa (NTAXA) (Jones 2016; Lyman 2008). In the Room 28 assemblage, the faunal material from the backdirt is dramatically richer than that from the subfloor (table 7.5). This is partly a reflection of the size of these two assemblages. It has been well demonstrated that as sample size (NISP) increases, so too does NTAXA (Grayson 1984; Grayson and Delpech 1998; Lyman 2008). However, in this case, factors other than sample size are likely also involved. As discussed earlier, there are noteworthy differences in depositional history between the backdirt and subfloor assemblages. These differences are likely responsible, at least in part, for the greater richness of the backdirt assemblage. The subfloor faunal material is more fragmentary than the material from the backdirt, and these specimens also have a much higher rate of digestive corrosion. These factors reduced the identifiability of specimens in the subfloor assemblage, making them less likely to be identifiable to the order level: while 59.96% of the backdirt assemblage was identified to taxon, only 31.83% of the subfloor assemblage was identifiable.

Difference in the original deposits that produced these two assemblages is another probable explanation for the difference in richness. The data presented here

and in Ainsworth and colleagues (2018) indicate that the backdirt assemblage was influenced by human ritual behavior as well as the incidental incorporation of small mammal remains, while the subfloor assemblage may relate largely to human subsistence activity.

EVENNESS Evenness is the degree to which taxa are equally distributed within a set (Jones 2004; Magurran 2004). For example, in an assemblage composed of two taxa, A and B, if taxon A has a NISP of 50 and taxon B also has a NISP of 50, then the assemblage is completely even. If taxon A has a NISP of 90 and taxon B has a NISP of 10, then the assemblage is uneven.

We measured evenness using the reciprocal of Simpson's index (1/D). Simpson's index (D) is a measure of species dominance: as a single taxon becomes more frequent, the value of D increases. Conversely, 1/D is a measure of evenness: the more even the assemblage, the higher the value of 1/D (Magurran 2004). This measure is less affected by sample size variability than other commonly used evenness measures and thus is especially appropriate for archaeological assemblages (Conrad 2015; Jones 2004; Stiner and Munro 2011).

In the Room 28 archaeofauna, the backdirt assemblage is more even than the subfloor assemblage (table 7.5). This reflects the dominance of lagomorph remains in the subfloor assemblage: although lagomorph remains are also common in the backdirt assemblage, their abundance is offset by a similarly high number of rodent remains and by the larger number of taxa.

Discussion

In characterizing the Room 28 faunal assemblage, several themes emerge. First, the unusual abundance of rodents in this assemblage, coupled with a low rate of the surface modifications associated with human processing behavior, supports the excavators' initial impression

TABLE 7.5. **Measures of richness and evenness calculated at the order level for the faunal assemblages from Room 28**

PROVENIENCE	NTAXA (ORDERS)	1/D (ORDERS)
Backdirt	16	2.27
Subfloor	4	1.39

NTAXA = number of identified taxa; 1/D = reciprocal of Simpson's index.

that a substantial portion of this assemblage may be of recent or nonhuman origin.

Second, the avian assemblage stands out as unusual in the high number of taxa represented. The richness of this avifauna relative to its size sets this assemblage apart from other Chacoan sites (see Ainsworth et al. 2018 for a full discussion of the 2013 Room 28 avifaunal assemblage; see also Bishop and Fladd 2018). Analyses indicate that these remains were part of a ritual deposit, likely in the form of wing fans. This material was most likely placed in Room 53 either as storage for future use, as an offering, or as part of a termination ritual.

Finally, the subfloor assemblage is markedly different from the backdirt assemblage. The two assemblages differ in the overall number of taxa (richness), the relative proportions of the taxa they have in common (evenness), and the frequency of surface modifications. These differences stem from the fact that the subfloor fauna, which represent the only in situ animal remains recovered from Room 28, were not subject to the same disturbance as the rest of the assemblage. The subfloor data may therefore be suited to answering questions about prehispanic human subsistence, which cannot be addressed with data from the backdirt assemblage.

INTRUSIVE RODENTS

Our analysis of intrusive specimens (specimens incorporated into the faunal assemblage by some means other than human deposition) in the Room 28 assemblage focuses on burrowing rodents. There are numerous indications that the Room 28 archaeofauna may contain a substantial number of intrusive rodents. During the excavation, archaeologists found complete rodent skeletons in the backdirt, and in Level 10a an entire rodent nest was uncovered (Crown, chapter 2, this volume). During the identification process, we noted a large number of clean and complete skeletal elements, and as discussed earlier, we also observed a high incidence of gnawed bones (table 7.4). Closer examination of the data shows that rodent gnawing, rather than carnivore gnawing, is most prevalent in this assemblage. The frequency of rodent gnawing in the Room 28 assemblage suggests the presence of live rodents subsequent to the assemblage's deposition; rodent incisors grow continually, and these animals must gnaw to wear their teeth down (Lyman 1994).

The Room 28 data contrast with those from the Pueblo

Bonito mounds: gnawing is rare in the mounds assemblage (affecting only 0.8% of NISP), and the majority of identified gnaw marks were the result of carnivore, not rodent, activity (figure 7.5). Finally, the fact that Room 28 was previously excavated and backfilled is of particular significance because intrusive animals in archaeological sites are often represented by fossorial (i.e., burrowing) or semi-fossorial mammals. Common burrowing mammals include small-bodied rodents and insectivores, such as gophers (Geomyidae), moles (Talpidae), prairie dogs (Cynomys sp.), and kangaroo rats (Dipodomyinae) (Bocek 1986). Because backdirt is typically loose and easy to burrow into (Hovezak and Schniebs 2002; Miksicek 1987:232), Room 28 would have been attractive to these species. Additionally, while backdirt in Room 28 and the Pueblo Bonito mounds have similar matrices—loosely deposited sediment with organic remains—the higher rate of rodent activity in Room 28 compared to the Pueblo Bonito mounds could be due to the open nature of the mounds versus the shelter of Room 28. This pattern is not limited to Pueblo Bonito. At Pueblo Alto, for instance, rodent gnawing was more prevalent than expected in floor fill and, more generally, within structures (Akins 1987:509), possibly indicating rodents' strategies for avoiding predation. Since Room 28 was left open for a season, there were multiple opportunities for rodents to burrow into the room. It should be noted, however, that even if optimal burrowing conditions are present, extremely high concentrations of rodent bones are not expected at archaeological sites except in the case of one or more mass mortality events (Stahl 1996; Morlan 1994). A mass mortality event (also referred to as a mass failure or burrowing failure) is most often caused by flooding or burrow collapse and results in the simulta-

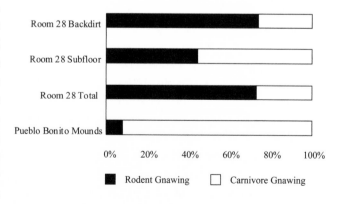

FIGURE 7.5. Relative frequency of rodent versus carnivore gnawing in the Room 28 and Pueblo Bonito mounds assemblages.

TABLE 7.6. **Surface modifications on rodent remains in the backdirt assemblage of Room 28**

NAME	BURNING	CARNIVORE GNAWING	RODENT GNAWING	CUT MARKS	DIGESTIVE CORROSION
Prairie dogs (*Cynomys* sp.)	yes	yes	yes	yes	none
Kangaroo rats (*Dipodomys* sp.)	none	none	none	none	none
Woodrats (*Neotoma* spp.)	yes	none	yes	none	none
Stephen's woodrat (*N. stephensi*)	none	none	none	none	none
Mexican woodrat (*N. mexicana*)	none	none	none	none	none
Squirrels and prairie dogs (Sciuridae)	none	none	none	none	none
Small rodents	yes	none	yes	none	yes
Large rodents	yes	yes	none	yes	yes
Indeterminate rodents	none	none	none	none	none

neous death and deposition of a large number of rodent remains. The concentration of intrusive remains and the presence of articulated skeletons suggest that one or more mass mortality events—which can result from flooding due to heavy rain—may have occurred in Room 28 sometime after Pepper's excavation (see Stahl 1996 for a discussion of mass mortality in micro-vertebrates).

Identifying which taxa are intrusive and which were deposited by prehispanic humans is not simple (e.g., Badenhorst 2008; Bocek 1986; Hockett and Haws 2002; Morlan 1994; Rodríguez-Hidalgo et al. 2013; Shaffer 1992; Shaffer and Neely 1992; Stahl 1996; Stiner and Munro 2011). While some analysts have simply assumed that any burrowing rodents in an assemblage must be intrusive, humans do often eat rodents (Stahl 1996; Szuter 1991). In the American Southwest, ethnographic evidence indicates that small-bodied rodents were part of the diet, and archaeological evidence supports this (e.g., Akins 1985; Schollmeyer and Driver 2013; Szuter 1991).

A number of techniques have been used to infer the quantity of intrusive remains in an archaeological assemblage (Andrews 1990a, 1990b; Andrews and Evans 1983; Bocek 1986; Fisher 1995; Lyman 1994; Szuter 1991). Here, we use four lines of evidence to identify which rodents were intrusive and which may reflect human subsistence activity: (1) frequency of surface modifications suggesting human consumption or butchery (cut marks, digestive corrosion, and burning); (2) frequency of cranial elements; (3) frequency of complete skeletal elements; and (4) distribution by depth. While weathering and root etching have been used to identify intrusive remains in other assemblages, the complex history of exposure and deposition in Room 28 complicates the use of these measures since older intrusive remains may show these surface modifications while more recent in-

trusives may not. We therefore did not use weathering or root etching to identify intrusive specimens.

We treat mice (family Cricetidae) differently than other rodent taxa since the variation in frequency of these extremely small specimens likely primarily reflects changes in the screening protocol during excavation (Crown, chapter 2, this volume). In addition, we limit our analysis to the remains recovered from discrete excavated levels; specimens recovered from floor sweepings or within postholes were excluded from analysis.

Surface Modification

The absence of bone surface modifications resulting from human activity—such as cut marks and burning—can suggest the presence of intrusive specimens. The majority of the rodent specimens in the Room 28 assemblage (with mice, $N = 1{,}220$ or 91.61%; without mice, $N = 362$ or 89.16%) show no traces of cut marks or digestive corrosion (table 7.6). The few rodents that do show evidence of modification are primarily larger taxa documented elsewhere as Ancestral Puebloan subsistence items, such as prairie dogs (*Cynomys* sp.) and woodrats (*Neotoma* spp.).

Interpretation of burnt bone (or lack thereof) is more contextually dependent. Burning on archaeological bone can result from human activities, such as cooking, but since Rooms 28 and 28a were burned upon abandonment, much of the burnt bone in the Room 28 assemblage likely reflects this post-depositional fire. Intrusive rodents would have entered the assemblage after the fire, and so these specimens should not be burned. Only 4.19% ($n = 17$ of 406) of the rodents show traces of burning; when mice are included, this decreases to 1.34% ($n = 18$ of 1,347). This suggests two conclusions: first, the mice in the Room 28 archaeofauna are, by and large, intrusive; and second, the majority of the rodents derive from backfill from the excavations of Rooms 53 and 56 (which did not burn) rather than backfill from Room 28a.

Cranial Element Abundance

Intrusive remains are often characterized by a high frequency of cranial elements compared to axial and appendicular elements (Bocek 1986; Thomas 1971b). We therefore calculated the relative abundance of cranial elements in the Room 28 rodent assemblage. Since teeth indicate the presence of crania, we included them in this analysis.

Cranial elements comprise 24.52% (N = 97) of total rodent element NISP (N = 334 or 24.45% when mice are excluded). This is not significantly different than the frequency of crania among non-rodent mammals (19%, or N = 300; χ^2 = 0.961, p = 0.327).

Our analysis of cranial elements thus does not suggest the presence of intrusive remains in the Room 28 assemblage. However, the skeletal remains of rodents are less robust than those of larger mammals. These specimens are therefore more likely to be damaged during excavation and, subsequently, more likely to be unidentifiable during analysis. The fragility of rodent crania could account for the limited number of cranial elements recovered during the reexcavation of Room 28. The lack of cranial elements in the Room 28 assemblage is not conclusive in and of itself; we thus turn to other potential signs of intrusiveness.

Completeness

As mentioned earlier, the Room 28 assemblage contains numerous complete and clean rodent skeletal elements. This is in contrast to most zooarchaeological assemblages, in which fragmented remains are common, whether due to human processing or post-depositional processes, such as trampling (Cannon 2013; Lyman 2008; Otarola-Castillo 2010; Wolverton 2002). While small fauna used in human subsistence are often prepared whole and so appear as complete elements, in archaeofaunal assemblages the frequency of complete elements should still be higher in assemblages containing a large number of intrusive specimens than in those created by human subsistence activities (Szuter 1991).

Among the non-rodent mammals in the Room 28 assemblage, only 34.78% (N = 551) of elements are complete. For rodents, however, 64.37% (N = 867) or, when mice are excluded, 52.53% (N = 212) of all rodent elements are complete. The Room 28 rodents thus do contain a relatively high frequency of complete skeletal elements, as would be predicted in the case of a faunal assemblage containing a large proportion of intrusive specimens. However, the decrease when mice (Cricetidae) are excluded suggests there is variability in skeletal completeness among rodent taxa. A chi-square analysis supports this hypothesis (χ^2 = 17.10, p = 0.00). Pocket gophers (Geomyidae) and squirrels and prairie dogs (Sciuridae) both have more incomplete (and fewer complete) elements than expected when compared to other rodents, while mice (Cricetidae) have more complete (and fewer incomplete) elements than expected.

These results suggest that most of the mice in the Room 28 assemblage are intrusive. Conversely, pocket gophers, squirrels, and prairie dogs may, in at least some cases, have been part of the diet at Pueblo Bonito. Squirrels and prairie dogs are known to have been part of the diet in the Ancestral Puebloan world (Akins 1985; Badenhorst 2008; Vivian et al. 2006). Although pocket gophers are fossorial animals and are often thought to be intrusive for this reason, they also may (like prairie dogs) be taken during garden hunting (Shaffer 1992). The completeness analysis suggests that this may have been the case for the remains recovered from Room 28.

Abundance by Depth

Because rodents burrow to specific depths, some researchers use abundance by depth to identify how different taxa were introduced into an assemblage. In general, the first 50–60 cm below ground surface (sometimes known as the "rodent zone") often contains the greatest concentration of recent intrusive mammal specimens (Bocek 1986). However, intrusive specimens can be found below this depth. Not only do different taxa have different maximum burrowing ranges (some sciurids, for instance, burrow as deep as 2 m; see Van Vuren and Ordeñana 2012), but as sediment accumulates in a site, the depth of the rodent zone will change.

The first 60 cm of the Room 28 assemblage contained few rodents, suggesting that recent rodent activity was relatively limited. Instead, rodents from the families Geomyidae, Heteromyidae (kangaroo rats, kangaroo mice, and pocket mice), and Sciuridae were concentrated in the 200–240 cm range (figure 7.6). This shared concentration, just above the room floor, suggests that this depth range may have been the rodent zone in years past. The floor itself would have been densely packed

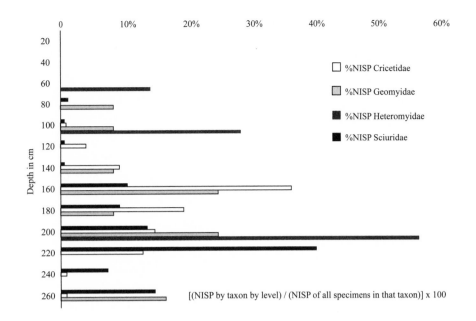

FIGURE 7.6. Frequency of rodent orders by depth in the Room 28 assemblage.

[(NISP by taxon by level) / (NISP of all specimens in that taxon)] x 100

□ %NISP Cricetidae
▨ %NISP Geomyidae
■ %NISP Heteromyidae
■ %NISP Sciuridae

Depth in cm

and may have acted as a barrier to deeper burrowing. Alternatively, this pattern may indicate that much of the rodent activity (and rodent death) dates to the period in 1896–1897 when the room lay open. Whichever of these scenarios is correct, the fact that heteromyids occur primarily in this area of heavy rodent disturbance but not in the subfloor suggests that members of the taxon Heteromyidae were likely not subsistence items. Geomyids and sciurids, conversely, are found in the subfloor. While most of the specimens found between 200 cm and 240 cm below the surface probably are intrusive, other geomyid and sciurid specimens in the Room 28 assemblage may reflect human subsistence practices.

Mice show a different and interesting depth distribution, with a unimodal curve that begins at 100 cm and peaks at 160 cm (Level 9). This likely reflects the change in screening protocol; it is at approximately 120 cm that excavators began screening with sixteenth-inch mesh.

Summary

By using four discrete lines of evidence, we are able to reach several conclusions about intrusive rodents in this zooarchaeological assemblage. Most of the mice and the heteromyids are likely intrusive. These taxa show limited bone surface modification and are largely represented by complete skeletal elements; in addition, their distribution by depth seems to reflect their burrowing practice and/or changes in excavation methodology.

On the other hand, at least some of the pocket gophers seem to have been part of the diet. Our analysis

of skeletal element completeness statistically demonstrates that there are more incomplete pocket gopher skeletal elements than complete ones; in addition, cut marks are present on at least one pocket gopher specimen. Some of the prairie dog and squirrel remains also likely reflect prehispanic human subsistence activity. However, it is almost certain that not all pocket gophers, prairie dogs, and squirrels in the Room 28 backdirt assemblage were subsistence items; the concentration of these taxa in the 200–240 cm depth range suggests that some specimens were intrusive.

Overall, while the rodent assemblage in Room 28 likely represents a palimpsest of different activities, our analysis supports the hypothesis that a substantial portion of the rodent remains is intrusive.

THE SUBFLOOR ASSEMBLAGE: RABBITS AND PREHISPANIC SUBSISTENCE

Because the backdirt assemblage contains a high proportion of intrusive fauna as well as specimens likely initially deposited in other rooms, the subfloor assemblage—the fauna from the levels beneath Pepper and Wetherill's excavation—is the most likely part of the Room 28 archaeofauna to provide information about prehispanic diet. This assemblage differs markedly from that recovered from the backdirt layers (figure 7.7). The majority of specimens are mammals (98.61%) with minimal representation of birds (N = 7) and reptiles (N = 3).

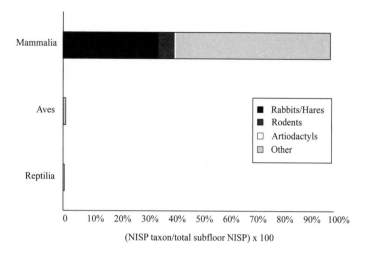

FIGURE 7.7. Taxonomic composition of the Room 28 subfloor assemblage.

Only nine taxa were identified (table 7.2). Of those specimens that could be assigned to a taxon lower than class (N = 301), lagomorphs—rabbits, including both cottontails (*Sylvilagus* spp.) and hares (*Lepus* spp.)—are by far the most abundant (N = 252, or 83.72%).

Our analysis of the subfloor assemblage therefore focuses on the lagomorphs, which likely represent trash deposited during the occupation of Room 28 (see Crown, chapter 2, this volume). We address two questions: (1) Were the subfloor lagomorphs deposited by humans or by some other agent (such as domestic dogs or raptors); and (2) how were these lagomorphs used?

Human versus Nonhuman Carnivore Collectors

Like other small mammals, rabbits can be introduced into archaeological sites by nonhuman predators (Hockett 1991, 1995, 1999). Lagomorph assemblages generated in such a way typically have a distinct signature similar to that of intrusive rodents: they contain many immature specimens; they do not bear traces of anthropogenic surface modification (such as cut marks or burning); they are complete; and they have surfaces marked by nonhuman carnivores.

The most common zooarchaeological method of assessing the presence of juveniles is analysis of epiphyseal fusion (Ruscillo 2014). Because the epiphyseal ends of elements fuse to the adjoining diaphysis in regular, predictable stages that correlate with age, this method can be used to identify immature animals in an assemblage. In the Room 28 subfloor assemblage, among those specimens for which epiphyseal fusion can be assessed,

the majority (N = 102, or 82.93%) are fully fused, suggesting that the Room 28 rabbits were largely adult. Few specimens show traces of burning (n = 2) or cut marks (n = 2). Both the focus on adults and the lack of obvious anthropogenic surface modifications are typical of rabbit assemblages created by human activity in the Chaco area (Akins 1985; Badenhorst 2008; Gillespie 1993) and in other times and places (e.g., Hockett 1995).

While lagomorph assemblages are usually not fragmented as intensely as artiodactyl ones, humans often process rabbits in a way that produces a distinct breakage pattern. Rabbit assemblages produced by human consumption typically have a significant percentage of long bones from which the ends have been removed to get at marrow. The resulting long bone diaphyses are sometimes called "rabbit tubes" and are a widely used marker of human-generated rabbit assemblages (e.g., Hockett and Bicho 2000; Jones 2006). The subfloor lagomorph assemblage from Room 28 does indeed contain many rabbit tubes (N = 35, or 63.64% of all lagomorph long bones), suggesting these specimens were consumed by humans.

The argument that this assemblage was created by humans is further supported by the lack of surface modification characteristic of nonhuman predators. Puncture marks and gnawing are typical by-products of nonhuman carnivore consumption; only three specimens (less than 1%) in the subfloor rabbit assemblage contain traces of nonhuman carnivores. As discussed earlier in this chapter, there is a high degree of digestive corrosion on many specimens; however, such corrosion can result from human consumption, and in this situation that appears to be the case.

The accumulated evidence thus suggests that the Room 28 subfloor lagomorph assemblage accumulated through human, rather than nonhuman carnivore, activity. The question then becomes, what can these rabbits tell us about prehispanic human subsistence at Pueblo Bonito during the late Basketmaker III/Pueblo I time period represented by the subfloor assemblage?

Rabbits and Subsistence Patterns in Room 28

While in some contexts the relative abundance of cottontails and jackrabbits can provide information about local environments (see Driver and Woiderski 2008), in the case of the Room 28 assemblage, cottontails and jackrabbits are both significantly represented (63.69% cottontails and 36.30% jackrabbits; table 7.2). This dis-

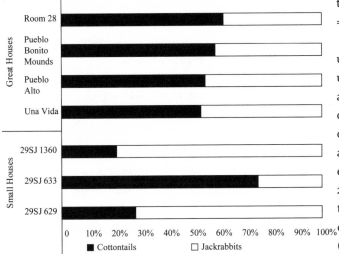

FIGURE 7.8. Relative abundance of cottontails and jackrabbits at Chacoan great house and small house sites.

TABLE 7.7. **Skeletal elements (NISP) of the subfloor lagomorphs of Room 28**

ELEMENT	COTTONTAILS (Sylvilagus spp.)	JACKRABBITS (Lepus spp.)	INDETERMINATE LEPORIDS
Cranial			
mandibles	7	6	10
maxillae	2	0	0
other	9	3	4
Axial			
scapulae	11	2	0
vertebrae	9	5	16
innominates	13	12	0
sacra	1	0	0
Appendicular			
humeri	4	4	2
radii	11	1	0
ulnae	2	2	0
femora	8	8	1
tibiae	11	9	2
tarsals	8	3	1
metatarsals	2	1	0
metapodials	3	4	7

tribution is similar to that of the lagomorphs from the Pueblo Bonito mounds assemblage (cottontails: N = 288, or 59%; jackrabbits: N = 199, or 41.00%; Badenhorst et al. 2016) and to that of Chacoan great house assemblages of similar age (figure 7.8; see also Akins 1985). This suggests that great house inhabitants exploited lagomorphs in similar ways regardless of specific location (Chacoan small house leporid assemblages appear to be more variable; see Akins 1985; Gillespie 1993). A chi-square test for independence supports this hypothesis, showing no statistically significant difference in lagomorph

taxonomic distribution for great house assemblages (χ^2 = 7.44, p = 0.06).

The distribution of skeletal elements is one way to understand past butchery and consumption patterns using zooarchaeological assemblages. Relative skeletal abundance studies have been used in the identification of prey transport techniques (Faith and Gordon 2007), on-site animal processing for hides and tallow (Conrad et al. 2015; Spielmann et al. 2009), ethnicity-specific butchery practices (Craw 2012), ritual activity (Ainsworth et al. 2018), and food preparation techniques (Bovy 2012). In the Room 28 subfloor assemblage, the distribution of lagomorph skeletal elements suggests that axial elements (those elements in the trunk of the body) are lower in frequency than might be expected, while cranial fragments are higher (table 7.7). In a complete rabbit skeleton, the ratio of axial to appendicular to cranial elements is 64:43:3 (excluding phalanges and ribs, which were not included in these analyses). A chi-square goodness-of-fit test confirms that axial elements are underrepresented in the Room 28 assemblage, while cranial elements are overrepresented (χ^2 = 176.82, p = 0.00). The overrepresentation of cranial elements likely is a result of differential fragmentation, but even when cranial elements are excluded from the analysis, axial elements appear to be less common than expected based on a complete lagomorph skeleton (χ^2 = 7.34, p = 0.01). In addition, the distribution of lagomorph elements differs significantly from that of the rodents in the subfloor assemblage (χ^2 = 22.80, p = 0.00), suggesting that this bias reflects some activity specific to the rabbit assemblage.

Underrepresentation of axial and overrepresentation of appendicular elements is present in the Pueblo Bonito mounds rabbits (Badenhorst et al. 2016) and has been identified in other prehispanic assemblages from what is now the US West as well (see, for example, Muir and Driver 2003; Schmidt 1999; Ugan 2010). Analysts typically invoke two (non–mutually exclusive) explanations for this phenomenon. First, Numic-speaking peoples of southern Utah and Colorado historically ground rabbit bones, particularly vertebrae and other axial portions, into a paste, which was then added to stews and mushes (Stewart 1942:253; Ugan 2010). While this type of processing has been more widely reported among hunter-gatherers than agriculturalists, it is possible that Ancestral Puebloans also used lagomorph axial skeletal elements as food, particularly given the reported use of rodent bones as a subsistence item (albeit processed

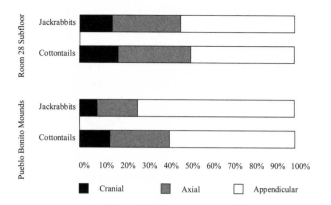

FIGURE 7.9. Relative proportion of cranial, axial, and appendicular elements for jackrabbits and cottontails from the Room 28 subfloor and the Pueblo Bonito mounds assemblages.

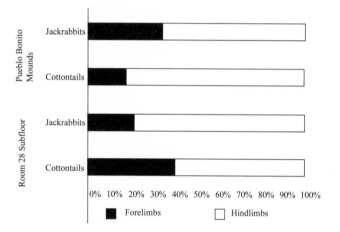

FIGURE 7.10. Relative proportion of forelimbs and hindlimbs for jackrabbits and cottontails from the Room 28 subfloor and the Pueblo Bonito mounds assemblages.

in a different manner; Cushing 1920; Szuter 1991). Alternatively, the preponderance of limb elements may reflect a preference for those cuts of meat—and possibly especially the marrow contained in limb bones (e.g., Hockett and Bicho 2000).

Although the overrepresentation of cranial elements and underrepresentation of axial elements is present among both cottontails and jackrabbits in the Room 28 fauna, there are differences in relative skeletal abundance between these two taxa (table 7.7). Compared to the cottontails from Room 28 and both the jackrabbits and cottontails from the Pueblo Bonito mounds, the Room 28 jackrabbits have a significantly different distribution of appendicular, axial, and cranial elements (χ^2 = 16.09, p = 0.01), with more axial elements represented

than for jackrabbits in other assemblages (figure 7.9). This suggests the Room 28 jackrabbits may have been butchered and/or consumed differently than the other Pueblo Bonito lagomorphs.

Unusual relative skeletal abundances in jackrabbit assemblages may result from targeted procurement strategies. In the ethnohistoric West, jackrabbits were sometimes the targets of a particular hunting strategy known as a "rabbit drive" (Driver and Woiderski 2008; Schollmeyer and Driver 2013; Shaffer and Gardiner 1995). In one prehispanic southwestern archaeofaunal assemblage, high frequencies of jackrabbit hindlimb elements (among other patterns) were interpreted as evidence of a rabbit drive (Schmidt 1999). The Room 28 jackrabbits do contain a higher frequency of hindlimb elements than forelimb elements (figure 7.10), and this frequency is higher than would be expected by chance (χ^2 = 4.64, p = 0.03). The Room 28 cottontails do not show this pattern, with forelimbs and hindlimbs instead being more or less equally represented (χ^2 = 0.16, p = 0.69). Although these results are suggestive, unfortunately the small size of the jackrabbit assemblage from the Room 28 subfloor limits our ability to test the possibility that it resulted from rabbit drives or similar targeted hunting events.

Even if we cannot determine the reason, however, these data do show that the jackrabbits and cottontails in the Room 28 assemblage were consumed differently. The relatively even distribution of forelimbs and hindlimbs among cottontails suggests that they were prepared and consumed whole. Jackrabbit consumption, on the other hand, seems to have focused on the meaty hindlimbs.

Summary

The small size of the Room 28 subfloor assemblage means that definitive conclusions about subsistence practices are difficult to make. We can, however, identify similarities to and differences from other Chacoan assemblages. As in other great house assemblages (Akins 1985), the Room 28 lagomorphs are roughly evenly split between cottontails and jackrabbits, suggesting a consistent exploitation strategy across great houses. The overall distribution of skeletal elements in the lagomorph remains from Room 28 is similar to that found at the Pueblo Bonito mounds, with axial or trunk elements underrepresented. The distribution of forelimbs and hindlimbs, however, indicates different preparation and consumption patterns for the Room 28 cottontails and jackrabbits.

CONCLUSIONS

The Room 28 faunal collection is a large assemblage with a complex formation history. The assemblage incorporates a mixture of specimens from human subsistence activities and ritual, as well as specimens introduced through non-anthropogenic actions. Our analysis of this material has led to several meaningful conclusions. First, the high proportion of lagomorph remains in the backdirt assemblage suggests that rabbits may have been an important dietary staple, while the low proportion of both artiodactyl and turkey remains in the Room 28 assemblage raises interesting questions suitable for future investigations of subsistence practices at Pueblo Bonito. The avian assemblage from the Room 28 backdirt is remarkable for its level of diversity, given its small size. Additional analysis of this portion of the assemblage by Ainsworth and colleagues (2018) indicated that this relates to the high level of ritual activity associated with this area of Pueblo Bonito (i.e., the northern burial group; Bishop and Fladd 2018; Neitzel, ed. 2003; Plog and Heitman 2010).

Our analysis of the rodent remains from the backdirt assemblage indicates a high proportion of intrusive remains. Such an abundance of intrusive specimens is unusual, even when optimal burrowing conditions are present (Morlan 1994). Interestingly, while the majority of the rodents in this assemblage may be intrusive, our results indicate that the prehispanic inhabitants of Pueblo Bonito also incorporated rodents into their diet. The distinction between subsistence items and later intrusions did not strictly follow taxonomic lines, emphasizing the need for the more nuanced analytical approach used here, incorporating multiple lines of evidence, in order to distinguish intrusive remains.

Finally, findings from our analysis of the subfloor material speak to subsistence practices during the Basketmaker III/Pueblo I period at Pueblo Bonito. The subfloor assemblage is also dominated by rabbit remains, and our analysis confirms that this portion of the assemblage accumulated through human, rather than nonhuman carnivore, activity. Patterns in the subfloor lagomorph assemblage indicate consistent exploitation across great house assemblages and suggest that different approaches were used for jackrabbits versus cottontails.

The Room 28 faunal assemblage is an example of how an archaeofauna resulting from a complex interaction of depositional agents and excavation histories can provide useful information.

ACKNOWLEDGMENTS

We thank Cyler Conrad, Joseph Cook, Robin Cordero, Jon Dunnum, Andrew B. Johnson, Christopher C. Witt, the Museum of Southwestern Biology, and the 2013 UNM zooarchaeology class for their analytical assistance; two anonymous reviewers for their thoughtful comments; and Patricia Crown for the opportunity to work on this assemblage, for helpful suggestions on this chapter, and above all, for her unflagging support.

FIGURE 8.1. Map of select sites in Chaco Canyon. Village sites are designated by circles and great houses are designated by triangles. Adapted from Mathien 2005:5.

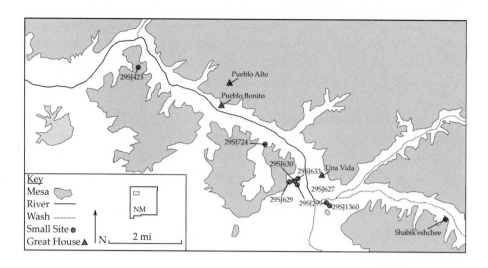

TABLE 8.1. **Turkey bone and eggshell remains from sites in Chaco Canyon**

SITE	DATE (AD)	PERIOD	BONE NISP	% AVES	EGG NISP	EGG MASS (grams)	EGGSHELL SCREEN SIZE (inches)
Una Vida	950–1050	PII–PIII	16	0.6			
	1050–1220	PII–PIII	1	0.2			
Pueblo Alto	920–1020	PII–PIII	3	0.1	26	0.31	.25/.125/.0625
	1020–1120	PII–PIII	68	0.4	1,408	49.065	
	1120–1220	PII–PIII	878	9.1	508	16.87	
Shabik'eshchee Village	600–750	BMIII–PI	1	0.3			
29SJ299	600–700	BMIII	0	0			
	780–820	PI	8	7.2			
	920–1020	PII–PIII	2	5			
29SJ627	1000–1050	PII–PIII	65	3.2	780	9.691	"fine screen"
	1050–1080	PII–PIII	15	3			
	1130–1200	PII–PIII	15	1.3			
29SJ628	700–820	BMIII–PI	24	0.5			
29SJ629	850–950	PII–PIII	13	0.9	1,470	33.21	no screening
	975–1040	PII–PIII	8	1.5			
	1100–1150	PII–PIII	2	0.7			
29SJ633	1020–1120	PIII	3	0.9			
	1220–1250	PIII	681	20			
29SJ721	650–850	BMIII–PI	0	0	1[a]	2.73	no screening
29SJ724	780–820	PI	1	0.2	92	2.07	no screening
29SJ1360	920–1020	PII	18	2.5	1,382	30.8	no screening
Pueblo Bonito mounds	~900–1140	PI–PIII	13	0.3	15[b]	unknown	.25/.125/.0625
Pueblo Bonito Room 28	~900–1140	PI–PIII	6	5.2	99[c]	1.63	.25/.125/.0625

Sources: Dates, turkey bone number of identified specimens (NISP), and percentage of total bird specimens (% Aves) for non-Bonito sites (29SJ628, 29SJ633) are from Akins 1985:370. Eggshell NISP, mass, and screening data from Pueblo Alto are from Windes 1987c; 29SJ627, 29SJ721, and 29SJ724 data are from Windes 1977; 29SJ629 data are from Windes 1993; 29SJ1360 data are from McKenna 1984; the Pueblo Bonito trash mounds data are from Badenhorst et al. 2016; the Room 28 turkey bone data are from Ainsworth et al., this volume, and the eggshell data are from this study.

BMIII = Basketmaker III; PI = Pueblo I; PII = Pueblo II; PIII = Pueblo III.

[a] 15 eggshell fragments came from a single turkey egg recovered in situ (Windes 1977).

[b] Eggshell specimens from the trash mounds were identified as "medium birds" (Badenhorst et al. 2016).

[c] Only 98 of these eggshells are identified as turkey.

CYLER CONRAD

CHAPTER EIGHT

Eggshells and Gastroliths from Room 28
Turkey Husbandry at Pueblo Bonito

Ethnographic and archaeological data indicate that birds were an important part of the prehispanic Pueblo world in what is now the US Southwest. There is recorded use of birds, feathers, eggs, and bird imagery in Puebloan ritual and ceremony (Beidleman 1956; Durand and Durand 2008; Hargrave 1965; Lang and Harris 1984; Potter 1997; Reed 1951; Senior and Pierce 1989), and birds play a large role in the oral traditions, stories, and myths of Puebloan peoples (Gunn 1917; Miller 1898; Tyler 1991). The physical remains of birds in burial or food waste contexts also provide evidence of their use and role in the Southwest (Akins 1985; Badenhorst and Driver 2009; Beacham and Durand 2007; Driver 2002; Durand and Durand 2008; Lipe et al. 2016; Muir and Driver 2002; Munro 2011; Windes 1987c). In this chapter, I examine the avian eggshell assemblage and gastroliths from Room 28 at Pueblo Bonito for evidence of human-avian interaction during Pueblo II–III in Chaco Canyon (figure 8.1).

BIRDS IN PREHISPANIC PUEBLO BONITO

Avifauna, feathers, imagery, ornaments, and effigies confirm that birds were a significant component of prehispanic life at Pueblo Bonito, and this is particularly true for the northern burial cluster rooms (Bishop and Fladd 2018). For example, archaeologists recovered from Room 32 a piece of hematite that was carved into the shape of a bird with inlaid turquoise bands and a shell tail (Pepper 1920:134–35). Ceremonial sticks cached in Room 32 originally had feathers tied to their ends (Pepper 1920:144). In the adjacent Room 33, excavations recovered bird-shaped turquoise pendants and several decorated flageolets (flutes), some made of bird long bones (Pepper 1909, 1920:164). Room 33 also

produced four shell pendants shaped into birds (Pepper 1920:173–74). To the northeast in Room 35, turkey quills were recovered alongside ceremonial sticks (Pepper 1920:179). And in Room 38, directly east of Room 35, excavations revealed a chalcedony "beak-like object" and the remains of 14 scarlet macaws (*Ara macao*)—at least 2 intentionally buried—and 4 Steller's jays (*Cyanocitta stelleri*). These bird-shaped artifacts and feather specimens recovered in the vicinity of Room 28 at Pueblo Bonito help emphasize the importance of birds at this site.

Given these data, the avian eggshells and gullet stones from the 2013 University of New Mexico excavations of Room 28 provide an opportunity to further examine human-bird interactions in Chaco Canyon. Presently, turkey (*Meleagris gallopavo*) specimens dominate the eggshell record from Pueblo Bonito and additional sites in Chaco (table 8.1; Badenhorst et al. 2016; Windes 1977, 1987c). However, turkey bone remains are relatively rare (Ainsworth et al., this volume; Ainsworth et al. 2018; Akins 1985, 1987; Badenhorst et al. 2016). By focusing on the Room 28 eggshells and gullet stones, it is thus possible to investigate how birds, including potentially turkeys, were husbanded and exploited during the Pueblo II–III period at Pueblo Bonito.

EGGSHELLS

Archaeological deposits in Room 28 are composed of backfill (Levels 1–12) and undisturbed subfloor contexts (Levels 13 and lower; Crown, chapter 2, this volume). The majority of turkey eggshells from Room 28 were recovered from backfill deposits (table 8.2). As excavation and contextual records demonstrate, this room was backfilled using deposits from nearby rooms, probably Room 28a to the east and Rooms 53 and 56 to the north, and thus the eggshells likely do relate to prehispanic

TABLE 8.2. Number of identified eggshell and gastrolith specimens by level and context in Room 28, Pueblo Bonito

PROVENIENCE	M. gallopavo	cf. M. gallopavo	Unknown taxon	Gastroliths
Level 6	2			4
Level 7	9			2
Level 7a	4			2
Level 8	13			10
Level 8a	9			10
Level 9a	21	3	1	5
Level 10a	5			3
Level 11	8			5
Level 12	2			7
Level 13	11			18
Level 14				17
Level 15	4			
Level 16				1
Posthole 2				1
Posthole 5	1			
Posthole 24				3
2 mm float, FS 511, subfloor surface		4		
4 mm float, FS 511, subfloor surface		2		
Ashpit				3
Ashpit A				2
East wall cleaning				1
Southeast door cleaning				3
Southeast quadrant				3
Slit trench along north wall				1
Subfloor surface				5
Thermal feature				1
West wall cleaning				4

FIGURE 8.2. (*a*) A turkey inner eggshell (PBE002) and (*b*) a non-turkey inner eggshell (PBE067) from Room 28. Photographs by Cyler Conrad.

human activity (Crown, chapter 2, this volume; see also Pepper 1920). While it is impossible to know the exact routing of eggshell into the Room 28 backfill deposits (see Ainsworth et al., this volume), it is probable that all excavated turkey eggshells from Room 28 (including backfill and subfloor) were deposited within the immediate vicinity in this area of Pueblo Bonito.

Methods of Analysis

I cataloged and analyzed all avian eggshells from the Room 28 excavations at Pueblo Bonito, Chaco Canyon, in the Department of Anthropology, University of New Mexico, during July 2016. My analysis followed standard protocols by examining the eggshells under a high-powered microscope, weighing the eggshells to the nearest 0.01 gram on a Carolina digital scale (SLB302), assessing pigmentation using a Munsell chart, and measuring eggshell thickness to the nearest 0.01 mm using Mitutoyo Absolute Digimatic calipers. My taxonomic identification followed standard comparative morphological guides (Beacham 2006; Beacham and Durand 2007; Di Peso et al. 1974; Lamzik 2013; Reed 1965; Sidell 1993a, 1993b).

Results

There are a total of 99 eggshell fragments in the Room 28 assemblage (table 8.2). Of these, 77 derive from backfill levels, 21 from subfloor deposits, and 1 from a distinct posthole context at the subfloor level (see Crown, chapter 2, this volume). Only 3 eggshell specimens are burnt (charred), all from Level 9a.

Of the 99 eggshells, the majority (NISP [number of identified specimens] = 98) are turkey. The turkey eggshells vary in thickness (0.27–0.59 mm) and mass (0.01–0.11 grams) throughout Room 28. A single eggshell from Level 9a (PBE067) is unidentifiable to taxon. This specimen, while falling within the thickness range for turkey, has distinct variation in pigmentation and mammillary cone morphology (figure 8.2). I analyzed this specimen against domestic chicken (*Gallus gallus domesticus*) eggshell since George Pepper and Richard Wetherill introduced historical refuse, including domesticated animal remains, into the Room 28 backfill during their late nineteenth-century excavations (Ainsworth et al., this volume; Brewer, this volume; Crown, chapter 2, this volume). The results indicate that this eggshell is not chicken. In comparison to turkey, eggshell specimen PBE067 has mammillary cones that are smaller in diameter and more widely dispersed throughout the inner shell matrix.

Turkey eggshells from Room 28 match known Munsell color descriptions for this species: typically pale brown and yellow (Windes 1977, 1987c). A turkey shell from Level 6 (PBE002) has an outer surface value of 10YR-8/4 (very pale brown) and an inner surface value of 10YR-7/6 (yellow). In contrast, the unidentified eggshell from Level 9a (PBE067) has an outer surface value of 10YR-6/2 (light brownish gray) and an inner surface value of 10YR-4/3 (dark brown).

To further assess taxonomic identification, I compared the Room 28 turkey eggshell thickness values against measurements from Tijeras Pueblo (LA 581; Fletcher and Merkt 2016) and Arroyo Hondo Pueblo (LA 12; specimens from Conrad et al. 2016). Eggshell thickness measurements from Tijeras and Arroyo Hondo Pueblos support the turkey species identification for the Room 28 specimens (figure 8.3). In general, turkey eggshell thickness values for Room 28 fall within published standards for wild and domesticated turkeys (table 8.3).

Given the vertical distribution of turkey eggshells throughout the Room 28 stratigraphy, the variation in

TABLE 8.3. Published values for turkey eggshell thickness

TYPE	NUMBER OF SAMPLES	THICKNESS OR RANGE (MM)	REFERENCE
Modern turkey	5	0.325–0.350	Sidell 1993b:13
Modern possibly turkey	2	0.407–0.498	Lamzik 2013:70
Modern wild turkey	1	0.420–0.459	Lamzik 2013:70
Modern domestic turkey	1	0.332–0.434	Lamzik 2013:70
Modern turkey	unknown	0.35	Windes 1977
Modern domestic turkey	42	0.341–0.377	Mróz et al. 2014:199
Holland turkey	1	0.41	Romanoff and Romanoff 1949:150
Archaeological turkey	7	0.432–0.495	Lamzik 2013:71
Archaeological turkey	unknown	0.30–0.35	Beacham 2006:51
Archaeological turkey	1	0.53	Lapham et al. 2016:539

Note: These researchers used several different types of measuring instruments (calipers, digital microscope, scanning electron microscope). Therefore, this is a relatively broad summary. See the references for specifics.

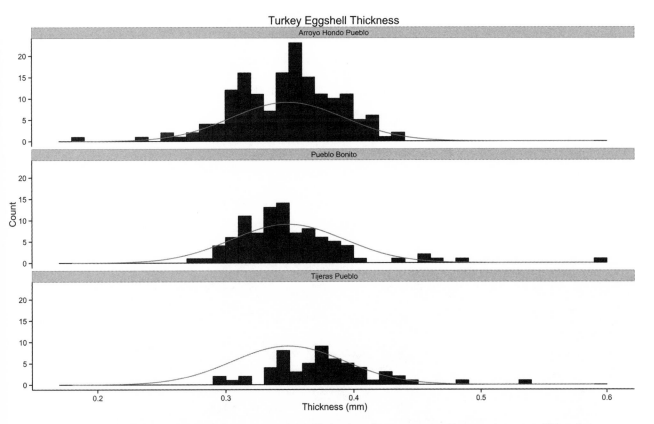

FIGURE 8.3. Eggshell thickness histograms for Arroyo Hondo Pueblo (LA 12; *top*), Room 28 at Pueblo Bonito (LA 226; *middle*), and Tijeras Pueblo (LA 581; *bottom*). A normal distribution line is plotted over the histograms.

eggshell thickness and mass, and the relatively large number of specimens, I argue that these fragments originate from multiple individual eggs. The Room 28 turkey eggshell assemblage does not include any restorable or partially restorable eggs, in contrast to other sites in Chaco Canyon and throughout the northern Southwest (figure 8.4; Lang and Harris 1984; Senior and Pierce 1989; Windes 1977). This makes it difficult to quantify the original number of eggs. Clearly, however, the turkey eggshell assemblage is highly fragmented with a NISP-to-mass ratio of ~62.0 (98:1.58; see Conrad et al. 2016). Furthermore, when I apply a whole egg weight estimation metric (Windes 1977, 1987c, 1993; but see comments in Conrad et al. 2016), the total number of estimated eggs in Room 28 (based on a whole egg mass of 7.25 grams) is only 0.22 eggs. These values suggest that the Room 28 turkey eggshells are from multiple, highly fragmented eggs, rather than from less than a quarter of a single egg.

GASTROLITHS

The 2013 UNM excavations in Room 28 yielded 111 of what are variously called gullet stones, gizzard stones, or gastroliths (table 8.2). These are small pieces of stone that are swallowed to aid in digestion in bird gizzards.

All birds have gizzards, but not all birds use this organ with stones for digestion. Ground-feeding Galliformes, including turkeys, swallow stones that act like teeth, grinding up food. Over time, these stones become polished and too smooth to function properly; they are then regurgitated or passed through the digestive tract. Diagnostic markers for gullet stones are high polish, rounded edges, and few pits and crevices (Brooks 2012; Munro 1994). Turkeys have been shown to ingest debitage (Munro 1994), and this feature is reflected in the Room 28 gullet stone assemblage (figure 8.5). Both Pepper (1920) and Judd (1954) also recovered gastroliths in their excavations at Pueblo Bonito.

The sizes of turkey gastroliths vary, but when they are passed through the digestive system they are typically too small for recovery in a quarter-inch screen (e.g., Ortman 2000). Gastroliths smaller than one-quarter inch (approximately 6 mm) are likely from turkey droppings; those larger may be related to butchering or regurgitation.

Methods of Analysis

Jacqueline Kocer analyzed all gastroliths from Room 28 using the identification criteria specified above. The stones were measured with calipers and weighed with a digital scale.

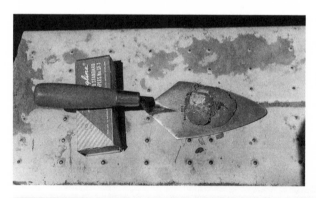

FIGURE 8.4. A partial turkey egg from site 29SJ627 in Chaco Canyon (see figure 8.1). This egg was photographed after excavation from the plaza, next to Cist 4 (a firepit), on July 19, 1974. Windes (1977:n.p.) noted that "most of one egg [is] present." Photograph courtesy of the Chaco Culture National Historical Park Photo Archives, Image no. 0002/016.004-1, NPS #9741.

FIGURE 8.5. Swallowed debitage turkey gastroliths from Room 28.

Results

Table 8.2 shows the distribution of gastroliths by level for Room 28. The excavations recovered gullet stones both in backfill (believed to have come from the excavations of Rooms 28a, 53, and 56) and in situ Room 28 contexts, including the floor and subfloor. There is no way to prove that the gastroliths from Room 28 came from turkeys, but since no other Galliformes besides turkey were identified in the faunal assemblage, these stones are likely from this species. The maximum dimension of the Room 28 gastroliths averaged 6.55 mm with the largest at 17.68 mm and the smallest at 2.64 mm (figure 8.6). The distribution suggests that the stones derive both from droppings and regurgitation or butchering. The material types of these gastroliths are chalcedony (52.3%), petrified wood (20.7%), chert (19.8%), and Narbona Pass chert (7.2%). Most of the stones are thus of locally available materials, but even the exotic Narbona Pass chert was widely used for creating chipped stone tools at Pueblo Bonito and thus pieces would have been available to local turkeys.

DISCUSSION

Archaeological turkey remains from Pueblo Bonito are relatively rare. The trash mound excavations recovered only 13 turkey bone specimens (Badenhorst et al. 2016), and the Room 28 reexcavation recovered only 6 (Ainsworth et al., this volume). However, this eggshell analysis, a spatial analysis of turkey remains at Pueblo Bonito, and complementary ancient DNA (aDNA) and strontium isotope data (Grimstead, Reynolds, et al. 2016; Speller 2009; Speller et al. 2010) suggest the presence of prehispanic turkey husbandry at Pueblo Bonito.

Quantitative data on turkey eggshells from Pueblo Bonito are limited. Fifteen eggshell fragments in the Pueblo Bonito trash mounds are potentially turkey, but these are not confirmed identifications (table 8.1; Badenhorst et al. 2016). If these specimens are accepted as turkey, then there are 6.5 times more turkey eggshells in Room 28 than in the trash mounds (perhaps the result of differences in screening sizes used in the two excavations). Since turkey eggshell is traditionally a marker of turkey husbandry in the Southwest (Beacham and Durand 2007; Conrad et al. 2016; Di Peso et al. 1974; Munro 2011; Windes 1987c), this evidence provides initial support for prehispanic husbandry activity in Pueblo Bonito.

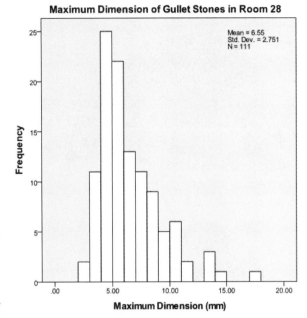

FIGURE 8.6. Distribution of the maximum dimension of gullet stones in Room 28.

A critical examination of the spatial distribution and abundance of turkey remains and by-products from Pueblo Bonito also suggests at least small-scale management and husbandry of turkeys. While turkey eggshells and gastroliths are present throughout the site, this analysis identified an important cluster in Room 28 (figure 8.7). In addition to eggshells and gastroliths, quills/feathers and turkey dung deposits are clustered in the immediate vicinity of Room 28. Turkey bones (and bone artifacts, like beads and awls) appear throughout Pueblo Bonito: they are found in at least eight kivas and, again, clustered in some of the northern rooms. This spatial analysis is largely based on excavation records from the Chaco Research Archive (2016) and therefore aggregates several distinct temporal periods in the Pueblo Bonito construction sequence (Windes 2003; Windes and Ford 1996). However, it is suggestive.

The presence of abundant turkey eggshells in Room 28 and the associated turkey by-products recovered from the northern room block cluster both provide evidence to support turkey husbandry activity at Pueblo Bonito. In theory, an additional line of evidence that would help support this argument is the presence of turkey pens (Munro 2006, 2011). Unfortunately, turkey pens are rare in Chacoan sites (Akins 1985), but in Room 92 (to the west of Room 28) at Pueblo Bonito (figure 8.7) excavators recorded "turkey droppings" in their notes (Chaco

EGGSHELL AND GASTROLITHS

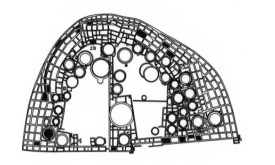

QUILL / FEATHERS

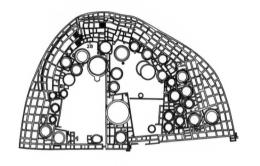

DROPPINGS

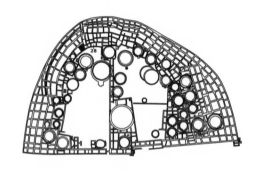

BONE

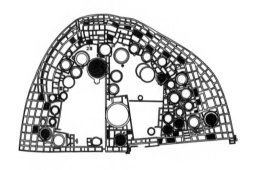

50m

FIGURE 8.7. Distribution of turkey eggshells and gastroliths, quills/feathers, bones, and dung in Pueblo Bonito. Black-shaded rooms indicate presence of the artifact type. Data from Chaco Research Archive 2016; Pepper 1920; and Judd 1954. The Pueblo Bonito trash mounds are not shown (see Crown 2016). Adapted from Windes and Ford 1996:296.

Research Archive 2016). This, in addition to the refuse and architectural features identified in Room 92, raises the possibility that it served as a turkey pen.

Pepper (1920:298–300) described a "great deal of corn," a "bunch of bean bushes," "masses of beans from the same plant, that were still green," "corn on the cob," and "beans in the pod" in Room 92. The association of plants and turkey dung suggests that these may reflect turkey feed. Stable isotope studies support the possibility of husbanded southwestern turkeys eating at least some of these plant foods (Conrad et al. 2016; Jones et al. 2016; Lipe et al. 2016; McCaffery et al. 2014; Rawlings and Driver 2010), and unpublished carbon stable isotope data from two turkey bone collagen specimens in Room 28 indicate a C4 plant–based diet (Patricia Crown, personal communication, 2017). Finally, the door of Room 92 is also suggestive of a restricted passage, which may have been built for a turkey pen: "the doorway in the central part was of the old type, narrow at the bottom and broad at the top, possibly, as has been suggested, to allow a person to enter with a bundle on his back" (Pepper 1920:299).

In addition, aDNA and strontium isotope studies support the presence of prehispanic turkey husbandry at Pueblo Bonito. A genetic analysis of turkey specimens from the trash mounds identified four individuals with the ancient haplotype aHap1, which represents the extinct prehispanic Southwest domesticated turkey lineage (table 8.4; Speller 2009; Speller et al. 2010). Only one turkey specimen analyzed from the trash mounds is wild and related to extant Merriam's turkey (*Meleagris gallopavo merriami*) populations. These results indicate that while only 54% (7 of 13) of the trash mound turkey specimens received aDNA analysis, 57% (4 of 7) of those that did are domestic, and only 14% (1 of 7) are not. Two turkey specimens analyzed for aDNA failed to produce results.

The genetic analysis of turkey specimens provides one of the most direct approaches for identifying husbandry activity and, in conjunction with the eggshell results, supports the presence of this activity at Pueblo Bonito. But since recent aDNA and stable isotope research (Jones et al. 2016) indicates that prehispanic southwesterners practiced complex husbandry strategies (i.e., domestic but free range), it is necessary to examine strontium isotope data from prehispanic turkeys in Chaco Canyon to improve our understanding of this process.

Turkey bone apatite strontium isotope data also sug-

TABLE 8.4. Ancient DNA (aDNA) results for turkey samples analyzed from the Pueblo Bonito trash mounds

SAMPLE	ELEMENT	SIDE	PORTION	D-LOOP HAPLOTYPE	PROVENIENCE
TU136	tibiotarsus	right	distal	failed	FS 557, box 2-12 (5104), West Mound
TU137	ulna	left	proximal	aHap1	FS 399, box 2-8, Level 9, 491N, 562E, East Mound
TU138	tarsometatarsus	left	proximal	aHap1	FS 2666, box 1-4 (1101), East Mound
TU139	tarsometatarsus	right	distal	aHap1	FS 2939, box 1-2 (1023), East Mound
TU140	tibiotarsus	—	distal	aHap1	FS 2819, box 1-4 (1023), West Mound
TU141	tarsometatarsus	—	distal	aHap2	FS 2819, box 1-4 (1023), West Mound
TU142	tarsometatarsus	left	distal	failed	FS 2736, box 1-4 (1240), West Mound

Sources: Speller 2009; Speller et al. 2010.

gest the presence of prehispanic husbandry activity in Chaco Canyon (Grimstead, Reynolds, et al. 2016). An analysis of specimens from Pueblo Alto (n = 10), Una Vida (n = 1), 29SJ628 (n = 1), and 29SJ629 (n = 4) indicates that turkeys in the canyon have low—and statistically overlapping—variance in strontium ($^{87}Sr/^{86}Sr$) isotope values (table 8.5). Given the analysis of both juvenile and adult turkeys from throughout Chacoan sites in this strontium study, these data help support the presence of prehispanic husbandry by identifying the restricted mobility of turkeys in the canyon. If, as suggested elsewhere (Vivian et al. 2006; Windes 1977), the bulk of turkeys at Chaco were husbanded outside the region and imported into the canyon, possibly from the north, then there should be significant variance in turkey $^{87}Sr/^{86}Sr$ values. Since current strontium evidence from turkeys suggests the opposite, this indicates that either local domesticated but feral (or free-range) turkeys were being exploited or that local domesticated and husbanded turkeys were being exploited. Combined, the turkey eggshell, gastrolith, feather, dung, and bone data from Pueblo Bonito; the aDNA data from the trash mounds; and the strontium isotope data from throughout Chaco Canyon support the latter scenario, specifically that at least some turkeys were husbanded in the Puebloan period at Pueblo Bonito.

In chapter 2, Crown suggests that the upper story of Rooms 28 and 28a may have been used as a turkey pen late in the sequence of occupation. This may be correct, but the recovery of gastroliths and eggshells below the floor of Room 28 indicates that turkeys were being exploited at Pueblo Bonito prior to construction of the room in the late AD 800s or early 900s.

CONCLUSIONS

Turkeys clearly held an important ritual, ceremonial, and subsistence role in Puebloan society (Akins 1985; Beidleman 1956; Hill 2000; Judd 1954; Lipe et al. 2016; Munro 1994; Reed 1951). Room 28 at Pueblo Bonito has a relatively large assemblage of turkey eggshells, a single non-turkey eggshell specimen, and numerous turkey gastroliths. Small amounts of turkey bone and a large and diverse assemblage of non-turkey birds represented by low numbers of individuals (Ainsworth et al., this volume; Ainsworth et al. 2018) are also present in the deposits. The clustering of turkey products and specimens in the northern block cluster (figure 8.7), in direct association with diverse bird species (many of which have colorful plumage), and the rich and dynamic artifactual record, including objects crafted in the shape of birds, support the important role that birds played in Chacoan culture and the presence of turkey husbandry at Pueblo Bonito.

In conjunction, these records allow a preliminary interpretation for turkey exploitation and husbandry at Pueblo Bonito throughout the Pueblo II period and likely earlier. Small numbers of turkeys, either domesticated forms or wild-caught individuals (or both), were likely penned in nearby rooms (e.g., Room 92) to facilitate easy and restricted access to turkey feathers and eggs. Feathers and eggs were collected for the creation of ceremonial objects, and eggs were used for food, as were turkeys themselves (at least during the AD 1100s, when there is an increase in buried turkey bones; Windes 1987c). This process, while small-scale, is supported by several lines of evidence, including the presence of turkey eggshells, gastroliths, dung, feathers, and bone remains, as well as

TABLE 8.5. **Strontium isotope results for analyzed turkey samples from Chaco Canyon**

SITE	DATE	LOCATION	FS	SPECIES	AGE	ELEMENT	$^{87}Sr/^{86}Sr_{apatite}$
Alto/29SJ389	AD 1050–1100	Kiva 13	4227-124	*Meleagris gallopavo*	adult	distal coracoid	0.709507
Alto/29SJ389	Post–AD 1150	Room 145, roof fall	2198-70	*Meleagris gallopavo*	adult	tibiotarsus shaft	0.709269
Alto/29SJ389	Post–AD 1150	Plaza grid 275, upper	4275-1	*Meleagris gallopavo*	adult	distal femur	0.709359
Alto/29SJ389	Post–AD 1150	East Plaza, unit 1	3405-3	*Meleagris gallopavo*	adult	distal radius	0.709368
Alto/29SJ389	Post–AD 1150	Kiva 16	4196-32	*Meleagris gallopavo*	adult	radius shaft	0.709376
Alto/29SJ389	Post–AD 1150	East Plaza, unit 1	3411-27	*Meleagris gallopavo*	adult	tibiotarsus	0.709410
Alto/29SJ389	Post–AD 1150	Kiva 15, floor fill	5341-16	*Meleagris gallopavo*	adult	fibula	0.709429
Alto/29SJ389	Post–AD 1150	Room 112, surface 1	7079-24	*Meleagris gallopavo*	adult	carpometacarpus	0.709433
Alto/29SJ389	Post–AD 1150	Room 103, floor 1	1138-2	*Meleagris gallopavo*	adult	ulna	0.709446
Alto/29SJ389	Post–AD 1150	Room 142, roof fall	2728-2	*Meleagris gallopavo*	adult	distal femur	0.709450
29SJ629	Pre–AD 950	Pithouse 3, lower	3036-2	*Meleagris gallopavo*	adult	proximal ulna	0.709118
Una Vida/29SJ391	Pre–AD 950	Room 83, floor 2	115-12	*Meleagris gallopavo*	adult	proximal[a]	0.709176
29SJ629	Pre–AD 950	Early trash	1534-19	*Meleagris gallopavo*	adult	sternum fragment	0.709244
29SJ629	Pre–AD 950	Middle trash	1602-1	*Meleagris gallopavo*	immature	coracoid	0.709334
29SJ629	Pre–AD 950	Pithouse 3, lower	2609-22	*Meleagris gallopavo*	adult	distal humerus	0.709429
29SJ628	Pre–AD 950	Pithouse E, level 1	535	*Meleagris gallopavo*	immature	tibiotarsus	0.709446

Source: Grimstead, Reynolds, et al. 2016.

[a] No element listed in original publication.

aDNA and strontium isotope analyses in Room 28 and elsewhere throughout Chaco Canyon.

From the morphology of eggshell alone, it is impossible to determine if the turkey eggshells present in Room 28 at Pueblo Bonito represent wild or domesticated forms. Both wild and domesticated turkeys are present at the site (Speller et al. 2010), and although I argue that there was husbanding of turkeys at Pueblo Bonito, it is also possible that wild turkeys and/or their eggs were collected and brought to this location (Akins 1987; Windes 1977). For instance, historically documented residents of Taos Pueblo apparently only raised turkeys that were born in the wild, captured in the mountains, and held in confinement at the pueblo (Schorger 1961:140).

While analysis of the Room 28 avian eggshells and gastroliths helps highlight the complex nature of turkey husbandry in the prehispanic Southwest and specifically in Chaco Canyon at Pueblo Bonito, future genetic, stable/radio isotope, and spatial analyses of turkey remains are required to help clarify and further these interpretations.

ACKNOWLEDGMENTS

Thank you to Patricia Crown for providing the opportunity to analyze and discuss the eggshells and gastroliths from Room 28 in this volume. I am extremely grateful to Emily Jones for providing invaluable comments and suggestions on this chapter. Finally, thank you to Caitlin S. Ainsworth, Milford Fletcher, Stephanie E. Franklin, Jacqueline M. Kocer, Kathryn Lamzik, Brenna Lissoway, Camilla Speller, Hannah Van Vlack, and Tom Windes, for assistance during this project.

KAREN R. ADAMS

CHAPTER NINE

Archaeobotanical Evidence from Room 28, Pueblo Bonito

Pueblo Bonito is located in northwestern New Mexico within a biotic community characterized as the Plains and Great Basin Grassland (Brown 1982a). This biotic community has been considerably altered historically by grazing, fire suppression, and shrub invasion. In its more natural form, broad stretches of perennial grasses are usually intermixed with shrubs, such as saltbush (*Atriplex*), sagebrush (*Artemisia*), and rabbitbrush (*Chrysothamnus*), and a diversity of herbaceous perennials. The uplifted sandstone feature of Chaco Mesa supports Great Basin Conifer Woodland (Brown 1982b), which has an additional suite of trees and shrubs, including pinyon (*Pinus edulis*), various junipers (*Juniperus scopulorum, J. osteosperma*), mountain mahogany (*Cercocarpus* spp.), and bitterbrush (*Purshia tridentata*). Cottonwood (*Populus*) and willow (*Salix*) trees are found near riparian areas, such as along Chaco Wash, Escavada Wash, Gallo Wash, and the Chaco River.

METHODS

The types of archaeological plant samples collected during excavation provide information regarding subsistence and nonsubsistence resources of importance to ancient communities. Macrobotanical samples, including recognizable maize (*Zea mays*) specimens, comprise the larger plant parts that are easily recognized and collected directly from site excavation units or archaeological screens. In contrast, smaller plant parts, such as seeds and other tiny reproductive parts that are difficult to recognize during excavation, are retrieved from site sediment samples routinely collected for flotation processing. The best archaeobotanical interpretations rely on both the larger macrobotanical samples and the smaller plant parts to reveal a balanced view of ancient plant use.

This chapter includes my analysis of data from 11 macrobotanical samples, 7 flotation samples, and 10 *Zea mays* cob segments/fragments collected separately (table 9.1). Most macrobotanical samples and *Zea mays* cob specimens were recovered from the backfill put back into the room during its original excavation in 1896. In addition, flotation samples and a few *Zea mays* cob specimens were collected in 2013 from previously unexcavated levels that were under the floor exposed in 1896. These subfloor features included ephemeral thermal features with some ash/charcoal in them and postholes.

Macrobotanical Samples

The contents of each macrobotanical sample were spread out on lab trays, so that all items were visible. Specimens were sorted into groups of the separate plant taxa/parts recognized. Each taxon/part group was then counted, and the condition of specimens was noted. All specimens were identified under a Zeiss binocular microscope at magnifications ranging from 8× to 50× and were compared to an extensive Colorado Plateau collection of modern plant materials backed by voucher specimens deposited in the University of Arizona Herbarium.

Flotation Samples

Flotation samples are sediment samples from which plant remains are extracted in the laboratory using a water-separation technique (Bohrer and Adams 1977). Jacqueline Kocer processed the Room 28 flotation samples, ranging in size from 0.40 to 5.19 L, at the University of New Mexico. The resulting light fraction, composed of buoyant plant specimens that float on the surface of water, was skimmed off and dried. These light fraction volumes, ranging from 13.5 to 104 mL, were passed through a series of US Geological Survey standard graduated sieves with mesh sizes of 4 mm, 2 mm, 1 mm, and

TABLE 9.1. **Context of archaeobotanical samples analyzed**

FS	LEVEL	CONTEXT	SAMPLE TYPE	DEPTH (M)	NOTES
20	3	backfill	*Zea mays*	99.22–99.02	
65	6	backfill	macrobotanical	98.62–98.42	modern seeds
106	8	backfill	macrobotanical	98.22–98.02	seeds
118	8A	backfill	macrobotanical	98.22–98.02	seeds, probably from a different room thrown into Room 28
119	8A	backfill	*Zea mays*	98.22–98.02	probably from a different room; no burned material and a high frequency of ornaments
139	9A	backfill	macrobotanical	98.02–97.82	seed, probably from a different room thrown into Room 28
140	9A	backfill	*Zea mays*	98.02–97.82	cob segment, probably from a different room thrown into Room 28
140	9A	backfill	*Zea mays*	98.02–97.83	cob segment, probably from a different room thrown into Room 28
140	9A	backfill	*Zea mays*	98.02–97.84	cob segment, probably from a different room thrown into Room 28
179	10a	backfill	macrobotanical	97.82–97.62	
204	11	backfill	macrobotanical	97.62–97.42	seed, probably in backfill from adjacent rooms
222	12	backfill	macrobotanical	97.42–97.24	seeds
239	13	backfill and cleaning above Pepper's floor	macrobotanical	97.32–97.10	seed within the last material above the floor of the room
282		north wall cleaning	*Zea mays*		north wall cleaning
299	13	burned area on north wall	flotation	to depth of 97.19	from within an ashy, shallow, ephemeral thermal feature located along the north wall of the room direcly at floor level and with clay beneath it
307	14	southeast quadrant	*Zea mays*	97.19–96.87	from subfloor that predates Room 28
308	14	southeast quadrant	macrobotanical	97.19–96.87	from a subfloor surface that predates Room 28, apparently a plaza in front of rooms adjacent to Room 28
331	14	southeast quadrant	flotation	97.19–96.87	soil sample from subfloor area that predates Room 28
332	15	ash stain in southeast quadrant	flotation	96.70	from ash stain located in western half of southeast quadrant near a posthole
362		Ashpit A, center	flotation	97.09–96.88	another ash-filled thermal feature located about the center of the room
363		Ashpit B, center	flotation	97.09–96.89	north of Ashpit A, from an ephemeral ashy thermal pit feature; hard to determine sides
368		Posthole 24, fill	macrobotanical	96.30 at deepest part	in southern part of room adjacent to southeast quadrant taken to sterile
374	16	southeast quadrant	macrobotanical	96.63–96.00	from a 50 × 50 cm square taken down to foundation clay in northeast corner of southeast quadrant
384	16	southeast quadrant	*Zea mays*		sweeping from surface in southeast quadrant, predates Room 28
403	13		*Zea mays*	97.32–97.10	room cleaning for lidar
415		subfloor surface	*Zea mays*	97.01, surface 2	subfloor surface with ash, wood fragments, and pottery; float sample 511 is from this same surface, predating Room 28
510	13	floor, southwest corner	flotation	97.24–97.10	at floor level, taken when large post pulled from southwest corner of room
511		subfloor surface	flotation	97.01	subfloor surface in center of room; good ashy surface with ash, bits of charcoal, lots of pieces of wood, and small bones; surface may predate the east and south walls and represent plaze surface with ash dumps and construction debris

0.5 mm. I examined separately the material from each size fraction under a binocular microscope using 8× to 50× magnification. Subdividing material into size fractions allows for the use of a constant focal depth while examining each fraction. The larger fractions were examined first, because larger and more easily recognized plant parts sometimes provide clues for the identification of fragmented specimens in smaller fractions. Materials that passed through the 0.5 mm sieve were not analyzed; this fraction is assumed to consist primarily of nonorganic silt, unidentifiable organics, and small fragments of specimens that were likely recognized in the larger size fractions. For every flotation sample, the heavy fraction, which sank during processing, was also dried, bagged up, and then examined. Heavy fractions are primarily composed of rocks and clay chunks but can also include water-logged plant specimens, tiny bone fragments, lithic flakes, beads, and ceramic sherds.

Reproductive and nonreproductive plant parts were removed from the samples and segregated into separate vials or envelopes. Reproductive plant parts can include seeds, fruits, flowers, grass grains and embryos, achenes, nutshell fragments, and pieces of maize cobs. Nonreproductive plant materials can include wood fragments, small twigs, juniper scale leaves, pine bark scales and needles, and spines. Reproductive parts were identified to the most specific taxonomic category possible by using modern comparative collections and referring to published seed identification guides (Adams and Murray 2004; Bohrer and Adams 1976; Egginton 1921; Martin and Barkley 1961). The term "cheno-am" is utilized here to describe seeds that are so similar in appearance that they might belong to either the genus *Chenopodium* (goosefoot) or *Amaranthus* (pigweed). Some of these annuals provided radiocarbon dates, as discussed in chapter 2.

Charred fragments of wood in the archaeobotanical samples were identified in the following manner. For each flotation sample, 20 charred wood pieces were selected from the > 4 mm size fraction. If fewer than 20 pieces were present in that size fraction, then pieces from the 2–4 mm size fraction were included. To facilitate identification, I snapped the charred wood fragments for a clear cross-section view and then examined them under high (50×) magnification. Each wood specimen was identified to the most specific taxonomic category possible via the use of modern comparative collections and published wood identification

guides (Adams and Murray 2004; Hoadley 1990; Minnis 1987).

Charred plant remains from open archaeological sites are considered more likely to be related to human activities than are uncharred specimens (Minnis 1981; Pearsall 1989:224–26). Uncharred specimens generally owe their presence to post-occupational intrusion into archaeological sites. However, conditions in portions of Room 28 at Pueblo Bonito appear to have protected both charred and uncharred items. Some of these uncharred items are considered cultural, as I argue below.

RESULTS

A minimum of 27 plant taxa and their parts were preserved in the samples examined (table 9.2). Use of the word "type" in the table indicates that the charred specimen most closely resembles the taxon named, but the condition and age of the specimens make it difficult to identify some of them with absolute certainty. This conservative approach acknowledges the similarity in appearance of various southwestern US plant taxa, especially when specimens have been carbonized and/or damaged. For ease of use, I indicate "type" only in table 9.2, but the word is implied in all text and tables. Representative examples of charred and uncharred plant specimens from Room 28 are shown in figures 9.1–9.3 (reproductive parts) and figures 9.4–9.6 (nonreproductive parts). The complete sample data can be found in appendix B. Ethnographic literature relevant to what is now the US Southwest (Castetter 1935; Yanovsky 1936; summarized in Rainey and Adams 2004) and previous summaries of the southwestern US archaeobotanical record (Adams 1988; Adams and Fish 2006; Huckell and Toll 2004) all provide substantial evidence of use of these plants through time.

I first present the macrobotanical sample data. These are uncharred plant specimens that could owe their presence in Room 28 to humans, rodents, or both. Then, I discuss the charred specimens recovered from flotation samples. I present the flotation sample data as taxon ubiquity, which tallies the number of analyzed samples in which a given plant and its parts occur and which provides insight into the frequency of use of a plant resource in prehistory. Ubiquity is generally converted to a percentage to compare/contrast among plant taxa/ parts, although caution is needed when low sample numbers are involved.

TABLE 9.2. **Plant taxa and parts recovered in Room 28 samples**

TAXON	COMMON NAME	PARTS	CONDITION
Amaranthus type	pigweed	seed	uncharred
Amelanchier/Peraphyllum type	serviceberry/peraphyllum	wood	charred
Artemisia type	sagebrush	wood	charred
Atriplex type	saltbush	wood	charred
Celtis reticulata type	hackberry	seed half	uncharred
Cercocarpus type	mountain mahogany	twig, wood	charred
Cheno-am	goosefoot-pigweed	seed	charred, uncharred
Chrysothamnus type	rabbitbrush	twig, wood	charred
Cucurbita moschata type	butternut squash	seed, seed fragment	uncharred
Descurainia	tansy mustard	seed (tentative ID)	charred
Echinocereus type	hedgehog cactus	seed	charred, uncharred
Forestiera type	New Mexico privet	wood	charred
Fraxinus type	ash	wood	charred
Gossypium type	cotton	twine fragment; tentative ID	charred
Juniperus type	juniper	seed	uncharred
Juniperus type	juniper	wood	charred
Mentzelia albicaulis type	stickleaf	seed	charred
Opuntia type	prickly pear	seed, seed fragment	uncharred
Physalis type	tomatillo	seed	charred
Pinus edulis type	pinyon	seed fragment, seed	uncharred
Pinus ponderosa type	ponderosa pine	wood	charred
Populus/Salix type	cottonwood/willow	twig, wood	charred
Pseudotsuga type	Douglas fir	wood	charred
Quercus type	oak	wood	charred
Rhus aromatica type	lemonade berry	twig	charred
Sarcobatus type	greasewood	wood	charred
Sphaeralcea type	globe mallow	seed	uncharred
Unknown	unknown	bone?	uncharred
Unknown	unknown	fruit fragment, nutshell fragment	charred
Unknown	rodent	pellet	charred
Zea mays	corn, maize	cob fragment, cob segment, cupule, kernel	charred
Zea mays	corn, maize	cob segment	uncharred

DISCUSSION

Backfill Samples

Macrobotanical samples from backfill preserved evidence of four different plant taxa, none of them charred (table 9.3). The origins of these plant specimens may well be diverse. Reasonably, the pigweed (*Amaranthus*) population of more than 1,000 seeds may have been carried in by rodents, although no rodent evidence (pellets, nest material, or gnaw marks) was preserved with these seeds. The same could be said for the globe mallow (*Sphaeralcea*) seeds. Pigweed plants are annuals that can produce large quantities of seeds following the onset of summer monsoons. Globe mallow plants are annuals or herbaceous perennials also capable of producing quantities of seeds from midsummer through the first frost of fall. The loose backfill may have provided locations that rodents found acceptable for caching these potentially abundant seeds.

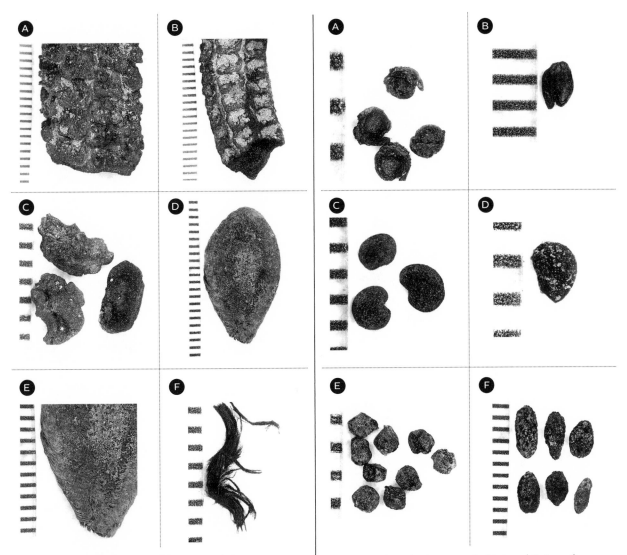

FIGURE 9.1. Reproductive parts of domesticated plants: (*a*) charred maize (*Zea mays*) cob segment, 14 rows, FS 282; (*b*) charred maize cob segment, 12 rows, FS 140; (*c*) three charred maize cupules, FS 363; (*d*) uncharred squash (*Cucurbita moschata*) seed, FS 118; (*e*) close-up of wavy, fringed edge of the same squash seed (*lower left*); (*f*) charred twine fragment with kinked seed hairs, likely cotton (*Gossypium*), FS 362. Scales are in mm. Photographs by Karen R. Adams.

FIGURE 9.2. Reproductive parts of wild plants (all charred), plus evidence of rodents: (*a*) four goosefoot/pigweed (cheno-am) seeds with encircling embryo, FS 363; (*b*) a likely tansy mustard (*Descurainia*) seed, FS 363; (*c*) three tomatillo (*Physalis*) seeds, FS 363; (*d*) a hedgehog (*Echinocereus*) cactus seed with large opening (*lower left*), FS 299; (*e*) nine stickleaf (*Mentzelia albicaulis*) seeds with beaded surface and blocky shape, FS 299; and (*f*) six rodent pellets, FS 299, suggesting rodents may have raided food stores. Scales are in mm. Photographs by Karen R. Adams.

The pinyon (*Pinus edulis*) and butternut squash (*Cucurbita moschata*) seed evidence preserved in the backfill is more difficult to interpret. Although pinyon trees grow in the region, they would have had to grow relatively close to Pueblo Bonito for their seeds to be carried in by rodents. Some pinyon (*Pinus edulis*) seeds clearly appear to have been gnawed by rodents, which left evidence in the form of striations made by their incisors. The possibility exists that some pinyon seeds were originally gathered and stored by Pueblo Bonito occupants and

were eventually discovered by rodents, which damaged them. The *Cucurbita moschata* seeds, representative of a domesticated squash whose seeds are identified on the basis of a "thin, ragged, often wavy or fringed . . . margin" (Cutler and Whitaker 1961:478), could only owe their presence to ancient agriculturalists.

Subfloor Features

The uncharred macrobotanical sample evidence from subfloor features helps clarify the possible interpreta-

FIGURE 9.3. Reproductive parts of wild plants (continued) (all are uncharred). (*a*) five prickly pear (*Opuntia*) seeds, three lower ones with rodent damage, FS 510; (*b*) a pinyon (*Pinus edulis*) seed fragment with slanted edges indicative of rodent gnawing, FS 239; (*c*) a hackberry (*Celtis reticulata*) seed, FS 374; (*d*) six globe mallow (*Sphaeralcea*) seeds, FS 65; (*e*) numerous pigweed (*Amaranthus*) seeds, FS 65; (*f*) close-up of the shiny exterior surfaces of pigweed seeds. Scales are in mm. Photographs by Karen R. Adams.

FIGURE 9.4. Charred wood and twigs of trees and shrubs. Transverse views at 50× magnification unless otherwise noted. (*a*) serviceberry/peraphyllum (*Amelanchier/Peraphyllum*), FS 331; (*b*) sagebrush (*Artemisia*), FS 511; (*c*) tangential view of sagebrush showing lenticels (narrow openings), FS 510; (*d*) saltbush (*Atriplex*), FS 511; (*e*) transverse view (8×) of mountain mahogany (*Cercocarpus*) twigs, FS 510; (*f*) mountain mahogany (*Cercocarpus*) wood, FS 331. Photographs by Karen R. Adams.

tions of the backfill specimens discussed above. A subfloor feature that predated Room 28 (FS 308), some posthole fill (FS 368), and a square taken down to foundation clay (FS 374) preserved uncharred specimens of pinyon seed fragments, butternut squash seed fragments, and a hackberry (*Celtis reticulata*) seed half (table 9.3). Since this evidence from subfloor features is similar to backfill evidence, it supports the notion that some portion of the backfill plant specimens above the floor may have been collected by humans and later raided by rodents.

Charred rodent pellets (figure 9.2f) recovered in a flotation sample from a burned area on the north wall (FS 299) likely burned when people occupied the pueblo.

Flotation samples from subfloor features shed more light on the diversity of plants gathered in the past. The charred plant specimens identified in seven flotation samples represent a variety of plants and their parts, which were sought as subsistence and nonsubsistence resources (table 9.4): domesticates, wild plants, and trees that grew some distant away.

Domesticated Maize (*Zea mays*)

Maize specimens were preserved in all seven flotation samples, suggesting an important role for this domesticate, which ripens in the fall. Seven charred and one uncharred maize cob segments recovered separately from backfill and subfloor locations were complete around their circumference, allowing an accurate determination of the number of kernel rows (table 9.5). These specimens indicate a landrace of maize with 10–14 rows of kernels. One nearly whole cob segment (FS 20), which tapered toward the apex and base, measured 4.4 cm in length, suggesting that the landrace produced rather small, cigar-shaped ears. When compared to published traits of southwestern US maize (Adams 1994:277, 296–97), the best match is to small to medium ears categorized as Basketmaker/Hohokam, Pima/Papago, or Chapalote maize with a cigar shape (tapering to both apex and base) and flint and/or pop kernels. Some charred maize specimens from Chaco Culture National Historical Park site 29SJ519, representing an earlier Basketmaker III (AD 600s)

occupation of the canyon, were identified as flint maize with an average of 12 kernel rows, also similar to Basketmaker/Hohokam or Pima/Papago maize (Adams 2010).

The Chaco era great house site of Chimney Rock in southwestern Colorado, dating to the eleventh century, contained a well-preserved collection of maize remains (Adams 2011). Analyses of charred maize ears, cobs, kernels, and shanks (stalks that attach the ears to the stems) suggest that at least two landraces were grown by Chimney Rock farmers. The cigar-shaped ear/cob specimens, kernels with husk striations across the top, and an average kernel row number of 12, coupled with the presence of flint and/or pop kernels in the assemblage, suggest maize similar to Chapalote and/or Basketmaker landraces. Other Chimney Rock maize specimens—with a gradual ear/cob taper, possible flour kernels, relatively large shanks, and 14 or 16 rows of kernels—bear some resemblance to historic Rio Grande pueblo large-eared flour maize landraces, except the Chimney Rock pueblo specimens are not nearly as large.

TABLE 9.3. **Uncharred macrobotanical specimens from backfill and subfloor features**

FS	TAXON	PART	QUANTITY	NOTES
From backfill above the floor				
65	Amaranthus	seed	1,000+	cache? no rodent pellets
65	Sphaeralcea	seed	18	cache? no rodent pellets
65	Unknown	bone?	1	rodent?
106	Cucurbita moschata	seed fragment	6	wavy fringed edge
106	Pinus edulis	seed fragment	5	one is gnawed
106	Unknown	bone?	1	
118	Cucurbita moschata	seed	1	whole
118	Cucurbita moschata	seed fragment	2	wavy fringed edge
139	Pinus edulis	seed	2	with rodent gnaw marks
139	Pinus edulis	seed fragment	8	no gnaw marks
179	Pinus edulis	seed fragment	1	no gnaw marks
204	Cucurbita moschata	seed fragment	6	wavy fringed edge
204	Pinus edulis	seed fragment	7	no gnaw marks
222	Cucurbita moschata	seed fragment	5	wavy fringed edge
222	Pinus edulis	seed fragment	8	one is gnawed
239	Pinus edulis	seed fragment	7	with rodent gnaw marks
From subfloor features				
308	Cucurbita moschata	seed fragment	8	one with wavy fringed edge
308	Pinus edulis	seed fragment	5	not gnawed
368	Pinus edulis	seed fragment	4	
374	Celtis reticulata	seed half	1	

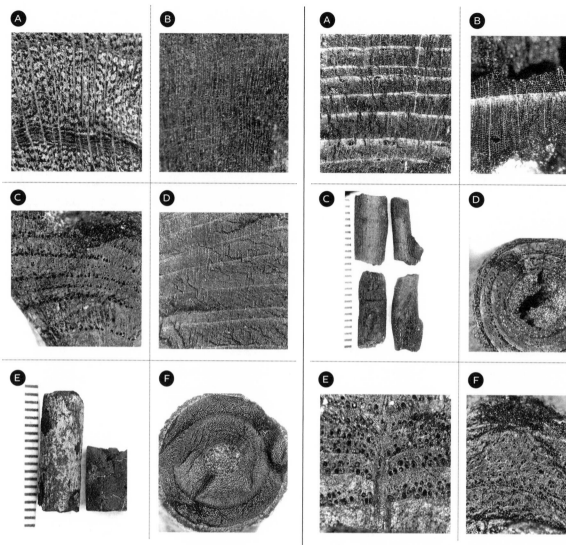

FIGURE 9.5. Charred wood and twigs of trees and shrubs (continued). Transverse views at 50× magnification unless otherwise noted. (*a*) rabbitbrush (*Chrysothamnus*), FS 332; (*b*) New Mexico privet (*Forestiera*), FS 511; (*c*) ash (*Fraxinus*), FS 362; (*d*) juniper (*Juniperus*), FS 331; (*e*) tangential view of two cottonwood/willow (*Populus/Salix*) twigs at 8×, FS 510 (scale is in mm); (*f*) one cottonwood/willow twig at 8×, showing two growth rings and pith. Photographs by Karen R. Adams.

FIGURE 9.6. Charred wood and twigs of trees and shrubs (continued). Transverse views at 50× magnification unless otherwise noted. (*a*) ponderosa pine (*Pinus ponderosa*) at 32×, showing larger resin canals within and near shiny bands of latewood, FS 510; (*b*) Douglas fir (*Pseudotsuga*) with tiny resin canals visible within latewood, FS 299; (*c*) tangential views of four lemonade berry (*Rhus aromatica*) twigs at 8× (scale is in mm), FS 510; (*d*) a lemonade berry twig at 8×, showing at least three growth rings and pith; (*e*) oak (*Quercus*), FS 510; (*f*) greasewood (*Sarcobatus*), FS 362. Photographs by Karen R. Adams.

Wild Plant Subsistence Resources

The flotation samples preserved charred evidence of wild plants sought as foods. Wild tomatillo (*Physalis*) seeds indicate use of the tiny fruit, which ripen in the late summer through fall. A single tansy mustard (*Descurainia*) seed and a small cache of stickleaf (*Mentzelia albicaulis*) seeds represent plants that ripen in the spring (Kearney and Peebles 1960:349; Bohrer 1978:12), documenting collection in the early part of the growing season. Hedgehog cactus (*Echinocereus*) fruits were also harvested; different species of hedgehog cactus flower as early as February and as late as July (Kearney and Peebles 1960:570–73), and their tiny, sweet, fleshy fruits ripen some weeks later.

Uncharred wild seeds were also identified in flotation samples from subfloor features (table 9.6). For example, a posthole in the southwest corner of the room (FS 510) preserved uncharred tomatillo, cheno-am, hedgehog,

TABLE 9.4. **Charred subsistence and nonsubsistence resources preserved within seven flotation samples from subfloor features**

TAXON	PART	NUMBER AND PERCENTAGE OF SAMPLES CONTAINING TAXON (%)
Subsistence resources		
Zea mays	cob fragment, cupule, kernel	7 (100)
Physalis	seed	2 (28.6)
Cheno-am	seed	1 (14.3)
Descurainia	seed	1 (14.3)
Echinocereus	seed	1 (14.3)
Mentzelia albicaulis	seed	1 (14.3)
Nonsubsistence resources		
Juniperus	wood	6 (85.7)
Sarcobatus	wood	6 (85.7)
Cercocarpus	twig, wood	5 (71.4)
Populus/Salix	twig, wood	5 (71.4)
Amelanchier/Peraphyllum	wood	4 (57.1)
Atriplex	wood	4 (57.1)
Fraxinus	wood	4 (57.1)
Artemisia	wood	2 (28.6)
Chrysothamnus	twig, wood	2 (28.6)
Forestiera	wood	2 (28.6)
Pinus ponderosa	wood	1 (14.3)
Pseudotsuga	wood	1 (14.3)
Quercus	wood	1 (14.3)
Rhus aromatica	twig	1 (14.3)

juniper (*Juniperus*), and prickly pear (*Opuntia*) seeds. A soil sample taken from a subfloor area (FS 331) preserved uncharred seeds of tomatillo, hedgehog, prickly pear, and pinyon (*Pinus edulis*) seeds. A subfloor surface (FS 511) preserved cheno-am and prickly pear seeds, and an ash-filled thermal feature (FS 362) and an ephemeral thermal pit feature (FS 363) preserved uncharred tomatillo seeds and pinyon seeds, respectively. Some of these uncharred specimens displayed rodent damage (figures 9.3a and 9.3b). The most reasonable explanation for these uncharred seeds is rodent entry. However, when seeds have been lightly parched, but not turned black by exposure to fire, they could well be evidence of gathering and processing by human groups. Three of these uncharred seed types (*Physalis*, cheno-am, and *Echinocereus*) were also recovered in charred condition, supporting an interpretation that some likely represent human foods at Pueblo Bonito.

Seasonality Implications

The seasons that plant parts are available give some indication of when people occupied or visited landscapes, with the exception of wood, which can be gathered throughout the year. However, because groups often store foods for future use, it becomes harder to link the season of availability with the season of use (Adams and Bohrer 1998). The tansy mustard and stickleaf seed evidence in Room 28 indicates the presence of harvesters in the spring. Weedy cheno-am (goosefoot-pigweed) plants that thrive in disturbed habitats often germinate

TABLE 9.5. **Well-preserved maize (*Zea mays* L.) cob segments and fragments collected separately**

FS	PART	CONDITION	NUMBER	ROWS	LENGTH (cm)	DIAMETER (cm)	NOTES
20	cob segment	charred	1	10	4.4	1.3	nearly whole
119	cob segment	charred	1	12	2.5	1.3	
140	cob fragment	charred	1				
140	cob segment	charred	1	12	2.8	1	curved
140	cob segment	charred	1	12	1.8	0.8	
282	cob segment	charred	1	14	3.3	1.5	partial
307	cob segment	uncharred	1	10	2.2	1	
384	cob fragment	charred	1				
403	cob segment	charred	1	10	1.3	1.5	in 3 pieces
415	cob segment	charred	1	10	2.1	1.2	

TABLE 9.6. Uncharred wild seeds recovered within seven flotation samples

TAXON	PART	NUMBER OF SAMPLES CONTAINING TAXON (%)	ALSO PRESENT IN CHARRED CONDITION
Opuntia	seed, seed fragment	3 (42.9)	no
Physalis	seed, seed fragment	3 (42.9)	yes
Cheno-am	seed	2 (28.6)	yes
Echinocereus	seed	2 (28.6)	yes
Pinus edulis	seed fragment	2 (28.6)	no
Juniperus	seed	1 (14.3)	no

TABLE 9.7. Charred twigs from the subfloor surface where a large post was pulled from Posthole 22 in the southwest corner of Room 28

TAXON	DIAMETER (cm)	NUMBER OF GROWTH RINGS
Cercocarpus	1.0	~10
Cercocarpus	0.8	~10
Cercocarpus	0.7	~10
Cercocarpus	0.6	~10
Populus/Salix	0.6	2
Populus/Salix	0.6	4
Rhus aromatica	0.5	3–6
Rhus aromatica	0.5	3–6
Rhus aromatica	0.5	3–6
Rhus aromatica	0.4	3–6
Rhus aromatica	0.4	3–6
Rhus aromatica	0.4	3–6

with each succeeding summer monsoon rain, providing people with a long harvest period for greens and seeds, starting in July. Later in the summer–fall, tomatillo fruits ripen. Mature maize ears could be harvested in September–October. Unless some/all of these resources were carried into the Pueblo Bonito great house from outside of Chaco Canyon, the Room 28 plant record suggests the presence of some people in the local area throughout the growing season.

Wood Usage

The charred wood types identified in flotation samples indicate an interest in a broad range of local and nonlocal woody plants (table 9.4). There was a clear preference for juniper (*Juniperus*) and greasewood (*Sarcobatus*) wood, followed closely by mountain mahogany (*Cercocarpus*) and cottonwood/willow (*Populus/Salix*) wood. Branches and twigs from rose family members, such as serviceberry (*Amelanchier*) or peraphyllum (*Peraphyllum*), plus saltbush (*Atriplex*) were also carried in regularly. Less often, woody materials from sagebrush (*Artemisia*), rabbitbrush (*Chrysothamnus*), and New Mexico privet (*Forestiera*) were gathered. Although a few ponderosa pine (*Pinus ponderosa*) trees may have been locally available, for the quantities of large trees needed for roofing and support elements, people likely traveled some distances, certainly for Douglas fir (*Pseudotsuga*) construction elements. Locally, they also sought oak (*Quercus*) and lemonade berry (*Rhus aromatica*) wood.

When a large juniper support post was pulled from the southwest corner of Room 28, a number of charred twigs were recovered from a large (5.19 L) floor-level flotation sample (FS 510). These represent mountain mahogany (*Cercocarpus*), lemonade berry (*Rhus aromatica*), and cottonwood/willow (*Populus/Salix*). They are all similar in size, ranging from 0.4 cm to 1.0 cm in diameter and having fewer than 10 growth rings (table 9.7). They may have served as a layer in roofing or for something like a room divider, drying rack, or ramada cover. Perhaps they were part of the shelving that held the cylinder jars at this end of the room. One partially charred shelf fragment displays the transverse anatomy of Douglas fir (*Pseudotsuga*) wood, whose main distinguishing features are a limited number of very small resin canals in the latewood and tracheid cells easily visible at low magnification (8×–10×).

ROOM 28 IN THE PUEBLO BONITO CONTEXT

Previous archaeological projects in Chaco Canyon presented data on plant use in Pueblo Bonito. Judd (1954) and Pepper (1920) focused on larger plant parts visible to the naked eye and did not include smaller plant parts in their analyses. Toll (1981, 1985) did include a small component of reproductive parts in her analysis of 13 coprolites from Pueblo Bonito. When compared to this previous research, my analysis in this chapter both reinforces previous knowledge and adds further information about Pueblo Bonito plant choices in the past.

It is clear that Pueblo Bonito occupants had access

to domesticated maize, squash, and beans (table 9.8). I found maize remains to be ubiquitous in the flotation samples, likely representing a landrace with relatively small ears having 10–14 rows of kernels. A single charred cob segment suggests that the maize may have been similar to a landrace called Chapalote, which tapers to the apex and base and is known to generally have flint and/or pop kernels. I also found that some of the squash seeds represent a species similar to butternut squash (*Cucurbita moschata*), whose seeds have wavy, fringed edges. Toll (1985) reported that squash peduncles previously found in Pueblo Bonito conform to characteristics of *Cucurbita pepo*, which is the jack-o'-lantern type of pumpkin. I documented no examples of domesticated beans (*Phaseolus vulgaris*). However, my findings do suggest that people had access to cotton (*Gossypium*): a charred twine fragment was preserved, the only cotton evidence tentatively identified in the samples examined.

Charred reproductive parts in all seven Room 28 flotation samples confirm a reliance on maize. In addition, people gathered seeds of weedy plants, such as cheno-ams (goosefoot-pigweed), which would have occupied agricultural fields and other locally disturbed locations, such as trash middens and pathways. Previous reports documented additional wild resources, such as pinyon seeds, walnuts, yucca fruit, and beeweed seeds (table 9.8). I add stickleaf (*Mentzelia albicaulis*) seeds, which ripen in the spring, to the list of likely foods. I also add hedgehog cactus (*Echinocereus*) and tomatillo (*Physalis*) fruits, which ripen later in the growing season. Reasonably, the uncharred pinyon (*Pinus edulis*) seeds recovered in the macrobotanical samples from backfill and subfloor features, along with uncharred prickly pear (*Opuntia*) seeds in subfloor features, were carried in by humans and then subsequently damaged by rodents. The recovery of charred rodent pellets confirms rodent presence in prehistory. Caches of uncharred pigweed (*Amaranthus*) and globe mallow (*Sphaeralcea*) seeds in the backfill could owe their presence solely to rodents, although they are both recognized as ancient human subsistence resources (Huckell and Toll 2004). An uncharred hackberry (*Celtis reticulata*) seed half from a subfloor feature and an uncharred juniper (*Juniperus*) seed may also have entered via rodent activity.

Studies of ancient wood recovered from Chaco Canyon archaeological sites have generally focused on building timbers and their source areas. However, Room 28 provided an opportunity to assess the diversity of wood types from trees and shrubs that likely served a range of everyday needs, including fuels for cooking and heating, and raw materials useful in making tools, drying racks, shelving, and room dividers. Heavy demand likely required travel to distant uplands for Douglas fir (*Pseudotsuga*) timbers and for some of the ponderosa pine (*Pinus ponderosa*) timbers. Roofing timbers perhaps became charred during room fires or when their use changed from roof timber to fuel for cooking and heating. People locally sought twigs of mountain mahogany (*Cercocarpus*), cottonwood/willow (*Populus/Salix*), and lemonade berry (*Rhus aromatica*) for some needs; these twigs range between 0.4 cm and 1 cm in diameter and represent relatively short (< 10 years) periods of growth. People also carried in wood of other trees (*Juniperus, Fraxinus, Forestiera, Quercus*) and numerous shrubs (*Sarcobatus, Atriplex, Artemisia, Chrysothamnus, Amelanchier/Peraphyllum*). This wood record helps us to understand the everyday plant needs at Pueblo Bonito beyond roofing requirements.

SUMMARY

My Room 28 archaeobotanical study contributes a number of new insights into Pueblo Bonito plant use. Data from 11 macrobotanical samples, 10 *Zea mays* cob segments/fragments collected separately, and 7 flotation samples together indicate use of at least 24 plant taxa and their associated parts. Both charred and uncharred specimens have contributed to this story.

The archaeobotanical samples indicate a reliance on maize. Limited observations on maize cob segments suggest that a landrace with small to medium, possibly cigar-shaped ears was grown, similar to Basketmaker/Hohokam, Pima/Papago, or Chapalote maize known from the Chimney Rock great house and from an earlier Basketmaker III site (29SJ519) in Chaco Canyon. People also had access to butternut squash (*Cucurbita moschata*) fruits with distinctive seeds and to cotton (*Gossypium*) fibers, which were fashioned into twine.

Ancient people incorporated a number of wild foods into their diets. Charred evidence of hedgehog cactus (*Echinocereus*) and tomatillo (*Physalis*) fruits and of cheno-am (goosefoot-pigweed), tansy mustard (*Descurainia*), and stickleaf (*Mentzelia albicaulis*) seeds reflects the use of these resources, which might have accidentally burned during preparation. This suite of subsistence resources spans seasons from spring through

**TABLE 9.8. Pueblo Bonito archaeobotanical analyses
that reported reproductive plant parts**

TAXON	PART	NUMBER OF SPECIMENS PER EACH ANALYSIS			
		Pepper 1920	Judd 1954	Toll 1981*	Adams (this chapter)
Domesticates					
Zea mays	kernel	108	34	19	present
	other parts	present	present		present
Cucurbita	seed	88	present	present	
Cucurbita moschata	rind	561	present	present	present
	peduncle	46	present	present	
Phaseolus vulgaris	seed	62			
Gossypium	fiber				present
Wild plants					
PERENNIALS					
Celtis reticulata					present**
Echinocereus					present
Juglans		present	present		
Juniperus		present			present**
Opuntia			present		present
Oryzopsis				present	
Pinus edulis		present	present	present	present
Physalis					present
Solanum				present	
Sporobolus				present	
Rumex		present			
Vitis			present		
Yucca		present			
ANNUALS					
Amaranthus					present**
Cleome			present	present	
Cheno-am					present
Descurainia				present	present
Helianthus				present	
Mentzelia albicaulis					present
Portulaca				present	
Solanum			present		
Sphaeralcea					present**

Shaded cells indicate new information.

* Coprolite study.

** Reasonably likely to have been carried in by rodents.

monsoon and into fall. Reasonably, at least some residents of Pueblo Bonito occupied their pueblo during the growing season. As for other wild plants, rodents likely carried in pigweed (*Amaranthus*) and globe mallow (*Sphaeralcea*) seeds, a hackberry (*Celtis reticulata*) seed half, and a juniper (*Juniperus*) seed. Rodents also may have raided stores of pinyon (*Pinus edulis*) seeds and prickly pear (*Opuntia*) fruits carried in by Pueblo Bonito occupants, since they left evidence in the form of gnaw marks on some seeds. That rodents were present during the occupation of Pueblo Bonito is suggested by charred rodent pellet evidence.

ACKNOWLEDGMENTS

Many thanks to Patty Crown for guiding this project to completion and for hosting specialists in the field during her Chaco excavation sessions in Room 28, so we could see the excavated portions of the site firsthand. Thanks also to palynologist Susan Smith, who shared her pollen sample analysis results throughout this project and who joined with me in presenting the Room 28 data at professional meetings.

SUSAN J. SMITH

CHAPTER TEN

Pollen Results from Room 28, Pueblo Bonito

Thirteen pollen samples were analyzed from sediment collected below the floor of Room 28 primarily from the southeast quadrant of the room (table 10.1). One sample (FS 480) was taken from the center of the room beneath a large flat rock. The pollen assemblages have preserved a rich record of cultigens and native plants, which provides a glimpse through time to when Pueblo Bonito was occupied. In this chapter, I present the pollen analysis methods and results with a comparison to previous research at Chaco Canyon and to select projects from the surrounding region.

METHODS

The samples were processed at the Palynology Laboratory at Texas A&M University, utilizing protocols developed and tested by Vaughn Bryant Jr. Ten grams of sediment were subsampled from sample bags and spiked with a known concentration (18,583 spores) of clubmoss spores (*Lycopodium*). These spores provide an artificial marker to monitor degradation from laboratory chemicals and are used to calculate pollen concentrations. Pretreatment steps included sieving to remove coarse material (rocks, roots, charcoal, etc.) and using hydrochloric acid to dissolve carbonates. Samples were next treated with hydrofluoric acid to reduce silicates, followed by a density separation in zinc bromide. Lignin and other organic plant materials were oxidized by chemical acetolysis, and the final residues were transferred to vials and stored in glycerol.

Drops from the extracted samples were spread and sealed onto microscope slides, which I analyzed on a Reichert Microstar compound microscope at 400× magnification. For each sample, I identified pollen grains across successive transects until more than 200 grains were tallied. I counted aggregates (clumps of the same

pollen type) as one grain per occurrence and recorded the taxon and size separately. Following the standard counts, I scanned the entire slide at 100× magnification to search for larger grains of approximately 30 microns (0.03 mm). Larger grains include maize, cotton, squash, agave, cacti, pines, and some herbs.

Pollen identifications were made to the lowest taxonomic level possible based on published keys (Fægri et al. 1989; Kapp et al. 2000). I documented two unknowns.

TABLE 10.1. **Pollen samples analyzed from Room 28**

FS	CONTEXT	DEPTH (m)	DESCRIPTION
477	deep test, column 1, north profile	95.75	Control: Pre—Pueblo Bonito
472-1	deep test column 2, north profile	96.65	
472-2	deep test, column 2, north profile	96.80	
472-3	deep test, column 2, north profile	96.90	
472-4	deep test, column 2, north profile	97.00	
475	deep test, Posthole 21	96.50	Posthole 21, part of east wall
474	deep test, Posthole 20	96.65	Posthole 20, part of east wall
479	deep test, south profile	96.95	below masonry step
480	center of room by Postholes 4 and 5	97.00	below large stone
473-1	southeast quadrant	97.03	northeast corner under rock
473-2	southeast quadrant	97.03	northwest corner under sherds
473-3	southeast quadrant	97.03	southwest corner
473-4	southeast quadrant	97.03	southeast corner

Floor surface at 97.09 m.

Unknown 1 is a tricolpate, prolate grain (longest dimension approximately 30 microns) with transverse furrows and an exine characterized by coarse reticulate sculpturing, which may represent sumac (*Rhus*). The second unknown is a large, tricolpate (possibly tricolporate), prolate grain (longest dimension approximately 40 microns), which may represent a genus from the knotweed family (Polygonaceae).

Pollen from the grass family can be separated into only three categories based on grain diameters: maize (greater than 60 microns), large grass type (40–60 microns), and all other grasses (less than 40 microns) (Fægri et al. 1989:284–86). The large grass type subsumes imported cereal grasses (wheat, oats, and rye) and three native genera: little barley (*Hordeum*), panic grass (*Panicum*), and Indian ricegrass (*Achnatherum hymenoides*). Maize is common in Room 28 samples, and the pollen grains are generally large with diameters of 100 microns (median value from 48 grains measured in 5 samples). In 6 samples, a large grass type was identified with diameters ranging from 30 to 40 microns, and 12 samples contained smaller grass grains (less than 30 microns).

My identifications of another broad pollen group, the Asteraceae (sunflower family), are divided into four taxa: a low spine form counted as ragweed (*Ambrosia*); grains with high spines, which encompass most of the sunflower genera; the sagebrush type (*Artemisia*); and a long spine grain that compares well with sunflower (*Helianthus*). Pine pollen grains are present in most samples, and these I separated by size into two types:

ponderosa (*Pinus ponderosa*) with grains greater than 70 microns and smaller grains counted as pinyon (*Pinus edulis*) (Jacobs 1985).

I calculated three numerical measures from the data: pollen percentages, taxon richness, and sample pollen concentration. Percentages represent the relative importance of each taxon in a sample ([taxon count/pollen sum] × 100), and richness is the number of different pollen types identified per sample. Pollen concentration is an estimate of the absolute abundance or density of pollen grains and is calculated by taking the ratio of the sample pollen count to the tracer count and multiplying by the initial tracer concentration. Dividing this result by the sample weight yields the number of pollen grains per gram of sediment.

RESULTS

The data are documented in table 10.2, which includes for each sample the taxon counts listed by both common and scientific names, summary measures (pollen concentration and taxon richness), and provenience information.

Room 28 samples produced 33 pollen types, 2 distinct unknowns, and fossil palynomorphs. Palynomorphs are spores and pollen derived from erosion of the Cretaceous sedimentary layers visible in the cliffs bounding Chaco Canyon and tributary drainages (Hall 1975). Microphotographs of pollen grains from a few select taxa and one of the unknowns are in figure 10.1. The pollen preservation

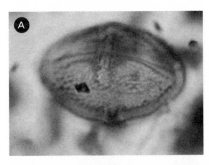
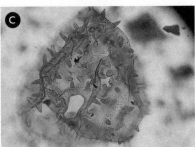
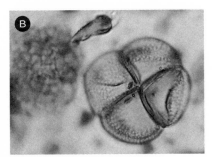
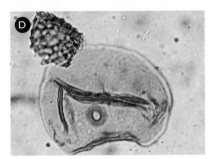

FIGURE 10.1. (*a*) FS 479 includes an unknown tricolpate pollen grain with transverse furrows, longest dimension approximately 30 microns; (*b*) cattail (*Typha latifolia*) from FS 473-2, with four pollen grains in tetrad, longest dimension approximately 40 microns; (*c*) squash pollen grain from FS 473-4, longest dimension approximately 120 microns; (*d*) maize pollen grain from FS 473-4, longest dimension approximately 100 microns. Microphotographs at greater than 400× magnification. Photographs by Susan J. Smith.

TABLE 10.2. **Room 28 pollen data raw counts**

FS	477	472-1	472-2	472-3	472-4	475	474	479	480	473-1	473-2	473-3	473-4
Context	deep test, column 1	deep test, column 2	deep test, column 2	deep test, column 2	deep test, column 2	deep test, PH 21	deep test, PH 20	deep test, south profile	by PH 4 and 5	SEQ, sample 1	SEQ, sample 2	SEQ, sample 3	SEQ, sample 4
Depth (m)	95.75	96.65	96.80	96.90	97.00	96.50	96.65	96.95	97.00	97.03	97.03	97.03	97.03
Description	north profile, sample 1	north profile, sample 1	north profile, sample 2	north profile, sample 3	north profile, sample 4	PH 21	PH 20	below masonry step	below large stone	northeast corner, under rock	northwest corner, under sherds	southwest corner	southeast corner
Sample weight (grams)	10	10	10	10	10	10	10	10	10	10	10	10	10
Tracers (initial concentration 18,583 spores)	46	48	83	14	22	37	31	30	38	42	11	46	13
Pollen sum	218	236	200	230	256	208	216	214	259	238	246	274	267
Pollen concentration (grains/gram)	8,807	9,137	4,478	30,529	21,624	10,447	12,948	13,256	12,666	10,530	41,558	11,069	38,167
Taxon richness	13	16	15	17	14	18	15	16	17	15	21	20	18

COMMON NAME	TAXON	477	472-1	472-2	472-3	472-4	475	474	479	480	473-1	473-2	473-3	473-4
Ragweed type	Ambrosia		2				1	2			1		1	1
Carrot family	Apiaceae													1
Sagebrush	Artemisia	4	7	4	5	2		3	2	1	5	3	1	1
Sunflower family	Asteraceae	19	30	36	26	22	32	24	10	23	31	15	15	10
Mustard family	Brassicaceae	2	2		1		1							
Cheno-am	cheno-am	104	71	56	40	29	93	135	31	71	58	20	69	16
Beeweed	Cleome	3	27	3	3	34	10		12	26	14	21	8	16
Squash	Cucurbita		1		1		X		X	X		1	X	1
Juniper family	Cupressaceae	6	5	3		1	12	3		2	3	1	1	
Cholla	Cylindropuntia		X	X	8	1		X		3	2	X	8	X
Sedge	Cyperaceae						1							
Mormon tea	Ephedra	1			1		1	1	1	1		1		X
Buckwheat	Eriogonum				3									
Spurge family	Euphorbiaceae	1	1		1			1	1	1				
Pea family	Fabaceae								1	1				
Long spine type	Helianthus type											1		
Evening primrose family	Onagraceae		1											
Pinyon	Pinus edulis	5	12	9	13	1	13	8		4	8	2	3	2
Large pine	Pinus ponderosa	5	8	6	14	4	10	13	6	8	14	2	12	3
Prickly pear	Platyopuntia		X	X		1	X		1	1	1	1	1	
Grass family	Poaceae	7	7	3	4	2	2	2	3	6	5	5	5	

Taxon	1	2	3	4	5	6	7	8	9	10	11
Large grass — Poaceae, large	2	1	2	2		1	1		1	1	2
Phlox type — Polemoniaceae										1	X
Cottonwood type — Populus type						18				3	
Oak — Quercus				1							
Sumac, lemonade berry type — Rhus type				1					1		
Rose family — Rosaceae		2				1			1		
Willow — Salix									1		
Greasewood — Sarcobatus	1	33	1	4	12	1		5	3	39	8
Nightshade family — Solanaceae						1					
Globe mallow — Sphaeralcea		4	2		1					1	1
Cattail — Typha latifolia		2	94	2		75	53	34	90	33	100
Maize — Zea	22	26	46	1	1	41	16	32	64	30	82
Degraded	36	41	13	23	7	17	22	22	10	32	18
Unknown	2	5	3		2	10	2	2		8	4
Unknown 1: prolate tricolpate with transverse furrows, possibly sumac (Rhus) type						1					
Unknown 2: large prolate, tricolpate/tricolporate, possibly Eriogonum or Polygonum	2				1						
Total Aggregates	2	1				1			1	1	1
Cheno-am aggregates	1(8)	1(20+)	1(4)								
Maize aggregates	1(4)	X(8)	X(4)								
Beeweed aggregates	1(7)										
Grass aggregates									1(8)	1(10+)	
Palynomorph: P3 type	2	1								1	
Palynomorph: Rhamnus type										1	
Trilete spores	2										

Pollen aggregate notation shows the number of aggregates with the size of the largest clump in parentheses.

PH = posthole, SEQ = southeast quadrant; X = scan-identified taxon presence.

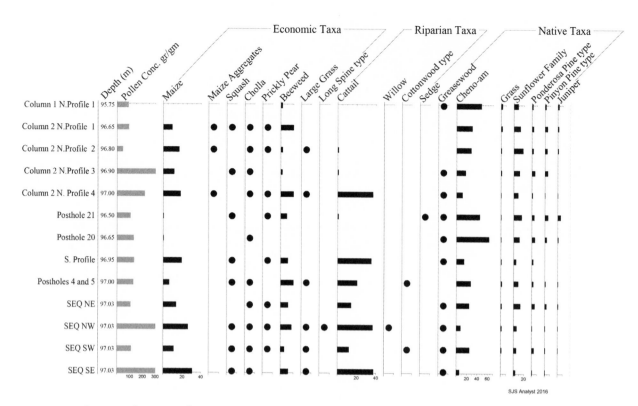

FIGURE 10.2. Summary of Room 28 pollen. Data are presented as pollen percentages; a black dot indicates a taxon's presence.

is exceptional as measured by the low percentages of degraded grains (average 11%; N = 13). Typical deteriorated pollen frequencies in archaeological samples range from 20% to 40%.

The overall variety of pollen types from just 13 samples is high and matches the number of taxa identified from 58 samples analyzed for the reexcavations of the Pueblo Bonito trash mounds (Wills et al. 2016). The rich assemblages from Room 28 undoubtedly relate to the many activities that engaged the people living at Pueblo Bonito. The pollen spectra are dominated by maize, cattail, and cheno-am (figure 10.2), which is an unusual signature for US Southwest archaeological contexts, which are typically overwhelmed by weedy cheno-am and sunflower family pollen.

Cattail is especially notable with counts of 30–100 grains in seven samples, and there are high maize counts (range of 20–82 grains) in nine samples (table 10.2). The cattail pollen occurs in a tetrad form—four conjoined grains (figure 10.1b), which I tallied as one grain in the sample counts. The tetrad is diagnostic to broadleaf cattail (*Typha latifolia*), a widely distributed global species known from every state in the United States except Hawaii. Cattail plants are a source of food and practical

products (table 10.3) around the world and are important in religious and ritual ceremonies (table 10.4). Even the pollen from flowering spikes is valued for food and ceremony. Curtin (1997:2) cited the food value of cattail roots as a source of starch equal to corn and rice. Clans among several Native American tribes are named for cattail, for example, in New Mexico, the San Juan Tewa Ye Clan (Austin 2007).

Environmental conditions for cattail are not limited to perennial aquatic habitats since these adaptable plants can thrive in less than an inch of water or in wet mud and can also survive dry periods (Gucker 2008). Cattail plants are wind-pollinated and produce abundant pollen, but their reproductive ecology evolved to essentially self-pollinate, which is a strategy that conserves pollen within local populations. This syndrome is an especially important survival mechanism in the arid US Southwest where riparian habitats are limited. The maximum downwind distance of cattail pollen, as measured by modern air samplers arrayed around natural stands of the plant, is less than one kilometer from parent populations (Krattinger 1975). Mud samples collected around cattail plants at Pecks Lake in the Verde Valley of Arizona (Hevly 1974) and on the Pajarito Plateau in New Mexico

TABLE 10.3. **Ethnobotanical uses of cattail (*Typha*)**

PART OF PLANT	SUBSISTENCE USES	COLLECTION TIME
Newly emergent stalks or culms cut from rhizomes	*Food*: eaten fresh (reported to taste like celery); new tender shoots salted and eaten	spring
Roots	*Food*: eaten fresh or lightly roasted, dried, and stored; dried roots ground to meal and mixed with water to make mush, which could be formed into cakes and roasted	spring and fall
	Medicine: poultice of crushed roots applied to infection; pulverized root and white base of leaves taken for abdominal cramps; used to treat kidney stones; poultice for strains; chewed for gonorrhea	
Green spikes of the flowering and seed-bearing heads	*Food*: eaten fresh	May and June
	Medicine: young flowering heads eaten for diarrhea	
Pollen	*Food*: pollen of flowering heads tapped into baskets, mixed with water, kneaded into cakes, and baked on coals between layers of cattail leaves or in small leaf pouches (made a sweet bread or cake that could be stacked and stored); cooked into mush	July
	Medicine: Mescalero Apache unspecified application	
Seed-bearing fluff	*Tools and household*: used for stuffing and padding	late summer
	Medicine: poultice of fluff applied to burns; used as wound dressing; used on infants to prevent chafing	
Seeds	*Food*: seed fluff burned off, leaving small, toasted black seeds that were winnowed and ground to meal on flat stones; dry meal mixed with water and eaten; boiled meal made into cakes and sun-dried	late summer
Leaves	*Other*: woven into bags and a variety of textiles; used for parts of sandals, ties, string, mats, boats, roof thatch, construction material; Northern Paiutes built houses, ramadas, and wind breaks with cattail leaves and made duck decoys for hunting	year round

Sources: Buskirk 1986; Curtin 1997; Dunmire and Tierney 1997; Fowler 1992:89–101, 122–127; Moerman 1998.

TABLE 10.4. **Ceremonial, religious, and ritual uses of cattail (*Typha*)**

PART	TRIBES (REFERENCES)
Pollen	Mescalero Apaches (Moerman 1998; Opler 1969:21)
	Navajos (Austin 2007:281; Mayes and Bayless Lacy 1989:25)
	Havasupais (used in face paint; Weber and Seaman 1985:208)
	Shasta legend "The Lost Brother": "That night Erikaner took out the little snake and the little mouse, sat by the door and watched while the snake caused lightning by its tongue and the mouse spread cattail pollen down over all" (Holsinger 1982:33).
Seed fluff	Salish (Pacific Northwest) buried their dead with seed fluff (Ostapkowicz et al. 2001)
Leaves	Navajos hung mats of cattail leaves to keep their hogans safe from lightning (Mayes and Bayless Lacy 1989:25)
	Navajos made ceremonial necklaces and wristbands with leaves (Mayes and Bayless Lacy 1989:25)
	Mescalero Apaches used leaves as ground covering during puberty rituals (Moerman 1998:576)
Stalks	California Cahuillas made ceremonial bundles from stalks (Moerman 1998:576)

(Smith 2008a:120) contained cattail pollen only within sediment from the parent stands. In light of the specialized ecology of cattail plants, the pollen abundance in samples from beneath Room 28 is strong evidence that cattail pollen and/or the flowering spikes were culturally introduced onto surfaces associated with the sampled levels. The cattail signature also indicates an accessible wetland where plants could be harvested.

Ranking samples by the abundance of maize pollen is one way to identify other important economic indicators, based on the assumption that maize is a pointer to culturally influenced samples. In table 10.5, pollen concentrations provide a measure of abundance expressed as the density of pollen grains in sample sediments (grains/gram). The ranked samples highlight the following economic resources: cattail, squash, cholla, prickly pear, beeweed, cheno-am, and possibly large grass. These pollen types represent plants documented in the ethnographic literature as important resources for food, medicine, and a variety of practical products (e.g., Moerman 1998), and most are consistently recovered in archaeobotanical studies (Adams and Fish 2011; Huckell and Toll 2004). A single occurrence of long spine sunflower (cf. *Helianthus*) in FS 473-2 may reflect an additional harvested resource.

Squash is generally rare in archaeological samples, but eight samples from Room 28 contain squash pollen. This high frequency complements the recovery of squash seeds (*Cucurbita moschata*) in three backfill samples and in one sample collected beneath Room 28 (FS 308) in the southeast quadrant at depths comparable to the pollen samples (97.19–96.87 m) (see Adams, this volume).

All of the cacti, including cholla, are insect-pollinated, and characteristics of this biology include low production of pollen grains and short dispersal distances, which means cacti pollen is uncommon in natural soil. The presence of cholla pollen in 10 of the project samples—with high counts of eight grains in 2 samples—is notable, especially since cholla plants are missing from the modern landscape. Cholla is a food resource often cited in ethnographic accounts from throughout the US Southwest (Dunmire and Tierney 1997; Moerman 1998). The fruits were collected, dried, and ground to flour, and the immature joints could be eaten, but the most valuable food is the unopened cholla flower buds, which were gathered usually in May, pit roasted or dried, and consumed or stored (Hodgson 2001). Ceremonial uses are also documented, including at Isleta Pueblo, where arrowheads made from cholla wood were believed to be infectious (Jones 1931), and stems were used for torches and spines for tattooing (Swank 1932). At Zuni, a fraternity-cultivated garden of cholla was used in special ceremonies (Stevenson 1915:95).

In the archaeological record, macrobotanical evidence of cholla is rare because the soft flower buds quickly degrade, but one striking example comes from a Basketmaker site near Mexican Springs (located north of Gallup), where a vessel filled with cholla flower buds was excavated from a pithouse that also contained evidence of ceremonial use of *Datura* (Brandt 1996). Prehispanic use of cholla is generally recognized through pollen data because the harvested flower buds are full of pollen. The absence of cholla plants in the modern landscape and the strong pollen representation from Room 28 together raise questions about the source of cholla at Pueblo Bonito. Several archaeobotanists suspect that cholla farming was widespread and common throughout the prehispanic Southwest (Bohrer 1991; Fish 1984:119–20; Hodgson 2001:115–16). East of Chaco Canyon in the Jemez Mountains, there are examples of cholla growing on archaeological sites beyond the species' natural range (Housely 1974; Smith 2008b). Given the ethnographic and archaeological history of cholla and the pollen expression in Room 28 samples, it is reasonable to at least consider the possibility that cholla farming was part of the local economy. Alternatively, cholla flower buds could have been a trade commodity imported to Chaco Canyon.

Another striking pattern evident in table 10.5 is the distribution of economic pollen by stratigraphic depths. The pollen assemblage from sample FS 477 at 95.75 m with no economic taxa serves as a control since it represents sterile sediment predating Pueblo Bonito. The interpreted economic pollen types all occur above sample FS 477, between 97.03 and 96.5 m, and the highest representations by pollen concentration or raw count (table 10.5) are in samples centered around 97 m (97.03–96.9 m), excluding samples from postholes. The postholes appear to have filled with sediment not influenced by cultural materials. Cheno-am abundance is generally highest in samples with the lowest representation of economic pollen, which indicates a background environmental signature probably related to the dense native saltbush (*Atriplex canescens*) community covering the floor of Chaco Canyon.

FS	CONTEXT	DEPTH	POLLEN CONCENTRATION (grains/gram × 100)				RAW COUNT			
			Maize	Cattail	Beeweed	Cheno-am	Squash	Cholla	Prickly pear	Large grass
473-4	SEQ, southeast corner	97.03	117	143	23	23	1	X		2
473-2	SEQ, northwest corner	97.03	108	152	35	34	1	X	1	1
472-4	deep test, column 2, north profile	97.00	39	79	29	24		1	1	2
472-3	deep test, column 2, north profile	96.90	35	3	4	53	1	8		
479	deep test, south profile, bleow step	96.95	25	46	7	19	X		1	
473-1	SEQ, northeast corner, under rock	97.03	14	15	6	26		2	1	
473-3	SEQ, southwest corner	97.03	12	13	3	28	X	8	1	1
472-1	deep test, column 2, north profile	96.65	9		10	27	1	X	X	
480	center of room by PH 4 and 5, below large stone	97.00	8	26	13	35	X	3		1
472-2	deep test, column 2, north profile	96.80	7		1	13		X	X	1
474	deep test, PH 20	96.65	1			81		X		
475	deep test, PH 21	96.50	1	1	5	47	X		X	
477	deep test, column 1, north profile, Pre—Pueblo Bonito	95.75			1	42				

Room floor surface at 97.09 m.

PH = posthole; SEQ = southeast quadrant; X = scan-identified taxa.

COMPARISON TO PREVIOUS POLLEN STUDIES

The abundance and high representation of economic pollen taxa from Room 28 samples are emphasized in these results, but how great is that expression when compared to other studies? Early research at Chaco Canyon, primarily by Cully (1982, 1985), did not include pollen concentration data, which excludes comparing pollen abundance with those studies. The more common method of analyzing archaeobotanical data is to calculate ubiquity or simple taxon presence within a sample set. In table 10.6, sample ubiquities of four selected economic pollen types are listed for four previous studies and Room 28. Previous investigations used samples from a variety of residential contexts, such as structure floors, mealing

bins, thermal features, and pits. Context is a primary architect of pollen assemblages (Adams and Smith 2011), and therefore my use of lumped data in table 10.6 is a broad-brush approach that averages and smooths the results. However, the numbers are striking in that the 13 samples from Room 28 register significantly higher frequencies of all economic pollen types compared to 134 samples from the other projects.

At Pueblo Alto, three samples from Cully's (1985) research begin to match the abundance of maize pollen documented from Room 28. The Pueblo Alto samples are from three mealing bins in the west room block's Room 110, where maize counts of 20–130 grains were recovered (Room 28 maize counts range from 20 to 82 grains). A Pueblo Alto pollen sample from Room 112 (west room block) included a high count of 54 cattail grains. Cully

TABLE 10.6. **Select pollen types as percentage of samples by project**

LOCATION	CHACO CANYON				ESCAVADA WASH
Project	Pueblo Bonito beneath Room 28	Pueblo Bonito mounds	Pueblo Alto[a]	Site 29SJ627[b]	Bis sá ani
Reference	Smith (this chapter)	Wills et al. 2016	Cully 1985	Cully 1985	Cully 1982
Number of sites	1	1	1	1	13
Number of pollen samples[c]	13	54	28	19	33
% OF SAMPLES BY PROJECT					
Cattail	77	—	14	21	3
Cholla	77	24	—	—	—
Maize	92	57	89	84	48
Squash	62	4	21	16	6

[a] Pollen samples were collected from nine rooms and Kiva 15.

[b] This is a room block located southwest of Pueblo Bonito in Marcia's Rincon.

[c] Number of samples excludes surface control, sterile, and coprolite samples.

(1985:208, 218) speculated that higher proportions of economic taxa from the west room block reflected the processing and storage of harvested crops and other resources.

CONCLUSIONS

The 13 pollen samples from Room 28 produced a record that is exceptional for the near-perfect preservation of pollen grains and a stratigraphic profile of economic taxa abundance that peaks in samples collected from below the room floor. This zone of enriched pollen is interpreted as a use area, room, or plaza space that predated Room 28, where cultivated and gathered plant resources were stockpiled, processed, and possibly stored.

There are several research themes that can be explored with the archaeobotanical record documented in this volume. It should be clear that Chacoans were accomplished farmers, a theme explored in detail by Heitman and Geib (2015) with regional pollen data. And it is clear that people used a wide variety of native plants. Whenever we say that, however, there is an underlying modern perception that wild foods are somehow inferior to the bounty of cultivated fields of corn and other crops. This mind-set is due in part to the typically meager recovery of wild plant taxa in most archaeobotanical records. It is difficult to build much of a story on a few fragments of some seed. It is also a fact that the majority of sites

with archaeobotanical records were relatively small endeavors and not the urban center that was Chaco. In the combined Room 28 record of pollen and macrobotanical remains (see Adams, this volume), we find quantities of plants that could well have supplied gourmet ingredients for a traditional cuisine exotic to most contemporary people's palates. These resources include oily blazing star and tansy mustard seeds, sweet and juicy cactus fruits, cattail pollen cakes, the artichoke-like texture of cholla flower buds, and the nutty taste of amaranth seeds and meals. Through the pollen lens, Room 28 is also remarkable for an abundance of cattail pollen, which is a food resource and also may be a glimpse of materials important in the rich pageant of ceremony and ritual at Pueblo Bonito.

The overall variety of pollen and the diverse environments represented in the plant record underscore another research theme: the intimate knowledge that people had of their home landscape. Chacoans knew where to find specific resources, and they understood the seasonal cycles for crucial products, such as when sap might flow in trees and woody shrubs or the best time to collect different fruits and pollen from maize and cattail. Finally, it is important to remember that the presence in the archaeological record of plant taxa that today are rare or absent at Chaco, such as cattail and cholla, indicates a different Pueblo period landscape from what we see today.

KATHERINE L. BREWER

Historical Artifacts from Room 28

CHAPTER ELEVEN

The 2013 excavations of Room 28 uncovered several historical artifacts believed to be associated with late nineteenth-century excavations by the Hyde Exploring Expedition (HEE). In this chapter I describe the historical artifacts and what they indicate about the dates they were discarded as well as the activities occurring at Pueblo Bonito, such as food consumption and leisure pursuits. As discussed in chapters 1 and 2, evidence now suggests that these historical artifacts might have been left by either the HEE excavators or the Moorehead group, which excavated in nearby rooms in the spring of 1897. For comparison, I also discuss artifacts left behind by HEE excavators in other rooms at Pueblo Bonito.

METAL

The University of New Mexico excavators recovered 12 complete iron wire nails and 3 iron wire nail fragments in seven different levels (table 11.1). Two of the nails are broken into several pieces, while a third nail is incomplete. At least 3 metal cans are also represented in this assemblage. Two of the cans were excavated with all the pieces together. The third can was excavated along with pieces that may or may not represent additional cans. All 3 appear to have had a circle cut out of the base of the can. Some of the rim pieces of the cans have triangular portions folded over where the top of the can was cut open, indicating that these were likely cans of non-liquid food items (Rock 1987:113). All 3 of the cans are cylindrical in shape with a side seam. The majority of the can fragments were found in Levels 10 and 10a, while the remaining 16 pieces (comprising 1 can) were uncovered as part of a floor cleaning. Both the cans and the nails are potentially within the date range for either the HEE or Moorehead excavations. Finally, the UNM excavations uncovered 1 aluminum pull tab, likely from a soda can and certainly a late twentieth-century intrusion.

GLASS

The UNM excavations uncovered two items of glass: one small shard of amber glass, likely from a bottle, and an almost complete amber porter bottle, broken into three pieces that mend to form a single bottle (figure 11.1, table 11.1). The base of the bottle is embossed with an anchor above the letters L. G. Co. The number 28 occurs below the letters. The most likely maker of the bottle itself is the Lindell Glass Company, which was in operation from 1875 to 1890, when it may have become part of the United States Glass Company (Bottle Research Group 2016; Glass Bottle Marks 2016; von Mechow 2017). The body of the bottle has a label that is now covered with patina, but was visible when first uncovered. The label showed that the bottle was used by the American Brewing Company of St. Louis, Missouri, which was in business between 1890 and 1906 (Old Breweries 2004). The glass itself also has patina. The cork used as a closure still rests inside the bottle. The dates for the American Brewing Company are consistent with dates for either the HEE or Moorehead excavations.

OTHER

In addition to the artifacts discussed above, the excavations uncovered one piece of a cork object with a partial hole (table 11.1). The cork appears to be from the lining of an indeterminate object. Additional historical items include a fragment of wool and seeds described in chapters 6 and 9, respectively.

TABLE 11.1. **Historical artifacts recovered from Room 28**

ARTIFACT	QUANTITY	MEASUREMENTS (MM)	LEVELS	NOTES
Iron wire nails	12	52.02, 52.37, 54.12, 54.23, 54.61, 55.01, 55.05, 61.61, 79.77, 81.25, 85.09	9a, 10a, 11, 12, 13; Hyde Exploring Expedition: excavation in front of the door to Room 28	one nail was too fragmented to measure
Iron wire nail fragments	3	indeterminate	8	
Metal cans	2	105.18 (w) × 114.72 (h); 111.24 (w) × 127.96 (h)	10, 10a; southeast floor clean	
Metal can fragments	58	indeterminate	10	can fragments include 16 pieces of a third can, but it is unclear which of the other fragments are part of this can
Aluminum pull tab	1	n/a	2	
Glass porter bottle	1	n/a	11	
Glass fragment	1	n/a	12	
Cork object	1	n/a	2	

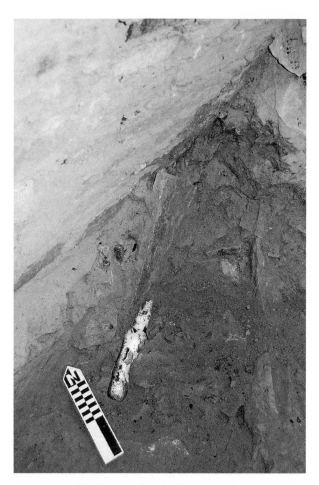

FIGURE 11.1. A porter bottle found in Room 28 resting in burned sand, perhaps the remains of a campfire in the room in 1897. Chaco Collections, CHCU 124552.

HISTORICAL ARTIFACTS IN OTHER ROOMS

In June 1992, Chaco Culture National Historical Park and the Getty Conservation Institute reexcavated Rooms 20, 62, 83, 85, 97, and 348 in Pueblo Bonito to verify the possibility of using backfilling in room stabilization (Wendy Bustard, personal communication, November 2018). George Pepper and Richard Wetherill initially excavated all of these rooms except Room 348. The 1992 reexcavations uncovered a variety of materials, including glass, metal, ceramics, macrobotanical remains, and fabric.

A portion of the metal artifacts found were associated with firearms: one spent .45-caliber lead bullet, one .45 Colt shell casing with W. D. Co on the base, one .44-caliber shell casing with W. H. Co. and .44 on the base, one .22-caliber compressed shell casing, and one shotgun shell casing labeled Winchester 10 New Rival (dated to the early twentieth century) (Cartridge Corner 2018). The reexcavations also found 22 can fragments, a long wire nail, several pieces of brass hardware, a safety pin fragment, and a copper store token labeled "F. E. Hyde, Jr. Putnam, New Mexico" on one side and "For 5 in Merchandise" on the other. The store token directly connects these artifacts with the Pepper and Wetherill excavations since F. E. Hyde Jr. was Frederick Hyde, one of the two brothers who lent their name to the Hyde Exploring Expedition (Lister and Lister 1981:23, 41).

The 1992 project recovered 60 shards of glass in varying colors, including green, clear, milk glass, and black, as well as 2 glass beads, 1 blue and 1 green. Eleven brown glass fragments came from a humidor with an intact label that read "Air Tight—F. R. Rice Mercantile Cigar Co.—Mercantile—Colorado." One large fragment was also incised with "An Air Tight Humidor Cigar . . . Patented Nov. 10 94 Jan 15 95" and the letters "ILE . . . T . . . RS . ." Excavators also found 4 porcelain sherds, a squash seed, carbonized plant material, cloth, an electrical insulator, and a 4-hole shell button.

CONCLUSION

While only one artifact from the 2013 excavations can be exclusively attributed to the period in question, all of the artifacts, excluding the aluminum pull tab and the indeterminate cork object, are consistent with the period 1896–1897, when the HEE and the Moorehead group excavated in this part of Pueblo Bonito. The porter bottle can be attributed to the end of the nineteenth century, given the bottle manufacture date between 1875 and 1890. Reuse or storage would explain why the bottle was in use after the date at which the manufacturer ceased to make bottles. I therefore conclude that the historic artifacts from Room 28 were left by one of the two excavations, with the exception of the indeterminate cork object and the aluminum pull tab, which resulted from later loss or deposition. Pull tabs were not in use until 1962 (Rock 1987:15).

The artifacts excavated by the Chaco Culture National Historical Park and the Getty Conservation Institute are also consistent with the time period in which Wetherill and Pepper were operating at Pueblo Bonito, and they correspond with the Room 28 artifacts. The artifacts are items that workers living at the camp would have used in their everyday lives. The shell casings indicate the presence of firearms. The plant remains and the fragments of food cans are from eating. The glass fragments from bottles that contained much-needed liquid refreshment, the sherds from their dishware, and even the fragments from a humidor meant to hold cigars also point to daily life. Together, these artifacts provide a glimpse into the lives of the HEE excavators, including what they ate and drank and leisure activities, such as cigar smoking.

ACKNOWLEDGMENTS

Thank you to Patricia Crown for providing me the opportunity to analyze the historical artifacts from Room 28. Thank you to Wendy Bustard for providing me with comparative National Park Service data from twentieth-century excavations and allowing me to use those data in my analysis. Finally, thank you to my friends and family for supporting me and listening to my ideas while I worked on this chapter.

PATRICIA L. CROWN

CHAPTER TWELVE

Conclusions
Understanding Room 28 in Pueblo Bonito

The research reported in this volume began with a series of questions about why most of the known Chacoan cylinder jars were found in one room in Pueblo Bonito. The 1896 HEE excavations had left many issues unresolved, including when the cylinder jars were placed in Room 28, where they were placed, why the room burned, and the chronology of events in the room. Reopening Room 28 offered the only way to answer these questions. In this chapter, I synthesize the results of our investigation to provide a comprehensive history of Room 28 and the space it occupied. I also place Room 28 in broader context by discussing the surrounding rooms.

A BRIEF HISTORY/BIOGRAPHY OF ROOM 28

Use of the area that became the site for Room 28 changed over time. Prior to the construction of the room, it was an outdoor activity space located adjacent to earlier rooms and used for processing various foods and materials, as described in chapters 9 and 10. A series of earlier surfaces show clearly in the southeast subfloor unit (figure 2.2). As described in chapter 3, ceramics from beneath the floor suggest use of the area between AD 650 and 900. The earliest of these surfaces may have been used during the Basketmaker III (AD 450–750) occupation of the area. Prior to the construction of the masonry pueblo at Pueblo Bonito, at least two pithouses were constructed and occupied several meters under what became the West Court (Judd 1964).

By the early 800s, a tub room was constructed directly to the east of Room 28, under the later Room 28a (figure 12.1; Crown and Wills 2018). Tub rooms had square to rounded masonry walls with floors that included a central, bathtub-shaped depression 20–40 cm deep, surrounded by shelves 15–25 cm wide (Windes 1993). The floor of the tub room under Room 28a is 76 cm deeper than the later floor in Room 28a (figure 12.2), which is assumed to be contemporaneous with and at the same level as the only clearly identified floor in Room 28. Strata beneath the Room 28 floor that are probably contemporaneous with the structure under Room 28a contain large numbers of turkey gastroliths, suggesting that turkeys were kept there (chapter 8). Impressions of splinters of wood around postholes reveal the level at which builders shaped posts to construct Room 28, although it is possible that the posts originally were constructed to support a ramada because ramadas are common structures adjacent to tub rooms (Crown and Wills 2018).

The east and south walls of Room 28 were constructed of 6–7 courses of wall-wide slabs of sandstone, each separated by about 10 cm of mud. The builders then placed posts 25–30 cm apart on the interior of each wall, with horizontal cross-pieces of wood attached to the posts to create a wattlework wall. This wattlework was covered with about 10 cm of earthen plaster. Handprints are common on the east wall particularly. The west "wall" of the room during the excavations was simply debris from the collapse of the room; the actual wall is not in the space excavated by the Hyde Exploring Expedition. I believe that there was a wall just west of this debris wall, but we could not test this because we could not undercut the later upper-story wall further. We do not know what the original north wall looked like because it was replaced later. AMS (accelerator mass spectrometry) and tree-ring dates confirm the original room construction in the late 800s or early 900s (chapter 2). The presence of several informal fire pits suggests that the room was initially used as a domestic space; as described in chapter 9, the archaeobotanical remains from these pits reveal food preparation using a wide variety of economic plant species.

FIGURE 12.1. Photograph from 1897 of excavations in Room 28a. (*a*) upper-story wall constructed around AD 1071; (*b*) lower-story wall constructed approximately AD 850–925; (*c*) lower-story floor; (*d*) shelf-like projections of probable tub room. The worker is standing on the tub room floor, and the sloping backfill sits in Room 28 to the west. Catalog # HEE 184. Courtesy of the Division of Anthropology, American Museum of Natural History. Image modified by Patricia Crown.

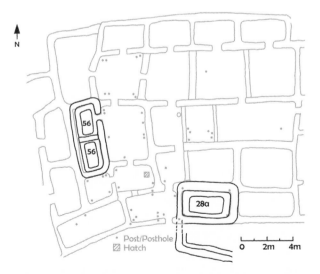

FIGURE 12.2. Lower-story rooms in the northern portion of Pueblo Bonito. The possible tub rooms are outlined in black; later first-story rooms and known postholes are outlined in gray. Drawing by Drew Wills.

The room floor was tamped earth with bits of gypsum. There were many posts associated with the floor level. Those on the plaza (south) side of the room had plaster cone-shaped collars surrounding them (Crown and Wills 2018), a feature of the plaza-side posts along the western side of Pueblo Bonito as well (Judd 1964). Two sets of double posts had figure 8–shaped plastered collars. The use of multiple sets of double posts suggests the symbolic importance of twinning. The use of wood in Room 28 seems excessive for a single-story room, but wood had symbolic importance at Pueblo Bonito (Wills 2000).

Tree-ring dates indicate a hiatus in building activity throughout Pueblo Bonito between approximately AD 975 and 1040. People may have abandoned part or all of the site during this interval. Although occupation of the existing rooms (without new construction) may have continued, areas of the village were "left unmaintained and then partly collapsed before new construction in the A.D. 1040s" (Windes and Ford 1996:301). Remodeling was such a continuous process at Pueblo Bonito that the absence of dates in this interval is striking; there are no dates to verify occupation of Room 28 during these decades, so the room may well have stood empty.

Around AD 1050, a new north wall was constructed of Type II masonry. This wall rested on a clay foundation that sat atop the original Room 28 floor level, so by the time the wall was constructed, the floor level was several centimeters higher. This north wall had two doors, one leading into Room 32 and one leading into Room 51a. Centered between the two doorways was a pinyon post surrounded by masonry and plaster, so it would not have been visible. A second post was placed immediately south of the post built into the wall, and they were connected by plaster. This created a small partition between the western and eastern parts of the room. It is possible that at one time, a partition wall ran across the entire room from north to south at this location, dividing the room into two roughly equal halves. Builders also constructed a room-wide shelf running north-south on the western end of the room. On the south wall, the shelf was socketed into the existing wall and surrounded by thick plaster tamped into place by an individual with six toes on their left foot. Other footprints, rock art, artifacts, and human remains indicate that polydactyly was valued at Pueblo Bonito (Crown et al. 2016).

When construction resumed at Pueblo Bonito in the 1000s, the surface of the West Court had risen so

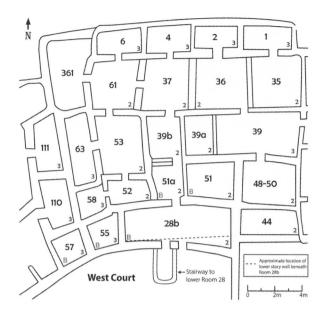

FIGURE 12.3. Upper-story rooms in the northern portion of Pueblo Bonito. A "B" indicates a burned room, and the small numbers indicate the number of stories. Drawing by Drew Wills.

much that it was approximately level with the roofs of the first-story rooms. Judd (1964:60) suggested that wind-blown sand built up to this level. Sand also piled up against the rear rooms, and new rooms were constructed on the accumulated sand (Lekson 1984:133). While Judd saw these deposits as natural accumulation, Stein and colleagues (2003:50) argued that occupants of Pueblo Bonito raised the surface level artificially. The deposits may represent both natural and cultural accumulation, particularly since excavation of large kivas may have deposited material around them. In the case of Room 28, which had a door leading to the West Court, the higher ground surface made this entrance inaccessible.

Around AD 1070, an upper story was built above Room 28. To support this upper story, a new ground-story wall was added on the West Court side of the entire arc of rooms from Room 28a to Room 57 (figure 12.3). The new south wall for these rooms was two stories high along the northern part of the West Court and set onto a foundation 0.53 m high (Judd 1964). It must have been constructed by digging out the accumulated wind-blown sand deposits and placing the wall parallel to and just south of the existing wall. The new wall arc has a smaller diameter than the room walls it parallels, sitting atop part of the south wall of Room 28 but then curving away from the walls of the adjacent rooms to

an ever-greater extent. This created a bench-like feature, where the lower-story ceilings sat. The upper-story rooms were thus slightly larger than the lower-story rooms. The new rooms also had curved walls, while the lower-story rooms had straight walls. Tree-ring dates from the new upper-story rooms suggest construction in AD 1071—a date that matches the Type IV masonry style (Lekson 1984:19). The new upper-story Room 28b covered both lower Rooms 28 and 28a and was fitted with two side-by-side T-shaped doorways.

There is some controversy about whether there was a room adjacent to Room 28 to the south. Pepper (1920:199) excavated in this area in 1897 and believed there was a room, which he numbered Room 40. In the room, he found a feature that he called a "bin" located on the north wall, directly beneath one of the two T-shaped doorways that separate this area from Room 28b. In contrast, Judd (1954) argued that there was no room south of Rooms 28 and 28a and that the "bin" was a stairway framed inside masonry/mud walls that led from the West Court down to the lower Room 28 (Judd 1954: 27), permitting individuals to enter and leave the lower room once it was underground (figure 12.3). We used ground-penetrating radar in this area, and the results suggested the presence of stairs (Jennie Sturm, personal communication, June 2014). Other rooms adjacent to the West and East Courts feature "bin"-like features that are probably stairs necessitated by the rising plaza level that buried these lower-story rooms. The stairway and entry into Room 28 would have been the primary access to the underground rooms of the northern portion of Pueblo Bonito from the West Court. If Room 40 existed, the stairway would lead from Room 28 to the roof of that room; I believe the evidence for there being a Room 40 is strong. According to Judd's (1964:figure 14) cross-section B–B', the roofline of Room 40 would have been at the same level as the roofs of Kivas R and Q to the south of it.

Evidence indicates that Room 28 and probably many of the adjacent underground rooms were used after this time primarily for storage, particularly the storage of objects used in rituals, including the cylinder jars. The function of the original upper-story Room 28b is not known. Pepper did not find any features to identify the use of the room, but the original floor collapsed when the room burned, so any features that may have been present collapsed into the lower room with the burning floor. The location of Room 28b at the northern center of the arc of Pueblo Bonito suggests that it might have been an important room, and the presence of the twin T-shaped doorways leading from Room 28b into the West Court suggests that it had a special function tied to that part of the settlement. I have posited (Crown 2018) that it served as a preparation room for ritual processions into the West Court, with the participants processing through the twin doorways onto the roof of the adjacent Room 40 and then into the public space.

Room 28 burned around AD 1100, a date based on a combination of the latest ceramic type present (Chaco-McElmo Black-on-white) and the absence of any McElmo or Mesa Verde Black-on-white pottery. The actual date for the room burning could be a decade or so later.

Evidence is strong that the conflagration in Room 28 was not an accident. It is unusual for pueblo rooms to burn on their own. In the case of Room 28, there is no evidence of the fire starting from a hearth or fire pit. Instead, our excavation shows that the fire began in the western area of the room around a post and beneath the room-wide shelving that held the cylinder jars and other vessels. The floor there is vitrified and deep red in color. The fire then spread upward from the post to the shelving and the ceiling. It then moved down other posts in the room, burning all of them to about half of their original length. When the ceiling collapsed, it smothered the fire. All posts in the room burned, but the heaviest burning was along the western end of the floor and the southwestern corner of the wall, particularly around where the shelving was socketed into that wall. The wall in the southwestern corner partially melted down onto the post that sat in that corner. In other parts of the room, the posts burned, but the walls show less evidence of high-temperature burning; they are not reddened or even hardened to the same extent as the walls on the western side of the room.

Two of the three doors of the room appear to have been sealed prior to the fire. The northwest door to Room 32 was filled with masonry. We have no way of knowing when it was closed: years before the fire or just prior to the fire. Outside the southeast doorway, Pepper (1920) found a stone slab in the stairway area that leads from Room 28 to the West Court. I suggest that this slab was not a lapidary stone, as Pepper (1920:200) implied, but rather a door placed to seal Room 28 from the court side. The lack of burning on the second story's exterior wall directly above the door suggests that some-thing blocked the fire from escaping the room, and that something was most likely the stone slab. Photographs (e.g., figure 2.11) show the stone slab positioned upright against the wall where the door was located, again providing evidence that it was a door used to seal Room 28 from the outside. Only a single door was left open: the door between Room 28 and Room 51a.

On the day that Room 28 burned, 127 ceramic vessels, including 99 cylinder jars, sat on the shelving at the western end of the room. Thirty ceramic vessels and several baskets were placed in a pile in front of the northeast doorway to Room 51a, essentially blocking egress in that direction. As described in chapter 5, the large number of ornaments found in and among the vessels in the room indicates that the individuals charged with preparing the room placed ornaments in some vessels and sprinkled more ornaments over the piles of vessels. It was probably these same individuals who then laid fuel around one of the posts on the lower floor, a post directly adjacent to the shelving. Given the oily stains on some vessels, these people may have poured grease over some of the vessels. They then started the fire that destroyed the room. They probably exited through the south door, sealing it with the door slab, and as they climbed the stairs to the West Court they placed hundreds more turquoise and shell ornaments as offerings. Pepper (1920:200) found so many ornaments in this "bin" or stairway area that he interpreted it as an ornament workshop. Probably at the same time, many adjacent rooms burned, including Room 28a to the east, Rooms 55 and 57 to the west, and probably Room 51 to the north. This part of the settlement, the arc of rooms between the West Court and the northern burial rooms, was destroyed.

At some time after Room 28 burned, the debris filling the lower-story room was leveled and a plaster floor laid over the debris. A new partition wall of sloppy masonry was placed atop the debris between Rooms 28 and 55. The T-shaped doorways to the West Court were at least partially filled with masonry. It is unclear if the resulting large Room 28b was ever rerooofed. We cannot date this reuse of Room 28b precisely. There are no late tree-ring dates to suggest a roof, and Pepper did not find any evidence of one. So this may have been an unroofed space, perhaps used as a turkey pen or for other activities that required four walls but no roof.

Room 28b eventually was abandoned. Hyde Exploring Expedition photographs suggest that it filled with sand

and chunks of masonry over time, becoming indistinguishable from the surrounding rooms.

There is no known mention of Room 28 until around August 10, 1896, when George Pepper and Richard Wetherill had Navajo workers begin excavations on the room. Pepper (1920:117) stated that this part of Pueblo Bonito was "a mound on which greasewood thrived." Initially, the excavators opened the full Room 28b, but once they encountered the partition wall between the lower Rooms 28 and 28a, they only worked on Room 28, leaving Room 28a until 1897.

The workers began finding artifacts, including bits of turquoise and a piece of hammered copper, at about 60 cm. At 1 m, they encountered the burned remains of the upper story, and on August 20, a worker identified only as Juan discovered the first cylinder jar (Pepper 1920:117). We do not know where they threw the backdirt from Room 28, although the historic photographs of the room suggest that most of it was thrown just outside the walls in all directions. By August 29, they had completed their excavation of the room, and one of the Wetherill brothers removed the stones from the door to the adjoining Room 32, and they began excavating there. Most of the rest of the 1896 season entailed excavation of Rooms 32 and 33; the expedition left Chaco Canyon on September 23, 1896.

George Pepper (1896a:diary entry for September 16, 1896) stated in his field notes that fill from the burials in Room 33 was thrown into Room 28. At least some of that fill was subsequently moved near Wetherill's tent northwest of Pueblo Bonito to facilitate the search for ornaments (Pepper 1896a:diary entries for September 18, 21, and 22, 1896). Given that the only entry to Room 32 was located almost at floor level at the northwest end of Room 28, it was imperative to keep the room clear enough to reach that doorway. Yet the backdirt from Rooms 32 and 33 would have more than filled Room 28, so keeping the doorway open would have required moving the majority of that backdirt out of Room 28. Steps were taken to make moving the backdirt from those rooms into Room 28 easier: the stone threshold of the door to Room 32 was removed, enlarging the size of the doorway; and a hole adjacent to the door on the Room 28 side was excavated or perhaps just created by the constant movement of people in and out of the door. However, despite the archival indications that backfill from Rooms 32 and 33 was shoveled initially into Room 28, we did not find any material in Room 28 that un-

questionably fit vessels, sherds, or other artifacts from Rooms 32 or 33. Indeed, the lack of any indication that material from Rooms 32 or 33 was left in Room 28 is somewhat baffling. Where did that fill go? A photograph taken from the mesa top of the western end of Pueblo Bonito on September 20, 1896 (AMNH 411867) shows piles of backfill just north and south of Room 28. It also shows wagon tracks circling through the East Court toward the West Court. It is possible that backdirt was moved by wagon to the area near Wetherill's tent, where the matrix was searched for ornaments. In any event, we found no physical evidence that backdirt from Rooms 32 and 33 was in Room 28 when we reexcavated it in 2013.

We did find that the doorway to Room 32 was blocked haphazardly with chunks of masonry, but we do not know when this was done; perhaps the door was blocked before the HEE excavators left the canyon in September. This would have effectively kept curious visitors and animals out of the rooms, but we have no way of knowing if that material was placed in the doorway in 1896. The archaeologist Warren Moorehead did not enter the northern rooms through this passageway when he worked at Pueblo Bonito in April 1897, suggesting that this doorway was blocked by the time he arrived in the canyon. The rest of Room 28 almost certainly remained open. A photograph taken three days before the HEE group left the canyon was shot at an angle that does not show all of Room 28, but it does show part of the room, which appears to be empty of backfill. I conclude from this that Room 28 remained largely open between late September 1896 and April 1897.

Fortunately, various types of evidence provide strong indications of where the backfill did come from. As described in chapter 2, the fill we excavated in 2013 contained two different deposits. One was heavily burned with abundant chunks of charcoal; we took almost 1,800 pieces of charcoal for tree-ring dating from the burned matrix, which disappeared in the level above the floor. Both Pepper's notes and an 1897 photograph (figure 12.1; Crown and Wills 2018:figure 6) indicate that this fill came from the adjacent Room 28a. The backdirt from Room 28a was the source of the burned matrix that extended from the surface down 2.2 m, indicating that Room 28 remained partially open when Room 28a, which was the ninth room opened during that season, was excavated in 1897. The other fill we encountered had no burned material but abundant unburned wood and chunks of masonry; this fill was a discrete unit that extended from the surface to the floor. As discussed in chapter 3, my ceramic refitting studies indicate that ceramics found in the Room 28 fill from 0.2 to 2.6 m below the surface refit sherds and partial vessels from Rooms 53 and 56. These rooms, located two rooms north of Room 28, were excavated by Moorehead in April 1897 just before the HEE returned in May. With a group of farmers recruited in Farmington, New Mexico, Moorehead tore down walls to enter the underground rooms. This group threw material over a wide area, as indicated both by the ceramic distributions and by Kerriann Marden's (2011:205–10) reassociation of burials found in Rooms 53 and 56. Marden found that the remains of individual skeletons were scattered from Room 56 to the adjacent Rooms 53 and 61 and to Room 39b, indicating that Moorehead's excavators threw backdirt widely (figure 3.13). Pepper's (1897b:1) field notes from May 1897 described the piles of backdirt left by Moorehead's work. Pepper and Wetherill had to remove this backdirt to excavate the other rooms in this area, and Room 28 was one of the few locations open for disposing of the piles of debris at the beginning of the 1897 field season. Thus, Moorehead's group might have thrown some backdirt from Rooms 53 and 56 into Room 28 and/or Pepper and Wetherill may have chosen to do the same. The pattern of backdirt in Room 28 provides additional evidence. The unburned backfill is piled highest along the south side of the room, sloping almost to the floor on the north (figure 2.14). This pattern indicates that it was thrown against the south wall from the north; Rooms 53 and 56 are north of Room 28. In contrast, the burned matrix is highest on the west side of the room and slopes toward the east, indicating it was thrown from the east; Room 28a is east of Room 28.

Room 28 did not have human remains when it was excavated in 1896. No burials were found or described in Pepper's field notes or published account (Pepper 1920). But as documented in appendix C, in 2013 we encountered 155 individual specimens of human remains in the backfill of Room 28. When we encountered these remains, we followed the Chaco Culture National Historical Park policy on inadvertent discoveries of human remains: to immediately cease excavations and hold a consultation with the descendant tribes. We stopped excavations on June 23, and the tribes responded on June 30, allowing us to resume excavations. A reburial was planned at the end of the field season. The park required an inventory of the human remains prior to reburial, so

we asked Emily Lena Jones to come to Chaco and analyze the materials while we continued excavations. Some additional human remains were found during the analysis in Albuquerque, and these were identified by Caitlin S. Ainsworth and reburied after inventory as well.

The human remains were consistently recovered in the unburned backfill. Two phalanges were found inside a tin can recovered next to the southern door in Room 28. There is no question that these were thrown into the room with the unburned backfill. As with the other remains, the question became whether these were from the Rooms 32 and 33 burials or the Rooms 53 and 56 burials. The results of our analysis indicate that the skeletal elements came from at least four individuals: two adults (one likely female, one likely male, one of them an older adult), one adolescent (9–15 years of age), and one perinatal infant (appendix C). After the material was reburied, I asked Marden, who has conducted extensive research on the human remains from the northern burial rooms, to examine our inventory of remains and evaluate whether they likely came from Rooms 32 and 33 or 53 and 56. Her response was that most of the bones could have come from either set of rooms, but the frontal bone could only have come from the burials found in Rooms 53 and 56.

All of the remains listed here seem consistent with the burials we already know about. . . . Since we already know that there were partial remains of at least three infants accessioned with the remains from the northern cluster (two with Room 33 and one from Room 53/56), there's no reason to think that the infant remains described are not from one of these three children. Likewise, the adult bones— all of these seem consistent with the remains we already have knowledge of, and since Moorehead made such a mess of 53/56, the presence of an unassociated frontal bone is unsurprising. We have a couple of unassociated mandibles that Pepper found in Moorehead's debris the following season, and since Moorehead sold off a couple of skulls in the *Antiquarian*, we'll never know how many individuals were present or what the burial context was, other than the presence of two distinct sub-floor graves (although the number of interments in each is also unknown). But the ribs, hand and foot bones, hyoids and thyroid/cricoid cartilages, etc., could be from either room, because the hands and

feet in Room 33 were incompletely represented. . . .
So, the presence of the frontal bone tells me that at
least some of the remains you found are from Room
53/56. The rest could be from either room, and
there's really no way to know without the chance to
compare the elements. (Kerriann Marden, personal
communication, September 3, 2015)

Given that the ceramic evidence indicates that the
unburned fill came from Rooms 53 and 56, it seems likely
that the human remains also came from these rooms and
were thrown into Room 28 with the backfill from those
rooms by either Moorehead or the Hyde Exploring Expedition in 1897. Based on this interpretation, we can also
infer that the other artifacts and ecofacts found in the
unburned fill, including the ornaments and fauna, came
from Rooms 53 and 56. Ainsworth and colleagues (2018)
have made this argument for the high numbers of bird
elements and species recovered from the unburned fill.

Based on this evidence, either Moorehead or the HEE
excavators filled some of Room 28 with backfill from
Rooms 53 and 56 in April or May 1897. Then, the HEE
workers filled in the remainder of the room with the
burned fill from Room 28a when they excavated the
room later in the field season.

The final part of this brief history of Room 28 concerns our own University of New Mexico excavations.
As described in chapter 1, we excavated and recorded
Room 28 for 23 days between June 4 and July 13, 2013.
The CCNHP stabilization crew then filled the postholes
with clean white sand and filled the remainder of the
room with the backdirt we had removed. Plywood and
screwjacks originally placed for safety reasons were left
in place to keep the walls from collapsing.

ANSWERS TO RESEARCH QUESTIONS

As described in chapter 1, the reexcavation of Room
28 was guided by several research questions that, we
argued, could only be answered by reopening the room.
We were able to collect data to answer all of these questions. Here, I review the answers to these questions and
the data supporting them.

1. What was the sequence of events from construction of the lower room to construction of the upper room?

This sequence is described above and in chapter 2, so I
summarize the events here. The site on which Room 28
was built had originally served as an outdoor activity
area or ramada adjacent to what was likely a tub room
under Room 28a to the east (Crown and Wills 2018).
The lower Room 28 was constructed in the late 800s to
early 900s. The room probably originally had four walls
constructed of sandstone courses widely spaced with
abundant mortar and a facing of wattlework. Plaster
covered the wattle, with particularly heavy plaster at
the rounded room corners. Although no western wall
has been found, I believe one existed, which was hidden
by the debris under the upper partition wall. The room
may have been abandoned between about AD 975 and
1040, when there is a hiatus in building activity in Pueblo
Bonito (Windes and Ford 1996:301). Then around AD
1040/50, the north wall was torn down and replaced with
a new wall. A room-wide shelf was constructed running
north-south across the western part of the room. The
stairs from the West Court to Room 28 may have been
built at this time or slightly later, when the upper story
was added. Construction of the upper story around AD
1070 included placing a second wall on the plaza side of
the south wall of Room 28; this wall was curved, creating a new north wall for the West Court and a sturdy
foundation for the upper story of Room 28. Finally, the
room burned and collapsed around AD 1100.

2. What are the absolute dates for each of these events?

Dates for the area's pre-room activity use are based on
ceramics found in the subfloor excavations, indicating
use about AD 650–875. A single AMS date from a corncob has a 95% probability of dating between cal AD 800
and 906 (Cruz and Hodgin 2016). Dates for the room
construction are based primarily on the AMS dates
from posts throughout the room. Although charred
wood samples were sent to the Laboratory of Tree-Ring
Research at the University of Arizona, only a few were
able to be dated, and the dates indicate a lack of outer
rings (Towner 2014). Construction of the north wall
was dated based on three lines of evidence. First, the
masonry is Type II, which is usually dated between AD
1020 and 1060 (Judd 1964). The wall itself was built on a
foundation of heavy clay that sits *above* the original floor

level of Room 28, indicating later construction. Finally, a post built into the wall had both a tree-ring date (933 +vv) and a calibrated AMS date (877–992). It is possible that this post was a beam taken from another location and reused when this north wall was constructed. Given the hiatus in building activity in Pueblo Bonito between AD 975 and 1040, I suggest that this north wall was built around AD 1050. Dates for the construction of the upper story are based on tree-ring dates taken from the upper-story room and a tree-ring date (1069 +L) from a sample recovered in Room 28 that probably came from the backdirt from the adjacent Room 28a. As discussed in chapter 2, cutting dates from the upper story of adjacent rooms indicate construction of the upper story in or close to AD 1071.

3. Were the cylinder jars associated with the lower or upper room?

The reexcavation of Room 28 indicates that 10 of the cylinder jars were smashed on the upper-story floor, and the remaining 102 were associated with the lower room. Of those in the lower room, 99 were placed on shelving above the floor, and the remaining three were on the floor. The burning of the shelving created the pattern of burning (fireclouds primarily) on the side of the jars contacting the shelving, which made it appear initially that they had been sitting on the upper-story floor.

4. Was the surface on which the jars were found the earliest floor in the room?

The HEE excavators reached the first (and probably only) floor in most of Room 28. They did not clear to the floor level in all areas of the room, so, for instance, the posthole collars were not completely cleared. I believe that sand had accumulated on the original floor surface during the time when Room 28 was used as a storage room for the cylinder jars, and so the vessels "on the floor" actually sat in this sand, which may have only been a few centimeters thick. In some areas, it appeared that Pepper and his crew did not completely clear this sand, but for the most part, they reached the original floor. Beneath this floor, we found only a series of outdoor activity surfaces. The level at which the room was built was clearly identifiable based on shavings of wood around the postholes. These were directly below the floor level. I had thought that the HEE excavators had not reached the original floor based partly on a photograph of the doorway to Room 32, which appeared to show the

doorsill at almost the same level as the floor. Excavation showed that this was due to the excavators removing the sill to make getting into and out of Room 32 easier. The original sill would have been about 5 cm higher than indicated in the photograph. The two doorways in the north wall of Room 28 were placed only about 15 cm above the floor, based on the photographs of those doorways.

ROOM 28 IN THE CONTEXT OF PUEBLO BONITO AND THE NORTH BURIAL CLUSTER

Resolving questions about Room 28 and the cylinder jars found in it were important objectives of reopening the room, and we were able to answer all of the questions we posed for the project. The surprise was that we also learned a great deal about surrounding rooms. In this section, I review what we learned about nearby rooms during the Room 28 excavations.

Early Bonito

Excavations beneath the floor of Room 28 revealed a series of surfaces identifiable by dark staining atop the yellowish sand that characterizes this part of the canyon. Sterile soil was reached at 96.6 m, indicating a slightly sloping surface from the Chaco Wash because the mounds reached depths closer to 93 m (Wills et al. 2016), and Neil Judd (1964:figure 14) excavated a pit structure 80 m south of Room 28 at 94.74 m. The first construction in the northern area of Pueblo Bonito included what we have suggested were at least four tub rooms: one under Room 28a, one along the south wall of Room 28a into Room 40, and two under Room 56 (Crown and Wills 2018). As noted above, tub rooms had square to rounded masonry walls with floors that had a central, bathtub-shaped depression 20–40 cm deep, surrounded by shelves 15–25 cm wide (Windes 1993). The tub room beneath Room 28a is described in chapter 2 (see also figures 12.1 and 12.2).

Immediately to the south of this possible tub room and at approximately the same elevation, Judd (1964:76–77) found the remains of a second possible tub room. He described a quadrangular structure, a packed-clay floor, and a "bench" 24 inches wide and 34 inches high, with repeated plastering and smoke blackening. The location of the "bench" places it in line with the wall that Pepper found under the Room 28a partition wall, and so this feature is probably a continuation of that wall. Given the location and description, this may be another tub room and has to predate the initial construction of Rooms 28 and 28a around AD 880–900.

Based on stratigraphy and depth, two additional rooms found under Room 56 are probably contemporaneous (Pepper 1920). These rooms are described as having held burials on either side of a wall dividing the room just below the floor. It seems possible that the burials were placed in the "tub" portion of the rooms.

Later rooms adjacent to these four tub rooms have high numbers of posts (figure 12.2). As discussed in chapter 2, posts along the southern or West Court side of Room 28 had adobe collars (or cones). Likewise, three rooms along the West Court (Rooms 323, 325, and 326) excavated by Neil Judd (1964:325) also had adobe-collared posts on the West Court side of the rooms. As noted in chapter 2, these posts may have supported ramadas running along the margin in the West Court, ramadas that were later replaced by masonry-walled rooms. Additional work examining the archives for these rooms may resolve this issue, or a future reopening of these rooms may help determine if they were originally constructed as ramadas.

Late 800s–900s

Terrestrial lidar of the western part of Pueblo Bonito as a whole included Room 28 after excavation and the intact rooms to the west of it. This revealed that the floor of Room 28 was constructed at the same elevation as the floor of the intact Room 3b, which is two rooms west and one room north of Room 28. This equivalence in floor level suggests that these rooms were built roughly contemporaneously. The roof of Room 3b has four tree-ring dates: 845 vv, 852 vv, 860 v, and 860 v (Laboratory of Tree-Ring Research 2015). These dates suggest construction in the 860s, perhaps twenty years earlier than the AD 880–900 date suggested for Room 28.

As discussed above, our excavations revealed two distinct sources of backdirt: backdirt from a burned room, which undoubtedly came from the adjacent Room 28a, and backdirt with no evidence of burning, which at least partially came from Rooms 53 and 56. The analyses presented in the preceding chapters provide information relevant to the interpretation of these rooms, so each is discussed here. Table 12.1 collates data on these rooms from our 2013 excavations, from Pepper's 1920 publication, from the HEE catalog at the AMNH, from Moore-

head's 1906 description of his "excavations" in Pueblo Bonito, and from the online catalog of the Robert S. Peabody Institute of Archaeology (2018). In creating this compilation, I placed any artifacts from the Room 28 fill excavated in 2013 that showed evidence of burning in the column for Room 28a, and any artifacts that did not show burning in the column for Rooms 53 and 56. I used dissertations by Jolie (2018), Marden (2011), and Mattson (2015) to help with the counts and the identification of items. I consider the numbers presented to be minimum counts of objects in each category. Hopefully, additional archival research will help determine the actual numbers.

ROOM 28A Excavated in 1897, Room 28a is described in Pepper (1920:127–28) without much detail. The upper-story room is a single long room that covered both Rooms 28 and 28a. It is sometimes designated Room 28b. The east wall of Room 28 serves as the partition of this space for the lower story and thus is the west wall of Room 28a. Pepper definitely dug all of the western portion of Room 28b as part of the Room 28 excavations in 1896, but he probably left some of the eastern portion of Room 28b unexcavated until 1897, when he returned to excavate Room 28a. Most of my description here focuses on the lower Room 28a, but some of the material found in the fill of Room 28 may have come from the upper-story Room 28b if portions remained unexcavated until 1897.

Above the possible tub room, there was a floor in Room 28a at the same level as the Room 28 floor. On that lower floor, the excavators found a number of stone objects: five metates; six sandstone manos; two comales; a grinding stone with red pigment on one side; a sandstone disk; a fragment of chalcedony; two natural pebbles; and a jar cover. In addition, they found a heavy handle for a bowl and a fragment of a clay pipe (Pepper 1920:128). The room had burned to such an extent that Pepper (1920:127) suggested it had served as a granary because the sand floor had vitrified. The Room 28 fill that came from the adjacent Room 28a was bright red to orange in color and filled with charred wood and burned daub. The charred wood included more than 1,000 charred sticks. My research assistant Jill Jordan measured a sample of 496 of these and examined them for modification. The mean diameter of the sticks was 7.74 mm. They were quite fragmentary, ranging from 5 to 37 mm in length. These measurements are smaller than

TABLE 12.1. **Comparison of the contents of Rooms 28, 28a, 53, and 56**

	ROOM 28[a]	ROOM 28a[b]	ROOMS 53 AND 56[c]
Ceramic vessels	174 (p)		4 (p), 22 (u), 5 (m)
Gray ware sherds	6 (p)	138 (u)	138 (u)
White ware sherds	31 (p)	7 (u)	493 (u)
Red/brown ware sherds	2 (p)		119 (u)
Chipped stone debitage		85 (u)	120 (u)
Projectile points	5 (p)		7 (u)
Other chipped stone tools		18 (u)	28 (u)
Metates	1 (p)	5 (p)	1 (p), 1 (u)
Jar covers	88 (p)	1 (p)	2 (p), 1 (u)
Ground stone (includes fragments)	10 (u)		1 (p), 68 (u)
Ornaments	698 (p), 1,723[d] (u)		4,382[d] (p), 2,000[d] (u)
Shell trumpets	at least 2[d]		at least 1[d]
Copper	hammered object and copper ore (p)		
Textiles	yucca cordage (p, u)	cotton textile, feathered object?[e] (u)	cotton cloth, feather blankets/robes[e] (p, u, m)
Baskets	at least 1 bowl and 1 cylinder basket (p)		polychrome probable cylinder basket[f]
Sandal			1[f]
Matting			5 fragments[f]
Ceremonial sticks	maybe (p)	yes (u)	yes (p)
Fauna	15 worked antler segments (p)	40 mammal bones[g] (u)	bird wings of many species[g] (u), unknown bones (p)
Gullet stones	at floor level (p)		yes[h] (u)
Bone tools	2 awls (p)		
Human burials	none;1 human tooth	none	7 adults, 2 adolescents, 1 infant[i] (m,p)
Other items	crystal, shark's tooth, mica, square perforated wooden object, bowl sherd with feathers attached (p)	2 comales, pipe bowl (p)	wooden slab, stone slab, cradleboard (p); possibly a sandal stone, stone "sword," ground stone with square hole (m); also possibly a wooden sword, throwing stick, rope

[a] Based on Pepper 1920, Hyde Exploring Expedition catalog and field notes.

[b] Based on Pepper 1920, Hyde Exploring Expedition catalog and field notes; burned objects recovered in 2013 in Room 28 fill, including sooted ceramics.

[c] Based on Hyde Exploring Expedition catalog and field notes; Moorehead 1906; Pepper 1920; Robert S. Peabody Institute of Archaeology 2018; National Park Service 2008; unburned objects recovered in 2013 in Room 28 fill, including ceramics without soot and ceramics that refit material in museum collections from these rooms.

[d] Data from Mattson 2015; Mattson and Kocer, this volume.

[e] Data from Webster, this volume.

[f] Data from Jolie 2018.

[g] Data from Ainsworth, Franklin, and Jones, this volume.

[h] Data from Conrad, this volume.

[i] Data from Marden 2011.

p = recovered by Hyde Exploring Expedition; m = recovered by Moorehead; u = recovered in Room 28 fill by University of New Mexico.

TABLE 12.2. Modified charred sticks found in backfill in Room 28 that originated from Room 28a (identified by Karen Adams)

FS	LOCATION	TAXON	PART	CONDITION	QUANTITY	NOTES
22-1	Level 3	*Cercocarpus*	twig	charred	1	cut/abraded to a point on one end; cut? on the other end
22-2	Level 3	*Populus/Salix*	twig	charred	1	cut on one or both ends
35-1	Level 4	*Cercocarpus*	twig	charred	1	cut on one or both ends
35-2	Level 4	*Cercocarpus*	twig	charred	1	cut/abraded to a point on one end; cut? on the other end
35-3	Level 4	*Cercocarpus*	twig	charred	1	cut/abraded to a point at one end; cut at the other end
36	Level 4	*Juniperus*	wood	partially charred	1	cut into a rectangle
46-1	Level 5	*Populus/Salix*	twig	charred	1	cut/abraded at one end; cut at the other end; one diagonal cut mark present
46-2	Level 5	*Populus/Salix*	twig	charred	1	cut/abraded to a point on one end; cut? on the other end
46-3	Level 5	*Atriplex*	twig	charred	1	cut/abraded to a point on one end; cut? on the other end
46-4	Level 5	*Populus/Salix*	twig	charred	1	cut on one end; cut/abraded on the other end
57	Level 6	*Pinus edulis*	wood	charred	2	one cut into a rectangle; one possibly cut on two sides (of four)
57-1	Level 6	*Populus/Salix*	twig	charred	1	cut/abraded at both ends
57-2	Level 6	*Juniperus*	twig	charred	1	cut/abraded to a sharp point at one end
58	Level 6	*Juniperus*	wood	partially charred	1	cut into a rectangle; 4 diagonal cuts across one flat side
73	Level 7	*Populus/Salix*	twig	charred	1	cut/abraded to a point on one end; cut on the other end
81	Level 7a	*Populus/Salix*	twig	charred	2	pieces fit together to make one; both ends cut
89-1	Level 6	*Populus/Salix*	twig	charred	1	cut/abraded to a point on one end; cut on the other end
103-1	Level 8	*Populus/Salix*	twig	charred	1	cut/abraded to a point on one end; cut on the other end
103-2	Level 8	*Populus/Salix*	twig	charred	1	cut/abraded to a point on one end; cut on the other end
103-3	Level 8	*Juniperus*	wood	partially charred	1	cut into a small slab; cut/abraded to a point on one end
127-1	Level 9	*Populus/Salix*	twig	charred	1	cut/abraded on one end; cut? flat on the other end
127-2	Level 9	*Juniperus*	twig	partially charred	1	cut into a square; abraded to a point and charred on one end
138-1	Level 9a	*Populus/Salix*	twig	charred	1	cut/abraded to a point on one end; cut? on the other end
138-2	Level 9a	*Cercocarpus*	twig	charred	1	cut/abraded to a point on one end
175-1	Level 10a	*Populus/Salix*	twig	charred	1	cut/abraded to a point on one end; cut? on the other end
175-2	Level 10a	*Populus/Salix*	twig	charred	1	cut/abraded to a point on one end; cut? on the other end
227-1	Level 13	Angiosperm	twig	charred	1	cut/abraded to a sharp point at one end; cut on the other end
227-2	Level 13	*Populus/Salix*	twig	charred	1	cut/abraded to a point on one end; cut? on the other end
227-3	Level 13	*Chrysothamnus*	twig	partially charred	1	cut/abraded at one end
227-4	Level 13	*Juniperus*	wood	partially charred	1	cut into a square; cut/abraded to a point and charred on one end
227-5	Level 13	*Juniperus*	wood	partially charred	1	cut flat on 2 sides and along both edges; charred on one end
245	Posthole 2	*Atriplex*	wood	charred	1	abraded to a tapered end
297	Floor level	*Juniperus*	twig	partially charred	1	cut/abraded to a round shape with a point on one charred end

the ceremonial sticks found by Pepper (1920:143–58) in Room 32. In chapter 2, I argue that most of the charred sticks were probably part of rush mats used for roofing in Room 28b, because such mats were used for roofing in later rooms in Pueblo Bonito (Judd 1964:26; Lekson 1984:31). Support for this argument comes from both the large number of charred sticks recovered and measurements taken from burned daub found in the same contexts, which showed impressions of reeds averaging 9.6 mm in diameter. Given the differential shrinkage of wood versus daub, the measurements of the sticks and the measurements of the reed impressions are close enough to suggest they are related.

While most of the sticks were probably part of rush mats, some showed evidence of modification, perhaps for use as prayer sticks, arrows, gaming pieces, or ceremonial sticks, so these were examined further. Karen Adams analyzed 35 shaped sticks, identifying the wood species and examining them under a microscope for any purposeful modification. As shown in table 12.2, the sticks are cottonwood/willow (16), juniper (8), mountain mahogany (5), saltbush (2), pine (2), angiosperm/flowering plant (1), and *Chrysothamnus*/sunflower family shrub (1). Of these, 21 showed abrading of one end into a tapered point. The others showed various types of modification, including cutting, shaping, and abrading. We do not know what these were used for, but they might have been ceremonial sticks, similar to those found by Pepper (1920) in Room 32. Pepper (1920) provided diameters for the Room 32 ceremonial sticks of 1–2 cm and described four types of modified objects. The sticks found in Room 28 most resemble those shown in Pepper's (1920) figure 55b–c, which are cottonwood and average 1.2 cm in diameter. They taper to a point at one end. Pepper (1920:157) stated that there were no markings to indicate their use, although he included them with the "ceremonial sticks." Charring might account for the difference in diameter. Such worked sticks might have served multiple functions, but overall they demonstrate that some sort of modified sticks were originally placed in either the lower-story Room 28a or the upper-story Room 28b prior to burning.

Other perishables came from Room 28a as well. Laurie Webster's analysis of the small assemblage of textiles found in the fill of Room 28 (chapter 6) shows that a cotton blanket and feather blanket or feather-wrapped cordage also burned in Room 28a.

It is difficult to separate out the ceramics found in the burned fill from the ceramics found in the unburned fill because ceramics can show evidence of burning from use over a fire. The column for Room 28a in table 12.1 includes the sherds with evidence of soot or burning found in the Room 28 fill. Most are utility ware (gray ware), with only 7 white ware sherds and no red or brown ware (exotic) sherds. However, gray ware includes cooking vessels, so these may or may not have actually come from Room 28a; they might have been cooking vessels and sooted from use over a fire. As discussed in chapter 4, 41% of all chipped stone debitage shows evidence of burning, along with 18 of the non–projectile point chipped stone tools. No ornaments were unquestionably burned, which would typically be apparent from calcined gray shell or blackened turquoise. The faunal analysis in chapter 7 found only 40 bones that show burning, and these are all mammals.

Based on all of this information, I interpret Room 28a as having been a storage room at the time it was burned. Artifacts were not abundant in the room, and most were ground stone or discarded fragments. The perishables, including textiles and modified sticks, found in the burned matrix from Room 28 may have come from the upper Room 28b, which overlay both Room 28 and Room 28a. The other artifacts found in the fill might also have come from this upper room, except those found by Pepper (1920). The lack of floor features makes it difficult to interpret the use of the room further. But there do not seem to be unusual objects that would suggest use as a storage room for ritual objects similar to the use of the adjacent Room 28.

ROOMS 53 AND 56   Rooms 53 and 56 were excavated first by Warren Moorehead in April 1897 and then a couple of months later by George Pepper (1920:210–13, 216–18) and the Hyde Exploring Expedition. They are combined here because the work by Pepper (1920) and Marden (2011) makes it clear that materials from Room 56 were tossed into Room 53, so it is not possible to distinguish exactly what came from which of the two rooms. Some of the fill from one or both rooms ended up in Room 28, where we reexcavated it in the summer of 2013. As discussed previously, evidence indicates that the unburned fill from Room 28 came from these two rooms, and so it is described here along with an overview of what Pepper described in his publication. Moorehead (1906) has a brief description of what he found in the rooms, but it is difficult to figure out which rooms he is describing, and in some cases he appears to assign the same material to two different locations. The artifacts recovered from Rooms 53 and 56 are at the Robert S. Peabody Institute of Archaeology in Andover, Massachusetts, and the American Museum of Natural History in New York City. Marden (2011) discovered that at least some of the bones from the burials in these rooms were sold to the Field Museum in Chicago, so it is possible that some artifacts ended up there as well.

Room 53 is directly north of Room 32 and attached to it by a doorway. So, one way to enter Room 53 would have been to enter Room 28 and pass through the northwest doorway into Room 32 and then into Room 53. Room 53 is a large two-story room, but the material was found in the lower room. Room 56 is west of Room 53 and entered by a doorway from Room 53. Room 56 is a three-story room directly north of the important burial room, Room 33. There was another set of rooms beneath Room 56, as evidenced by the discovery of a wall at floor level that cut the room in half. Moorehead found burials on either side of that wall. As discussed above, Kerriann Marden (2011) reassociated the human remains from the northern burial rooms. Marden's work indicates that human remains were scattered from Room 56 into Room 53, and from there into Rooms 39b and 61. Her evaluation of the scattered human remains found in the unburned backfill of Room 28 indicates that those probably came from Room 56 as well. If this is the case, these remains do not increase the number of individuals found in Rooms 53 and 56, but they fill in missing bones.

Marden's (2011) research indicates that all of the burials, with the possible exception of an infant, were found originally in Room 56 and then scattered from there. There were seven adults (three males, four females), two adolescent males, and one infant. The human remains we recovered in the fill of Room 28 included a male and a female adult, an adolescent, and an infant; these are almost certainly isolated bones from the individuals already known in the collections, which Marden confirmed to us. So, seven individuals were originally buried in Rooms 53 and 56, with all but the infant likely originally buried in Room 56. Two were apparently found in subfloor graves, but the remainder may have come from above these graves. The infant may have been found with the cradleboard recovered in Room 53, or that may have been thrown there by Moorehead and his crew of farmers.

Apart from the human remains, many other types of materials were found in these rooms in 1897 and later (table 12.1). Moorehead found two cylinder jars, which are at the Robert S. Peabody Institute of Archaeology. One of these is a Gallup Black-on-white double cylinder jar, the only one found in Chaco Canyon. We found the missing pieces of this cylinder jar in the fill of Room 28. The second cylinder jar at the Peabody is a reconstructed unpainted white ware jar. Pepper found a partial Puerco Black-on-white cylinder jar when he cleaned up Moorehead's work. We found the remainder of that jar in Room 28 as well. We also found parts of five Gallup Black-on-white cylinder jars, two of which match sherds found in Room 39b, which is directly east of Room 53. We recovered part of a Black Mesa Black-on-white cylinder jar with a perforated rim; part of this jar was also found in Room 39b. We found portions of five additional white ware cylinder jars, including one for which we were able to locate most of the sherds and one that matches sherds from Room 39b. This makes a total of at least 14 cylinder jars that were once located in Rooms 53 and 56, but were scattered over a wide area by Moorehead's work, including into Rooms 28 and 39b.

Pepper located one bowl in Rooms 53 and 56; we found fragments of an additional nine bowls: Little Colorado White Ware, Gallup Black-on-white, McElmo Black-on-white, Mesa Verde White Ware, Cibola White Ware (unknown type, a learner vessel), Woodruff Brown Smudged–Sand, Woodruff Red Smudged–Sand, Showlow Red Smudged, and Showlow Red. I found additional sherds from the McElmo Black-on-white bowl in the AMNH collections from Room 39b.

Finally, Pepper recovered two pitchers from Rooms 53 and 56. Moorehead (1906:34) stated that some pottery was found with a subfloor burial in what we know was Room 56. Some of it is illustrated in his figure 13, which shows four pitchers. The NAGPRA (Native American Graves Protection and Repatriation Act) Notice of Inventory Completion for the Robert S. Peabody Institute of Archaeology (National Park Service 2008) indicates that three pitchers were found with that burial, so it is possible that three of the four pitchers shown in Moorehead's figure 13 came from Room 56. The four pitchers illustrated appear to be one Escavada Black-on-white, two Gallup Black-on-white, and one Mesa Verde White Ware. We recovered one partial large Red Mesa Black-on-white jar and one partial Chaco Black-on-white pitcher from the room. Together, this makes six pitchers and one jar.

The vessels in Rooms 53 and 56 thus once numbered

at least 31, including a minimum of 14 cylinder jars, 10 bowls, 6 pitchers, and 1 jar. Significantly, they include a range of intrusive vessels: a cylinder jar from the Tusayan area, bowls from the Little Colorado area and the Mesa Verde area, and four red and brown ware bowls from the Puerco Valley or Mogollon areas. Thus, at least 8 of the 31 vessels are intrusive, coming from the north, west, and southwest. This is a remarkably diverse collection, with a higher percentage of intrusive vessels (26%) than was found in Room 28.

As shown in table 12.1, Moorehead, Pepper, and our UNM reexcavations found a wide variety of other materials in Rooms 53 and 56, including 7 projectile points, 2 metates, 3 jar covers, and a variety of other ground and chipped stone. The combined total for turquoise, shell, jet, and shale ornaments is 6,382, including at least 81 mosaic tesserae (chapter 5, this volume), perhaps indicating the presence of an object covered with turquoise mosaic, such as the cylindrical basket found in Room 33. At least 1 shell trumpet was found as well (chapter 5, this volume). Textiles recovered include a feather robe, which Moorehead (1906:34) reported was 1.3 × 2 m in size and found with a burial in Room 56. Pepper (1920) found fragments of additional feather blankets in cleaning up Moorehead's debris, and Marden (2011:206) states that four of the burials she reassociated from Room 56 had adherent feathers, and one additional burial had adherent textile material. The UNM excavations recovered unburned cotton cloth and a fragment of feather-covered textile (chapter 6, this volume), probably a fragment of a feather blanket from Room 56. There was a probable cylinder basket with polychrome painted designs and a sandal (Jolie 2018), although Moorehead (1906) stated that he found two sandals. Ed Jolie (2018) also found five fragments of mats, and the Peabody NAGPRA inventory reports both a reed mat and a wood mat.

From the unburned fill of Room 28, we recovered a remarkable assemblage of bird bones from a variety of different species (chapter 7, this volume; Ainsworth et al. 2018). Pepper (1920) recovered a wooden slab, a stone slab, and pieces of a cradleboard, while Moorehead (1906) reported finding a sandal-shaped stone, a stone sword, a wooden sword, and rope (Marden 2011:286).

Rooms 53 and 56 thus had an assemblage of unusual and varied objects, particularly notable for the number of perishable items recovered. We will never know the full extent of the objects found or thrown out of these rooms by Moorehead. As noted, I found that a number

of sherds that Pepper excavated from Room 39b (located just east of Room 53) reattached to sherds found in the fill of Room 28 or in the fill of Room 52 (just south of Room 53). In other words, Moorehead clearly threw backdirt from Rooms 53 and 56 into at least Rooms 28, 39b, and 52. Marden's (2011) work reassociating the burials from Rooms 53 and 56 found the same thing: the burials had been thrown into several adjacent rooms. This calls into question some of the items found on the upper stories of these rooms. For instance, Pepper (1920:199) stated that he found portions of 19 broken cylinder jars (I have only located 15 of these, so his numbers may be off) in Room 39b, along with 29 stone jar covers, 2 hammerstones, an elk bone club, and many potsherds. As noted, the "many potsherds" include sherds that refit vessels from Rooms 53 and 56. Therefore, we must consider the possibility that the other items, including the 19 cylinder jars, originally came from Rooms 53 and 56 and were thrown out of them into Room 39b by Moorehead's careless excavations. Pepper (1920:210) also found a fragmented cylinder jar in Room 52 (directly south of Room 53); table 2 in his volume (Pepper 1920:359) erroneously listed 20 cylinder jars from Room 52, but there is only 1, with about 20 sherds reconstructing the vessel. Pepper (1920:210) stated that other items found in Room 52 included fragments of shell bracelets and fragments of matting and cloth. It seems quite possible that these items were actually thrown from Rooms 53 and 56 into Room 52 by Moorehead. Fragments of matting and cloth are relatively rare and likely to have come from a burial context, so the possibility that items found in Room 52 actually came originally from Rooms 53 and 56 must be entertained. If the cylinder jars found in Rooms 39b and 52 actually came from Rooms 53 and 56, then the total number of cylinder jars once placed in Rooms 53 and 56 is at least 30: 3 found in Rooms 53 and 56 in 1897, 11 recovered in Room 28 in 2013, 15 recovered in Room 39b in 1897, and 1 recovered in Room 52 in 1897. Further work reassociating all of the jars may resolve whether this interpretation is correct or not.

Regardless of the actual numbers, Rooms 53 and 56 clearly held special, unusual items, which were placed either with the burials in Room 56 or in storage in Room 53. I believe that Rooms 28, 32, and 53 were not only connected physically, but all were used as storage rooms for powerful ritual items. Access to these rooms was probably restricted to individuals charged with taking care of these items and individuals involved in their use.

ROOMS 55 AND 57 Rooms 55 and 57 were located directly west of Room 28. In the absence of a partition wall, these three rooms, which were separated on the upper story, would all have been connected into a single long, curved room on the lower story. However, as I argue in chapter 2, I believe that there was some type of partition wall between Room 28 and Room 55, but Rooms 55 and 57 were a single lower-story room. If there was a partition wall, then the ground-floor Room 28a, Room 28, and combined Rooms 55 and 57 would have been roughly the same size and dimensions. They each had relatively straight, parallel walls. Thus, in the late 900s, the arc of the northern wall of Pueblo Bonito was not created by having curved walls, but rather by offsetting each room slightly so that they created a sort of jogged curve rather than a smooth one.

ROOM 40 As discussed previously, Pepper (1920:199–200) designated the space directly south of Room 28 as Room 40. The Hyde Exploring Expedition did not finish excavating that space; in his field notes, Pepper (1897b:11) stated, "The room was not dug out fully at the Southern end, the measurements being at the point of discontinuation. The digging was hard and nothing was found." Judd (1964:131) called it the "non-existent Room 40," because he did not believe there was a room south of Room 28. However, the newer north wall of the West Court at that location has an unmistakable roof ledge at the height of a lower-story room just south of Rooms 28 and 28a, so there must have been a roof or ramada south of Room 28. The stairs from Room 28 are built into a walled space that ascends just to the level of where the roofline sits. In other words, the stairs would have led to the roof of Room 40. All of the evidence suggests that there was a room just south of Rooms 28 and 28a, that it was only a single story high, and that the stairs from Room 28 led to the roof of that room. Further excavation could resolve this issue.

AD 1000s–1100s
Around the 1070s, construction began on the upper stories of Rooms 28, 28a, 55, and 57. The arc of rooms that we view today in the park as adjacent to the northern edge of the West Court was added in the 1070s. By this time, the lower-story rooms were subterranean and the upper-story rooms were at or close to ground level. A new two-story south wall was added to the rooms, changing the profile of this wall from a series of straight walls offset to make a curve to an actual curved wall. Doors were built into this south wall, including two side-by-side T-shaped doorways leading to Room 28b and a rectangular door leading to Room 57. The dark lower-story rooms appear to have been used largely for storage after this time, and the upper-story rooms were used for activities that left few traces. Most of the rooms to the north of these rooms already had upper stories—sometimes more than one upper story. The addition of an upper story along this northern edge of the West Court changed the configuration of rooms in this part of Pueblo Bonito, creating that iconic curve and altering access to the northern burial cluster rooms.

Within about three decades, or around AD 1100, the front row of rooms was deliberately set on fire. That act may not have permanently closed off the northern burial cluster rooms, but it certainly changed the way they could be entered. Rooms 28, 28a, 55, and 57 collapsed, effectively closing off most of the early lower-story rooms. Room 32 could probably still be entered through a hatchway in the eastern part of the room, and this hatchway may have been the only means to enter many of the lower-story rooms in this part of Pueblo Bonito. That the rooms continued to be entered is suggested by the presence of Mesa Verde Black-on-white ceramics in some of them. There is little to suggest that these rooms continued to be used on a regular basis though, with entry perhaps restricted to ritual personnel.

Use of this part of Pueblo Bonito continued, as the possible use of Room 28 as a turkey pen suggests, but there is little known about the late use of the area. Much of Pueblo Bonito may have been abandoned by this time, and this northern part of the site shows little evidence of continuing use or upkeep.

PRODUCTION OF FOOD AND CRAFTS
The UNM excavations in Room 28 showed how the space changed over time from an outdoor activity space to a domestic room to a storage room. Beginning with the pre-room outdoor activity spaces, here I review evidence of production, and I focus on Room 28 alone, rather than the backfill from Rooms 28a, 53, and 56.

Evidence of food preparation was abundant under the floor in contexts that predate the late AD 800s. In chapter 10, Smith discusses the excellent preservation of pollen. Most of the pollen samples analyzed from the subfloor had evidence of cactus, cattail, maize, squash, and beeweed. She suggests that cholla may have been farmed. The high amount of cattail pollen indicates that either flowering spikes or pollen was introduced. Cattail pollen can be an important ritual or food resource, and cattail fluff is used to make plaster in some parts of the world. As Smith notes, every part of the cattail is edible or useful for construction or artifacts. As documented in chapter 9, maize was found in the archaeobotanical samples taken from the subfloor, along with uncharred butternut squash, pinyon nuts, prickly pear cactus, and hedgehog cactus. These results indicate a diet rich in a wide variety of wild and domesticated plants. Finally, the authors of chapter 7 show that lagomorphs (cottontails and jackrabbits) were important parts of the diet in the time periods represented by the subfloor material. As noted in that chapter, the lagomorph percentages for the subfloor assemblage are consistent with those from great houses in Chaco, indicating long-term patterns of exploitation of these species. Evidence of turkeys in the subfloor deposits includes eggshells identified as turkey and gullet stones almost certainly from turkeys (chapter 8).

The subfloor unit revealed a series of pre-room surfaces, too many to excavate separately in the short time we had. Evidence of activities associated with specific surfaces is lacking, but we have general information about subfloor materials. There is no specific evidence of pottery production in this location. Forty-eight pieces of chipped stone debitage were recovered in subfloor contexts, suggesting that at least some activities on those early surfaces involved creating chipped stone tools (chapter 4, this volume). A single fragment of ground stone was found in the subfloor as well. The authors of chapter 5 report seven ornament-related artifacts recovered from the subfloor: one bead, one mosaic fragment, three mineral specimens, and two pieces of lapidary debris (turquoise). Although modest, these finds suggest that there was some ornament production in the vicinity prior to the construction of the room.

Materials found in Room 28 provide additional information on productive activities. As I described in chapter 2, three thermal features were located at floor level in Room 28. Flotation samples from all three features produced economic plants, including tomatillo, maize, chenoam, mustard seeds, pinyon nuts, stickleaf seeds, and a cactus seed. Fauna from these features were primarily lagomorphs and rodents. Food was clearly processed in the room, and the ceramics associated with these ephemeral features suggest that it continued to be an activity in the room up to the late AD 1000s. There were no formal, lined hearths, and the small informal features were probably used as needed, but not on a regular basis.

Other evidence of productive activities in the room is fairly scant and comes from the 1896 excavations. At the level of the lower Room 28 floor, excavations recovered large numbers of finished artifacts, including a large number of ceramics; a few baskets; an obsidian projectile point; hundreds of turquoise, jet, and shell beads and tesserae; and ground stone jar lids. Most of the ceramics are serving vessels, with only a single partial corrugated jar recovered. Corrugated jars might have been used for cooking or storage. Artifacts associated with production are less frequent. At floor level, there were two bone awls and a bone "implement" that was unfortunately discarded. A jasper pebble suggests the possibility of ceramic production, because it might have been used for polishing vessels. A single metate suggests food processing, perhaps associated with the foods identified in the thermal features. Some raw turquoise suggests the possibility of ornament production in the room, although the minerals could also have been offerings. Turkey gullet stones at floor level suggest that turkeys were either kept in the room or killed in the room. At the time the room was in use, turkeys were primarily kept for their feathers rather than for food. So, the gullet stones might be associated with the production of feather crafts, as might the twine found in the flotation sample. All of these possible craft activities lack evidence of intense or sustained production in the room, and the scant artifacts associated with them might have simply been placed in the room for storage or lost.

Artifacts from the "general debris" and the upper level provide a glimpse of possible productive activities on the upper story of Room 28, also designated Room 28b. The excavations produced many unusual items in the matrix above the floor, including 15 sections of deer antler with rounded ends averaging 7 cm in length (Pepper 1920:126), hammered copper and a piece of raw copper ore, a crystal, a fossil shell, mica, and shell and turquoise beads. These layers also produced ceramics and jar lids, 4 projectile points, and a knife point. The evidence of production activities includes the knife and the raw shell and turquoise. The antler sections were probably used for some type of craft activity, but it is not clear what craft required antler sections with rounded ends. The other materials suggest the special nature of the activities that took place in the upper Room 28b.

EXCHANGE AND INTERACTION

The Room 28 assemblage is remarkable for the diversity and quantity of objects found, particularly for the high number of exotic or nonlocal objects recovered. But even the subfloor assemblage shows evidence of exchange. As I discuss in chapter 3, 23% of the subfloor ceramics are intrusive, with most (19%) of these coming from the Chuska area to the west. The remainder of the intrusive sherds come from the Mesa Verde area (2.5%) and the Puerco Valley/Mogollon area (1%). Chipped stone includes 1 piece of Narbona Pass chert and 1 piece of obsidian, with the intrusive materials equaling 3.7% of the total (54 pieces). The ornaments found in the subfloor included a jet bead, an argillite mosaic piece, and 2 pieces of turquoise lapidary debris, but only the turquoise is definitely intrusive. Unfortunately, we do not know where the obsidian or the turquoise came from outside the canyon. These results do show, however, that there was exchange with groups living in the Chuska, Mesa Verde, and Puerco Valley/Mogollon areas prior to construction of the room around AD 880–900, a finding that adds to what is already known about exchange relations during this time period.

Evidence from the room floor and the upper story adds further information on exchange, although most of it comes from the HEE excavations. The whole vessels were given ware designations whenever possible. Unfortunately, I was not always able to determine the temper for the whole vessels, particularly when there are no breaks of any kind on the vessel. Only 6 of the vessels are unquestionably intrusive: 4 are Chuska White Ware cylinder jars, 1 is a Chuska Gray Ware utility jar, and 1 is Showlow Red Ware. It is surprising that no vessels identifiably came from the Mesa Verde or Tusayan areas. This is true also for the sherds collected by George Pepper from the floor of the room: only 1 of the 15 sherds is definitely intrusive, and it is Chuska Gray Ware. The sherds found in the fill and probably from the upper floor include more intrusives, with 4 of the 24 sherds definite intrusives: 1 Chuska Gray Ware, 1 Chuska White Ware, 1 St Johns Polychrome/White Mountain Red Ware (a relatively rare type in Chaco), and 1 Puerco Valley/Mogollon Brown Ware. As discussed in chapter 4, few pieces of chipped stone were saved by the HEE excavators, but these include 5 projectile points, 2 of which are obsidian. The HEE excavations did include the collection of large quantities of turquoise and shell ornaments,

probably made locally on intrusive materials, as discussed in chapter 5. We do not know the sources for the turquoise, but the shell includes *Olivella* (*O. dama*), *Conus*, *Strombus*, *Glycymeris*, *Spondylus*, and *Chama* from the Gulf of California and the vicinity of the Baja Peninsula, as well as *Haliotis* sp. and *Murex* sp., which are found along the Pacific coast. The hammered copper object and copper ore are intrusive as well, although we do not know the source. A piece of mica found in the room debris and probably originally from the upper-story room also came from outside the canyon. Douglas fir identified in the tree-ring samples taken in 2013 may have been roofing material from Room 28b (the upper story), and it came from a distance; other wood might have come from outside the canyon as well. The probable shelving plank identified as Douglas fir would also have come from a distance, indicating perhaps both the use of a high-value wood for the shelving and a connection with higher elevations. Studies of cylinder jars from other rooms indicate that they contained cacao and/or holly-based drinks. Both plants are exotic. The cacao would have to come from the neo-tropics of Mesoamerica and the holly from either the Gulf coast or Mesoamerica, so they are evidence of long-distance exchange. Organic residues do not survive extreme heat well, and previous tests showed differing results for ceramics from Room 28 (Crown et al. 2015; Washburn et al. 2011); I believe it is unlikely that plant residues survived the conflagration in Room 28. Regardless, the results from cylinder jars from other contexts confirm the presence of cacao or holly plant residues.

On the whole, the material from Room 28 confirms known exchange relations based on other excavations in the canyon. Ties with populations in the Chuska and Mesa Verde areas are clear. Either exchange or travel to the sources for turquoise, obsidian, shell, copper, and mica indicates the importance of these colorful materials, which have valued properties, such as iridescence and luster. The high quantity and variety of intrusive objects in the room confirms the special nature of Room 28 and the upper Room 28b. Objects made of nonlocal materials outnumber objects made from local materials by a large magnitude, but they tend to be fairly portable, small, and durable items, such as turquoise, shell, obsidian, or copper. Breakable pottery is a less frequent intrusive item. Most of the turquoise, shell, obsidian, and copper probably entered the canyon as raw material; some of it was transformed in the canyon while some was deposited as raw material. The origin of the copper bells is a matter of continuing debate (Mathien 2003), and the two pieces of copper found in Room 28 have never been analyzed for source, probably because the various analysts have focused on copper bells rather than other copper objects. Three of the 21 copper bells/fragments reported by Judd (1954:109, figures 28d–f) came from "removal of debris previously thrown out of Rooms 55 and 57." Rooms 55 and 57 are the rooms directly adjacent to Room 28 to the west. How Judd knew that the debris came from these rooms is a mystery, although presumably the backdirt was found adjacent to the rooms in the West Court. The fact that they came from those rooms is quite interesting, particularly because both rooms burned when Room 28 did, likely as part of the same termination ritual. Finally, residues from other contexts confirm exchange or acquisition at the source for cacao and holly for preparing caffeinated drinks.

CONSUMPTION: DRINKING PERFORMANCE AND POLITICS

In a previous publication (Crown 2018), I discussed the use of cylinder jars in consumption rituals in Chaco Canyon. I summarize that information here, focusing particularly on the Room 28 assemblage and consumption practices. Cylinder jars are one of the later drinking vessel forms in Chaco, first made around AD 900, at the same time that both pitchers and gourd effigy vessels were in use. The earliest cylinder jars are quite large and wide, and there are only three known, none from Room 28. They are too large to have been personal drinking vessels, and they likely served as communal drinking/serving vessels (Hamilakis 2008:11). As I discuss in chapter 3, the earliest cylinder jars would have required two hands to hold. The low number of these vessels may indicate that the drinking was an exclusive activity and/or that the drink ingredients were scarce. One advantage of ceramic vessels is that they are opaque, disguising the actual quantity of the drink.

Beginning about AD 1030, when Gallup Black-on-white became the dominant decorative style, potters began crafting more and smaller cylinder jars, some of which could be held with one hand. The cylinder vessels found in Room 28 date to this time period. Average orifice diameter shifted from more than 15 cm to less than 10 cm. Potters often created sets of two to four vessels with identical shapes and lug configurations, indicating a level of standardization not recognized in other Chacoan ceramics (Toll 1990:284). In other parts of the world, drinking sets are associated with social competition and status (Anderson 2009:186; Stockhammer 2012:19; Wright 2004). The Chacoan sets might have been used to froth the drinks, employing a method used by both the Mayas and the Aztecs (Coe and Coe 2007:48, 86), which involved pouring the drink from a jar held at chest height into a jar set on the ground. This shift to the use of drinking sets suggests the presence of a shared social etiquette surrounding the consumption of drinks. Room 28 held several complete sets and portions of other sets. For instance, of the four Showlow Red jars, one was recovered in Room 28 and the other three in a single room in Pueblo del Arroyo (Judd 1959:156). We will never know if these particular jars were salvaged from Room 28 before it was burned.

The association of the cylinder jars with sandstone jar lids suggests the possibility that Chacoans preferred their drinks hot, with the lids used to retain heat; indeed, the cylinder shape has superior heat retention properties (Crown 2018). Public preparation of the drinks may have become an important part of their use.

The 112 cylinder jars found in Room 28 suggest large-scale consumption events, but only if all of the vessels were used at once. It is possible that only a few sets were in use at any one time. The designs indicate that new sets were added over time. However, as I note in chapter 3, most show moderate to heavy external use wear, and about a quarter show reslipping/repainting layers, which have been interpreted as renewal over time (Crown and Wills 2003), so at least some were used on multiple occasions. Toll (1990:296) suggested that the number of jars represents the number of participating communities in the system at AD 1100. The presence of jars of Showlow Red and Chuska White Ware in Room 28 does support the idea that these drinking events included participants from outside the canyon.

The distinctive cylinder jar shape was likely made to be recognized at a distance in public displays. The variety of designs, shape profiles, and lug shapes suggests the importance of differentiating the drinkers in such settings (Hamilakis 2008:11). Forty-seven of the 112 cylinder jars from Room 28 were plain white when found, but these probably had brightly decorated post-firing pigment designs on stucco (Crown and Wills 2003). Many jars have scouring marks (tiny vertical drag marks from being cleansed with sand or sandstone), so the plastered vessels might have been cleansed after use and then repainted before the next use. As animated objects, the cylinder jars accumulated biographies through these episodes of repainting/stuccoing/use followed by scouring/cleansing/storage (Gosden and Marshall 1999:176). The lug handles probably facilitated dressing/decorating them with ornaments or feathers. But they did not apparently only come to life in performance; the distinctive shape would have given them meaning outside of the ceremonial realm. The evidence from Room 28 suggests that they were revered and feared as powerful objects.

As discussed above, by the time Room 28 was used for storing the cylinder jars, it was an underground room that had a stairway up to the West Court of Pueblo Bonito. As Mills (2008:105) argued, storage of most cylinder jars in Room 28 adjacent to the West Court suggests their use in that space. The consumption practices associated with cylinder jars probably involved ceremonial processions in the West Court, a pattern seen in other parts of the world (Knappett 2011:163). Participants could have processed from the lower-story Room 28 up the stairs and into the West Court or through the twin T-shaped doorways of the upper-story Room 28b into the West Court.

I have argued that cylinder jars signal intensified drinking activity at Pueblo Bonito in the mid- to late 1000s, with feasts or rituals surrounding drinking becoming more common there. Such visually distinctive drinking forms likely became an important means of social differentiation. Drinking activity may have become competitive either within Pueblo Bonito or among the great houses in the canyon, with factions vying for followers. Consumption involving the cylinder jars was centered on Pueblo Bonito, and the activity was apparently successful in drawing participants from a distance for some decades in the late AD 1000s. The single burial with an associated cylinder jar is an adult female (Marden 2011), suggesting that the drinking events involved both women and men.

Cylinder jars were neither widely traded prestige items nor widely emulated or copied. A few potters outside of Chaco created cylinder jars, but almost all of those vessels were then brought to Pueblo Bonito rather than kept locally. Because so few Chacoan cylinder jars exist outside of Pueblo Bonito, there must have been control over their creation and use (see also Toll 1990:296).

This consumption pattern contrasts with earlier Maya practices. At feasts among the Classic Mayas (AD 250–900), elites provided cacao drinks to guests and then gifted the drinking vessels, which were cylinder jars with painted scenes (Reents-Budet 2006:222). In contrast, outsiders brought cylinder jars to Pueblo Bonito, where the jars remained. Perhaps gifting the vessels provided entrée for these outsiders.

The multiple forms of drinking vessels (pitchers, cylinder jars, gourd effigies) present in the eleventh century in Chaco may signal multiple recipes, ritual groups, social classes, or competitive factions. Following the ideas put forward by Dietler (1990), one group in Chaco may have adopted cacao and cylinder jars as a means of symbolically tying themselves to Mesoamerican groups that used cylinder vessels and thus differentiating themselves from other Chaco groups. However, if the Chacoan cylinder vessel is an emulation of Mesoamerican vessels (Washburn 1980, 2008:299), it is the form and contents only that are emulated, not the designs. If they do mimic the Mesoamerican forms, cylinder jar production using local materials and designs on a foreign shape may have helped to encourage acceptance of a new drinking ritual. As I have suggested previously (Crown 2018), the cylinder jar may thus have been a consciously hybrid form, incorporating aspects of cacao consumption to the south with local craft traditions and thus combining the familiar with the exotic. Both form and substance might have been viewed as holding positive sources of sacred power, in part through appropriation of that distinctive shape (Pugh 2009; Taussig 1993:19). Outside participants who brought cylinder jars made using their own wares and designs simultaneously announced their local identity and their shared identity with the ritual enacted at Pueblo Bonito.

Drinking of special elixirs generally occurs in the context of religious or secular rituals, including feasts, so these were likely contexts of consumption in Chaco as well. If all of the jars were used simultaneously, or even if each participant used a set of two vessels, the quantity of drink required and the labor needed to prepare it would have been quite high. Drinking rituals tend to be practiced against a backdrop of competing claims to authority, because when there is no competition or factionalism, there is no need for such display. When leadership is contested, competitive events recruit followers (Hayden 1995; LeCount 1999:242), and providing drinks can be a route to status and power—particularly when exchanging drinks for work (Dietler 1990:380).

Providing drinks to participants from outside Chaco would undoubtedly have created social debt (Dietler 1990; Henderson and Joyce 2006:141).

The other vessels found in Room 28 may indicate more about the ritual activity associated with the cylinder jars. The four bowls more than 30 cm in diameter are all Gallup Black-on-white with strap handles on the exterior. These large bowls are relatively shallow for their height. The large size suggests their use as serving vessels for feasts, perhaps in the same ritual feasting described above for the cylinder jars. Other objects found in the room may have been used to prepare food and drink. Because of the fire, organic residues are unlikely to have survived to aid with further identification of the foods consumed from the vessels.

DISCARD PATHWAYS

Archaeologists recover a variety of items ranging from large, heavy metates to invisible residues. The way that these items enter the archaeological record varies. Some were left as refuse where productive activities occurred; some were lost; some were deposited as trash in a different location from where the productive activities occurred, often in a defined refuse pile; some were recycled for a different purpose (sherds as temper, or ground stone as masonry); some were usable items left where they were used, often because they were too heavy or cumbersome to move; some were used or stored in a location and left when that location was abandoned; and some were purposefully placed into what some archaeologists call "structured" deposits (Richards and Thomas 1984). Structured deposits are materials that were arranged in formal or symbolic positions, including layers, where the arrangement of the materials and their relationship to one another had significance (Pollard 2008; Walker 2002). They can include cutting as well as layering strata (McAnany and Hodder 2009). They might include foundation deposits, offerings, retirement or termination deposits, burial deposits, or any other ritual/symbolic deposits. Some scholars have critiqued this approach and argued that all deposits have a structure of some kind, that everyday activities can lead to deposits that have structure, and that archaeologists have lumped too many varied types of deposits under the "structured deposits" label (Garrow 2012; Mills and Walker 2008; Pollard 2008:43). The focus on the structure of the deposits may also ignore the perfor-mative aspects of their creation (Garrow 2012; Pollard 2008).

What were the discard pathways found in the HEE and UNM excavations? The artifacts found beneath the floor in what I interpret as a pre-room outdoor activity area are everyday refuse associated with household activities and perhaps some crafts production. The sherds or chipped stone recovered do not refit into vessels or tools. They are debris that was scattered, lost, or left unswept by the people who used this area. The small ornament and turquoise debris may have been lost there. The area we excavated was close to the adjacent early room wall under Room 28a, so perhaps the artifacts had been swept to this location. The few artifacts found in the three thermal features appear to have been everyday refuse as well. Incorporated into the ashy fill of these thermal features, these were mostly small items that were probably simply part of the refuse present in households that was not cleared away.

Most of the sherds recovered by the HEE excavators were probably simply discarded as well; there were no refits among those sherds. Rooms in Pueblo Bonito typically do not have huge amounts of trash unless they were used specifically for trash disposal, which Room 28 was not. While the HEE excavators undoubtedly were biased in what they collected from the fill of Room 28, they selected a variety of sherds of many different types for shipment to New York.

Artifacts were sometimes reused/recycled in the architecture. As I describe in chapter 2, at least three broken ground stone tools were used as masonry to build the Room 28 walls. The roof and floor daub had sherds, chipped stone, and ornaments incorporated into it—perhaps accidentally, to get rid of some trash, or as "temper" in the thick mud.

I have argued that Room 28 was used initially as a domestic space and later for storage of cylinder jars and other ceramic vessels. Construction of the shelving and placement of the cylinder jars on that shelving suggests that this was the location where the jars were stored between uses. The shelving thus provides evidence of storage in the room, a form of temporary deposition.

The other depositional practices apparent in the room are associated with less common practices than storage, loss, trash disposal, or construction. These practices are methods of depositing material that is ritualized. Bell (1992:74) argued that "ritualization is a way of acting that is designed and orchestrated to distinguish and privilege what is being done in comparison to other, usually more quotidian, activities." One important aspect of the ritualizing of these depositional practices is that the deposition had a performative aspect that resulted in unique deposits. Rather than accumulating over time, they were created in events. In most cases, the deposits were not visible, but perhaps they were remembered by some, assumed by others, and told to yet others.

There are three distinct deposits in Room 28 that fall into this category and may be thought of as ceremonial deposits. The first are the foundation deposits or offerings placed in the postholes prior to seating the posts. As discussed in chapters 2 and 5, these consisted of turquoise and/or shell beads and lapidary debris. These offerings were similar to those described ethnographically for Pueblo peoples. For instance, Parsons (1939:296, 479) described the placement of a shell mixture (white shell and turquoise, sometimes with other shell, coral, or hematite) under a new house, or turquoise placed in the corners of a new house. Saile (1977:75) described a number of rituals associated with house building among Pueblo peoples, including offerings of bread, tobacco, cornmeal, eagle feathers, prayer sticks, and prayer feathers. Saile (1977:76) argued, "When something was constructed it had to take its proper place in the scheme of things, as part of the world framework. It had to be made real, 'animated,' 'endowed with a 'soul.'" Such ensouling practices make homes safe and proper, and they are found elsewhere in the Americas, including among the modern Mayas (Stross 1998; Vogt 1998). The offerings in Room 28 might have been considered nourishment for the posts or the house (McAnany and Hodder 2009:15; Mock 1998; Mock, ed. 1998). Saile (1985:100) noted, "Excavations in the earth . . . made connections with the spiritual world and were often very dangerous places. They were made very carefully and with appropriate sequences, prayers, rituals and thoughts." Digging postholes and foundation trenches made "a break in the earth level, a potential link with the underworld" (Saile 1977:78), and these powerful alterations of the surface needed to be sanctified. Similar practices were also present among the Classic Mayas (Mock 1998:5). It is likely then that the entire process of creating the posthole and setting the post was ritualized, including digging the hole, placing a sandstone slab at the base, placing the offering on the slab, seating the post, and placing cobble-size pieces of sandstone with lignite chinking around the post to hold it in place. As I discuss in chap-

ter 2, this process describes some of the posts in Room 28; other posts lack the sandstone/lignite lining, and yet others lack the turquoise/shell offering. Heitman (2015) associates lignite with the color black and the nadir in Pueblo cosmology, although noting that lignite may have a functional purpose as well as a symbolic one. If the practice at Room 28 was analogous to those found among the historic Pueblo peoples, proper placement of the foundation deposits brought the room to life, made it safe for use, and perhaps provided for its nourishment.

The second ritualized deposit was the small, bowl-shaped depression on the floor directly south of the door connecting Room 28 to Room 32. As I describe in chapter 2, that bowl was filled with powdered hematite, and a round worked sherd was pressed down into the hematite. The type, Red Mesa Black-on-white, possibly dates to the period when the room was constructed around AD 880–900, suggesting that the feature was created at that time. Like the ornaments placed in postholes, this small floor feature was likely placed to ensoul or animate the room. The hematite would have provided an excellent medium for holding prayer feathers or prayer sticks upright around the worked sherd. Red is associated with the South among Pueblo peoples, so the red ocher filling a small depression in front of a door in the northwest part of the room does not particularly fit with a strict view of Puebloan cosmology. Alternatively, one could view the feature as located directly south of the door to Room 32; however, the wall with that door was constructed about 150 years after the room was originally built. Perhaps the earlier wall that was replaced around AD 1040/50 had a door in the same location. It is possible that this small pit filled with a powerful substance helped protect the room from the spirits of the dead housed in Room 33 adjacent to Room 32. Whatever the beliefs associated with the small pit, the ocher, and the sherd, the entire feature undoubtedly had ritual/ceremonial importance and symbolism.

The final ritualized deposit involves the event that destroyed the room and buried its contents. As described previously, the event began with preparing the room and ended with the collapse of the burning room. Most of the objects in the room were probably stored there already, and others may have been brought to the room for placement prior to the fire. I describe the event in detail above, but there are several aspects of it that must be emphasized. First, powerful objects were stored and gathered in Room 28 and the upper Room 28b. Those placed in the upper room may have been smashed there, because the vessels were so fragmentary when excavated. Alternatively, they may have broken when the room collapsed or the roof fell on them. The vessels placed in front of the lower northeast doorway that led to Room 51a almost certainly were placed there immediately prior to the room being set on fire, because they completely blocked that doorway. The ornaments were certainly also placed in the room immediately prior to the burning because they were found in and on the piles of vessels. Second, the deposition included many exotic objects: copper, turquoise, shell, mica, obsidian, and ceramics from the Chuska and Puerco Valley/Mogollon areas. The recovery of these exotics as a group suggests relations among them; that is, the various materials were either viewed as similar or viewed as distinctive parts of a whole, with power accruing and magnified by the presence of all of them together (Zedeño 2009). Third, the placement of objects had layering that was undoubtedly significant in the overall tableau created prior to lighting the whole on fire. Layer 1 was the floor of the lower room, where items were placed near doorways, some in stacks of objects. For instance, there was a stack of nested bowls and baskets placed near the doorway to Room 51a. Layer 2 was the doorsill and plaster feature adjacent to the doorway and stairs leading to the West Court. The doorsill was raised above a rounded step and had an adjacent plaster feature. Vessels were placed on the sill and the plaster, both raised above the floor. Layer 3 was the wooden shelving on the western end of the room, which was filled with vessels, particularly 99 cylinder jars. Above this was the ceiling/roof for the lower room, which constituted Layer 4. Layer 5 consisted of the items on the upper floor, which included some vessels, ornaments, and copper objects. The last layer was the ceiling/roof for the upper room, Room 28b. Finally, what was *not* present in Room 28 or 28b is significant as well: there were no living things, no burials of macaws, parrots, eagles, turkeys, or humans.

In chapter 1, I outlined the research questions that drove the project. One of these concerned the nature of the materials in Room 28, whether so many objects were simply abandoned in the room or were part of a desecratory or reverential termination ritual. In table 1.3, I provided expectations for each of these possibilities. Reviewing these expectations, it is clear that the deposits found in Room 28 represent a reverential termination ritual. But what exactly was being terminated:

the room or the materials in it? Room 28 was not the only room burned in this ritual event. The entire sweep of rooms on the northern side of the West Court was burned: Rooms 55, 57, 28, and 28a. And while it would have been possible for the fire to spread from room to room, the pattern of floor vitrification in Rooms 28 and 28a indicates that these fires were set separately. So, the termination of Room 28 was part of a larger process of room closure that included several adjacent rooms. The collapse of Room 28 effectively shut off entry to the adjacent rooms from the West Court. While Room 32 had a hatchway, providing continuing entry into Rooms 32 and 33, entry into Room 51a may have required moving through a series of rooms. But if closing the rooms was the major purpose, why place so many valuable objects in them? It is possible that the vessels and other objects placed in Room 28 were put there to honor the room prior to its destruction. However, the placement of so many vessels in the room and the reverential placement of ornaments over and in the vessels suggests that it was the *vessels* in particular that were being terminated (along with the room in which they had been stored). If this is correct, the ornaments were placed to honor or thank the vessels prior to their destruction. I suggest it was the cylinder jars that were of most relevance among the objects in the room, in part because they dominate the assemblage, but also because the 112 cylinder jars terminated on that day represent more than half of all known cylinder jars, few of which exist outside of Pueblo Bonito. If the termination was performed to retire the old structure and its contents, the purpose was to contain and destroy the accumulated power of both. The magnitude of the event indicates both the respect and fear with which the cylinder jars were viewed. As animate objects, those jars held power that had to be neutralized, in this case by burning the room in which they were stored so that it collapsed and buried them.

This termination event shares features with termination events elsewhere in the US Southwest (Adams 2016) and Mesoamerica (Mock 1998; Mock, ed. 1998). But there are some differences as well. In acts of "de-sanctification" (Mock 1998:8) in the Maya area, lintels were often destroyed or roofs torn down. This was a means to "close their sacred portals" (Mock 1998:8). While the portals into and out of Room 28 were unquestionably closed by the fiery termination, the architecture was not damaged in the ways described for the Mayas. The doorways remained intact.

There are several possible reasons that the materials and room were terminated. The occupants of Pueblo Bonito might have held a reverential termination ritual if the last practitioner capable of performing the ritual associated with the cylinder jars died. The clan or sodality that owned the cylinder jars and the associated ritual might have terminated the room prior to moving from Pueblo Bonito. The vessels might also have been terminated by "Pueblo Bonito's last ceremonial community, consisting of a dwindling population in the late 1100s" (Mills 2008:105), if abandonment of the site was planned. Or the vessels might have been terminated in association with a cyclical ritual destruction of objects or structures prior to rebuilding and renewal (Crown and Wills 2003). In Mesoamerica, the destruction of earlier materials sometimes precedes rebuilding, perhaps to "ensoul the new incorporative structure with the genealogical power of the old" (Mock 1998:8).

The timing of the termination is important in teasing these possibilities apart, and I have noted in this volume that the evidence suggests termination around AD 1100 or shortly thereafter. I have made this argument on the basis of a few lines of evidence. The date must be around or after AD 1100 based on the pottery types present in the room. The latest ceramics found in the room were one Chaco-McElmo Black-on-white jar and one Nava Black-on-white jar, dating to AD 1100–1275. But I suggest that the date was not much later than AD 1115 because there were no Mesa Verde White Ware vessels in the room (which would likely indicate a later date), as there were in Rooms 32 and 53 to the north. Furthermore, there were no mugs in the room, a form most associated in Chaco with post-1100s dates (Crown 2018). Also, the upper story was reused after the fire and after leveling the debris, indicating that the rooms were not burned at the time the entire site was abandoned. So, the termination of the jars and the room most likely date to around AD 1100, suggesting that the room and its contents were burned while Pueblo Bonito was occupied, and then the upper, unroofed space continued to be used after the burning.

I have suggested (Crown 2018) that the termination of the cylinder jars reflects the end of their ritual use, perhaps the end of the competitive events in which they were used, or the emigration or even expulsion of the group that used them (see Rabinowitz 2009). The storage of the vessels in Room 28 and their rare occurrence as burial objects supports their ownership by a clan or sodality rather than by individuals; if individuals owned them, we would expect to find these important vessels more often in burials. So, the termination was likely by the clan or sodality that owned them. Whatever value and status the use of cylinder jars once held was gone, but the animated jars still held power that had to be destroyed through respectful termination. This was undoubtedly a time of upheaval since one form of drinking vessel (the cylinder jar) and the behavior and rituals associated with it disappeared, and a new form of drinking vessel (the mug) appeared, probably accompanied by changes in manners and standards of behavior (Elias 1994:79). The termination of the cylinder jars in Room 28 appears to have been accompanied by a complete rejection of this form (Crown 2018).

The termination may be seen then as part of a broader shift involving destruction and separation from the old rituals and adoption of the new. The disorder or chaos associated with burning part of Pueblo Bonito would then have been replaced by a new order (Mock 1998:10). The finding of three mugs inside Room 32 directly on the other side of the closed doorway from Room 28 suggests that the use of mugs in drinking activity lay symbolically on the other side of the closing of Room 28 and termination of the cylinder jars.

The other items destroyed in the fire were probably used by the same social group that owned the cylinder jars and perhaps as part of the same ritual activity. These items were linked, perhaps through their use lives but certainly through their deposition (Pollard 2008:49). Although initially built probably for use as a domestic space, all of the evidence indicates that Room 28 had become a storage room used by a clan or ritual sodality. The destruction not only of Room 28 but the rooms adjacent to it suggests that the clan or sodality owned and closed off this part of Pueblo Bonito adjacent to the West Court. While other nearby underground rooms apparently continued to be entered and used to store important ritual paraphernalia (particularly Rooms 32 and 53), entry into those spaces was made more difficult by the destruction of Room 28, and it was no longer possible to enter the West Court from the underground stairway in Room 28, emerging from the symbolic below into the public space above. The twin T-shaped doorways of the upper Room 28b were likely filled with masonry at the time of the burning, effectively closing those doorways as a means of entering the West Court as well. So, the destruction of those rooms had a lasting impact on ritual performance in Pueblo Bonito, not only because of the termination of the ritual involving the cylinder jars, but also because of the termination of the room and its doorways connecting to the West Court.

THE HOUSE OF THE CYLINDER JARS

From around AD 880 to 1100, the space occupied by Room 28 transformed from a locus for outdoor activities, then perhaps to a ramada, and then to a domestic space. After a building hiatus that might signal an abandonment, people returned to Pueblo Bonito in the middle decades of the 1000s and remodeled old rooms north of the West Court. They replaced the north wall of Room 28 to accommodate a room-wide shelf for storing vessels used for cacao-drinking rituals. In doing so, they transformed a house for people into a house for animated objects, ritual sacra. In the Pueblo world, spirits, including the sun, the wind, katsinas, clouds, and the dead, have houses (Parsons 1939:199–200). "Without appropriate houses, spirits and powers were dangerous and unpredictable" (Saile 1977:75), and houses, in this sense, were places for communication with the spirit world through their placement and connection with the above and the below of the Pueblo universe.

The clan or sodality that implemented these changes built an elaborate stairway to the now aboveground West Court. They built a second wall on the West Court side of the room, altering the arc of the wall to create the sweeping curve we see today. They constructed an upper story with twin T-shaped doorways onto the West Court, allowing ritual practitioners/participants to exit Room 28b in two lines of side-by-side processions. Whether the two lines were male and female or two equal social groups, or whether they were meant to symbolize twinning, we will likely never know. But the configuration and location of the room, sited at the apex of the curved inner wall of Pueblo Bonito and directly north in this central position, must have had symbolic import. Inside the room, the small, bowl-shaped cup filled with red ocher and a worked sherd may have served as a means of communicating with the below or as a locus for placing prayer sticks. But as I note in chapter 2, it also had the appearance of an eye; perhaps it symbolized a guardian watching or protecting the doorway to Room 32. By the mid-1000s, Room 28 was below ground rather than a surface room, possibly providing a more direct connection with the below, much like a kiva. The stairway would have provided a means of reaching the above, the courtyard and center of the village.

The room itself was ensouled by the rituals performed when it was constructed. The jars stored in the room also were animated, and therefore they had potential power that required control. "Stored" may be the wrong word here, because the vessels "lived" in the room, and thus it was their house. They were probably fed, as important ritual objects are among the Pueblo peoples today. Room 28 must be seen then as having concentrated power due to its location, features, and contents.

The termination involved scarring, smashing, or otherwise altering the vessels; pouring fuel on some; and burning the entire room until it collapsed on them. The termination must be seen as a genuine and extreme act to remove the power of the vessels and other objects in the room. The termination effectively removed the power the cylinder jars once had, burying them under tons of debris. Yet while the jars and destroyed rooms were not visible, memories of the dramatic termination event must have remained. Eventually, the burned debris was leveled over, and the space was used again for some period of time. Given the power associated with the room and its contents, this reuse is somewhat surprising. The new room space used three of the burn-scarred walls, along with a new partition wall. Thus, it occupied the same footprint that Room 28b had. This is important because it indicates that the space was not avoided, nor was a new space offset from the old one (McAnany and Hodder 2009:15). Had the memory of the termination and the reasons for it faded by that point? Were the builders consciously occupying and linking with that powerful space? The fact that avoidance was not practiced is undoubtedly significant, but we cannot know the reasons, and we do not know the timing. Despite this later use of the space over the leveled debris, the individuals who set Room 28 on fire did their best to destroy the house of the cylinder jars to prevent anyone from ever accessing and using the powerful objects it contained. They succeeded so well that the members of the Hyde Exploring Expedition did not know they would find anything in Room 28 when the excavation started in August 1896.

EPILOGUE

By September 1, 1896, George Pepper and the HEE excavators had packed the Room 28 cylinder jars in boxes and loaded the boxes onto a wagon. Excavations had shifted to the adjacent Rooms 32 and 33 for the duration of the season. The vessels and other contents of Room 28 began a long journey by wagon and then by train to New York City. The vessels are now housed in storage drawers at the American Museum of Natural History; on shelving at the National Museum of the American Indian in Washington, DC; and at the Peabody Museum at Harvard University in Cambridge, Massachusetts. Their social lives continue today as scholars from all over the world come to visit and study them. Sometimes they are on display, where thousands of visitors can see them. They maintain a powerful hold on the imagination of the people who come into contact with them, or see photographs of them, or hear the tale of their use and destruction and rescue.

The wagon that carried the cylinder jars from Pueblo Bonito returned with supplies for the camp, including a luxury food from the tropics of Mesoamerica. Records indicate that George Pepper and Richard Wetherill drank hot chocolate on Sunday, September 13, after what was perhaps a 700-year hiatus in its consumption at Pueblo Bonito. Ironically, before Room 28 was filled with tons of backdirt, the excavators discarded a piece of modern material culture in the room that was yet another distinctive drinking vessel: an empty porter bottle (figure 11.1).

PATRICIA L. CROWN

Room 28
Whole Vessels

FIGURE A.1A–G. Room 28 cylinder jars in the collections of the American Museum of Natural History (catalog numbers beginning with H/), the National Museum of the American Indian (catalog numbers beginning with the numeral 5), and the Peabody Museum of Archaeology and Ethnology at Harvard University (catalog numbers beginning with A). The AMNH photographs are courtesy of the Division of Anthropology, American Museum of Natural History. The NMAI photographs are courtesy of the National Museum of the American Indian, Smithsonian Institution. The Peabody photographs are © 2020 President and Fellows of Harvard College, Peabody Museum of Archaeology and Ethnology, PM 30-18-10/A6918, PM 30-18-10/A6919, PM 30-18-10/A6921. All photographs by Patricia Crown and Marianne Tyndall. Composite illustration by Patricia Crown.

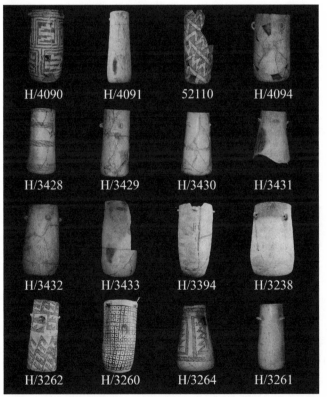

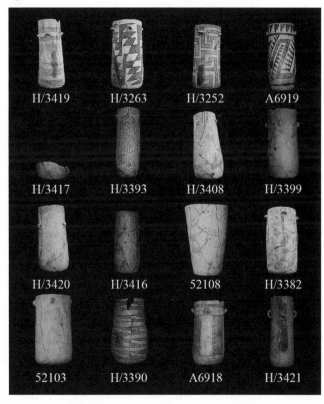

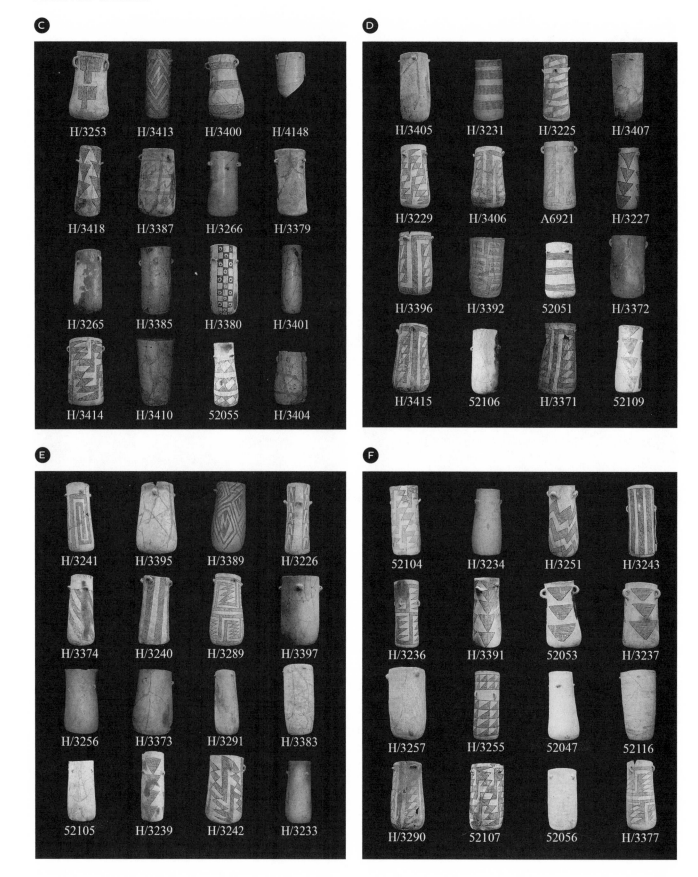

C

H/3253 H/3413 H/3400 H/4148

H/3418 H/3387 H/3266 H/3379

H/3265 H/3385 H/3380 H/3401

H/3414 H/3410 52055 H/3404

D

H/3405 H/3231 H/3225 H/3407

H/3229 H/3406 A6921 H/3227

H/3396 H/3392 52051 H/3372

H/3415 52106 H/3371 52109

E

H/3241 H/3395 H/3389 H/3226

H/3374 H/3240 H/3289 H/3397

H/3256 H/3373 H/3291 H/3383

52105 H/3239 H/3242 H/3233

F

52104 H/3234 H/3251 H/3243

H/3236 H/3391 52053 H/3237

H/3257 H/3255 52047 52116

H/3290 52107 52056 H/3377

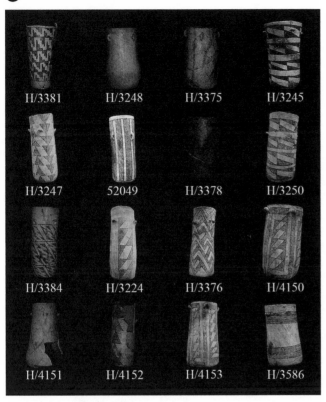

G

H/3381   H/3248   H/3375   H/3245

H/3247   52049   H/3378   H/3250

H/3384   H/3224   H/3376   H/4150

H/4151   H/4152   H/4153   H/3586

FIGURE A.2A–B. Room 28 pitchers and other vessels in the collections of the American Museum of Natural History (catalog numbers beginning with H/) and the National Museum of the American Indian (catalog numbers beginning with the numeral 5). The AMNH photographs are courtesy of the Division of Anthropology, American Museum of Natural History. The NMAI photographs are courtesy of the National Museum of the American Indian, Smithsonian Institution. All photographs by Patricia Crown. Composite illustration by Patricia Crown.

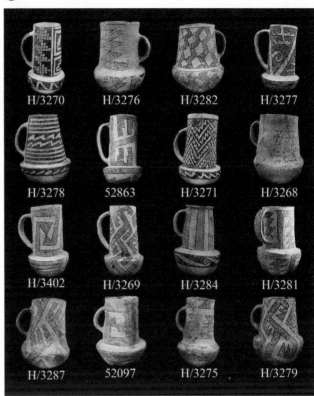

A

H/3270   H/3276   H/3282   H/3277

H/3278   52863   H/3271   H/3268

H/3402   H/3269   H/3284   H/3281

H/3287   52097   H/3275   H/3279

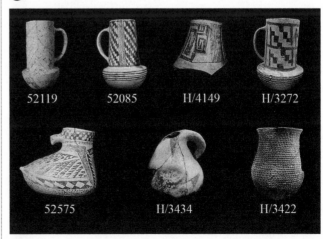

B

52119   52085   H/4149   H/3272

52575   H/3434   H/3422

FIGURE A.3A–C. Room 28 bowls in the collections of the American Museum of Natural History (catalog numbers beginning with H/) and the National Museum of the American Indian (catalog numbers beginning with the numeral 5). The AMNH photographs are courtesy of the Division of Anthropology, American Museum of Natural History. The NMAI photographs are courtesy of the National Museum of the American Indian, Smithsonian Institution. All photographs by Patricia Crown. Composite illustration by Patricia Crown.

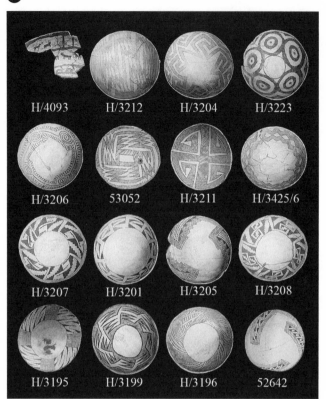

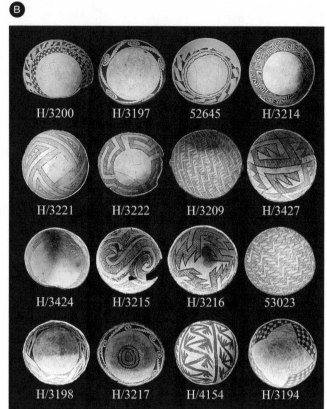

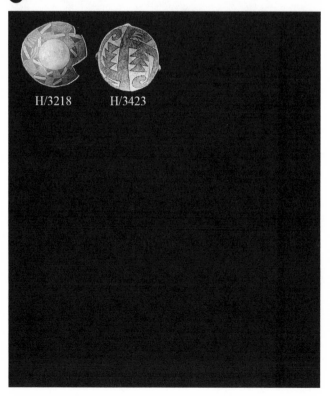

Archaeobotanical Remains

TABLE B.1. **Archaeobotanical remains: flotation (F) and macrobotanical (M) samples from Room 28**

FS	LEVEL	TAXON	PART	CONDITION	QUANTITY	NOTES	VOLUME (mL)	mL AVAILABLE	mL EXAMINED	SAMPLE TYPE
299	13	*Amelanchier/ Peraphyllum*	wood	charred	3		2,300	67	65	F
299	13	*Chrysothamnus*	wood	charred	2		2,300	67	65	F
299	13	*Echinocereus*	seed	charred	1		2,300	67	65	F
299	13	*Fraxinus*	wood	charred	15		2,300	67	65	F
299	13	*Mentzelia albicaulis*	seed	charred	50+		2,300	67	65	F
299	13	*Populus/Salix*	wood	charred	3		2,300	67	65	F
299	13	*Pseudotsuga*	wood	charred	1		2,300	67	65	F
299	13	*Sarcobatus*	wood	charred	8		2,300	67	65	F
299	13	Unknown rodent	pellet	charred	6		2,300	67	65	F
299	13	*Zea mays*	cob fragment	charred	2		2,300	67	65	F
299	13	*Zea mays*	cupule	charred	1		2,300	67	65	F
331	14	*Amelanchier/ Peraphyllum*	wood	charred	2		1,480	52	47	F
331	14	*Atriplex*	wood	charred	2		1,480	52	47	F
331	14	*Cercocarpus*	wood	charred	2		1,480	52	47	F
331	14	*Echinocereus*	seed	uncharred	1		1,480	52	47	F
331	14	*Juniperus*	wood	charred	3		1,480	52	47	F
331	14	*Opuntia*	seed fragment	uncharred	16	prickly pear	1,480	52	47	F
331	14	*Physalis*	seed fragment	uncharred	3		1,480	52	47	F
331	14	*Pinus edulis*	seed fragment	uncharred	7		1,480	52	47	F
331	14	*Sarcobatus*	wood	charred	11		1,480	52	47	F
331	14	*Zea mays*	cob fragment	charred	19		1,480	52	47	F
331	14	*Zea mays*	cupule	charred	21		1,480	52	47	F
331	14	*Zea mays*	kernel	charred	1		1,480	52	47	F
332	15	*Atriplex*	wood	charred	4		400	15	14	F
332	15	*Chrysothamnus*	twig	charred	2		400	15	14	F
332	15	*Juniperus*	wood	charred	5		400	15	14	F
332	15	*Populus/Salix*	twig	charred	1		400	15	14	F
332	15	*Populus/Salix*	wood	charred	3		400	15	14	F
332	15	*Sarcobatus*	wood	charred	10		400	15	14	F
332	15	Unknown	nutshell fragment	charred	8		400	15	14	F

FS	LEVEL	TAXON	PART	CONDITION	QUANTITY	NOTES	VOLUME (mL)	mL AVAILABLE	mL EXAMINED	SAMPLE TYPE
332	15	*Zea mays*	cob fragment	charred	1		400	15	14	F
332	15	*Zea mays*	cupule	charred	18		400	15	14	F
362		*Cercocarpus*	wood	charred	3		1,250	13.5	11.5	F
362		*Fraxinus*	wood	charred	1		1,250	13.5	11.5	F
362		*Juniperus*	wood	charred	3		1,250	13.5	11.5	F
362		*Physalis*	seed	uncharred	2		1,250	13.5	11.5	F
362		*Populus/Salix*	wood	charred	6		1,250	13.5	11.5	F
362		*Sarcobatus*	wood	charred	6		1,250	13.5	11.5	F
362		Unknown, possibly *Gossypium*	twine fragment	charred	1		1,250	13.5	11.5	F
362		*Zea mays*	cob fragment	charred	1		1,250	13.5	11.5	F
362		*Zea mays*	cupule	charred	1		1,250	13.5	11.5	F
363		*Amelanchier/ Peraphyllum*	wood	charred	10		2,200	104	87	F
363		*Atriplex*	wood	charred	6		2,200	104	87	F
363		*Cercocarpus*	wood	charred	8		2,200	104	87	F
363		Cheno-am	seed	charred	4		2,200	104	87	F
363		*Descurainia*	seed	charred	1	bent over embryo; tentative ID	2,200	104	87	F
363		*Forestiera*	wood	charred	2		2,200	104	87	F
363		*Fraxinus*	wood	charred	2		2,200	104	87	F
363		*Juniperus*	wood	charred	4		2,200	104	87	F
363		*Physalis*	seed	charred	3		2,200	104	87	F
363		*Pinus edulis*	seed fragment	uncharred	60+		2,200	104	87	F
363		*Sarcobatus*	wood	charred	6		2,200	104	87	F
363		Unknown	fruit fragment	charred	2	fleshy	2,200	104	87	F
363		*Zea mays*	cob fragment	charred	3		2,200	104	87	F
363		*Zea mays*	cupule	charred	18		2,200	104	87	F
510	13	*Artemisia*	wood	charred	2		5,190	87	82	F
510	13	*Cercocarpus*	twig	charred	4		5,190	87	82	F
510	13	*Cercocarpus*	wood	charred	3		5,190	87	82	F
510	13	Cheno-am	seed	uncharred	50+		5,190	87	82	F
510	13	*Echinocereus*	seed	uncharred	1		5,190	87	82	F
510	13	*Juniperus*	wood	charred	1		5,190	87	82	F
510	13	*Juniperus*	seed	uncharred	1		5,190	87	82	F
510	13	*Opuntia*	seed	uncharred	16+	prickly pear; systematic rodent damage	5,190	87	82	F
510	13	*Physalis*	seed	charred	3		5,190	87	82	F
510	13	*Physalis*	seed	uncharred	4		5,190	87	82	F
510	13	*Pinus ponderosa*	wood	charred	11		5,190	87	82	F
510	13	*Populus/Salix*	twig	charred	2		5,190	87	82	F
510	13	*Populus/Salix*	wood	charred	13		5,190	87	82	F
510	13	*Quercus*	wood	charred	1		5,190	87	82	F
510	13	*Rhus aromatica*	twig	charred	6		5,190	87	82	F
510	13	*Sarcobatus*	wood	charred	4		5,190	87	82	F
510	13	*Zea mays*	cupule	charred	5		5,190	87	82	F

FS	LEVEL	TAXON	PART	CONDITION	QUANTITY	NOTES	VOLUME (mL)	mL AVAILABLE	mL EXAMINED	SAMPLE TYPE
511		*Amelanchier/ Peraphyllum*	wood	charred	1		1,970	52	49	F
511		*Artemisia*	wood	charred	4		1,970	52	49	F
511		*Atriplex*	wood	charred	1		1,970	52	49	F
511		Cheno-am	seed	uncharred	50+		1,970	52	49	F
511		*Forestiera*	wood	charred	1		1,970	52	49	F
511		*Fraxinus*	wood	charred	1		1,970	52	49	F
511		*Juniperus*	wood	charred	14		1,970	52	49	F
511		*Opuntia*	seed	uncharred	10+	prickly pear	1,970	52	49	F
511		*Populus/Salix*	wood	charred	1		1,970	52	49	F
511		*Zea mays*	cob fragment	charred	2		1,970	52	49	F
511		*Zea mays*	cupule	charred	10		1,970	52	49	F
65		*Amaranthus*	seed	uncharred	1,000+	cache? No rodent pellets				M
65		*Sphaeralcea*	seed	uncharred	18	cache? No rodent pellets				M
65		Unknown	bone?	uncharred	1	rodent?				M
106		*Cucurbita moschata*	seed fragment	uncharred	6	wavy, fringed edge				M
106		*Pinus edulis*	seed fragment	uncharred	5	one is gnawed				M
106		Unknown	bone?	uncharred	1					M
118		*Cucurbita moschata*	seed	uncharred	1	whole				M
118		*Cucurbita moschata*	seed fragment	uncharred	2	wavy, fringed edge				M
139		*Pinus edulis*	seed	uncharred	2	with rodent gnaw marks				M
139		*Pinus edulis*	seed fragment	uncharred	8	no gnaw marks				M
179		*Pinus edulis*	seed fragment	uncharred	1	no gnaw marks				M
204		*Cucurbita moschata*	seed fragment	uncharred	6	wavy, fringed edge				M
204		*Pinus edulis*	seed fragment	uncharred	7	no gnaw marks				M
222		*Cucurbita moschata*	seed fragment	uncharred	5	wavy, fringed edge				M
222		*Pinus edulis*	seed fragment	uncharred	8	one is gnawed				M
239		*Pinus edulis*	seed fragment	uncharred	7	with rodent gnaw marks				M
308		*Cucurbita moschata*	seed fragment	uncharred	8	one with wavy, fringed edge				M
308		*Pinus edulis*	seed fragment	uncharred	5	not gnawed				M
368		*Pinus edulis*	seed fragment	uncharred	4					M
374		*Celtis reticulata*	seed half	uncharred	1					M

CAITLIN S. AINSWORTH AND EMILY LENA JONES

Human Remains

While human burials and scattered human remains were recovered from the four rooms north of Room 28 in previous excavations (see Marden 2011), Room 28 itself contained no burials, and no human remains had ever before been reported from this room. Therefore, the recovery of human remains was not expected during the 2013 reexcavation. During the course of the University of New Mexico project, it became evident that human skeletal material had been inadvertently incorporated into the backdirt that George Pepper and Richard Wetherill used to refill Room 28 in 1897. At the request of the National Park Service and following its policy for the inadvertent discovery of human remains, we inventoried these remains prior to their reburial. The details of this small assemblage of disarticulated human skeletal material are presented here.

A total of 155 specimens of human bone were recovered from the Room 28 fill. These represent the remains of at least four individuals: two adults, one older child/early adolescent (estimated age 9–15 years), and one perinatal infant. Ages at death of the subadult remains were estimated using the metric and fusion data compiled by Baker and colleagues (2005). The ages of the adult individuals could not be precisely estimated; however, the presence of three fragments of ossified thyroid cartilage indicates that at least one was a middle-aged or old adult. One adult individual has an estimated sex of female. This estimate is based on the morphology of the frontal bone. The second adult was significantly larger than the first, indicating a probable male. Evidence of pathology was identified on a total of three specimens of bone. A right and left intermediate cuneiform show evidence of osteoarthritis, and there is a healed fracture on the body of a left rib. Both of the tarsals are from an adult. It is not clear which individual the rib fragment is from.

TABLE C.1. **Human skeletal elements from Room 28, Pueblo Bonito**

Element		Side	Completeness (%)	Age	Notes
Cranial elements	frontal	R	80	adult	Probable female based on morphology
Teeth	lower incisor	R	100	adult	Very worn crown surface
	upper M1	R	100	adult	
Axial skeleton	hyoid, body	n/a	75% of body (50% of total bone)		Greater horns not fused to body, and lesser horns also unfused; since ossification of the hyoid is highly variable, this specimen not assigned to an age category
	hyoid, body	n/a	100% of body (60% of total bone)		Greater horns not fused to body
	ossified thyroid cartilage	n/a	10% of total cartilage	adult	Fragment, including one of the cornu
	ossified thyroid cartilage	n/a	15% of total cartilage	adult	Fragment, including one of the cornu
	ossified thyroid cartilage	n/a	5% of total cartilage	adult	Fragment, including one of the cornu
	C2/axis	n/a	85	adult	
	cervical vertebra (3–7)	n/a	95	adult	
	cervical vertebra (3–7)	n/a	75	adult	
	cervical vertebra (3–7)	n/a	97	adult	Specimen is broken into four refittable pieces; both epiphyses on centrum fully fused
	thoracic vertebra (lower)	n/a	85	adult	
	thoracic vertebra (lower)	n/a	95	adult	
	vertebra, fragment of articular facet	n/a	2	unknown	Probably a thoracic vertebra
	caudal vertebra (caudal 1)	n/a	100	adult	
	caudal vertebra	n/a	100	adult	
	coccyx, inferior portion (fused segments 2–4)	n/a	100% of inferior portion (75% of total coccyx)	unknown	Taphonomic damage; cortical bone in poor condition; segments 2–4 are complete and fully fused to each other
	rib 1	L	95	adult	Large individual
	rib 1	R	50	adult	
	central rib	R	80	adult	
	central rib	L	85	adult	
	central rib	R	30	adult	
	central rib	R	70	adult	Large individual
	central rib	R	40	adult	
	central rib	L	30	adult	
	central rib	R	80	adult	Burned
	central rib	L	80	adult	Large individual
	central rib	R	90	adult	Broken into two pieces; weathered
	central rib	L	80	adult	
	central rib	R	30	adult	
	lower rib	R	90	adult	Broken into two pieces; weathered

Element		Side	Completeness (%)	Age	Notes
Axial skeleton (continued)	rib body fragment	unknown	20	unknown	Large individual
	rib body fragment	unknown	50	unknown	
	rib body fragment	unknown	50	unknown	
	rib body fragment	unknown	55	unknown	Adult size
	rib body fragment	unknown	40	unknown	Adult size
	rib body fragment	unknown	15	adult	
	rib body fragment	unknown	15	adult	
	rib body fragment	unknown	35	unknown	
	rib body fragment	L	70	unknown	Pathology present: healed fracture
	rib body fragment	unknown	20	unknown	Adult size
	sternal rib end (fragment)	unknown	2	adult	Condition of cortex poor due to taphonomic damage; not enough present for precise aging, but morphology consistent with adult
	manubrium (sternum segment I)	n/a	100	adult	Not fused to body of sternum
	sternal body	n/a	100	adult	
	os coxa	unknown	20	adult	Fragment
Appendicular skeleton	ulna	L	97	adult	Missing styloid process
	scaphoid	L	100	adult	
	scaphoid	R	100	adult	
	lunate	L	100	adult	
	lunate	R	100	adult	Adult size and morphology; dense cortex
	triquetal	R	100	adult	
	triquetal	unknown	100	adult	
	trapezium	R	100	adult	
	trapezium	unknown	100	adult	
	trapezoid	unknown	100	adult	
	trapezoid	L	100	adult	Adult morphology and density
	trapezoid	L	100	adult	Adult morphology and density; large individual
	capitate	R	100	adult	Adult size and morphology; dense cortex
	capitate	L	100	adult	Adult morphology and density
	metacarpal III	R	80	adult	Burned
	proximal phalanx (finger)	unknown	100	adult	
	proximal phalanx (finger)	unknown	100	adult	
	middle phalanx (finger)	unknown	100	adult	
	middle phalanx (finger)	unknown	100	adult	Large individual
	middle phalanx (finger)	unknown	100	adult	Large individual
	middle phalanx (finger)	unknown	100	adult	
	middle phalanx (finger)	unknown	100	adult	
	middle phalanx (finger)	unknown	100	adult	
	distal phalanx (finger)	unknown	100	adult	
	distal phalanx (finger)	unknown	100	adult	

Element	Side	Completeness (%)	Age	Notes
Appendicular skeleton (continued)	distal phalanx (finger)	unknown	100	adult	
	distal phalanx (finger)	unknown	100	adult	
	distal phalanx (finger)	unknown	100	adult	
	distal phalanx (finger)	unknown	100	adult	
	patella	R	100	adult	Large individual
	talus	L	100	adult	
	talus	L	100	adult	
	calcaneus	L	95	adult	
	cuboid	L	100	adult	
	cuboid	L	100	adult	Adult morphology and density
	navicular	L	95	adult	Large individual
	navicular	unknown	100	adult	
	medial cuneiform	R	100	adult	Adult morphology and density
	intermediate cuneiform	L	100	adult	Evidence of osteoarthritis
	intermediate cuneiform	R	100	adult	Adult morphology and density; osteophytes on non-articular surfaces
	lateral cuneiform	R	100	adult	
	lateral cuneiform	R	100	adult	
	lateral cuneiform	L	100	adult	
	metatarsal I	L	100	adult	Large individual
	metatarsal I	L	100	adult	
	metatarsal II	L	100	adult	
	metatarsal II	L	100	adult	
	metatarsal II	R	100	adult	Large individual
	metatarsal II	R	100	adult	
	metatarsal IV	L	100	adult	
	proximal phalanx (toe); first digital ray	unknown	100	adult	
	proximal phalanx (toe)	unknown	100	adult	
	proximal phalanx (toe)	unknown	100	adult	
	proximal phalanx (toe)	unknown	100	adult	
	proximal phalanx (toe)	unknown	100	adult	
	proximal phalanx (toe)	unknown	100	adult	
	proximal phalanx (toe)	unknown	100	adult	
	proximal phalanx (toe)	unknown	100	adult	
	proximal phalanx (toe)	unknown	100	adult	
	proximal phalanx (toe)	unknown	100	adult	
	proximal phalanx (toe)	unknown	100	adult	
	proximal phalanx (toe)	unknown	100	adult	
	proximal phalanx (toe)	unknown	100	adult	
	proximal phalanx (toe)	unknown	100	adult	
	proximal pedal phalanx	unknown	35	adult	Complete proximal end plus 1/3 of diaphysis; epiphysis on proximal end completely fused
	middle phalanx (toe)	unknown	100	adult	
	middle phalanx (toe)	unknown	100	adult	
	middle phalanx (toe)	unknown	100	adult	
	middle phalanx (toe)	unknown	100	adult	Adult size and morphology; dense cortex; proximal epiphysis completely fused

Element		Side	Completeness (%)	Age	Notes
Appendicular skeleton (continued)	middle phalanx (toe)	unknown	100	adult	Adult size and morphology; dense cortex; proximal epiphysis completely fused
	middle phalanx (toe)	unknown	100	adult	Adult size and morphology; dense cortex; proximal epiphysis completely fused
	middle phalanx (toe)	unknown	100	adult	Adult size and morphology; dense cortex; proximal epiphysis completely fused
	middle phalanx (toe)	unknown	100	adult	Adult size and morphology; dense cortex; proximal epiphysis completely fused
	distal phalanx (toe); first digital ray	unknown	100	adult	
	distal phalanx (toe)	unknown	100	adult	
	distal phalanx (toe)	unknown	100	adult	
	distal phalanx (toe)	unknown	100	adult	
	distal phalanx (toe)	unknown	100	adult	
	distal phalanx (toe)	unknown	100	adult	
	distal phalanx (toe)	unknown	100	adult	Adult size and morphology; dense cortex; proximal epiphysis completely fused
	distal phalanx (toe)	unknown	100	adult	Adult size and morphology; dense cortex; proximal epiphysis completely fused
	distal phalanx (toe)	unknown	100	adult	Adult size and morphology; dense cortex; proximal epiphysis completely fused
	distal phalanx (toe)	unknown	100	adult	Adult size and morphology; dense cortex; proximal epiphysis completely fused
	distal phalanx (toe)	unknown	100	adult	Adult size and morphology; dense cortex; proximal epiphysis completely fused
	distal phalanx (toe)	unknown	100	adult	Adult size and morphology; dense cortex; proximal epiphysis completely fused
	distal phalanx (toe)	unknown	100	adult	Adult size and morphology; dense cortex; proximal epiphysis completely fused
	distal phalanx (toe)	unknown	100	adult	Adult size and morphology; dense cortex; proximal epiphysis completely fused

OLDER CHILD/ADOLESCENT (9–15 YEARS)

Element		Side	Completeness (%)	Age	Notes
	ulna, unfused distal epiphysis	L	100 (complete epiphysis)	older child/ adolescent	Styloid process is present (appears in late childhood), but epiphysis is unfused (fuses between 15 and 20 years of age); specimen is not adult size; morphology is more smooth, rounded, and less sharply defined than that of an adult

Element		Side	Completeness (%)	Age	Notes
Cranial elements	parietal	L	25	infant	Includes portions of sagittal and lambdoidal sutures; absence of sagittal sulcus and meningeal grooves indicates neonate or younger, as does bone texture, size, and thickness
	occipital	n/a	15	infant	Fragment is of the squama along the mendosal suture; mendosal suture still partly open, but supraoccipital part and interparietal parts are united
	occipital	n/a	20	infant	Fragment of the supraoccipital portion of the squama; size, morphology, and bone texture consistent with an infant
	cranial vault bone (frontal, parietal, or occipital)	n/a	approximately 10	infant	No suture edges present; specific element could not be determined, but degree of curvature suggests frontal or parietal; texture, size, and thickness of bone indicate infant/perinate
	mandible	L	45	infant	Posterior half of bone; taphonomic damage to condyle, coronoid process, tooth crypts/superior half of body; size, texture, and morphology consistent with perinate
Axial skeleton	central rib	R	97	infant	Consists of two pieces that refit; ventral portion is quite straight indicating one of the lower true ribs; size and morphology consistent with infant
	pedicle (vertebra, unfused)	n/a	100% (25% of total vertebra)	infant	
	pedicle (vertebra, unfused)	n/a	100% (25% of total vertebra)	infant	
	pedicle (vertebra, unfused)	n/a	100% (25% of total vertebra)	infant	
	pedicle (vertebra, unfused)	n/a	100% (25% of total vertebra)	infant	
	pedicle (vertebra, unfused)	n/a	100% (25% of total vertebra)	infant	
	pedicle (vertebra, unfused)	n/a	100% (25% of total vertebra)	infant	
	pedicle (vertebra, unfused)	n/a	100% (25% of total vertebra)	infant	
	pedicle (vertebra, unfused)	n/a	100% (25% of total vertebra)	infant	
	pedicle (vertebra, unfused)	n/a	100% (25% of total vertebra)	infant	
	pedicle (vertebra, unfused)	n/a	100% (25% of total vertebra)	infant	

Element		Side	Completeness (%)	Age	Notes
Appendicular skeleton	scapula	L	85	infant	Taphonomic damage to margins, acromion process, and portion of bone superior to the supraspinous fossa; size, morphology, and bone texture consistent with an infant
	humerus	R	90	infant	Diaphysis is complete; taphonomic damage to metaphyses; size is between 3rd trimester and perinate (see Baker et al. 2005); diaphysis unusually thin/gracile for perinate, but length seems closest to perinate
	radius	R	35	infant	Distal end present and complete, plus approximately 1/3 of shaft; size is consistent with a perinate (see Baker et al. 2005)
	femur	R	100	infant	
	femur	L	95	infant	

n/a = not applicable.

References Cited

Adams, E. Charles

2016 Closure and Dedication Practices in the Homol'ovi Settlement Cluster. *American Antiquity* 81:42–57.

Adams, Jenny L.

1993 Mechanisms of Wear on Ground Stone Surfaces. *Pacific Coast Archaeological Society Quarterly* 29(4):60–73.

1996 *Manual for a Technological Approach to Ground Stone Analysis.* Center for Desert Archaeology, Tucson, AZ.

1999 Refocusing the Role of Food-Grinding Tools as Correlates for Subsistence Strategies in the US Southwest. *American Antiquity* 64:475–98.

2002 *Ground Stone Analysis: A Technological Approach.* University of Utah Press, Salt Lake City.

Adams, Karen R.

1988 The Ethnobotany and Phenology of Plants in and Adjacent to Two Riparian Habitats in Southeastern Arizona. PhD dissertation, Ecology and Evolutionary Biology Department, University of Arizona.

1994 A Regional Synthesis of *Zea mays* in the Prehistoric American Southwest. In *Corn and Culture in the Prehistoric New World*, edited by Sissel Johannessen and Christine A. Hastorf, 273–302. Westview Press, Boulder, CO.

2010 Charred Maize (*Zea mays* L.) from Basketmaker III Site 29SJ519, Chaco Culture National Historical Park, New Mexico. Manuscript on file, Chaco Culture National Historical Park.

2011 Appendix E: Archaeobotanical Analysis. In *Chimney Rock Stabilization Project, Chimney Rock Great House (5AA83) Archuleta County, CO (Permit No. COL538)* by Brenda K. Todd. Submitted to the USDA San Juan National Forest, Pagosa District, and Chimney Rock Interpretive Association by Stephen H. Lekson, University of Colorado, Boulder. USFS Report No. 11-076.

Adams, Karen R., and Vorsila L. Bohrer

1998 Archaeobotanical Indicators of Seasonality: Examples from Arid Southwestern United States. In *Seasonality and Sedentism: Archaeological Perspectives from Old and New World Sites*, edited by T. R. Rocek and O. Bar-Yosef, 129–41. Peabody Museum Bulletin 6. Peabody Museum of Archaeology and Ethnology, Harvard University, Cambridge, MA.

Adams, Karen R., and Suzanne K. Fish

2006 Southwest Plants. In *Handbook of North American Indians: 3. Environment, Origins, and Population*, edited by Douglas Ubelaker, 292–312. Smithsonian Institution Press, Washington, DC.

2011 Subsistence through Time in the Greater Southwest. In *The Subsistence Economies of Indigenous North American Societies*, edited by Bruce C. Smith, 147–83. Smithsonian Institution Scholarly Press, Washington, DC.

Adams, Karen R., and Shawn S. Murray

2004 Identification Criteria for Plant Remains Recovered from Archaeological Sites in the Central Mesa Verde Region. http://www.crowcanyon.org/PlantID, accessed September 25, 2014.

Adams, Karen R., and Susan J. Smith

2011 Reconstructing Past Life-Ways with Plants: I. Subsistence and Other Daily Needs. In *Ethnobiology*, edited by E. N. Anderson, D. Pearsall, E. Hunn, and N. Turner, 149–71. Wiley-Blackwell, Hoboken, NJ.

Ainsworth, Caitlin S.

2017 Diet and Subsistence in the Middle Rio Grande Valley during the 18th and 19th Centuries: Evidence from the Los Ranchos Plaza (LA46638) Faunal Assemblage. Master's paper, Department of Anthropology, University of New Mexico, Albuquerque.

Ainsworth, Caitlin S., Patricia L. Crown, Emily Lena Jones, and Stephanie E. Franklin

2018 Ritual Deposition of Avifauna in the Northern Burial Cluster at Pueblo Bonito, Chaco Canyon. *Kiva* 184:110–35.

Akins, Nancy J.

1985 Prehistoric Fauna Utilization in Chaco Canyon: Basketmaker III through Pueblo III. In *Environment and Subsistence of Chaco Canyon, New Mexico*, edited by F. J. Mathien, 315–33. National Park Service, Department of the Interior, Albuquerque, NM.

1987 Faunal Remains from Pueblo Alto. In *Investigations at the Pueblo Alto Complex, Chaco Canyon: 3, pt. 2. Artifactual and Biological Analyses*, edited by F. J. Mathien, 445–645. National Park Service, Santa Fe, NM.

1997 The Abraders of Chaco Canyon: An Analysis of Their Form and Function. In *Ceramics, Lithics, and Ornaments of Chaco Canyon: Analyses of Artifacts from the Chaco Project, 1971–1978: Pt. 2. Lithics*, edited by F. J. Mathien, 701-945. Publications in Archaeology 18G, National Park Service, Santa Fe, NM.

2001 Chaco Canyon Mortuary Practices: Archaeological Correlates of Complexity. In *Ancient Burial Practices in the American Southwest*, edited by D. Mitchell and J. Brunson-Hadley, 167–90. University of New Mexico Press, Albuquerque.

Alden, Peter, and Peter Friederici

1999 *National Audubon Society Field Guide to the Southwestern States.* Knopf, NY.

Altschul, Jeffrey H.

1978 The Development of the Chacoan Interaction Sphere. *Journal of Anthropological Research* 34:109–46.

Anderson, Karen

2009 Tiwanaku Influence on Local Drinking Patterns in Cochabamba, Bolivia. In *Drink, Power, and Society in the Andes*, edited by Justin Jennings and Brenda J. Bowser, 167–99. University of Florida Press, Gainesville.

Andrefsky, W., Jr.

2005 *Lithics: Macroscopic Approaches to Analysis.* Cambridge University Press, NY.

Andrews, Peter

1990a *Owls, Caves, and Fossils.* Natural History Museum Publications, Chicago, IL.

1990b Small Mammal Taphonomy. In *European Neogene Mammal Chronology*, edited by E. H. Lindsay, 487–94. Plenum Press, NY.

Andrews, Peter, and Elizabeth M. Nesbit Evans

1983 Small Mammal Bone Accumulation Produced by Mammalian Carnivores. *Paleobiology* 9(3):289–307.

Arazi-Coambs, Sandra

2016 White Ware Ceramics from the Pueblo Bonito Mounds. In *The Pueblo Bonito Mounds of Chaco Canyon: Material Culture and Fauna*, edited by Patricia L. Crown, 53–92. University of New Mexico Press, Albuquerque.

Austin, Daniel F.

2007 Sacred Connections with Cat-tail (*Typha*, Typhaceae): Dragons, Water Serpents and Red-Maces. *Ethnobotany Research and Applications* 5:273–303.

Badenhorst, Shaw

2008 The Zooarchaeology of Great House Sites in the San Juan Basin of the American Southwest. PhD dissertation, Department of Archaeology, Simon Fraser University, Burnaby, BC.

Badenhorst, Shaw, and Jonathan C. Driver

2009 Faunal Changes in Farming Communities from Basketmaker II to Pueblo III (AD 1–1300) in the San Juan Basin of the American Southwest. *Journal of Archaeological Science* 36(9):1832–41.

Badenhorst, Shaw, Jonathan C. Driver, and David Maxwell

2016 Pueblo Bonito Fauna. In *The Pueblo Bonito Mounds of Chaco Canyon*, edited by P. L. Crown, 189–211. University of New Mexico Press, Albuquerque.

Baker, Brenda J., Tosha L. Dupras, Matthew W. Tocheri, and Sandra M. Wheeler

2005 *The Osteology of Infants and Children.* Texas A&M University Press, College Station.

Bayham, Frank E.

1977 Analysis of Faunal Remains and Animal Exploitation in Copper Basin. In *Archaeology in Copper Basin, Yavapai County, Arizona: Model Building for the Prehistory of the Prescott Region*, edited by M. D. Jeter, 339–67. Anthropological Research Paper No. 11. Arizona State University, Tempe.

Beacham, E. Bradley

2006 Eggshell and the Archaeological Record: A Developmental Study of Prehistoric Eggshell. MA thesis, Department of Anthropology, Eastern New Mexico University, Portales.

Beacham, E. Bradley, and Stephen R. Durand

2007 Eggshell and the Archaeological Record: New Insights into Turkey Husbandry in the American Southwest. *Journal of Archaeological Science* 34(10):1610–21.

Beidleman, Richard G.

1956 Ethnozoology of the Pueblo Indians in Historic Times. *Southwestern Lore* 22(2):17–28.

Bell, Catherine

1992 *Ritual Theory, Ritual Practice.* Oxford University Press, Oxford.

Bernardini, Wesley

1999 Reassessing the Scale of Social Action at Pueblo Bonito, Chaco Canyon, New Mexico. *Kiva* 64:447–70.

Binford, Lewis R.

1978 *Nunamiut Ethnoarchaeology.* Academic Press, NY.

1981 *Bones: Ancient Men and Modern Myths.* Academic Press, NY.

Bishop, Katelyn J., and Samantha G. Fladd

2018 Ritual Fauna and Social Organization at Pueblo Bonito, Chaco Canyon. *Kiva* 84:293–316.

Bocek, Barbara

1986 Rodent Ecology and Burrowing Behavior: Predicted Effects on Archaeological Site Formation. *American Antiquity* 51:603–14.

Bohrer, Vorsila L.

1978 Plants That Have Become Locally Extinct in the Southwest. *New Mexico Journal of Science* 18(2):10–19.

1991 Recently Recognized Cultivated and Encouraged Plants among the Hohokam. *Kiva* 56(3):227–35.

Bohrer, Vorsila L., and Karen R. Adams

1976 Guide to Learning: Prehistoric Seed Remains from Salmon Ruin, New Mexico. Unpublished manuscript on file, Crow Canyon Archaeological Center, Cortez, CO.

1977 *Ethnobotanical Techniques and Approaches at Salmon Ruin, New Mexico.* Contributions in Anthropology Vol. 8(1). Eastern New Mexico University, Portales.

Bottle Research Group

2016 Manufacturer's Marks and Other Logos on Glass Containers. https://sha.org/bottle/pdffiles/LLogoTable.pdf, accessed June 15, 2016.

Bovy, Kristine M.

2012 Why So Many Wings? A Re-Examination of Avian Skeletal Part Representation in the South-Central Northwest Coast, USA. *Journal of Archaeological Science* 39(7):2049–59.

Brand, Donald D.

1937 The Natural Landscape. In *Tseh So, a Small House Ruin, Chaco Canyon, New Mexico*, edited by Donald D. Brand, Florence M. Hawley, Frank C. Hibben, et al., 39–65. University of New Mexico Publication No. 308, Anthropological Series 2(2). University of New Mexico Press, Albuquerque.

Brandt, Carol

1996 Analysis of Plant Macro-Remains. In *The N30-31 Project: Investigations at Twenty-Two Sites between Mexican Springs and Navajo, McKinley County, New Mexico*, Vol. 3, pt. 2, 133–84. Zuni Archaeology Program and Zuni Cultural Resource Management, Report No. 466, Research Series No. 10. Zuni, NM.

Brody, Jerry J.

1991 *Anasazi and Pueblo Painting.* University of New Mexico Press, Albuquerque.

Bronk Ramsey, C.

2009 Bayesian Analysis of Radiocarbon Dates. *Radiocarbon* 51:337–60.

Brooks, Mark J.

2012 From Gizzards to Gastroliths: Early to Mid-Holocene Intensive Harvest and Processing of Migratory Waterfowl at a Carolina Bay in the Upper Coastal Plain of South Carolina. *Legacy* 16(1):22–25.

Broughton, Jack M.

1994 Declines in Mammalian Foraging Efficiency during the late Holocene, San Francisco Bay, California. *Journal of Anthropological Archaeology* 13:371–401.

1997 Widening Diet Breadth, Declining Foraging Efficiency, and Prehistoric Harvest Pressure: Ichthyofaunal Evidence from the Emeryville Shellmound, California. *Antiquity* 71:845–62.

1999 *Resource Depression and Intensification during the Late Holocene, San Francisco Bay: Evidence from the Emeryville Shellmound, California.* Anthropological Records 32. University of California Press, Berkeley.

Broughton, Jack M., and Frank E. Bayham

2003 Showing Off, Foraging Models, and the Ascendance of Large-Game Hunting in the California Middle Archaic. *American Antiquity* 68(4):783–89.

Broughton, Jack M., Michael D. Cannon, Frank E. Bayham, and David A. Byers

2011 Prey Body Size and Ranking in Zooarchaeology: Theory, Empirical Evidence, and Applications from the Northern Great Basin. *American Antiquity* 76(3):403–28.

Brown, David E.

1982a Plains and Great Basin Grasslands. In *Biotic Communities of the American Southwest: United States and Mexico*, special issue edited by David E. Brown. *Desert Plants* 4(1–4):115–21.

1982b Great Basin Conifer Woodland. In *Biotic Communities of the American Southwest: United States and Mexico*, special issue edited by David E. Brown. *Desert Plants* 4(1–4):52–57.

Bunzel, Ruth

1932 Introduction to Zuni Ceremonialism. In *Forty-Seventh Annual Report of the Bureau of American Ethnology*, 467–544. US Government Printing Office, Washington, DC.

Buskirk, Winfred

1986 *The Western Apache: Living with the Land before 1950.* University of Oklahoma Press, Norman.

Bustard, Wendy J.

1996 Space as Place: Small and Great House Spatial Organization in Chaco Canyon, New Mexico, AD 1000–1150. PhD dissertation, Department of Anthropology, University of New Mexico, Albuquerque.

2003 Pueblo Bonito: When a House Is Not a Home. In *Pueblo Bonito: Center of the Chacoan World*, edited by J. Neitzel, 80–93. Smithsonian Institution Press, Washington, DC.

Byers, David A., and Jack M. Broughton

2004 Holocene Environmental Change, Artiodactyl Abundances, and Human Hunting Strategies in the Great Basin. *American Antiquity* 69:235–56.

Byers, David A., Craig S. Smith, and Jack M. Broughton

2005 Holocene Artiodactyl Population Histories and Large Game Hunting in the Wyoming Basin, USA. *Journal of Archaeological Science* 32(1):125–42.

Cameron, Catherine

1997a The Chipped Stone of Chaco Canyon. In *Ceramics, Lithics, and Ornaments of Chaco Canyon: Analyses of Artifacts from the Chaco Project, 1971–1978*, Vol. 2, edited by F. J. Mathien, 531–609. Publications in Archaeology 18G, Chaco Canyon Studies, National Park Service, Santa Fe, NM.

1997b An Analysis of Manos from Chaco Canyon, New Mexico. In *Ceramics, Lithics, and Ornaments of Chaco Canyon: Analyses of Artifacts from the Chaco Project, 1971–1978*, Vol. 3, edited by F. J. Mathien, 997–1012. Publications in Archaeology 18G, Chaco Canyon Studies, National Park Service, Santa Fe, NM.

Cameron, Catherine M., and H. Wolcott Toll

2001 Deciphering the Organization of Production in Chaco Canyon. *American Antiquity* 66:5–13.

Campana, Douglas V.

1989 *Natufian and Protoneolithic Bone Tools: The Manufacture and Use of Bone Implements in the Zagros and the Levant.* British Archaeological Reports International Series No. 494. British Archaeological Reports, Oxford.

Cannon, Michael D.

2013 NISP, Bone Fragmentation, and the Measurement of Taxonomic Abundance. *Journal of Archaeological Method and Theory* 20(3):397–419.

Carr, Christopher, and D. Troy Case (editors)

2005 *Gathering Hopewell: Society, Ritual and Ritual Interaction.* Springer, NY.

Cartridge Collector's Exchange

2008 An Unlikely Candidate for a Paper-Patched Bullet. http://www.oldammo.com/january08.htm, accessed March 29, 2018.

Cartridge Corner

2018 Winchester Shotshell Headstamps. www.cartridge-corner.com/winch.htm, accessed March 29, 2018.

Castetter, Edward F.

1935 Uncultivated Native Plants Used as Sources of Food. University of New Mexico Biological Series 4(1). *University of New Mexico Bulletin* No. 266.

Chaco Research Archive

2016 Query the Database. http://www.chacoarchive.org, accessed September 2016.

Clark, Jamie L., and Bertrand Ligouis

2010 Burned Bone in the Howieson's Poort and Post-Howieson's Poort Middle Stone Age Deposits at Sibudu (South Africa): Behavioral and Taphonomic Implications. *Journal of Archaeological Science* 37(10):2650–61.

Coe, Sophie E., and Michael D. Coe

2007 *The True History of Chocolate.* Thames and Hudson, London.

Conrad, Cyler

2015 Archaeozoology in Mainland Southeast Asia: Changing Methodology and Pleistocene to Holocene Forager Subsistence Patterns in Thailand and Peninsular Malaysia. *Open Quaternary* 1(7):1–23.

Conrad, Cyler, Kenneth W. Gobalet, Kale Bruner, and Allen G. Pastron

2015 Hide, Tallow and Terrapin: Gold Rush–Era Zooarchaeology at Thompson's Cove (CA-SFR-186H), San Francisco, California. *International Journal of Historical Archaeology* 19(3):502–51.

Conrad, Cyler, Emily Lena Jones, Seth D. Newsome, and Douglas W. Schwartz

2016 Bone Isotopes, Eggshell and Turkey Husbandry at Arroyo Hondo Pueblo. *Journal of Archaeological Science* 10:566–74.

Crabtree, D. E.

1972 *An Introduction to Flintworking*. Occasional Papers of the Idaho State University Museum. Idaho State University Museum, Pocatello.

Craw, M. Maggie

2012 Faunal Remains. In *Urban Archaeology in the Capitol Complex Historic Neighborhood, Santa Fe, New Mexico*, edited by M. J. Barbour, 265–84. Archaeology Notes No. 403. Office of Archaeological Studies, Museum of New Mexico, Santa Fe.

Creel, Daryl, and Roger Anyon

2003 New Interpretations of Mimbres Public Architecture and Space: Implications for Cultural Change. *American Antiquity* 68:67–92.

Crown, Patricia L.

2007 Life Histories of Pots and Potters: Situating the Individual in Archaeology. *American Antiquity* 72(4):677–90.

2008 Chacoan Cylinder Jars. Paper presented in the symposium "The Chaco Stratigraphy Project: Ongoing Research and Preliminary Results" at the 73rd Annual Meeting of the Society for American Archaeology, Vancouver, BC.

2011 Chocolate, Cylinder Jars, and Ritual in Chaco Canyon, New Mexico. Proposal submitted to the National Endowment for the Humanities. Manuscript on file, Department of Anthropology, University of New Mexico, Albuquerque.

2016a Summary and Conclusions: Production, Exchange, Consumption, and Discard at Pueblo Bonito. In *The Pueblo Bonito Mounds of Chaco Canyon: Material Culture and Fauna*, edited by Patricia Crown, 213–37. University of New Mexico Press, Albuquerque.

2016b Acquisition, Use and Discard of Red and Brown Wares at Pueblo Bonito, Chaco Canyon. In *The Pueblo Bonito Mounds of Chaco Canyon: Material Culture and Fauna*, edited by Patricia Crown, 93–122. University of New Mexico Press, Albuquerque.

2018 Drinking Performance and Politics in Chaco Canyon. *American Antiquity* 83:387–406.

Crown, Patricia L. (editor)

2016 *The Pueblo Bonito Mounds of Chaco Chanyon: Material Culture and Fauna*. University of New Mexico Press, Albuquerque.

Crown, Patricia L., Jiyan Gu, W. Jeffrey Hurst, Timothy J. Ward, Ardith D. Bravenec, Syed Ali, Laura Kebert, Marlaina Berch, Erin Redman, Patrick D. Lyons, Jamie Merewether, David A. Phillips, Lori S. Reed, and Kyle Woodson

2015 Ritual Drinks in the Prehispanic US Southwest and Northwest Mexico. *Proceedings of the National Academy of Sciences* 112(37):11436–42.

Crown, Patricia L., and W. Jeffrey Hurst

2009 Evidence of Cacao Use in the Prehispanic American Southwest. *Proceedings of the National Academy of Sciences* 106:2110–13.

Crown, Patricia L., and W. James Judge (editors)

1990 *Chaco and Hohokam: Prehistoric Regional Systems in the American Southwest*. SAR Press, Santa Fe, NM.

Crown, Patricia L., Kerriann Marden, and Hannah V. Mattson

2016 Foot Notes: The Social Implications of Polydactyly and Foot Imagery at Pueblo Bonito, Chaco Canyon. *American Antiquity* 81(3):426–48.

Crown, Patricia L., and W. H. Wills

2003 Modifying Pottery and Kivas at Chaco: Pentimento, Restoration or Renewal? *American Antiquity* 68:511–32.

2018 The Complex History of Pueblo Bonito and Its Interpretation. *Antiquity* 92(364):890–904.

Cruz, Richard, and Greg Hodgins

2016 Radiocarbon Analytical Report. P. Crown (AA108152–AA108161). AMS Laboratory, University of Arizona, Tucson.

Cully, Anne C.

1982 Prehistoric Subsistence at Bis Sa Ani Ruin and Associated Small Sites: Evidence from Pollen Analysis. In *Bis sa' ani: A Late Bonito Phase Community on Escavada Wash, Northwest New Mexico*, edited by Cory D. Breternitz, David E. Doyel, and Michael P. Marshall, 1181–208. Navajo Nation Papers in Anthropology 14(3).

1985 Pollen Evidence of Past Subsistence and Environment at Chaco Canyon, New Mexico. In *Environment and Subsistence of Chaco Canyon*, edited by Frances Joan Mathien, 135–245. Publications in Archaeology 18E, Chaco Canyon Studies, National Park Service, Albuquerque, NM.

Curtin, Leonora S. M.

1997 *Healing Herbs of the Upper Rio Grande: Traditional Medicine of the Southwest*. Originally published in 1947. Revised and edited by Michael M. Moore. Western Edge Press, Santa Fe, NM.

Cushing, Frank Hamilton

1920 *Zuñi Breadstuff*. Indian Notes and Monographs, a Series of Publications relating to the American Aborigines Vol. 13. Museum of the American Indian, Heye Foundation, NY.

Cutler, Hugh C., and Thomas W. Whitaker

1961 History and Distribution of the Cultivated Cucurbits in the Americas. *American Antiquity* 26(4):469–85.

Dean, Rebecca M.

2007a Hunting Intensification and the Hohokam "Collapse." *Journal of Anthropological Archaeology* 26(1):109–32.

2007b The Lagomorph Index: Rethinking Rabbit Bones in Hohokam Sites. *Kiva* 73:7–30.

Dibble, H., and M. Bernard

1980 Comparative Study of Basic Edge Angle Measurement Techniques. *American Antiquity* 45:857–65.

Dietler, Michael

1990 Driven by Drink: The Role of Drinking in the Political Economy and the Case of Early Iron Age France. *Journal of Anthropological Archaeology* 9:352–406.

Di Peso, Charles, John Rinaldo, and Gloria Fenner

1974 *Casas Grandes: A Fallen Trading Center of the Gran Chichimeca: 8. Bone Perishables, Commerce, Subsistence and Burials*. Northland Press, Flagstaff, AZ.

Driver, Jonathan C.

2002 Faunal Variation and Change in the Northern San Juan Region. In *Seeking the Center Place: Archaeology and Ancient Communities in the Mesa Verde Region*, edited by M. D. Varien and R. H. Wilshusen, 143–60. University of Utah Press, Salt Lake City.

2005 Crow Canyon Archaeological Center Manual for the Description of Vertebrate Remains. https://core.tdar.org /document/4669/crow-canyon-archaeological-center-manual

-for-the-description-of-vertebrate-remains, accessed November 2, 2016.

Driver, Jonathan C., and Joshua R. Woiderski
2008 Interpretation of the "Lagomorph Index" in the American Southwest. *Quaternary International* 185(1):3–11.

Duff, Andrew, Jeremy M. Moss, Thomas C. Windes, John Kantner, and M. Steven Shackley
2012 Patterning in Procurement of Obsidian in Chaco Canyon and in Chaco-Era Communities in New Mexico as Revealed by X-Ray Fluorescence. *Journal of Archaeological Science* 39:2995–3007.

Dunmire, William W., and Gail D. Tierney
1997 *Wild Plants and Native Peoples of the Four Corners*. Museum of New Mexico Press, Santa Fe.

Durand, Kathy, and Stephen R. Durand
2008 Animal Bone from Salmon Ruins and Other Great Houses: Faunal Exploitation in the Chaco World. In *Chaco's Northern Prodigies: Salmon, Aztec, and the Ascendancy of the Middle San Juan Region after AD 1100*, edited by P. Reed, 96–112. University of Utah Press, Salt Lake City.

Earle, Timothy K.
2001 Economic Support of Chaco Canyon Society. *American Antiquity* 66(1):26–35.

Egeland, Charles P., Kristen R. Welch, and Christopher M. Nicholson
2014 Experimental Determinations of Cutmark Orientation and the Reconstruction of Prehistoric Butchery Behavior. *Journal of Archaeological Science* 49:126–33.

Egginton, George
1921 *Colorado Weed Seeds*. Bulletin No. 260. Agricultural Experiment Station, Fort Collins, CO.

Elias, Norbert
1994 *The Civilizing Process*. Translated by Edmund Jephcott. Blackwell, Oxford.

Emery, Kitty F.
2008 Techniques of Ancient Maya Bone Working: Evidence from a Classical Maya Deposit. *Latin American Antiquity* 19(2):204–21.
2009 Maya Bone Crafting: Defining the Nature of a Late/Terminal Classic Maya Bone Tool Manufacturing Locus. *Journal of Anthropological Archaeology* 28:458–70.

Fægri, Knut, Peter Emil Kaland, and Knut Kryzywinski
1989 *Textbook of Pollen Analysis*. 4th ed. Wiley, Chichester, England.

Faith, J. Tyler, and Adam D. Gordon
2007 Skeletal Element Abundances in Archaeofaunal Assemblages: Economic Utility, Sample Size, and Assessment of Carcass Transport Strategies. *Journal of Archaeological Science* 34(6):872–82.

Fish, Suzanne K.
1984 Agriculture and Subsistence Implications of the Salt-Gila Aqueduct Project Pollen Analysis. In *Hohokam Archaeology along the Salt-Gila Aqueduct, Central Arizona Project: Vol. 7, pt. 3. Environment and Subsistence*, edited by Lynn S. Teague and Patricia L. Crown, 111–38. Arizona State Museum Archaeological Series No. 150. University of Arizona, Tucson.

Fisher, John W.
1995 Bone Surface Modifications in Zooarchaeology. *Journal of Archaeological Method and Theory* 2(1):7–68.

Fletcher, Milford R., and Maynard Merkt
2016 Measurements of Turkey Egg Shell Fragments from Tijeras Pueblo. Unpublished manuscript on file at the Maxwell Museum of Anthropology, University of New Mexico, Albuquerque.

Fowler, Andrew
1991 The Anasazi Brownware/Redware Ceramic Tradition. *Kiva* 56:123–44.

Fowler, Catherine S.
1992 *In the Shadow of Fox Peak: An Ethnography of the Cattail-Eater Northern Paiute People of Stillwater Marsh*. Cultural Resource Series No. 5. US Department of the Interior, Fish and Wildlife Service, Region 1, Stillwater National Wildlife Refuge. US Government Printing Office, Washington DC.

Freidel, David, and Linda Schele
1989 Dead Kings and Living Temples: Dedication and Termination Rituals among the Ancient Maya. In *Word and Image in Maya Culture*, edited by W. F. Hanks and D. S. Rice, 233–43. University of Utah Press, Salt Lake City.

Fritz, John
1978 Paleopsychology Today: Ideational Systems and Human Adaptation in Prehistory. In *Social Archaeology: Beyond Subsistence and Dating*, edited by C. Redman, 37–59. Academic Press, NY.

Gallaga, Emiliano
2016 Introduction. *Manufactured Light: Mirrors in the Mesoamerican Realm*, edited by E. Gallaga and M. Blainey, 1–24. University Press of Colorado, Boulder.

Garrow, Duncan
2012 Odd Deposits and Average Practice: A Critical History of the Concept of Structured Deposition. *Archaeological Dialogues* 19:85–115.

Georgiev, G., W. Theuerkorn, M. Krus, R. Kilian, and T. Grosskinsky
2013 The Potential Role of Cattail-Reinforced Clay Plaster in Sustainable Building. *Mires and Peat* 13(9):1–13.

Gillespie, William B.
1993 Vertebrate Remains from 29SJ629. In *The Spadefoot Toad Site: Investigations at 29SJ629, Chaco Canyon, New Mexico*, Vol. 2, edited by T. C. Windes, 343–96. Reports of the Chaco Center No. 12. National Park Service, Santa Fe, NM.

Glass Bottle Marks
2016 The L.G.CO. Mark on Antique Glass Bottles and Jars. https://www.glassbottlemarks.com/l-g-co, accessed July 3, 2016.

Goetze, C., and B. Mills
1993 Classification Criteria for Wares and Types. In *Across the Colorado Plateau: Anthropological Studies for the Transwestern Pipeline Expansion Project*, Vol. 16, edited by B. Mills, C. Goetze, and M. Zedeño, 21–86. Office of Contract Archaeology and Maxwell Museum of Anthropology, University of New Mexico, Albuquerque.

Gosden, Chris, and Yvonne Marshall
1999 The Cultural Biography of Objects. *World Archaeology* 31:169–78.

Gould, R., D. Koster, and A. Sontz
1971 The Lithic Assemblage of the Western Desert Aborigines of Australia. *American Antiquity* 36:149–69.

Grayson, Donald K.
1984 *Quantitative Zooarchaeology*. Academic Press, NY.

1991 Alpine Faunas from the White Mountains, California: Adaptive Change in the Late Prehistoric Great Basin. *Journal of Archaeological Science* 18(4):483–506.

Grayson, Donald K., and Françoise Delpech

1998 Changing Diet Breadth in the Early Upper Paleolithic of Southwestern France. *Journal of Archaeological Science* 25:1119–30.

Greenfield, Haskel J.

2013 "The Fall of the House of Flint": A Zooarchaeological Perspective on the Decline of Chipped Stone Tools for Butchering Animals in the Bronze and Iron Ages of the Southern Levant. *Lithic Technology* 38(3):161–78.

Grimstead, Deanna N., and Frank E. Bayham

2010 Evolutionary Ecology, Elite Feasting, and the Hohokam: A Case Study from a Southern Arizona Platform Mound. *American Antiquity* 75(4):841–64.

Grimstead, Deanna N., Sharon M. Buck, Bradley J. Vierra, and Larry V. Benson

2015 Another Possible Source of Archeological Maize Found in Chaco Canyon, NM: The Tohatchi Flats Area, NM, USA. *Journal of Archaeological Science: Reports* 3:181–87.

Grimstead, Deanna N., Jay Quade, and Mary C. Stiner

2016 Isotopic Evidence for Long-Distance Mammal Procurement, Chaco Canyon, New Mexico, USA. *Geoarchaeology* 31(5):335–54.

Grimstead, Deanna N., Amanda C. Reynolds, Adam M. Hudson, Nancy J. Akins, and Julio L. Betancourt

2016 Reduced Population Variance in Strontium Isotope Ratios Informs Domesticated Turkey Use at Chaco Canyon, New Mexico, USA. *Journal of Archaeological Method and Theory* 23(1):127–49.

Gucker, Corey L.

2008 Typha latifolia. In *Fire Effects Information System*. US Department of Agriculture, Forest Service, Rocky Mountain Research Station, Fire Sciences Laboratory. https://www.feis-crs.org/feis, accessed December 3, 2019.

Gunn, John M.

1917 *Schat-Chen: History, Traditions, and Narratives of the Queres Indians of Laguna and Acoma*. Albright and Anderson, Albuquerque, NM.

Hagstrum, Melissa

2001 Household Production in Chaco Canyon Society. *American Antiquity* 66(1):47–55.

Hall, Stephen A.

1975 Stratigraphy and Palynology of Quaternary Alluvium at Chaco Canyon, New Mexico. PhD dissertation, Department of Geology, University of Michigan, Ann Arbor.

Hamilakis, Yannis

2008 Time, Performance, and the Production of a Mnemonic Record: From Feasting to an Archaeology of Eating and Drinking. In *DAIS: The Aegean Feast*, edited by Louise Hitchcock, Robert Laffineur, and Janice Crowley, 3–20. Aegaeum Vol. 29. Peeters Publishers, Leuven, Belgium.

Hamilton, Marian, Lee Drake, W. H. Wills, Emily Lena Jones, Cyler Conrad, and Patricia L. Crown

2018 The Importance of Modern Analogues in Stable Oxygen Isotope Sourcing: A Test Case from Chaco Canyon, New Mexico. *American Antiquity* 83:163–75.

Harbottle, Garman, and Phil C. Weigand

1992 Turquoise in Pre-Columbian America. *Scientific American* 266(2):78–85.

Hargrave, Lyndon L.

1965 Turkey Bones from Wetherill Mesa. *American Archaeology* 19:161–66.

Harrison-Buck, Eleanor, Patricia McAnany, and Rebecca Storey

2007 Empowered and Disempowered during the Late to Terminal Classic Transition: Maya Burial and Termination Rituals in the Sibun Valley, Belize. In *New Perspectives on Human Sacrifice and Ritual Body Treatments in Ancient Maya Society*, edited by Vera Tiesler and Andrea Cucina, 74–101. Springer, NY.

Hayden, Brian

1995 Pathways to Power: Principles for Creating Socioeconomic Inequalities. In *Foundations of Social Inequality*, edited by T. Douglas Price and Gary M. Feinman, 15–86. Plenum Press, NY.

Hays-Gilpin, K., and E. van Hartesveldt (editors)

1998 *Prehistoric Ceramics of the Puerco Valley: The 1995 Chambers-Sanders Trust Lands Ceramic Conference*. Museum of Northern Arizona Ceramic Series No. 7, Flagstaff.

Hegberg, Erin, and Patricia L. Crown

2016 Ground Stone from the Pueblo Bonito Mounds. In *The Pueblo Bonito Mounds of Chaco Canyon*, edited by Patricia L. Crown, 151–68. University of New Mexico Press, Albuquerque.

Heitman, Carrie C.

2015 The House of Our Ancestors: New Research on the Prehistory of Chaco Canyon, New Mexico, AD 800–1200. In *Chaco Revisited: New Research on the Prehistory of Chaco Canyon, New Mexico*, edited by Carrie C. Heitman and Stephen Plog, 215–48. University of Arizona Press, Tucson.

Heitman, Carrie C., and Phil R. Geib

2015 The Relevance of Maize Pollen for Assessing the Extent of Maize Production in Chaco Canyon. In *Chaco Revisited: New Research on the Prehistory of Chaco Canyon, New Mexico*, edited by Carrie C. Heitman and Stephen Plog, 66–95. University of Arizona Press, Tucson.

Heitman, Carrie C., and Stephen Plog

2005 Kinship and the Dynamics of the House: Rediscovering Dualism in the Pueblo Past. In *A Catalyst for Ideas*, edited by V. Scarborough, 69–100. SAR Press, Santa Fe, NM.

Henderson, John S., and Rosemary A. Joyce

2006 Brewing Distinction: The Development of Cacao Beverages in Formative Mesoamerica. In *Chocolate in Mesoamerica: A Cultural History of Cacao*, edited by Cameron L. McNeil, 140–53. University Press of Florida, Gainesville.

Hevly, Richard

1974 Recent Paleoenvironments and Geological History at Montezuma Well. *Journal of the Arizona Academy of Science* 9(2):66–75.

Hildebrandt, William R., and Kelly R. McGuire

2002 The Ascendance of Hunting during the California Middle Archaic: An Evolutionary Perspective. *American Antiquity* 67(2):231–56.

Hill, Erica

2000 The Contextual Analysis of Animal Interments and Ritual Practice in Southwestern North America. *Kiva* 65(4):361–98.

Hoadley, R. B.

1990 *Identifying Wood: Accurate Results with Simple Tools.* Taunton Press, Newton, CT.

Hockett, Bryan Scott

1991 Toward Distinguishing Human and Raptor Patterning on Leporid Bones. *American Antiquity* 56:667–79.

1995 Comparison of Leporid Bones in Raptor Pellets, Raptor Nests, and Archaeological Sites in the Great Basin. *North American Archaeologist* 16:223–38.

1999 Taphonomy of Carnivore-Accumulated Rabbit Bone Assemblage from Picareiro Cave, Central Portugal. *Journal of Iberian Archaeology* 1:251–57.

Hockett, Bryan Scott, and Nuno Ferreira Bicho

2000 The Rabbits of Picareiro Cave: Small Mammal Hunting during the Late Upper Palaeolithic in the Portuguese Estremadura. *Journal of Archaeological Science* 27:715–23.

Hockett, Bryan Scott, and Jonathan A. Haws

2002 Taphonomic and Methodological Perspectives of Leporid Hunting during the Upper Paleolithic of the Western Mediterranean Basin. *Journal of Archaeological Method and Theory* 9(3):269–302.

Hodgson, Wendy

2001 *Food Plants of the Sonoran Desert.* University of Arizona Press, Tucson.

Holsinger, Rosemary

1982 *Shasta Indian Tales.* Naturegraph Publishers, Happy Camp, CA.

Hosler, Dorothy

1986 The Origins, Technology, and Social Construction of Ancient West Mexican Metallurgy. PhD dissertation, University of California, Santa Barbara.

1994 *The Sounds and Colors of Power.* MIT Press, Cambridge, MA.

Housely, Lucile

1974 *Opuntia imbricata* Distribution on Old Jemez Indian Habitation Sites. MA thesis, Pomona College, Claremont, CA.

Hovezak, Timothy D., and LeeAnn Schniebs

2002 Vertebrate Faunal Remains. In *Archaeological Investigations in the Fruitland Project Area: Late Archaic, Basketmaker, Pueblo I, and Navajo Sites in Northwestern New Mexico: 5. Material Culture, Bioarchaeological, and Special Studies*, edited by T. D. Hovezak and L. M. Sesler, 415–51. La Plata Archaeological Consultants, Dolores, CO.

Huckell, Lisa W., and Mollie S. Toll

2004 Wild Plant Use in the North American Southwest. In *People and Plants in Ancient Western North America*, edited by Paul E. Minnis, 37–114. Smithsonian Books, Washington, DC.

Hull, Sharon, Mostafa Fayek, F. Joan Mathien, Phillip Shelley, and Kathy R. Durand

2008 A New Approach to Determining the Geological Provenance of Turquoise Artifacts Using Hydrogen and Copper Stable Isotopes. *Journal of Archaeological Science* 35:1355–69.

Hull, Sharon, Mostafa Fayek, F. Joan Mathien, and Heidi Roberts

2014 Turquoise Trade of the Ancestral Puebloan: Chaco and Beyond. *Journal of Archaeological Science* 45:187–95.

Jacobs, Bonnie F.

1985 Identification of Pine Pollen from the Southwestern United States. *American Association of Stratigraphic Palynologists Contribution Series* 16:155–68.

Jernigan, E. Wesley

1978 *Jewelry of the Prehistoric Southwest.* SAR, Santa Fe, and University of New Mexico Press, Albuquerque.

Jolie, Edward

2018 Sociocultural Diversity in the Prehispanic Southwest: Learning, Weaving and Identity in the Chaco Regional System, AD 850–1150. PhD dissertation, Department of Anthropology, University of New Mexico, Albuquerque.

Jones, Emily Lena

2004 Dietary Evenness, Prey Choice, and Human-Environment Interactions. *Journal of Archaeological Science* 31(3):307–17.

2006 Prey Choice, Mass Collecting, and the Wild European Rabbit (*Oryctolagus cuniculus*). *Journal of Anthropological Archaeology* 25:275–89.

2016 *In Search of the Broad Spectrum Revolution in Paleolithic Southwest Europe.* Springer Briefs in Archaeology. Springer International, NY.

Jones, Emily Lena, Cyler Conrad, Seth D. Newsome, Brian M. Kemp, and Jacqueline Marie Kocer

2016 Turkeys on the Fringe: Variable Husbandry in "Marginal" Areas of the Prehistoric American Southwest. *Journal of Archaeological Science: Reports* 10:575–83.

Jones, Emily Lena, and Caroline Gabe

2015 The Promise and Peril of Older Collections: Meta-Analyses in the American Southwest. *Open Quaternary* 1(6):1–13.

Jones, Volney

1931 The Ethnobotany of the Isleta Indians. MA thesis, University of New Mexico, Albuquerque.

Judd, Neil M.

1954 The Material Culture of Pueblo Bonito. Smithsonian Miscellaneous Collections Vol. 124. Smithsonian Institution, Washington, DC.

1959 Pueblo del Arroyo, Chaco Canyon, New Mexico. Smithsonian Miscellaneous Collections Vol. 138(1). Smithsonian Institution, Washington, DC.

1964 The Architecture of Pueblo Bonito. Smithsonian Miscellaneous Collections Vol. 147(1). Smithsonian Institution, Washington, DC.

Judge, W. James

1989 Chaco Canyon–San Juan Basin. In *Dynamics of Southwest Prehistory*, edited by L. S. Cordell and G. Gumerman, 209–61. Smithsonian Institution Press, Washington, DC.

Justice, Noel D.

2002 *Stone Age Spear and Arrow Points of the Southwestern United States.* Indiana University Press, Bloomington.

Kantner, John

1996 Political Competition among the Chaco Anasazi of the American Southwest. *Journal of Anthropological Archaeology* 15:41–105.

Kapp, Ronald O., Owen K. Davis, and James E. King

2000 *Guide to Pollen and Spores.* 2nd ed. American Association of Stratigraphic Palynologists Foundation, College Station, TX.

Kearney, Thomas H., and Robert H. Peebles

1960 *Arizona Flora.* 2nd ed. with suppl. University of California Press, Berkeley.

Kelly, Robert L.

    1988 The Three Sides of a Biface. *American Antiquity* 53:717–34.

Kelly, Robert L., and Lawrence C. Todd

    1988 Coming into the Country: Early Paleoindian Hunting and Mobility. *American Antiquity* 53:231–44.

Kim, Jangsuk, Arleyn Simon, Vincent Rinpoche, James Mayer, and King, Valerie

    2003 The Organization of Production of Chuska Gray Ware Ceramics for Distribution and Consumption in Chaco Canyon, New Mexico. PhD dissertation, Department of Anthropology, University of New Mexico, Albuquerque.

Knappett, Carl

    2011 *An Archaeology of Interaction: Network Perspectives on Material Culture and Society.* Oxford University Press, Oxford.

Kohler, Timothy A.

    1998 *Public Architecture and Power in Pre-Columbian North America.* Santa Fe Institute Paper 98-03-022, Santa Fe, NM.

Krattinger, K.

    1975 Genetic Mobility in *Typha. Aquatic Botany* 1:57–70.

Laboratory of Tree-Ring Research

    2015 Database of Chaco Canyon Great House Specimens. http://www.chacoarchive.org/cra/chaco-resources/tree-ring-database, accessed November 12, 2018.

Lamzik, Kathryn Elizabeth

    2013 "It All Began, like So Many Things, with an Egg": An Analysis of the Avian Fauna and Eggshell Assemblage from a 19th Century Enslaved African American Subfloor Pit, Poplar Forest, Virginia. MA thesis, Department of Anthropology, University of Tennessee, Knoxville.

Lang, Richard W., and Arthur H. Harris

    1984 *Faunal Remains from Arroyo Hondo Pueblo, New Mexico: A Study in Short-Term Subsistence Change.* SAR Press, Santa Fe, NM.

Lapham, Heather A., Gary M. Feinman, and Linda M. Nicholas

    2016 Turkey Husbandry and Use in Oaxaca, Mexico: A Contextual Study of Turkey Remains and SEM Analysis of Eggshell from the Mitla Fortress. *Journal of Archaeological Science: Reports* 10:534–46.

LeCount, Lisa

    1999 Polychrome Pottery and Political Strategies in Late and Terminal Classic Lowland Maya Society. *Latin American Antiquity* 10:239–58.

Lekson, Stephen H.

    1984 *Great Pueblo Architecture of Chaco Canyon.* Publications in Archaeology 18B, Chaco Canyon Studies, National Park Service, Albuquerque, NM.

    1999 Great Towns in the Southwest. In *Great Towns and Regional Polities in the Prehistoric American Southwest and Southeast,* edited by J. Neitzel, 2–22. University of New Mexico Press, Albuquerque.

    2006 Chaco Matters: An Introduction. In *The Archaeology of Chaco Canyon,* edited by S. Lekson, 3–44. SAR Press, Santa Fe, NM.

    2007 Great House Form. In *The Architecture of Chaco Canyon, New Mexico,* edited by Stephen H. Lekson, 7–44. University of Utah Press, Salt Lake City.

Lewis, Candace L.

    2002 Knowledge Is Power: Pigment, Painted Artifacts, and Cha-coan Leaders. Master's thesis, Department of Anthropology, Northern Arizona University, Flagstaff.

Lewis, Jason E.

    2008 Identifying Sword Marks on Bone: Criteria for Distinguishing between Cut Marks Made by Different Classes of Bladed Weapons. *Journal of Archaeological Science* 35(7):2001–8.

Lightfoot, Kent G., Rob Q. Cuthrell, Chuck J. Striplen, and Mark G. Hylkema

    2013 Rethinking the Study of Landscape Management Practices among Hunter-Gatherers in North America. *American Antiquity* 78(2):285–301.

Lipe, William D., R. Kyle Bocinsky, Brian S. Chisholm, Robin Lyle, David M. Dove, R. G. Matson, Elizabeth Jarvis, Kathleen Judd, and Brian M. Kemp

    2016 Cultural and Genetic Contexts for Early Turkey Domestication in the Northern Southwest. *American Antiquity* 81(4):1–17.

Lister, Robert H., and Florence C. Lister

    1981 *Chaco Canyon: Archaeology and Archaeologists.* University of New Mexico Press, Albuquerque.

Lodeiros, César, Gaspar Soria, Paul Valentich-Scott, Adrián Munguía-Veja, Jonathan Santana Cabrera, Richard Cudney-Bueno, Alfredo Loor, Adrian Marquez, and Stanislaus Sonneholzner

    2016 Spondylids of the Eastern Pacific Ocean. *Journal of Shellfish Research* 35(2):279–93.

Longacre, W. A., K. L. Kvamme, and M. Kobayashi

    1988 Southwestern Pottery Standardization: An Ethnoarchaeological View from the Philippines. *Kiva* 53(2):101–12.

Lucero, Lisa J.

    2008 Memorializing Place among Classic Maya Commoners. In *Memory Work: Archaeologies of Material Practices,* edited by Barbara J. Mills and William H. Walker, 187–205. SAR Press, Santa Fe, NM.

Lupo, Karen D.

    1994 Butchering Marks and Carcass Acquisition Strategies: Distinguishing Hunting from Scavenging in Archaeological Contexts. *Journal of Archaeological Science* 21:827–37.

Lyman, R. Lee

    1994 *Vertebrate Taphonomy.* Cambridge University Press, NY.

    2008 *Quantitative Paleozoology.* Cambridge University Press, NY.

Magurran, Anne E.

    2004 *Measuring Biological Diversity.* Blackwell, Malden, MA.

Magurran, Anne E., and Brian J. McGill

    2011 *Biological Diversity: Frontiers in Measurement and Assessment.* Oxford University Press, NY.

Manne, Tiina, João Cascalheira, Marina Évora, João Marreiros, and Nuno Bicho

    2012 Intensive Subsistence Practices at Vale Boi, an Upper Paleolithic Site in Southwestern Portugal. *Quaternary International* 264(20):83–99.

Marden, Kerriann

    2011 Taphonomy, Paleopathology and Mortuary Variability in Chaco Canyon: Using Bioarchaeological and Forensic Methods to Understand Ancient Cultural Practices. PhD dissertation, Department of Anthropology, Tulane University, New Orleans, LA.

Martin, Alexander C., and William D. Barkley

1961 *Seed Identification Manual*. University of California Press, Berkeley.

Mathien, Frances Joan

1985 Ornaments and Minerals from Chaco Canyon, National Park Service Project, 1971–1978. Manuscript on file, Chaco Culture National Historical Park. Museum Archive at the University of New Mexico, Zimmerman Library, Albuquerque.

1987 Ornaments and Minerals from Pueblo Alto. In *Investigations at the Pueblo Alto Complex, Chaco Canyon, New Mexico, 1975–1979: 3. Artifactual and Biological Analyses*, edited by F. J. Mathien and T. C. Windes, 381–428. Publications in Archaeology 19F, Chaco Canyon Studies, National Park Service, Albuquerque.

1988 Analysis of Ornaments, Minerals, and Cached Items. In *Historic Structure Report, Kin Nahasbas Ruin, Chaco Culture National Historical Park, New Mexico*, edited by F. J. Mathien and T. C. Windes, 249–73. Branch of Cultural Research, National Park Service, Santa Fe, NM.

1992 Ornaments and Minerals from 29SJ627. In *Excavations at 29SJ627, Chaco Canyon, New Mexico: 2. Artifact Analyses*, edited by F. J. Mathien, 265–318. Reports of the Chaco Center No. 11. Branch of Cultural Research, Division of Anthropology, National Park Service, Santa Fe, NM.

1993 Ornaments and Minerals from 29SJ629. In *The Spadefoot Toad Site: Investigations at 29SJ629, Chaco Canyon, New Mexico: 2. Artifactual and Biological Analyses*, edited by T. C. Windes, 269–316. Reports of the Chaco Center No. 12. Branch of Cultural Research, Division of Anthropology, National Park Service, Santa Fe, NM.

1997 Ornaments of the Chaco Anasazi. In *Ceramics, Lithics, and Ornaments of Chaco Canyon*, Vol. 3, edited by Frances Joan Mathien, 1119–207. Publications in Archaeology 18G, Chaco Canyon Studies. National Park Service, US Department of the Interior, Santa Fe, NM.

2001 The Organization of Turquoise Production and Consumption by the Prehistoric Chacoans. *American Antiquity* 66(1):103–18.

2003 Artifact Distributions at Pueblo Bonito. In *Pueblo Bonito: Center of the Chacoan World*, edited by J. Neitzel, 107–26. Smithsonian Institution Press, Washington, DC.

2005 *Culture and Ecology of Chaco Canyon and the San Juan Basin*. National Park Service, US Department of the Interior, Santa Fe, NM.

Mattson, Hannah V.

2015 Identity and Material Practice in the Chacoan World: Ornamentation and Utility Ware Pottery. PhD dissertation, Department of Anthropology, University of New Mexico, Albuquerque.

2016a Gray Ware from the Pueblo Bonito Mounds. In *The Pueblo Bonito Mounds of Chaco Canyon: Material Culture and Fauna*, edited by Patricia L. Crown, 13–52. University of New Mexico Press, Albuquerque.

2016b Ornaments as Socially Valuable Objects: Jewelry and Identity in the Chaco and Post-Chaco Worlds. *Journal of Anthropological Archaeology* 42:122–39.

2016c Ornaments, Mineral Specimens, and Shell Specimens from the Pueblo Bonito Mounds. In *The Material Culture of the Pueblo Bonito Mounds*, edited by Patricia L. Crown, 186–205. University of New Mexico Press, Albuquerque.

Mayes, Vernon O., and Barbara Bayless Lacy

1989 *Nanise': A Navajo Herbal*. Navajo Community College Press, Tsaile, AZ.

McAnany, Patricia, and Ian Hodder

2009 Thinking about Stratigraphic Sequence in Social Terms. *Archaeological Dialogues* 16(1):1–22.

McCaffery, Harlan, Robert H. Tykot, Kathy Durand Gore, and Beau R. Deboer

2014 Stable Isotope Analysis of Turkey (*Meleagris gallopavo*) Diet from Pueblo II and Pueblo III Sites, Middle San Juan Region, Northwest New Mexico. *American Antiquity* 79(2):337–52.

McKenna, Peter

1984 *The Architecture and Material Culture of 29SJ1360, Chaco Canyon, New Mexico*. National Park Service, Albuquerque, NM.

Medina, Matías E., Pablo Teta, and Diego Rivero

2012 Burning Damage and Small-Mammal Human Consumption in Quebrada del Real 1 (Cordoba, Argentina): An Experimental Approach. *Journal of Archaeological Science* 39(3):737–43.

Merrill, William L.

1979 The Beloved Tree: *Ilex vomitoria* among the Indians of the Southeast and Adjacent Regions. In *Black Drink: A Native American Tea*, edited by Charles M. Hudson, 40–82. University of Georgia Press, Athens.

Miksicek, Charles H.

1987 Formation Processes of the Archaeobotanical Record. *Advances in Archaeological Method and Theory* 10:211–47.

Miller, Mary, and Karl Taube

2003 *An Illustrated Dictionary of the Gods and Symbols of Ancient Mexico and the Maya*. Thames and Hudson, London.

Miller, Merton Leland

1898 *A Preliminary Study of the Pueblo of Taos, New Mexico*. University of Chicago.

Mills, Barbara J.

2002 Recent Research on Chaco: Changing Views on Economy, Ritual, and Society. *Journal of Archaeological Research* 10:65–117.

2004 The Establishment and Defeat of Hierarchy: Inalienable Possessions and the History of Collective Prestige Structures in the Southwest. *American Anthropologist* 106(2):238–51.

2008 Remembering while Forgetting: Depositional Practices and Social Memory at Chaco. In *Memory Work: Archaeologies of Material Practices*, edited by Barbara J. Mills and William H. Walker, 81–108. SAR Press, Santa Fe, NM.

2015 Unpacking the House: Ritual Practice and Social Networks at Chaco. In *Chaco Revisited: New Research on the Prehistory of Chaco Canyon, New Mexico*, edited by Carrie Heitman and Stephen Plog, 249–71. University of Arizona Press, Tucson.

Mills, Barbara J., and T. J. Ferguson

2008 Animate Objects: Shell Trumpets and Ritual Networks in the Greater Southwest. *Journal of Archaeological Method and Theory* 15:338–61.

Mills, Barbara J., and William H. Walker

2008 Memory, Materiality, and Depositional Practice. . In *Memory Work: Archaeologies of Material Practices*, edited by Barbara J. Mills and William H. Walker, 3–24. SAR Press, Santa Fe, NM.

Minnis, Paul E.

1981 Seeds in Archaeological Sites: Sources and Some Interpretive Problems. *American Antiquity* 46:143–52.

1987 Identification of Wood from Archaeological Sites in the American Southwest: I. Key to Gymnosperms. *Journal of Archaeological Science* 14:121–31.

Mock, Shirley Boteler

1998 Prelude. In *The Sowing and the Dawning: Termination, Dedication, and Transformation in the Archaeological and Ethnographic Record of Mesoamerica*, edited by Shirley Mock, 3–18. University of New Mexico Press, Albuquerque.

Mock, Shirley Boteler (editor)

1998 *The Sowing and the Dawning: Termination, Dedication, and Transformation in the Archaeological and Ethnographic Record of Mesoamerica*. University of New Mexico Press, Albuquerque.

Moerman, Daniel

1998 *Native American Ethnobotany*. Timber Press, Portland, OR.

Moorehead, Warren

1906 Explorations in Arizona, New Mexico, Indiana, etc. *Department of Archaeology Bulletin* No. 3. Phillips Academy, Andover, MA.

Morlan, Richard E.

1994 Dialogue: Rodent Bones in Archaeological Sites. *Canadian Journal of Archaeology / Journal Canadien d'Archéologie* 18:135–42.

Mróz, Emilia, Monika Stepinska, and Magdalena Krawczyk

2014 Morphology and Chemical Composition of Turkey Eggs. *Journal of Applied Poultry Research* 23:196–203.

Muir, Robert J., and Jonathan C. Driver

2002 Scale of Analysis and Zooarchaeological Interpretation: Pueblo III Faunal Variation in the Northern San Juan Region. *Journal of Anthropological Archaeology* 21(2):165–99.

2003 Faunal Remains. In *The Archaeology of Yellow Jacket Pueblo (Site 5MT5): Excavations at a Large Community Center in Southwestern Colorado*, edited by K. A. Kuckelman. https://www.crowcanyon.org/ResearchReports/YellowJacket/Text/yjpw_faunalremains.asp, accessed January 28, 2020.

Munro, Natalie D.

1994 An Investigation of Anasazi Turkey Production in Southwestern Colorado. MA thesis, Department of Anthropology, Simon Fraser University, Burnaby, BC.

2006 The Role of the Turkey in the Southwest. In *Handbook of North American Indians: 3. Environment, Origins, and Population*, 463–70. Smithsonian Institution Press, Washington, DC.

2011 Domestication of the Turkey in the American Southwest. In *The Subsistence Economies of Indigenous North American Societies: A Handbook*, edited by Bruce D. Smith, 543–55. Smithsonian Institution Press, Washington, DC.

Nagaoka, Lisa

2001 Using Diversity Indices to Measure Changes in Prey Choice at the Shag River Mouth Site, Southern New Zealand. *International Journal of Osteoarchaeology* 11(12):101–11.

2005 Differential Recovery of Pacific Island Fish Remains. *Journal of Archaeological Science* 32(6):941–55.

National Park Service

2008 Notice of Inventory Completion: Robert S. Peabody Museum of Archaeology, Phillips Academy, Andover, MA. Written by Sherry Hutt. *Federal Register* 73(234):73952–54.

Neitzel, Jill E.

1995 Elite Styles in Hierarchically Organized Societies: The Chacoan Regional System. In *Style, Society, and Person*, edited by Christopher Carr and Jill E. Neitzel, 393–417. Plenum Press, NY.

1999 Examining Societal Organization in the Southwest: An Application of Multiscalar Analysis. In *Great Towns and Regional Polities in the Prehistoric American Southwest and Southeast*, edited by J. Neitzel, 183–213. University of New Mexico Press, Albuquerque

2003a Artifact Distributions at Pueblo Bonito. In *Pueblo Bonito: Center of the Chacoan World*, edited by J. Neitzel, 143–50. Smithsonian Institution Press, Washington, DC.

2003b The Organization, Function, and Population of Pueblo Bonito. In *Pueblo Bonito: Center of the Chacoan World*, edited by Jill E. Neitzel, 143–49. Smithsonian Institution Press, Washington, DC.

2008 Maker's Marks on Pueblo Bonito Pottery. Paper presented at the Society for American Archaeology Meetings, March, Vancouver, BC.

Neitzel, Jill E. (editor)

2003 *Pueblo Bonito: Center of the Chacoan World*. Smithsonian Institution Press, Washington, DC.

Northrup, Stuart A.

1959 *Minerals of New Mexico*. Rev. ed. University of New Mexico Press, Albuquerque.

Old Breweries

2004 American Brewing Co.: MO 131i. http://www.oldbreweries.com/breweries-by-state/missouri/st-louis-mo-108-breweries/american-brewing-co-mo-131i/, accessed November 18, 2017.

Opler, Morris

1969 *Apache Odyssey: A Journey between Two Worlds*. Holt, Rinehart, and Winston, NY.

Ortman, Scott G.

2000 Artifacts. In *The Archaeology of Castle Rock Pueblo: A Thirteenth-Century Village in Southwestern Colorado*, edited by Kristin A. Kuckelman. Crow Canyon Archaeological Center, Cortez, CO. www.crowcanyon.org/ResearchReports/CastleRock/Text/crpw_artifacts_part_3.asp, accessed November 6, 2018.

Ostapkowicz, Joanna, Dana Lepofsky, Rick Shulting, and Albert McHalsie

2001 The Use of Cattail (*Typha latifolia* L.) Down as a Sacred Substance by the Interior and Coast Salish. *Journal of Ethnobiology* 21(2):77–90.

Otarola-Castillo, Erik

2010 Differences between NISP and MNE in Cutmark Analysis of Highly Fragmented Faunal Assemblages. *Journal of Archaeological Science* 37(1):1–12.

Pagliaro, Jonathan B., James Garber, and Travis Stanton

2003 Evaluating the Archaeological Signatures of Maya Ritual and Conflict. In *Ancient Mesoamerican Warfare*, edited by M. Katherine Brown and Travis Stanton, 75–89. AltaMira Press, Walnut Creek, CA.

Palmer, J.W., M. G. Hollander, P. S. Z. Rogers, T. M. Benjamin, C. J. Duffy, J. B. Lambert, and J. A. Brown

1998 Pre-Columbian Metallurgy: Technology, Manufacture, and Microprobe Analyses of Copper Bells from the Greater Southwest. *Archaeometry* 40(2):361–82.

Parry, W., and R. L. Kelly

1987 Expedient Core Technology and Sedentism. In *The Organization of Core Technology*, edited by Jay K. Johnson and Carol A. Morrow, 285–304. Westview Press, Boulder, CO.

Parsons, Elsie Clews

1939 *Pueblo Indian Religion*. University of Chicago Press.

Pearsall, Deborah M.

1989 *Paleoethnobotany: A Handbook of Procedures*. Academic Press, San Diego, CA.

Pepper, George H.

1896 Diary of G. H. Pepper from August 1st to September 28, 1896. Manuscript on file in the Archives of the Hyde Exploring Expedition, Department of Anthropology, American Museum of Natural History, NY. Chaco Research Archive accession 000157.

1897a Hyde Expedition, Field Notes 1, Folder 2: Pueblo Bonito Wetherill, R. Pepper, G. Records, 1897. American Museum of Natural History, NY. Chaco Research Archive accession 000159.

1897b Pueblo Bonito Field Notes, Pepper 1897: Folder 2. Manuscript on file in the Hyde Exploring Expedition, box 3. American Museum of Natural History, NY. Chaco Research Archive accession 000193.

1905 Ceremonial Objects and Ornaments from Pueblo Bonito, New Mexico. *American Anthropologist* 7:183–97.

1909 The Exploration of a Burial Room in Pueblo Bonito, New Mexico. In *Putnam Anniversary Volume: Anthropological Essays*, edited by His Friends and Associates, 196–252. Stechert Publishers, NY.

1920 *Pueblo Bonito*. Anthropological Papers of the American Museum of Natural History Vol. 27. American Museum of Natural History, NY.

Peregrine, Peter

2001 Matrilocality, Corporate Strategy and the Organization of Production in the Chacoan World. *American Antiquity* 66:36–46.

Plog, Stephen

2003 Exploring the Ubiquitous through the Unusual: Color Symbolism in the Pueblo Black-on-White Pottery. *American Antiquity* 68(4):665–95.

Plog, Stephen, and Carrie Heitman

2010 Hierarchy and Social Inequality in the American Southwest, AD 800–1200. *Proceedings of the National Academy of Sciences* 107(46):19619–26.

Pollard, Joshua

2008 Deposition and Material Agency in the Early Neolithic of Southern Britain. In *Memory Work: Archaeologies of Material Practices*, edited by Barbara J. Mills and William H. Walker, 41–59. SAR Press, Santa Fe, NM.

Potter, James M.

1997 Communal Ritual and Faunal Remains: An Example from the Dolores Anasazi. *Journal of Field Archaeology* 24(3):353–64.

Pugh, Timothy W.

2009 Contagion and Alterity: Kowoj Maya Appropriations of European Objects. *American Anthropologist* 111:373–86.

Quitmyer, Irvy R.

2004 What Kind of Data Are in the Back Dirt? An Experiment on the Influence of Screen Size on Optimal Data Recovery. *Archaeofauna* 13:109–29.

Rabinowitz, Adam

2009 Drinking from the Same Cup: Sparta and Late Archaic Commensality. In *Sparta: Comparative Approaches*, edited by Stephen Hodkinson, 113–92. Classical Press of Wales, Swansea.

Racusin, Jacob, and Ace McArleton

2012 *The Natural Building Companion: A Comprehensive Guide to Integrative Design and Construction*. Chelsea Green Publishing, Hartford, VT.

Rainey, Katharine D., and Karen R. Adams

2004 *Plant Use by Native Peoples of the American Southwest: Ethnographic Documentation*. http://www.crowcanyon.org/plantuses, accessed September 25, 2014.

Rawlings, Tiffany A., and Jonathan C. Driver

2010 Paleodiet of Domestic Turkey, Shields Pueblo (5MT3807), Colorado: Isotopic Analysis and Its Implications for Care of a Household Domesticate. *Journal of Archaeological Science* 37(10):2433–41.

Reed, Chester A.

1965 *North American Bird Eggs*. Dover, NY.

Reed, Erik K.

1951 Turkeys in Southwestern Archaeology. *El Palacio* 58(7):195–205.

Reents-Budet, Dorie

2006 The Social Context of Kakaw Drinking among the Ancient Maya. In *Chocolate in Mesoamerica: A Cultural History of Cacao*, edited by Cameron McNeil, 202–23. University Press of Florida, Gainesville.

Reimer, P. J., E. Bard, A. Bayliss, J. W. Beck, P. G. Blackwell, C. B. Ramsey, C. E. Buck, H. Cheng, R. L. Edwards, M. Friedrich, P. M. Grootes, T. P. Guilderson, H. H. I. Haflidason, C. Hatté, T. J. Heaton, D. L. Hoffmann, A. G. Hogg, K. A. Hughen, K. F. Kaiser, B. Kromer, S. W. Manning, M. Niu, R. W. Reimer, D. A. Richards, E. M. Scott, J. R. Southon, R. A. Staff, C. S. M. Turney, and J. van der Plicht

2013 Intcal13 and Marine13 Radiocarbon Age Calibration Curves 0–50,000 Years cal BP. *Radiocarbon* 55:1869–87.

Renfrew, Colin

2001 Production and Consumption in a Sacred Economy: The Material Correlates of High Devotional Expression at Chaco Canyon. *American Antiquity* 66:14–25.

Richards, Colin, and Julian Thomas

1984 Ritual Activity and Structured Deposition in Later Neolithic Wessex. In *Neolithic Studies: A Review of Some Current Research*, edited by R. Bradley and J. Gardiner, 189–218. Oxford University Press, Oxford.

Riggs, Marilyn

2016 Modified Sherds: The Value of Broken Ceramics in the Pueblo Bonito Mounds. In *The Pueblo Bonito Mounds of Chaco Canyon: Material Culture and Fauna*, edited by Patricia L. Crown, 123–29. University of New Mexico Press, Albuquerque.

Robert S. Peabody Institute of Archaeology

2018 Online Catalog. https://peabody.pastperfectonline.com, accessed September 14, 2018.

Robinson, William J., Bruce G. Harrill, and Richard L. Warren

1975 *Tree-Ring Dates from Arizona H-I: Flagstaff Area.* Laboratory of Tree-Ring Research, University of Arizona, Tucson.

Rock, Jim

1987 *A Brief Commentary on Cans.* US Forest Service, Klamath National Forest, CA.

Rodríguez-Hidalgo, Antonio J., Palmira Saldié, and Antoni Canals

2013 Following the White Rabbit: A Case of a Small Game Procurement Site in the Upper Paleolithic (Sala de las Chimeneas, Maltavieso Cave, Spain). *International Journal of Osteoarchaeology* 23(1):34–54.

Romanoff, A. L., and A. J. Romanoff

1949 *The Avian Egg.* Wiley, NY.

Root, W. C.

1937 The Metallurgy of Arizona and New Mexico. In *Excavations at Snaketown: Material Culture,* edited by Harold S. Gladwin, Emil W. Haury, E. B. Sayles, and Nora Gladwin, 276–277. Medallion Papers No. 25. Gila Pueblo, Globe, AZ.

Ruppert, Hans

1982 Zur Verbreitung und Herkunft von Turkis und Sodalith in Prakolumbischen Kulteren der Kordilleren. *Baessler-Archiv* 30:69–124.

1983 Geochemische Untersuchungen an Turkis und Sodalith in Prakolumbischen Kulteren der Kordilleran. *Berliner Beitrage zure Archaeometrie* 8:101–210.

Ruscillo, Deborah

2014 Zooarchaeology: Methods of Collecting Age and Sex Data. In *Encyclopedia of Global Archaeology,* edited by C. Smith, 8000–8010. Springer, NY.

Saile, David G.

1977 Making a House: Building Rituals and Spatial Concepts in the Pueblo Indian World. *Architectural Association Quarterly* 9:72–81.

1985 The Ritual Establishment of Home. In *Home Environments,* edited by Irwin Altman and Carol M. Werner, 87–112. Plenum Press, NY.

Saitta, Dean J.

1997 Power, Labor, and the Dynamics of Change in Chacoan Political Economy. *American Antiquity* 62:7–26.

Schelberg, J. D.

1997 The Metates of Chaco Canyon, New Mexico. In *Ceramics, Lithics, and Ornaments of Chaco Canyon: Analyses of Artifacts from the Chaco Project, 1971–1978: 3. Lithics and Ornaments,* edited by F. J. Mathien, 1013–118. Publications in Archaeology 18G, National Park Service, Santa Fe, NM.

Schmidt, Kari M.

1999 The Five Feature Site (AZ CC:7:55[ASM]): Evidence for a Prehistoric Rabbit Drive in Southeastern Arizona. *Kiva* 65:103–24.

Schollmeyer, Karen Gust, and Jonathan C. Driver

2013 Settlement Patterns, Source-Sink Dynamics, and Artiodactyl Hunting in the Prehistoric US Southwest. *Journal of Archaeological Method and Theory* 20(3):448–78.

Schorger, A. W.

1961 An Ancient Pueblo Turkey. *Auk* 78(2):138–44.

Sebastian, Lynne

1992 *The Chaco Anasazi: Sociopolitical Evolution in the Prehistoric Southwest.* Cambridge University Press, Cambridge.

Senior, Louise M., and Linda J. Pierce

1989 Turkeys and Domestication in the Southwest: Implications from Homol'ovi III. *Kiva* 54(3):245–59.

Shaffer, Brian S.

1992 Interpretation of Gopher Remains from Southwestern Archaeological Assemblages. *American Antiquity* 57(4):683–91.

Shaffer, Brian S., and Karen M. Gardiner

1995 The Rabbit Drive through Time: Analysis of the North American Ethnographic and Prehistoric Evidence. *Utah Archaeology* 8:13–25.

Shaffer, Brian S., and James A. Neely

1992 Intrusive Anuran Remains in Pit House Features: A Test of Methods. *Kiva* 57(4):343–51.

Shipman, Pat, and Jennie Rose

1983 Early Hominid Hunting, Butchering, and Carcass-Processing Behaviors: Approaches to the Fossil Record. *Journal of Anthropological Archaeology* 2:57–98.

Sidell, Elizabeth J.

1993a A Methodology for the Identification of Avian Eggshell from Archaeological Sites. *Archaeofauna* 2:45–51.

1993b *A Methodology for the Identification of Archaeological Eggshell.* University Museum of Archaeology and Anthropology, University of Pennsylvania, Philadelphia.

Smith, Susan J.

2008a Modern Pollen Analog Study, Los Alamos National Laboratory. In *The Land Conveyance and Transfer Data Recovery Project: 7000 Years of Land Use on the Pajarito Plateau:1. Baseline Studies,* edited by Bradley J. Vierra and Kari M. Schmidt, 97–121. LA-UR-07-6205. Los Alamos National Laboratory, Los Alamos, NM.

2008b Pollen's Eye View of Archaeology on the Pajarito Plateau. In *The Land Conveyance and Transfer Data Recovery Project: 7000 Years of Land Use on the Pajarito Plateau: 3. Artifact and Sample Analyses,* edited by Bradley J. Vierra and Kari Schmidt, 523–95. LA-UR-07-6205. Los Alamos National Laboratory, Los Alamos, NM.

Snow, David H.

1973 Prehistoric Southwestern Turquoise Industry. *El Palacio* 79:33–51.

Sofaer, Anna

1997 The Primary Architecture of the Chacoan Culture: A Cosmological Expression. In *Anasazi Architecture and American Design,* edited by Baker H. Morrow and V. B. Price, 88–132. University of New Mexico Press, Albuquerque.

Speller, Camilla

2009 Investigating Turkey (*Meleagris gallopavo*) Domestication in the Southwest United States through Ancient DNA Analysis. PhD dissertation, Department of Anthropology, Simon Fraser University, Burnaby, BC.

Speller, Camilla F., Brian M. Kemp, Scott D. Wyatt, Cara Monroe, William D. Lipe, Ursula M. Arndt, and Dongya Y. Yang

2010 Ancient Mitochondrial DNA Analysis Reveals Complexity of Indigenous North American Turkey Domestication. *Proceedings of the National Academy of Sciences* 107(7):2807–12.

Speth, John D.

2013 Thoughts about Hunting: Some Things We Know and Some Things We Don't Know. *Quaternary International* 297:176–85.

REFERENCES CITED

Spielmann, Katherine A., Tiffany Clark, Diane Hawkey, Katharine Rainey, and Suzanne K. Fish

2009 ". . . Being Weary, They Had Rebelled": Pueblo Subsistence and Labor under Spanish Colonialism. *Journal of Anthropological Archaeology* 28(1):102–25.

Stahl, Peter W.

1996 The Recovery and Interpretation of Microvertebrate Bone Assemblages from Archaeological Contexts. *Journal of Archaeological Method and Theory* 3:31–75.

Stanton, Travis W., M. Kathryn Brown, and Jonathan B. Pagliaro

2008 Garbage of the Gods? Squatters, Refuse Disposal and Termination Rituals among the Ancient Maya. *Latin American Antiquity* 19:227–47.

Stein, J. R., D. Ford, and R. Friedman

2003 Reconstructing Pueblo Bonito. In *Pueblo Bonito: Center of the Chacoan World*, edited by J. Neitzel, 33–60. Smithsonian Institution Press, Washington, DC.

Stein, John, and Stephen Lekson

1992 Anasazi Ritual Landscapes. In *Anasazi Regional Organization and the Chaco System*, edited by D. Doyel, 87–100. Anthropological Papers No. 5, Maxwell Museum of Anthropology, Albuquerque, NM.

Stevenson, Matilda Coxe

1915 *Ethnobotany of the Zuni Indians*. Bureau of American Ethnology Annual Report No. 30. Smithsonian Institution, Washington, DC.

Stewart, Omer C.

1942 Culture Element Distributions: XVIII. Ute–Southern Paiute. *University of California Anthropological Records* 6:213–360.

Stiner, Mary C.

2005 *The Faunas of Hayonim Cave (Israel): A 200,000-Year Record of Paleolithic Diet, Demography, and Society*. Peabody Museum of Archaeology and Ethnology, Harvard University, Cambridge, MA.

Stiner, Mary C., Ran Barkai, and Avi Gopher

2009 Cooperative Hunting and Meat Sharing 400–200 kya at Qesem Cave, Israel. *Proceedings of the National Academy of Sciences* 106(32):13207–12.

Stiner, Mary C., Steven L. Kuhn, Stephen Weiner, and Ofer Bar-Yosef

1995 Differential Burning, Recrystallization, and Fragmentation of Archaeological Bone. *Journal of Archaeological Science* 22(2):223–37.

Stiner, Mary C., and Natalie D. Munro

2011 On the Evolution of Diet and Landscape during the Upper Paleolithic through Mesolithic at Franchthi Cave (Peloponnese, Greece). *Journal of Human Evolution* 60(5):618–36.

Stockhammer, Philipp W.

2012 Performing the Practice Turn in Archaeology. *Transcultural Studies* 1:7–42.

Stross, Brian

1998 Seven Ingredients in Mesoamerican Ensoulment: Dedication and Termination in Tenejapa. In *The Sowing and the Dawning: Termination, Dedication, and Transformation in the Archaeological and Ethnographic Record of Mesoamerica*, edited by Shirley Mock, 31–40. University of New Mexico Press, Albuquerque.

Sturm, Jennie, and Patricia Crown

2015 Micro-Scale Mapping Using Ground-Penetrating Radar: An Example from Room 28, Pueblo Bonito, Chaco Canyon. *Advances in Archaeological Practice* 3:124–35.

Sullivan, Alan P., III, and Kenneth C. Rozen

1985 Debitage Analysis and Archaeological Interpretation. *American Antiquity* 50(4):755–79.

Swank, George R.

1932 The Ethnobotany of the Acoma and Laguna Indians. MA thesis, University of New Mexico, Albuquerque.

Szuter, Christine R.

1991 Hunting by Hohokam Desert Farmers. *Kiva* 56(3):277–91.

Tainter, J. A.

1979 The Mountainair Lithic Scatters: Settlement Patterns and Significance Evaluations of Low Density Surface Sites. *Journal of Archaeological Science* 6:643–69.

Taube, Karl

2016 Through a Glass, Brightly: Recent Investigations concerning Mirrors and Scrying in Ancient and Contemporary Mesoamerica. In *Manufactured Light: Mirrors in the Mesoamerican Realm*, edited by E. Gallaga and M. Blainey, 285–314. University Press of Colorado, Boulder.

Taussig, Michael

1993 *Mimesis and Alterity: A Particular History of the Senses*. Routledge, NY.

Thibodeau, Alyson M., John T. Chesley, Joaquin Ruiz, David J. Killick, and Arthur Vokes

2012 An Alternative Approach to the Prehispanic Turquoise Trade. In *Turquoise in Mexico and North America: Science, Conservation, Culture, and Collections*, edited by J. C. H. King, Caroline R. Cartwright, and Colin McEwan, 65–74. Archetype, London.

Thibodeau, Alyson M., David J. Killick, Saul L. Hedquist, John T. Chesley, and Joaquin Ruiz

2015 Isotopic Evidence for the Provenance of Turquoise in the Southwestern United States. *Geological Society of America Bulletin* 127(11):1617–31.

Thomas, David Hurst

1971a Prehistoric Subsistence-Settlement Patterns of the Reese River Valley, Central Nevada. PhD dissertation, University of California, Davis.

1971b On Distinguishing Natural from Cultural Bone in Archaeological Sites. *American Antiquity* 36:366–71.

Toll, H. Wolcott

1990 A Reassessment of Chaco Cylinder Jars. In *Clues to the Past: Papers in Honor of William M. Sundt*, edited by Meliha S. Duran and David T. Kirkpatrick, 273–306. Archaeological Society of New Mexico No. 16, Albuquerque.

1991 Material Distributions and Exchange in the Chaco System. In *Chaco and Hohokam: Prehistoric Regional Systems in the American Southwest*, edited by P. Crown and W. Judge, 77–107. SAR Press, Santa Fe, NM.

2006 Organization of Production. In *The Archaeology of Chaco Canyon: An Eleventh-Century Pueblo Regional Center*, edited by Stephen H. Lekson, 117–52. SAR Press, Santa Fe, NM.

Toll, H. Wolcott, and Peter McKenna

1997 Chaco Ceramics. In *Ceramics, Lithics, and Ornaments of Chaco Canyon: Analyses of Artifacts from the Chaco Project, 1971–1978*, edited by F. J. Mathien, 17–530. National Park Service, Publications in Archaeology 18G, Chaco Canyon Studies, Santa Fe, NM.

Toll, Mollie S.

1981 Macro-Botanical Remains Recovered from Chaco Canyon Coprolites. Manuscript on file, Division of Cultural Research, National Park Service, Albuquerque. Castetter Laboratory for Ethnobotanical Studies, Technical Series 38.

1985 An Overview of Chaco Canyon Macrobotanical Materials and Analysis to Date. In *Environment and Subsistence of Chaco Canyon, New Mexico*, edited by Frances Joan Mathien, 247–77. Publications in Archaeology 18E, Chaco Canyon Studies, National Park Service, Albuquerque, NM.

Towner, Ronald

2014 Report on Accession A2041: Tree-Ring Samples from Room 28, Pueblo Bonito. Laboratory of Tree-Ring Research, University of Arizona, Tucson.

Trowbridge, Meaghan

2007 Maker's Marks on Chacoan Black-on-White Ceramics. *Pottery Southwest* 25(3):14–20.

Tyler, Hamilton A.

1991 *Pueblo Birds and Myths*. Northland Publishing, Flagstaff, AZ.

Ugan, Andrew

2010 The Effect of Cooking on the Survivorship of Jackrabbit Skeletons (*Lepus californicus*) Presented to Desert Scavengers of the Eastern Great Basin, North America. *International Journal of Osteoarchaeology* 20:214–26.

Van Vuren, Dirk H., and Miguel A. Ordeñana

2012 Factors Influencing Burrow Length and Depth of Ground-Dwelling Squirrels. *Journal of Mammalogy* 93(5):1240–46.

Vargas, Victoria D.

1995 *Copper Bell Trade Patterns in the Prehispanic US Southwest and Northwest Mexico*. Arizona State Museum Archaeology Series No. 187. Arizona State Museum, University of Arizona, Tucson.

Vivian, R. Gwinn

1990 *The Chacoan Prehistory of the San Juan Basin*. Academic Press, NY.

Vivian, R. Gwinn, Carla R. Van West, Jeffrey S. Dean, Nancy J. Akins, Mollie S. Toll, and Thomas C. Windes

2006 Ecology and Economy. In *The Archaeology of Chaco Canyon: An Eleventh-Century Pueblo Regional Center*, edited by S. H. Lekson, 45–65. SAR Press, Santa Fe, NM.

Vogt, Evon Zartman

1998 Zinacanteco Dedication and Termination Rituals. In *The Sowing and the Dawning: Termination, Dedication, and Transformation in the Archaeological and Ethnographic Record of Mesoamerica*, edited by Shirley Mock, 21–30. University of New Mexico Press, Albuquerque.

von Mechow, Tod

2017 Soda and Beer Bottles of North America: Bottle Attributes: Beer and Soda Bottle Manufacturers. http://sodasandbeers .com/SABBottleManufBeerSoda.htm, accessed November 18, 2018.

Walker, William

1995 Ceremonial Trash? In *Expanding Archaeology*, edited by J. Skibo, W. Walker, and A. Nielsen, 67–79. University of Utah Press, Salt Lake City.

2002 Stratigraphy and Practical Reason. *American Anthropologist* 104:159–77.

Walker, William, Vincent LaMotta, and E. Charles Adams

2000 Katsinas and Kiva Abandonments at Homol'ovi: A Deposit-Oriented Perspective on Religion in Southwest Prehistory. In *The Archaeology of Regional Interaction*, edited by Michelle Hegmon, 341–60. University Press of Colorado, Boulder.

Warren, A. Helene

1967 Petrographic Analysis of Pottery and Lithics. In *An Archaeological Survey of the Chuska Valley and the Chaco Plateau*, edited by James Schoenwetter and Arthur H. Harris, 104–34. Museum of New Mexico Research Records No. 4. Albuquerque.

Washburn, D. K.

1980 The Mexican Connection: Cylinder Jars from the Valley of Oaxaca. *Transactions of the Illinois State Academy of Science* 72:70–85.

2008 The Position of Salmon Ruins in the Middle San Juan, AD 1000–1300: A Perspective from Ceramic Design Structure. In *Chaco's Northern Prodigies*, edited by Paul F. Reed, 284–308. University of Utah Press, Salt Lake City.

Washburn, D., William Washburn, and Petia Shipkova

2011 The Prehistoric Drug Trade: Widespread Consumption of Cacao in Ancestral Pueblo and Hohokam Communities in the American Southwest. *Journal of Archaeological Science* 38:1634–40.

Watson, Adam

2012 Craft, Subsistence, and Political Change: An Archaeological Investigation of Power and Economy in Prehistoric Chaco Canyon, New Mexico, 850 to 1200 CE. PhD dissertation, Department of Anthropology, University of Virginia, Charlottesville.

2015 Bones as Raw Material: Temporal Trends and Spatial Variability in the Chacoan Bone Tool Industry. In *Chaco Revisited: New Research on the Prehistory of Chaco Canyon, New Mexico*, edited by C. Heitman and S. Plog, 30–65. University of Arizona Press, Tucson.

Weber, Steven A., and P. David Seaman

1985 *Havasupai Habitat: A. F. Whiting's Ethnography of a Traditional Indian Culture*. University of Arizona Press, Tucson.

Webster, Laurie D.

2006 Survey and Photographs of Worked-Fiber Artifacts from Pueblo Bonito at the American Museum of Natural History, National Museum of the American Indian, and National Museum of Natural History. Notes and photographs in possession of Laurie Webster.

2008 An Initial Assessment of Perishable Relationships among Chaco, Salmon, and Aztec. In *Chaco's Northern Prodigies: Salmon, Aztec, and the Ascendency of the Middle San Juan Region after AD 1100*, edited by Paul F. Reed, 167–89. University of Utah Press, Salt Lake City.

2011 Perishable Ritual Artifacts at the West Ruin of Aztec, New Mexico: Evidence for a Chacoan Migration. *Kiva* 77(2):139–71.

Weigand, Phil C., and Garman Harbottle

1993 The Role of Turquoise in the Ancient Mesoamerican Trade Structure. In *The American Southwest and Mesoamerica: Systems of Prehistoric Exchange*, edited by Jonathan E. Ericson and Timothy G. Baugh, 159–77. Plenum Press, NY.

Weigand, Phil C., Garman Harbottle, and Edward Sayre

1977 Turquoise Sources and Source Analysis: Mesoamerica and the Southwestern USA. In *Exchange Systems in Prehistory*, edited by T. Earle and J. Ericson, 15–34. Academic Press, NY.

Wilkens, Barry

2003 Proton-Induced X-Ray Emission Analysis of Turquoise Artifacts from Salado Platform Mound Sites in the Tonto Basin of Central Arizona. *Measurement Science and Technology* 1 4:1579–89.

Wills, W. H.

1997 A Preliminary Analysis of Hammerstones from Chaco Canyon, New Mexico. In *Ceramics, Lithics, and Ornaments of Chaco Canyon: Analyses of Artifacts from the Chaco Project, 1971–1978*, edited by F. J. Mathien, 947–976. Publications in Archaeology 18G, National Park Service, Santa Fe, NM.

2000 Political Leadership and the Construction of Chacoan Great Houses, AD 1020–1140. In *Alternative Leadership Strategies in the Prehistoric Southwest*, edited by Barbara J. Mills, 19–44. University of Arizona Press, Tucson.

2001 Mound Building and Ritual in Chaco Canyon. *American Antiquity* 66:433–51.

Wills, W. H., David W. Love, Susan J. Smith, Karen R. Adams, Manuel Palacios-Fest, Wetherbee B. Dorshow, Beau Murphy, Jennie O. Sturm, Hannah Mattson, and Patricia L. Crown

2016 Water Management at Pueblo Bonito: Evidence from the National Geographic Society Trenches. *American Antiquity* 81(3):449–70.

Wills, W. H., and Adam Okun

2016 Chipped Stone from the Pueblo Bonito Trash Mounds. In *The Pueblo Bonito Mounds of Chaco Canyon: Material Culture and Fauna*, edited by Patricia L. Crown, 131–50. University of New Mexico Press, Albuquerque.

Wilmsen, Edwin. N.

1970 *Lithic Analysis and Cultural Inference: A Paleoindian Case*. University of Arizona Press, Tucson.

Wilshusen, Richard H., and Ruth M. Van Dyke

2006 Chaco's Beginnings. In *The Archaeology of Chaco Canyon: An Eleventh-Century Pueblo Regional Center*, edited by Stephen H. Lekson, 211–60. SAR Press, Santa Fe, NM.

Windes, Thomas C.

1977 Dwellers of the Wood ("Say, Who Are Those Turkeys?"): A Preliminary Eggshell Report. Manuscript (Chaco C51724/Coll. 0002/042.001-56) on file at the National Park Service, Chaco Culture National Historical Park, Albuquerque, NM.

1984 A View of the Cibola Whitewares from Chaco Canyon. In *Regional Analysis of Prehistoric Ceramic Variation: Contemporary Studies of the Cibola Whitewares*, edited by Alan P. Sullivan and Jeffrey L. Hantman, 94–119. Arizona State University, Tempe.

1987a Some Ground Stone Tools and Hammerstones from Pueblo Alto. In *Investigations at the Pueblo Alto Complex, Chaco Canyon, New Mexico, 1975–1979: 3, pt. 1, Artifactual and Biological Analyses*, edited by Frances Joan Mathien and Thomas C. Windes, 291–358. Publications in Archaeology 18F, Chaco Canyon Studies, National Park Service, Santa Fe, NM.

1987b *Investigations at the Pueblo Alto Complex, Chaco Canyon, New Mexico, 1975–1979: 1. Summary of Tests and Excavations at the Pueblo Alto Community*. Publications in Archaeology 18F, Chaco Canyon Studies, National Park Service, Department of the Interior, Santa Fe, NM.

1987c The Use of Turkeys at Pueblo Alto Based on the Eggshell and Faunal Remains. In *Investigations at the Pueblo Alto Complex,

Chaco Canyon, New Mexico, 1975–1979: 3, pt. 2. Artifactual and Biological Analyses*, edited by Frances Joan Mathien and Thomas C. Windes, 679–88. National Park Service, US Department of the Interior, Santa Fe, NM.

1992 Blue Notes: The Chacoan Turquoise Industry in the San Juan Basin. In *Anasazi Regional Organization and the Chaco System*, edited by D. E. Doyel, 159–68. Anthropological Papers No. 5. Maxwell Museum of Anthropology, University of New Mexico, Albuquerque.

2003 This Old House: Construction and Abandonment at Pueblo Bonito. In *Pueblo Bonito: Center of the Chacoan World*, edited by J. Neitzel, 14–32. Smithsonian Institution Press, Washington, DC.

Windes, Thomas C. (editor)

1993 *The Spadefoot Toad Site: Investigations at 29SJ629, Chaco Canyon, New Mexico: 2. Artifactual and Biological Analyses*. National Park Service, US Department of the Interior, Santa Fe, NM.

Windes, Thomas, and Dabney Ford

1992 The Nature of the Early Bonito Phase. In *Anasazi Regional Organization and the Chaco System*, edited by D. Doyel, 75–86. Maxwell Museum of Anthropology Anthropological Paper No. 5. University of New Mexico, Albuquerque.

1996 The Chaco Wood Project: The Chronometric Reappraisal of Pueblo Bonito. *American Antiquity* 61(2):295–310.

Wolverton, Steve

2002 NISP:MNE and %Whole [*sic*] in Analysis of Prehistoric Carcass Exploitation. *North American Archaeologist* 23(2):85–100.

Wolverton, Steve, Lisa Nagaoka, Julie Densmore, and Ben Fullerton

2008 White-Tailed Deer Harvest Pressure and Within-Bone Nutrient Exploitation during the Mid- to Late Holocene in Southeast Texas. *Before Farming* 2008(2):1–23.

Wolverton, Steve, Clara Otaola, Gustavo Neme, Miguel A. Giardina, and Adolfo Gil

2015 Patch Choice, Landscape Ecology, and Foraging Efficiency: The Zooarchaeology of Late Holocene Foragers in Western Argentina. *Journal of Ethnobiology* 35(3):499–518.

Wright, James C.

2004 Mycenaean Drinking Services and Standards of Etiquette. In *Food, Cuisine and Society in Prehistoric Greece*, edited by Paul Halstead and John C. Barrett, 90–104. Oxbow Books, Oxford.

Yanovsky, Elias

1936 *Food Plants of the North American Indians*. US Department of Agriculture Miscellaneous Publications 237. US Government Printing Office, Washington, DC.

Yoffee, Norman

2001 The Chaco "Rituality" Revisited. In *Chaco Society and Polity: Papers from the 1999 Conference*, edited by L. S. Cordell, W. J. Judge, and J. Piper, 63–78. Special Publications No. 4. New Mexico Archaeological Council, Albuquerque.

Young, Suzanne M., David A. Phillips, and Frances Joan Mathien

1994 Lead Isotope Analysis of Turquoise in the Southwestern USA and Mesoamerica. Paper presented at the 29th International Symposium on Archaeometry, May 1994, Ankara, Turkey.

Zedeño, María Nieves

2009 Animating by Association: Index Objects and Relational Taxonomies. *Cambridge Archaeological Journal* 19:407–17.

Contributors

KAREN R. ADAMS is an independent archaeobotanical consultant. She holds an undergraduate degree in archaeology (Miami University, Ohio) and a PhD in ecology and evolutionary biology (University of Arizona). For almost five decades, she has analyzed and reported on ancient plant specimens from archaeological sites throughout the greater US Southwest. Adams has synthesized the archaeological plant record at the plant, site, project, subregional, and regional levels, with a special focus on maize/corn (*Zea mays* L.) and indigenous domesticated and managed plants.

CAITLIN S. AINSWORTH is a PhD candidate at the University of New Mexico and a faunal analyst for the Museum of New Mexico, Office of Archaeological Studies. Her work and academic studies focus on the zooarchaeological record of New Mexico and northern Mexico and the diverse ways in which past humans interacted with animals and their environment.

KATHERINE L. BREWER is a PhD candidate at the University of New Mexico. She is a historical archaeologist specializing in Spanish colonial archaeology. Brewer analyzed the historical artifacts for Room 28 while cataloging artifacts for Chaco Culture National Historical Park Collections.

CYLER CONRAD is a zooarchaeologist who received his PhD in anthropology (archaeology) from the University of New Mexico. He is an adjunct assistant professor of archaeology at the University of New Mexico and serves as the archaeology technical lead at Los Alamos National Laboratory. Conrad specializes in the analysis of bird bones and eggs and contributed to this project by analyzing eggshell specimens from the Room 28 assemblage.

PATRICIA L. CROWN is an archaeologist with a PhD from the University of Arizona. She is the Leslie Spier Distinguished Professor of Anthropology at the University of New Mexico, where she has taught since 1993. She directed the reexcavation of Room 28 as part of her interest in cacao exchange and ritual in Chaco Canyon.

STEPHANIE E. FRANKLIN is an archaeologist for the Southwest Jemez Mountains Collaborative Landscape Restoration Project in the Santa Fe National Forest in New Mexico. She is a public archaeologist who studies zooarchaeology and manages archaeological sites on public lands.

EMILY LENA JONES is an associate professor of anthropology at the University of New Mexico. A zooarchaeologist who studies changes in human-environment interactions, she has worked on numerous projects based in prehispanic New Mexico as well as in other times and places.

JACQUELINE M. KOCER is a PhD candidate at the University of New Mexico; her dissertation research focuses on production practices in Gallina (AD 1100–1300) ceramics. She served on the crew for the 2013 excavation of Room 28 in Pueblo Bonito and has experience in lithic, ground stone, and ornament analysis. Kocer is a native New Mexican and an enrolled member of the Oglala Lakota. She plans to work with tribal entities after graduation.

HANNAH V. MATTSON is an assistant professor of anthropology at the University of New Mexico. She specializes in US Southwest archaeology and the study of social identity, ritual practice, and craft production and exchange. Mattson conducted her dissertation research on the personal ornaments from Pueblo Bonito and Aztec Ruin, New Mexico, and has been involved with UNM's Chaco Canyon research projects since 2005.

SUSAN J. SMITH hails from a small town in eastern Oregon, where she first fell in love with botany. For the past thirty years, she has specialized in archaeo-pollen studies in the western United States.

LAURIE D. WEBSTER is an anthropologist and independent scholar who specializes in textiles and other perishable material culture of the US Southwest. She received her PhD in anthropology from the University of Arizona. Her research interests include craft production, technological change, cultural affiliation, and the documentation and interpretation of older museum collections.

Index

Page numbers in *italic text* indicate illustrations.

termination rituals: acts, 179; cylinder jars and, 3, 5–8, *8*; evidence of, *9*; reason for, 5, 13

termination types, flaked stone, 68

terrestrial laser scanner. *See* lidar

tesserae, *84*, 85, 87, *95–96*, *98*, 169, 171

Texas A&M University, 144

textiles, Room 28: commercial wool yarn and fabric, 102; cotton plain-weave cloth, 101; cotton yarn, 101; discussion, 102–3; fragments from 2013 excavations, *100*; types, *101*; yucca cordage, 102

textiles, Room 56, 169

Thomas, David Hurst, 73

thread counts, 101

Tijeras Pueblo, eggshell thickness histograms for, *125*

tomatillos, 16, 27, 28, 138, 139, 140, 141, 171

tools: butchering, 73; choppers and hammerstones, 73–74, *74*; flaked stone, 68, 70–72, *71*, *72*, *73*; ground stone, 75–77; lithic, 85; non-tool debitage versus, 70, *71*; pronghorn ulna tool, 110, *110*; swords, 169

Towner, Ronald H., 32

trash disposal, 16, *16*, 35, 36, 39–40, 111, 175

trash mounds, 148; DNA results for turkey samples from Pueblo Bonito, *129*

tree rings: dating, 5, 7, 20, 21–22, 23, 25, 26, 33, 36, 156–60, 163; Laboratory of Tree-Ring Research, 12, 32, 162; sampling, 4, 10, 12, 32, 172

trees: charred wood and twigs of shrubs and, *136*, *138*, *166*; Douglas Fir, 20, 29, 140, 172; juniper, 17, 20, 140

Tribal Consultation Committee, 2

Tsegi Orange Ware, 60

tub rooms, 15, 156, 157, 162–64

tubular beads, 84, 95

turbation, taphonomy, 111

Turkey Pen Ruin, 102

turkeys: bone and eggshell remains from Chaco Canyon, 122; bones, 110, 122, 123, 128–29; distribution of quills/feathers, bones dung in Pueblo Bonito, *128*; DNA results analyzed from Pueblo Bonito trash mounds, *129*; dung, 127–28, *128*, 129; eggshell thickness, published values, *125*; feathers, 171; inner eggshell and non-turkey eggshell, *124*; *Meleagris gallopavo*, 109–10; partial egg from Chaco Canyon, *126*; pens, 36, 102, 127–29, 156, 159, 170; quills in Room 35, 123; strontium isotope results for analyzed Chaco Canyon samples, *130*; swallowed debitage gastrolith, *126*. *See also* eggshells and gastroliths, Room 28

turquoise: beads, 22, 26, 29, 91, 93, 171; disc beads, *84*, 90, 91; origins, 82; ornaments, 81; pendants, 87, 123; production debris, 80, 172; sources, 85; specimens, 81–82

Tusayan Gray Ware, 60

Tusayan White Ware, 60

twigs: from rose family members, 140; subfloor surface and charred, *140*; of trees and shrubs and charred wood, *136*, *138*, *166*

Type I masonry, 22

Type II masonry, 22–23, 30, 33, 36, 157

Type IV masonry, 30, 31, 33, 158

Typha. See cattail

ubiquity, 133, 151

United States Glass Company, 153

University of Arizona, 12

University of New Mexico reexcavation (2013), 4, 9; metal and glass from, 153, *154*; sherds recovered, 39–40, *40*, 60–66, *61–66*; textile fragments from, *100*

upper story, of Room 28, 30–31

use: cattail and ethnobotanical, *149*; description of utilized edges, 73; processes of abandonment and, 8; Room 28, 36; wood, 140

use wear, vessels, modification and residues, 55–57, *56–57*

utilization and retouch, flaked stone, 69

vessel forms and wares, 50; bowls, 54, 55; cylinder jars, 51, *51–53*, *53*; maker's marks on Room 28, 53; other, 54–55; pitchers, 53–54

vessels: bird effigy, 47, 48, 50; for cacao consumption, 179; ceramic type classifications for whole, *47*; cooking, 167, 171; cut marks on, 52, 57; decoration on, 82; in excavation "layers" for western part of Room 28, *50*; Gallup Black-on-white, 50; in large pile in southwestern portion of Room 28, 49; mortuary, 60; recovered in 1896 by location in Room 28, *48*; Room 53, 168–69; Room 56, 168–69; sitting on plaster, *20*; types and forms found in front of door to Room 51a, *49*; use wear, modification and residues, 55–57; whole, from 1896 excavation, 41–60, *42*, *43*, *44–51*, *53*, *55–59*, *181–84*. *See also* whole vessels, Room 28

Villa Grove turquoise source, 82

Vivian, R. Gwinn, 110

voles, 105

walls: Room 28, 17–23, *18–22*; Room 32, 23; Room 40, 27; Room 53, 21; Room 55, 22, 49, 170; Room 57, 170; between Rooms 39a and 39b, 22; tub room, 15

Washburn, D. K., 52, 55

Wetherill, Richard, 102, 127, 154; with cacao consumption, 180; doors and, 20; HEE

and, 1, 4; human remains and, 189; notes of, 5; Room 28 and, 14, 160; Room 33 and, 34; southern wall and, 19. *See also* Hyde Exploring Expedition

White Mountain Red Ware, 60, 67, 172

whole vessels, from 1896 excavation, *181–85*; abrasion lines on exterior wall of cylinder jar, *59*; bird's-eye view of Room 28, *43*; ceramic type classifications for, *47*; in context, 41–46; cylinder jar with cut marks near lug holes, *57*; cylinder jar with greasy-looking discoloration, *57*; cylinder jar with patch cut or ground from surface, *59*; in excavation "layers" for western part of Room 28, *50*; exterior basal use wear for, *56*; field numbers and vessels from Room 28, *44–46*; forms recovered, *48*; Gallup Black-on-white bowl found with ornaments inside, *54*, *55*; interior use wear for, *56*; lugs and straps on cylinder jars, *53*; maker's marks, *53*; modifications by form and type, *58*; mutilation and termination, 57–60; orifice diameters for cylinder jars, *51*; recovery contexts and types, 47–50, *47–50*; with reslipping, repainting and fired-out paint, *56*; scatter plot of bowl rim diameter by height, *55*; sherds, *42*; types and forms found in front of door to Room 51a, *49*; vessel forms and wares, 50–55; vessels in Layer 1 by door connecting Rooms 28 and 51a, *43*; vessel use wear, modification and residues, 55–57

whole vessels, Room 28: bowls, *184*; cylinder jars, *181–82*; pitchers, *183*

Wide Neckbanded Chuska Gray (ca. AD 850–925), 15, *16*

wildfires, 112

wild plants: reproductive parts of, *135*, *136*; subsistence resources, 138–39

Wills, Chip, 2, 74

Windes, Thomas C., 75

wood: cross-pieces, 18, 30, 156; floors and types of, 25; pinyon, 20, 21; roof timbers, 141; specimens, 133; swords, 169; twigs of trees and shrubs and charred, *136*, *138*, *166*; usage, 140; varieties, 29. *See also* posts

woodrats, 17, 105, 115

Woodruff Brown Smudged-Sand, 168

Woodruff Smudged Brown Ware, 41

wool, 102, 153

yarn, 101, 102

Ysleta del Sur Pueblo, 2

yucca cordage, 102

Zea mays. See domesticated maize

Zooarchaeology Laboratory, 105